Intermediate Units 6 and 7

RECORDING AND EVALUATING
COSTS AND REVENUES AND
PREPARING REPORTS AND RETURNS

For assessments in December 2003

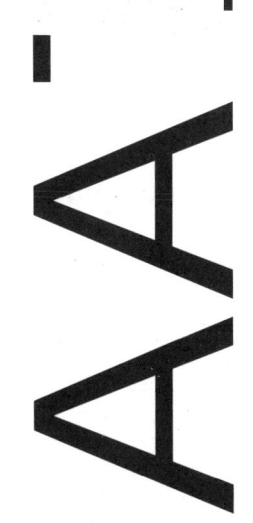

AAT

Interactive Text

In this May 2003 new edition

- For assessments under the **new standards**
- Layout designed to be easier on the eye – and easy to use
- Clear language and presentation
- Lots of diagrams and flowcharts
- Activities checklist to tie in each activity to specific knowledge and understanding, performance criteria and/or range statement
- Thorough reliable updating of material to 1 April 2003

FOR 2003 AND 2004 EXAM BASED AND SKILLS BASED ASSESSMENTS

BPP PROFESSIONAL EDUCATION

First edition May 2003

ISBN 0 7517 1129 2

British Library Cataloguing-in-Publication Data
A catalogue record for this book
is available from the British Library

Published by

BPP Professional Education
Aldine House, Aldine Place
London W12 8AW

www.bpp.com

Printed in Great Britain by Ashford Colour Press Ltd
Unit 600
Fareham Reach
Fareham Road
Gosport
Hampshire
PO13 0FW

All our rights reserved. No part of this publication may
be reproduced, stored in a retrieval system or
transmitted, in any form or by any means, electronic,
mechanical, photocopying, recording or otherwise,
without the prior written permission of BPP
Professional Education.

We are grateful to the Lead Body for Accounting for
permission to reproduce extracts from the Standards
of Competence for Accounting, and to the AAT for
permission to reproduce extracts from the mapping
and Guidance Notes.

©
BPP Professional Education
2003

Contents

Introduction

How to use this Interactive Text – Intermediate qualification structure –
Unit 6 Standards of competence – Unit 7 Standards of competence –
Assessment strategy – Building your portfolio

	Page	Answers to activities

UNIT 6 Recording and evaluating costs and revenues

		Page	Answers to activities
1	Introduction to recording and evaluating costs and revenues	3	–
2	Materials	15	461
3	Labour costs	43	467
4	Expenses	61	470
5	Overheads and absorption costing	77	472
6	Marginal costing and absorption costing	101	475
7	Cost behaviour	115	476
8	Recording costs and revenues	129	478
9	Costing systems	145	480
10	Process costing	161	483
11	Short term decisions	183	489
12	Long term decisions	205	491

UNIT 7 Preparing reports and returns

		Page	Answers to activities
13	The organisation, accounting and reporting	225	–
14	Business and accounting information	237	–
15	Statistical information	249	493
16	Presenting information: tables and charts	263	495
17	Presenting information: graphs	287	499
18	Averages and time series	309	502
19	Using index numbers	327	504
20	Reporting performance	339	506
21	Measuring performance	357	507

		Page	Answers to activities
22	Preparing reports and returns	371	509
23	The VAT charge and VAT returns	385	511
24	The computation and administration of VAT	417	516

Answers to activities 461

Discount factor tables 525

Index 529

Order form

Review form & free prize draw

Introduction

How to use this Interactive Text

Aims of this Interactive Text

> To provide the knowledge and practice to help you succeed in the assessment for Intermediate Unit 6 *Recording and Evaluating Costs and Revenues* and Intermediate Unit 7 *Preparing Reports and Returns*.

To pass the assessments successfully you need a thorough understanding in all areas covered by the standards of competence.

> To tie in with the other components of the BPP Effective Study Package to ensure you have the best possible chance of success.

Interactive Text

This covers all you need to know for the exam based and skills based assessments for Unit 6 *Recording and Evaluating Costs and Revenues* and Unit 7 *Preparing Reports and Returns*. Numerous activities throughout the text help you practise what you have just learnt.

Assessment Kit

When you have understood and practised the material in the Interactive Text, you will have the knowledge and experience to tackle the Assessment Kit for Unit 6 *Recording and Evaluating Costs and Revenues* and Unit 7 *Preparing Reports and Returns*. This aims to get you through the assessments, whether exam based or skills based.

Passcards

These short memorable notes are focused on key topics for Units 6 and 7, designed to remind you of what the Interactive Text has taught you.

Recommended approach to this Interactive Text

(a) To achieve competence in Units 6 and 7 (and all the other units), you need to be able to do **everything** specified by the standards. Study the Interactive Text carefully and do not skip any of it.

(b) Learning is an **active** process. Do **all** the activities as you work through the Interactive Text so you can be sure you really understand what you have read. There is a checklist at the end of each chapter to show which knowledge and understanding, performance criteria and/or range statement is covered by each activity.

(c) After you have covered the material in the Interactive Text, work through the **Assessment Kit**.

(d) Before you take the assessment, check that you still remember the material using the following quick revision plan for each chapter.

   (i) Read and learn the **key learning points**, which are a summary of the chapter. This includes key terms and shows the sort of things likely to come up in an assessment.

   (ii) Do the **quick quiz** again. If you know what you're doing, it shouldn't take long.

   (iii) Go through the **Passcards** as often as you can in the weeks leading up to your assessment.

This approach is only a suggestion. Your college may well adapt it to suit your needs.

Quick quizzes

> These include multiple choice questions, true/false and other formats not used by the AAT. However, these types of questions are usually very familiar to students and are used to help students adjust to otherwise unfamiliar material.

Remember this is a **practical** course.

(a) Try to relate the material to your experience in the workplace or any other work experience you may have had.

(b) Try to make as many links as you can to your study of the other Units at Intermediate level.

(c) Keep this text, (hopefully) you will find it invaluable in your everyday work too!

Intermediate qualification structure

The competence-based Education and Training Scheme of the Association of Accounting Technicians is based on an analysis of the work of accounting staff in a wide range of industries and types of organisation. The Standards of Competence for Accounting which students are expected to meet are based on this analysis.

The AAT issued new standards of competence in 2002, which take effect from 1 July 2003. This Text reflects the **new standards.**

The Standards identify the key purpose of the accounting occupation, which is to operate, maintain and improve systems to record, plan, monitor and report on the financial activities of an organisation, and a number of key roles of the occupation. Each key role is subdivided into units of competence, which are further divided into elements of competences. By successfully completing assessments in specified units of competence, students can gain qualifications at NVQ/SVQ levels 2, 3 and 4, which correspond to the AAT Foundation, Intermediate and Technician stages of competence respectively.

Whether you are competent in a Unit is demonstrated by means of:

- *Either* an Exam Based Assessment (set and marked by AAT assessors)
- *Or* a Skills Based Assessment (where competence is judged by an Approved Assessment Centre to whom responsibility for this is devolved)
- Or *both* Exam *and* Skills Based Assessment

Below we set out the overall structure of the Intermediate (NVQ/SVQ Level 3) stage, indicating how competence in each Unit is assessed. In the next section there is more detail about the Assessments for Units 6 and 7.

Both units 6 and 7 are assessed by Skills Based Assessment. Unit 7 is also assessed by Exam Based Assessment.

NVQ/SVQ Level 3

All units are mandatory. Units 21 and 22 need not be repeated if they have been completed at Level 2.

Unit 5	Maintaining Financial Records and Preparing Accounts	Element 5.1	Maintain records relating to capital acquisition and disposal
		Element 5.2	Measure income and expenditure
		Element 5.3	Collect and collate information for the preparation of accounts
		Element 5.4	Prepare the accounts of unincorporated organisations

Unit 6	Recording and Evaluating Costs and Revenues	Element 6.1	Record and analyse information relating to direct costs and revenues
		Element 6.2	Record and analyse information relating to the allocation, apportionment and absorption of overhead costs
		Element 6.3	Prepare and evaluate estimates of costs and revenues

Unit 7	Preparing Reports and Returns	Element 7.1	Prepare and present periodic performance reports
		Element 7.2	Prepare reports and returns for outside agencies
		Element 7.3	Prepare VAT returns

Unit 21	Working with Computers	Element 21.1	Use computer systems and software
		Element 21.2	Maintain the security of data

Unit 22	Contribute to the Maintenance of a Healthy, Safe and Productive Working Environment	Element 22.1	Contribute to the maintenance of a healthy, safe and productive working environment
		Element 22.2	Monitor and maintain an effective and efficient working environment

Unit 6 Recording and Evaluating Costs and Revenues

UNIT 6 IS ASSESSED BY SKILLS BASED ASSESSMENT AND EXAM BASED ASSESSMENT

Unit Commentary

This unit is concerned with how organisations record, analyse and report current and future costs and revenue data for use within the organisation. You will need to know that organisations build up costs and revenues in different ways. The way costs are recorded vary with the type of industry as well as the measurement rules chosen by the organisation. You have to understand the meaning and consequence of these different ways of recording costs and revenues and be able to apply them in relevant circumstances.

There are three elements. The first element focuses on direct costs and revenues, the second on overheads. You will need to apply both types of cost to the reporting of the organisation's expenses. In addition, you will need to apply both types of costing to the recording and analysing of unit and departmental costs. The third element is concerned with using cost and revenue information to help organisations make decisions. You will need to know about cost behaviour and apply it appropriately to managerial decisions for both short– and long-term planning purposes.

Elements contained within this unit are:

Element 6.1   Record and analyse information relating to direct costs and revenues

Element 6.2   Record and analyse information relating to the allocation, apportionment and absorption of overhead costs

Element 6.3   Prepare and evaluate estimates of costs and revenues

INTRODUCTION

Knowledge and understanding

To perform this unit effectively you will need to know and understand:

The business environment

1. The nature and purpose of internal reporting (Elements 6.1, 6.2 & 6.3)
2. Management information requirements (Elements 6.1, 6.2 & 6.3)
3. Maintaining an appropriate cost accounting system (Elements 6.1 & 6.2)

Accounting techniques

4. Recording of cost and revenue data in the accounting records (Elements 6.1 & 6.2)
5. Methods of stock control and valuation including First In First Out, Last In First Out and Weighted Average Cost (Element 6.1)
6. Methods for and calculation of payments for labour (Element 6.1)
7. Procedures and documentation relating to expenses (Elements 6.1 & 6.2)
8. Bases of allocating and apportioning indirect costs to responsibility centres: direct and step down methods (Element 6.2)
9. Marginal versus absorption costing for costing and reporting purposes (Elements 6.1 & 6.2)
10. The arbitrary nature of overhead apportionments (Element 6.2)
11. Bases of absorption (Element 6.2)
12. Calculation of product and service cost (Elements 6.1, 6.2 & 6.3)
13. Analysis of the effect of changing activity levels on unit costs (Elements 6.1, 6.2 & 6.3)
14. Methods of presenting information in written reports (Element 6.3)
15. The identification of fixed, variable and semi-variable costs and their use in cost recording, cost reporting and cost analysis (Elements 6.1, 6.2 & 6.3)
16. Cost-volume-profit analysis (Element 6.3)
17. The identification of limiting factors (Element 6.3)
18. Methods of project appraisal: payback and discounted cash flow methods (NPV and IRR) (Element 6.3)

Accounting principles and theory

19. Relationship between the materials costing system and the stock control system (Element 6.1)
20. Relationship between the labour costing system and the payroll accounting system (Element 6.2)
21. Relationship between the accounting system and the expenses costing system (Elements 6.1 & 6.2)
22. Marginal costing (Elements 6.1 & 6.3)
23. Absorption costing (Elements 6.2 & 6.3)
24. Cost behaviour (Element 6.3)
25. The principles of discounted cash flow (Element 6.3)

The organisation

26	Costing systems appropriate to the organisation: job, batch, unit and process costing systems (Elements 6.1, 6.2 & 6.3)
27	The sources of information for revenue and costing data (Elements 6.1, 6.2 & 6.3)

Element 6.1 Record and analyse information relating to direct costs and revenues

Performance criteria	Chapters in this Text
In order to perform this element successfully you need to:	
A Identify **direct costs** in accordance with the organisation's costing procedures	2, 3
B Record and analyse information relating to direct costs	2, 3
C Calculate direct costs in accordance with the organisation's policies and procedures	2, 3
D Check cost information for **stocks** against usage and stock control practices	2
E Resolve or refer queries to the appropriate person	2, 3

Range statement

Performance in this element relates to the following contexts:

Direct costs

- Materials
- Direct labour costs

Stocks

- Raw materials
- Part-finished goods
- Finished goods

INTRODUCTION

Element 6.2 Record and analyse information relating to the allocation, apportionment and absorption of overhead costs

Performance criteria	Chapters in this Text
In order to perform this element successfully you need to:	
A Identify **overhead costs** in accordance with the organisation's procedures	3, 4, 5
B Attribute overhead costs to production and service cost centres in accordance with agreed **bases of allocation and apportionment**	5
C Calculate overhead absorption rates in accordance with agreed **bases of absorption**	5
D Record and analyse information relating to overhead costs in accordance with the organisation's procedures	3, 4, 5
E Make adjustments for under and over recovered overhead costs in accordance with established procedures	5
F Review methods of allocation, apportionment and absorption at regular intervals in discussions with senior staff and ensure agreed changes to methods are implemented	4, 5
G Consult staff working in operational departments to resolve any queries in overhead cost data	4

Range statement

Performance in this element relates to the following contexts:

Overhead costs

- Fixed
- Variable
- Semi-variable

Bases of allocation and apportionment

- Direct methods
- Step down methods

Bases of absorption

- Labour hour methods
- Machine hour methods

Element 6.3 Prepare and evaluate estimates of costs and revenues

Performance criteria	Chapters in this Text
In order to perform this element successfully you need to:	
A Identify information relevant to estimating current and future revenues and costs	11, 12
B Prepare **estimates** of future income and costs	11, 12
C Calculate the effects of variations in capacity on product costs	11, 12
D Analyse critical factors affecting costs and revenues using appropriate accounting techniques and draw clear conclusions from the analysis	11, 12
E State any assumptions used when evaluating future costs and revenues	11, 12
F Identify and evaluate options and solutions for their contribution to organisational goals	11, 12
G **Present** recommendations to appropriate people in a clear and concise way and supported by a clear rationale	11, 12

Range statement

Performance in this element relates to the following contexts:

Estimates

- Short term decisions:
    - Break-even analysis
    - Margin of safety
    - Target profit
    - Profit volume ratio
    - Limiting factors
- Long term decisions:
    - Project appraisal using payback and discounted cash flow methods

Methods of presentation

- Verbal presentation
- Written reports

Unit 7 Preparing Reports and Returns

UNIT 7 IS ASSESSED BY SKILLS BASED ASSESSMENT

Unit Commentary

This unit relates to the preparation of reports and returns from information obtained from all relevant sources. You are required to calculate ratios and performance indicators and present the information according to the appropriate conventions and definitions to either management or outside agencies, including the VAT Office. The unit is also concerned with your communication responsibilities which include obtaining authorisation before despatching reports, seeking guidance from the VAT Office and presenting reports and returns in the appropriate manner.

Elements contained within this unit are:

Element: 7.1   Prepare and present periodic performance reports

Element: 7.2   Prepare reports and returns for outside agencies

Element: 7.3   Prepare VAT returns

INTRODUCTION

Knowledge and understanding

To perform this unit effectively you will need to know and understand:

The business environment

1. Main sources of relevant government statistics (Elements 7.1 & 7.2)

2. Relevant performance and quality measures (Element 7.1)

3. Main types of outside organisations requiring reports and returns: regulatory; grant awarding; information collecting; trade associations (Element 7.2)

4. Basic law and practice relating to all issues covered in the range statement and referred to in the performance criteria. Specific issues include: the classification of types of supply; registration requirements; the form of VAT invoices; tax points (Element 7.3)

5. Sources of information on VAT: Customs and Excise Guide (Element 7.3)

6. Administration of VAT: enforcement (Element 7.3)

7. Special schemes: annual accounting; cash accounting; bad debt relief (Element 7.3)

Accounting techniques

8. Use of standard units of inputs and outputs (Element 7.1 & 7.3)

9. Time series analysis (Element 7.1)

10. Use of index numbers (Element 7.1)

11. Main types of performance indicators: productivity; cost per unit; resource utilisation; profitability (Elements 7.1 & 7.2)

12. Ratios: gross profit margin; net profit margin; return on capital employed (Elements 7.1 & 7.2)

13. Tabulation of accounting and other quantitative information using spreadsheets (Elements 7.1 & 7.2)

14. Methods of presenting information: written reports; diagrammatic; tabular (Elements 7.1 & 7.2)

The organisation

15. How the accounting systems of an organisation are affected by its organisational structure, its administrative systems and procedures and the nature of its business transactions (Elements 7.1, 7.2 & 7.3)

16. The purpose and structure of reporting systems within the organisation (Element 7.1)

17. Background understanding that a variety of outside agencies may require reports and returns from organisations and that these requirements must be built into administrative and accounting systems and procedures (Element 7.2 & 7.3)

18. Background understanding that recording and accounting practices may vary between organisations and different parts of organisations (Elements 7.1, 7.2 & 7.3)

19. The basis of the relationship between the organisation and the VAT Office (Element 7.3)

INTRODUCTION

Element 7.1 Prepare and present periodic performance reports

Performance criteria	Chapters in this Text
In order to perform this element successfully you need to:	
A Consolidate **information** derived from different units of the organisation into the appropriate form	20
B Reconcile **information** derived from different information systems within the organisation	20
C Compare results over time using an appropriate method that allows for changing price levels	19
D Account for transactions between separate units of the organisation in accordance with the organisation's procedures	20
E Calculate **ratios** and **performance indicators** in accordance with the organisation's procedures	21
F Prepare reports in the appropriate form and present them to management within the required timescales	22

Range statement

Performance in this element relates to the following contexts:

Information

- Costs
- Revenue

Ratios

- Gross profit margin
- Net profit margin
- Return on capital employed

Performance indicators

- Productivity
- Cost per unit
- Resource utilisation
- Profitability

Methods of presenting information

- Written report containing diagrams
- Table

INTRODUCTION

Element 7.2 Prepare reports and returns for outside agencies

Performance criteria	Chapters in this Text
In order to perform this element successfully you need to:	
A Identify, collate and present relevant information in accordance with the conventions and definitions used by outside agencies	22
B Ensure calculations of **ratios** and performance indicators are accurate	21
C Obtain authorisation for the despatch of completed **reports and returns** from the appropriate person	22
D Present **reports and returns** in accordance with outside agencies' requirements and deadlines	22

Range statement

Performance in this element relates to the following contexts:

Ratios
- Gross profit margin
- Net profit margin
- Return on capital employed

Reports and returns
- Written report
- Return on standard form

Element 7.3 Prepare VAT returns

Performance criteria	Chapters in this Text
In order to perform this element successfully you need to:	
A Complete and submit VAT returns correctly, using data from the appropriate **recording systems**, within the statutory time limits.	23, 24
B Correctly identify and calculate relevant **inputs and outputs**.	23, 24
C Ensure submissions are made in accordance with current legislation	24
D Ensure guidance is sought from the VAT Office when required, in a professional manner	24

Range statement

Performance in this element relates to the following contexts:

Recording systems

- Computerised ledgers
- Manual control account
- Cash book

Inputs and outputs

- Standard supplies
- Exempt supplies
- Zero rated supplies
- Imports
- Exports

Assessment strategy

Unit 6 is assessed by **skills based assessment** and **exam based assessment**. Unit 7 is assessed by skills based assessment only.

Skills based assessment

Skills based assessment is a means of collecting evidence of your ability to **carry out practical activities** and to **operate effectively in the conditions of the workplace** to the standards required. Evidence may be collected at your place of work, or at an Approved Assessment Centre by means of simulations of workplace activity, or by a combination of these methods.

If the Approved Assessment Centre is a **workplace**, you may be observed carrying out accounting activities as part of your normal work routine. You should collect documentary evidence of the work you have done, or contributed to, in an **accounting portfolio**. Evidence collected in a portfolio can be assessed in addition to observed performance or where it is not possible to assess by observation.

Where the Approved Assessment Centre is a **college or training organisation**, devolved assessment will be by means of a combination of the following.

(a) Documentary evidence of activities carried out at the workplace, collected by you in an **accounting portfolio**.

(b) Realistic **simulations** of workplace activities. These simulations may take the form of case studies and in-tray exercises and involve the use of primary documents and reference sources.

(c) **Projects and assignments** designed to assess the Standards of Competence.

If you are unable to provide workplace evidence you will be able to complete the assessment requirements by the alternative methods listed above.

Possible assessment methods

Where possible, evidence should be collected in the workplace, but this may not be a practical prospect for you. Equally, where workplace evidence can be gathered it may not cover all elements. The AAT regards performance evidence from simulations, case studies, projects and assignments as an acceptable substitute for performance at work, provided that they are based on the Standards and, as far as possible, on workplace practice.

There are a number of methods of assessing accounting competence. The list below is not exhaustive, nor is it prescriptive. Some methods have limited applicability, but others are capable of being expanded to provide challenging tests of competence.

INTRODUCTION

Assessment method	Suitable for assessing
Performance of an accounting task either in the workplace or by simulation: eg preparing and processing documents, posting entries, making adjustments, balancing, calculating, analysing information etc by manual or computerised processes	**Basic task competence.** Adding supplementary oral questioning may help to draw out underpinning knowledge and understanding and highlight your ability to deal with contingencies and unexpected occurrences
General case studies. These are broader than simulations. They include more background information about the system and business environment	Ability to **analyse a system** and suggest ways of modifying it. It could take the form of a written report, with or without the addition of oral or written questions
Accounting problems/cases: eg a list of balances that require adjustments and the preparation of final accounts	Understanding of the **general principles of accounting** as applied to a particular case or topic
Preparation of flowcharts/diagrams. To illustrate an actual (or simulated) accounting procedure	**Understanding of the logic** behind a procedure, of controls, and of relationships between departments and procedures. Questions on the flow chart or diagram can provide evidence of underpinning knowledge and understanding
Interpretation of accounting information from an actual or simulated situation. The assessment could include non-financial information and written or oral questioning	**Interpretative competence**
Preparation of written reports on an actual or simulated situation	**Written communication skills**
Analysis of critical incidents, problems encountered, achievements	Your ability to handle **contingencies**
Listing of likely errors eg preparing a list of the main types of errors likely to occur in an actual or simulated procedure	Appreciation of the range of **contingencies** likely to be encountered. Oral or written questioning would be a useful supplement to the list
Outlining the organisation's policies, guidelines and regulations	Performance criteria relating to these aspects of competence. It also provides evidence of competence in **researching information**
Objective tests and short-answer questions	**Specific knowledge**
In-tray exercises	Your **task-management ability** as well as technical competence
Supervisors' reports	**General job competence**, personal effectiveness, reliability, accuracy, and time management. Reports need to be related specifically to the Standards of Competence
Analysis of work logbooks/diaries	**Personal effectiveness**, time management etc. It may usefully be supplemented with oral questioning
Formal written answers to questions	**Knowledge and understanding** of the general accounting environment and its impact on particular units of competence
Oral questioning	**Knowledge and understanding** across the range of competence including organisational procedures, methods of dealing with unusual cases, contingencies and so on. It is often used in conjunction with other methods

Exam based assessment

An exam based assessment is a means of collecting evidence that you have the **essential knowledge and understanding** which underpins competence. It is also a means of collecting evidence across the **range of contexts** for the standards, and of your ability to **transfer skills**, knowledge and understanding to different situations. Thus, although central assessments contain practical tests linked to the performance criteria, they also focus on the underpinning knowledge and understanding. You should, in addition, expect each central assessment to contain tasks taken from across a broad range of the standards.

Unit 6 Recording and evaluating costs and revenues

The examination will be consist of two sections and will be a case study based on a single organisation. This costing system will be appropriate to the needs of that organisation.

Section 1 will assess competence in elements 6.1 and 6.2. Examples of tasks which may be assessed in this section include:

- Methods of stock control and pricing of materials to include First In First Out, Last In First Out and Weighted Average Cost.
- Preparation of cost accounting entries for material, labour and overhead costs of the organisation.
- Calculation of direct labour costs.
- The allocation and apportionment of indirect costs to responsibility centres including direct and step down methods.
- Calculation of departmental absorption rates using different absorption bases.
- Calculation of product cost using absorption and marginal costing.

Section 2 will assess competence in element 6.3. Examples of tasks which may be assessed in this section include:

- The separation of variable and fixed costs and the effect of changing capacity levels.
- Preparation of estimates of future income and costs.
- Short term planning tasks involving cost-volume-profit analysis for a single product.
- Product mix decisions using limiting factor analysis.
- Long term planning tasks using net present value and payback techniques. Tasks will not be set which require the computation of a project's internal rate of return (IRR) but students should be aware of its meaning.
- Preparation of a report.

The tasks detailed above are indicative of those which may be assessed but are not exhaustive. It is important to understand that the examination is based on the Standards of Competence and that all areas in the Standard are assessable. Students should note that process costing is now included within the revised Unit 6 standard. Process costing will be examined to the following extent:

- The organisation will have no more than two processes.
- The student should be able to prepare process, normal loss, abnormal loss and abnormal gain accounts when there is no ending work in progress. This will include accounting for scrap sales.
- The calculation of unit costs where there is closing work in progress but neither opening work in progress nor process losses.
- By products and joint products will not be examined.

INTRODUCTION

Students should note that they could be required to prepare a report in section 2. Since competence must be demonstrated in both sections it is important that students practice their report writing. In this context, the following points should be borne in mind:

- Plan the report and check that the plan deals with the tasks set.
- Be aware of the context in which the report is written.
- Make sure all work is legible.
- A well constructed report needs to be expressed in clear and concise English.

The examination will be three hours in duration (with 15 minutes' reading time) and the two sections will normally take the same time to complete. Specific guidance will, however, be given on time allocation in the examination paper.

Exam based assessment technique

Completing exam based assessments successfully at this level is half about having the knowledge, and half about doing yourself full justice on the day. You must have the right **technique**.

The day of the exam based assessment

1. Set at least one **alarm** (or get an alarm call) for a morning exam.

2. Have **something to eat** but beware of eating too much; you may feel sleepy if your system is digesting a large meal.

3. Allow plenty of **time to get to where you are sitting the exam**; have your route worked out in advance and listen to news bulletins to check for potential travel problems.

4. **Don't forget** pens, pencils, rulers, erasers.

5. Put **new batteries** into your calculator and take a spare set (or a spare calculator).

6. **Avoid discussion** about the exam assessment with other candidates outside the venue.

Technique in the exam based assessment

1. **Read the instructions (the 'rubric') on the front of the assessment carefully**

   Check that the format hasn't changed. It is surprising how often assessors' reports remark on the number of students who do not attempt all the tasks.

2. **Read the paper twice**

   Read through the paper twice – don't forget that you are given 15 minutes' reading time. Check carefully that you have got the right end of the stick before putting pen to paper. Use your 15 minutes' reading time wisely. **From June 2003**, reading time can only be used for **reading**. You can not make notes or use a calculator during those 15 minutes.

3. **Check the time allocation for each section of the exam**

   Time allocations are given for each section of the exam. When the time for a section is up, you should go on to the next section.

4. **Read the task carefully and plan your answer**

   Read through the task again very carefully when you come to answer it. Plan your answer to ensure that you **keep to the point**. Two minutes of planning plus eight minutes of writing is virtually certain to produce a better answer than ten minutes of writing. Planning will also help you answer the assessment efficiently, for example by identifying workings that can be used for more than one task.

5. **Produce relevant answers**

   Particularly with written answers, make sure you **answer what has been set**, and not what you would have preferred to have been set. Do not, for example, answer a question on **why** something is done with an explanation of **how** it is done.

6. **Work your way steadily through the exam**

   Don't get bogged down in one task. If you are having problems with something, the chances are that everyone else is too.

INTRODUCTION

7 **Produce an answer in the correct format**

The assessor will state **in the requirements** the format which should be used, for example in a report or memorandum.

8 **Do what the assessor wants**

You should ask yourself what the assessor is expecting in an answer; many tasks will demand a combination of technical knowledge and business commonsense. Be careful if you are required to give a decision or make a recommendation; you cannot just list the criteria you will use, but you will also have to say whether those criteria have been fulfilled.

9 **Lay out your numerical computations and use workings correctly**

Make sure the layout is in a style the assessor likes.

Show all your **workings** clearly and explain what they mean. Cross reference them to your answer. This will help the assessor to follow your method (this is of particular importance where there may be several possible answers).

10 **Present a tidy paper**

You are a professional, and it should show in the **presentation of your work**. You should make sure that you write legibly, label diagrams clearly and lay out your work neatly.

11 **Stay until the end of the exam**

Use any spare time **checking and rechecking** your script. Check that you have answered all the requirements of the task and that you have clearly labelled your work. Consider also whether your answer appears reasonable in the light of the information given in the question.

12 **Don't worry if you feel you have performed badly in the exam**

It is more than likely that the other candidates will have found the assessment difficult too. As soon as you get up to leave the venue, **forget** that assessment and think about the next – or, if it is the last one, celebrate!

13 **Don't discuss an exam with other candidates**

This is particularly the case if you **still have other exams to sit**. Even if you have finished, you should put it out of your mind until the day of the results. Forget about exams and relax!

Building your portfolio

What is a portfolio?

A portfolio is a collection of work that demonstrates what the owner can do. In AAT language the portfolio demonstrates **competence**.

A painter will have a collection of his paintings to exhibit in a gallery, an advertising executive will have a range of advertisements and ideas that she has produced to show to a prospective client. Both the collection of paintings and the advertisements form the portfolio of that artist or advertising executive.

Your portfolio will be unique to you just as the portfolio of the artist will be unique because no one will paint the same range of pictures in the same way. It is a very personal collection of your work and should be treated as a **confidential** record.

What evidence should a portfolio include?

No two portfolios will be the same but by following some simple guidelines you can decide which of the following suggestions will be appropriate in your case.

(a) **Your current CV**

This should be at the front. It will give your personal details as well as brief descriptions of posts you have held with the most recent one shown first.

(b) **References and testimonials**

References from previous employers may be included especially those of which you are particularly proud.

(c) **Your current job description**

You should emphasise financial **responsibilities and duties**.

(d) **Your student record sheets**

These should be supplied by AAT when you begin your studies, and your training provider should also have some if necessary.

(e) **Evidence from your current workplace**

This could take many forms including **letters, memos, reports** you have written, **copies of accounts** or **reconciliations** you have prepared, **discrepancies** you have investigated etc. Remember to obtain permission to include the evidence from your line manager because some records may be sensitive. Discuss the performance criteria that are listed in your Student Record Sheets with your training provider and employer, and think of other evidence that could be appropriate to you.

(f) **Evidence from your social activities**

For example you may be the treasurer of a club in which case examples of your cash and banking records could be appropriate.

(g) **Evidence from your studies**

Few students are able to satisfy all the requirements of competence by workplace evidence alone. They therefore rely on simulations to provide the remaining evidence to complete a unit. If you are not working or not working in a relevant post, then you may need to rely more heavily on simulations as a source of evidence.

INTRODUCTION

(h) **Additional work**

Your training provider may give you work that specifically targets one or a group of performance criteria in order to complete a unit. It could take the form of questions, presentations or demonstrations. Each training provider will approach this in a different way.

(i) **Evidence from a previous workplace**

This evidence may be difficult to obtain and should be used with caution because it must satisfy the 'rules' of evidence, that is it must be current. Only rely on this as evidence if you have changed jobs recently.

(j) **Prior achievements**

For example you may have already completed the health and safety unit during a previous course of study, and therefore there is no need to repeat this work. Advise your training provider who will check to ensure that it is the same unit and record it as complete if appropriate.

How should it be presented?

As you assemble the evidence remember to **make a note** of it on your Student Record Sheet in the space provided and **cross reference** it. In this way it is easy to check to see if your evidence is **appropriate**. Remember one piece of evidence may satisfy a number of performance criteria so remember to check this thoroughly and discuss it with your training provider if in doubt.

To keep all your evidence together a ring binder or lever arch file is a good means of storage.

When should evidence be assembled?

You should begin to assemble evidence **as soon as you have registered as a student**. **Don't leave it all** until the last few weeks of your studies, because you may miss vital deadlines and your resulting certificate sent by the AAT may not include all the units you have completed. Give yourself and your training provider time to examine your portfolio and report your results to AAT at regular intervals. In this way the task of assembling the portfolio will be spread out over a longer period of time and will be presented in a more professional manner.

What are the key criteria that the portfolio must fulfil?

As you assemble your evidence bear in mind that it must be:

- **Valid**. It must relate to the Standards.
- **Authentic**. It must be your own work.
- **Current**. It must refer to your current or most recent job.
- **Sufficient**. It must meet all the performance criteria by the time you have completed your portfolio.

What are the most important elements in a portfolio that covers Unit 6?

You should remember that this unit is about recording and evaluating costs and revenues. Therefore you need to produce evidence not only demonstrating that you can carry out certain tasks, but also you must show that you can record and evaluate costs and revenues.

For Element 6.1 *Record and analyse information relating to direct costs and revenues,* you not only need to show that you can identify which costs are direct, you also need to demonstrate that you can code them correctly and resolve or refer any queries to the appropriate person.

The main evidence that you need for Element 6.2 *Record and analyse information relating to the allocation, apportionment and absorption of overhead costs* is detail of how overheads are correctly allocated, apportioned and absorbed in accordance with your organisation's procedures. You will also need to demonstrate that you consult staff working in operational departments if you need to resolve any queries in overhead cost data.

To fulfil the requirements of Element 6.3 *Prepare and evaluate estimates of costs and revenues* you need to demonstrate that you have prepared estimates of future income and costs. You will also need to show that you can present any recommendations to the appropriate personnel in a clear and concise way and supported by clear rationale.

What are the most important elements in a portfolio that covers Unit 7?

You should remember that the unit is about the **preparation** of **reports** and **returns**. Therefore you need to produce evidence not only demonstrating that you can carry out certain tasks, but also you must be able to show that you can prepare the relevant reports and returns.

For Element 7.1 *Prepare and present periodic performance reports* you not only need to show that you can produce periodic performance reports containing written information, you also need to demonstrate that you have used this information in order to produce charts and graphs. You will also need to provide evidence of having calculated ratios and performance indicators.

To fulfil the requirements of Element 7.2 *Prepare reports and returns for outside agencies* you need to demonstrate that you have completed standard returns and written reports for external bodies. You also need to provide evidence of correspondence with these bodies and evidence that you have sought authorisation for the despatch of any such correspondence.

For Element 7.3 *Prepare VAT returns* you need to show evidence of completed VAT returns (showing how you have calculated any input and output VAT). You will also need to show evidence of having sought guidance from the VAT office where necessary.

Finally

Remember that the portfolio is **your property** and **your responsibility**. Not only could it be presented to the external verifier before your award can be confirmed; it could be used when you are seeking **promotion** or applying for a more senior and better paid post elsewhere. How your portfolio is presented can say as much about you as the evidence inside.

> For further information on portfolio building, see the BPP Text *Building Your Portfolio*. This can be ordered using the form at the back of this Text or via the Internet: www.bpp.com/aat

UNIT 6

Recording and evaluating costs and revenues

chapter 1

Introduction to recording and evaluating costs and revenues

Contents

1. Introduction
2. Management information requirements
3. Cost accounting systems
4. Cost units and cost centres
5. Cost classification
6. Presentation of information to management

Knowledge and understanding

1. The nature and purpose of internal reporting
2. Management information requirements
3. Maintaining an appropriate cost accounting system
4. Recording of cost and revenue data in the accounting records
14. Methods of presenting information in written reports

1 Introduction

The aim of this chapter is to introduce you to the recording and evaluation of costs and revenues.

The main reason that an organisation records cost and revenues is in order to obtain information for management. As you probably know, managers (including your own manager!) are always asking for reports, analyses, schedules of costs and so on. Well, broadly speaking, these reports, analyses and schedules are part of what is known as **management information**. Management information, as we shall see, is most likely to be used for the following.

- Planning
- Control
- Decision making

2 Management information requirements

Information is sometimes referred to as **processed data.** Management have a constant need for information or processed data. The successful management of any company depends on information.

Example: Management information requirements

A company wishes to launch a new product. The company's pricing policy is to set the price at total cost + 20%. What should the price of the product be?

⇩

MANAGEMENT NEED INFORMATION ABOUT THE TOTAL COST OF THE PRODUCT

A company's bottle making machine has a fault and the company has to decide whether to repair the machine, to buy a new machine or to hire a machine. If the company aims to minimise costs, which decision should management take?

⇩

MANAGEMENT NEED COST INFORMATION RELATING TO THE FOLLOWING DECISIONS.
- REPAIRING THE CURRENT MACHINE
- BUYING A NEW MACHINE
- HIRING A SIMILAR MACHINE

The examples above show that information is a vital part of the following processes.

- Planning
- Control
- Decision making

2.1 Planning

Planning involves the following.

- Establishing **objectives** for the company
- Developing **strategies** in order to achieve the company's objectives

An **objective** is the aim or goal of an organisation.

A **strategy** is a possible course of action that might enable an organisation to achieve its objectives.

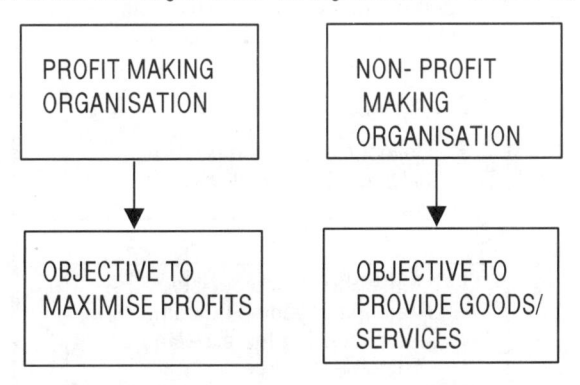

```
PROFIT MAKING              NON- PROFIT
ORGANISATION               MAKING
                           ORGANISATION
     |                          |
     v                          v
OBJECTIVE TO               OBJECTIVE TO
MAXIMISE PROFITS           PROVIDE GOODS/
                           SERVICES
```

The objectives of an organisation might include one or more of the following.

- Maximise profits
- Maximise shareholder value
- Minimise costs
- Maximise revenue
- Increase market share

Remember that the type of activity undertaken by an organisation will have an impact on its objectives.

2.2 Control

Control is the action of monitoring something in order to keep it on course. Most companies will set out a plan for a future period (for example, a **budget**) and then compare the actual results during the period with the budget. Any deviations from the budget can then be identified and corrected as necessary. Such deviations are known as **variances** (you studied variances at Foundation level in Unit 4).

You will go on to study variances and variance analysis in detail at Technician level in Unit 8 *Contributing to the Management of Performance and the Enhancement of Value*.

2.3 Decision making

Managers at all levels within an organisation take decisions. Decision making always involves a **choice between alternatives** and it is the role of the accounting technician to provide information so that management can reach an informed decision. It is therefore useful if accounting technicians understand the decision-making process so that they can supply the appropriate type of information.

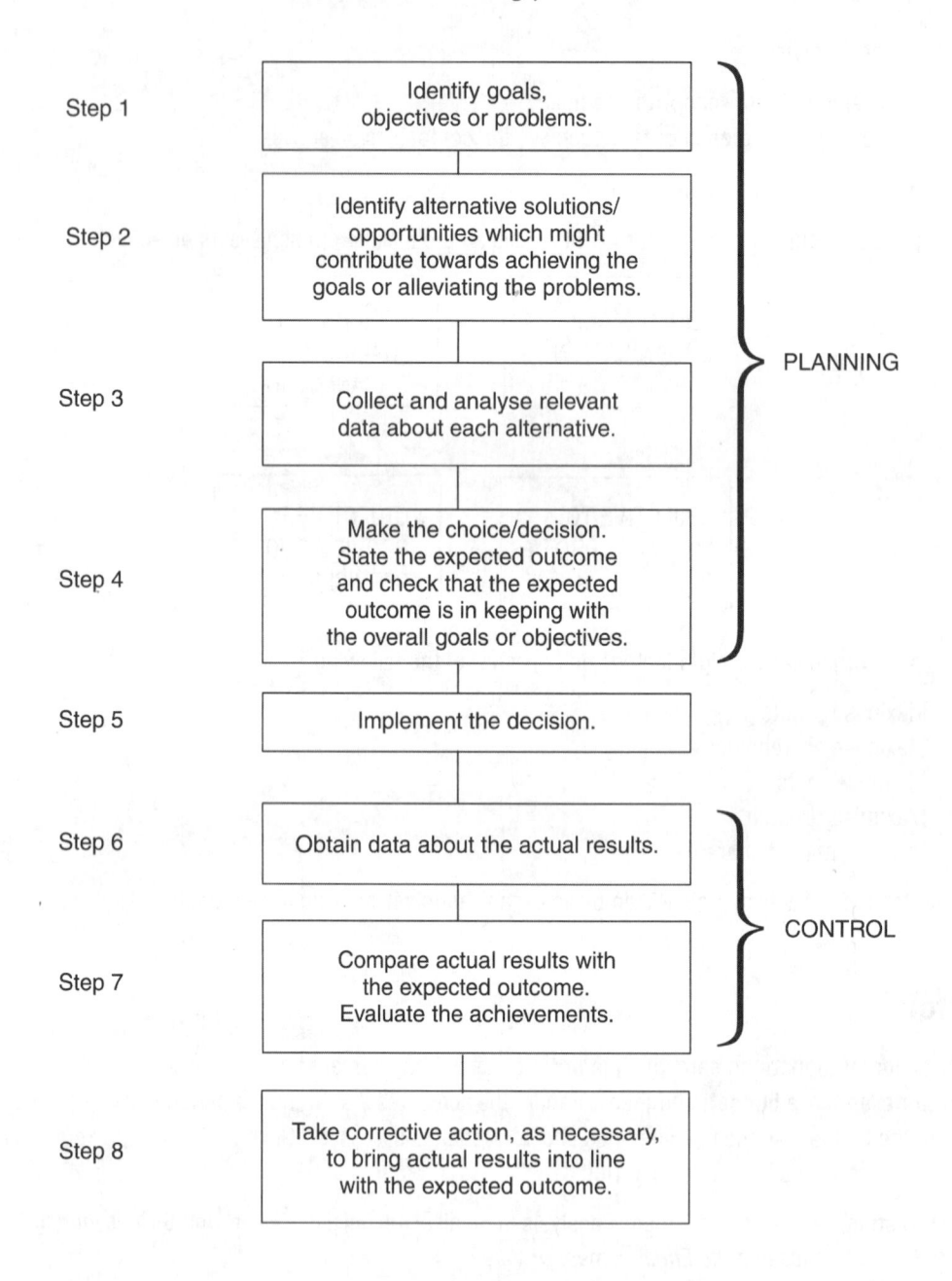

Decision-making process

Step 1	Identify goals, objectives or problems.
Step 2	Identify alternative solutions/ opportunities which might contribute towards achieving the goals or alleviating the problems.
Step 3	Collect and analyse relevant data about each alternative.
Step 4	Make the choice/decision. State the expected outcome and check that the expected outcome is in keeping with the overall goals or objectives.

Steps 1-4: PLANNING

Step 5	Implement the decision.
Step 6	Obtain data about the actual results.
Step 7	Compare actual results with the expected outcome. Evaluate the achievements.
Step 8	Take corrective action, as necessary, to bring actual results into line with the expected outcome.

Steps 6-8: CONTROL

3 Cost accounting systems

An organisation's cost accounting system is designed to record the organisation's costs and revenues. It provides information to assist management with planning, control and decision making and also accumulates historical costs to help establish stock valuations and provide profit and loss and balance sheet information.

3.1 Cost accounts

Cost accounting is concerned with the following.

- Preparing statements (eg budgets, costing)
- Cost data collection
- Applying costs to stock, products and services

Management accounting is concerned with using financial data and communicating it as information to users.

3.1.1 Aim of cost accounts

Cost accounting is part of management accounting. Cost accounting provides a bank of data for the management accountant to use. Cost accounts aim to establish the following.

- The **cost** of goods produced or services provided.
- The **cost** of a department or work section.
- What **revenues** have been.
- The **profitability** of a product, a service, a department, or the organisation in total.
- **Selling prices** with some regard for the costs of sale.
- The **value of stocks of goods** (raw materials, work in progress, finished goods).
- The **future costs** of goods and services (costing is an integral part of budgeting (planning)).
- **How actual costs compare with budgeted costs** (budgetary control).

It would be wrong to suppose that cost accounting systems are restricted to manufacturing operations, although they are probably more fully developed in this area of work. **Service industries**, **government departments** and **welfare activities** can all make use of cost accounting information. Within a manufacturing organisation, the cost accounting system should be applied not only to **manufacturing** but also to **administration**, **selling and distribution**, **research and development** and all other departments.

3.2 Financial accounts and management accounts

Management information provides a common source from which is drawn information for two groups of people.

- **Financial accounts** are prepared for individuals **external** to an organisation.
- **Management accounts** are prepared for **internal** managers of an organisation.

The data used to prepare financial accounts and management accounts are the same. The differences between the financial accounts and the management accounts arise because the data are analysed differently.

Financial accounts	Management accounts
Financial accounts detail the performance of an organisation over a defined period and the state of affairs at the end of that period.	Management accounts are used to aid management to record, plan and control the organisation's activities and to help the decision-making process.
Limited companies must, by law, prepare financial accounts.	There is no legal requirement to prepare management accounts.
The format of published financial accounts is determined by law (mainly the Companies Acts), by Statements of Standard Accounting Practice and by Financial Reporting Standards. In principle the accounts of different organisations can therefore be easily compared.	The format of management accounts is entirely at management discretion: no strict rules govern the way they are prepared or presented. Each organisation can devise its own management accounting system and format of reports.
Financial accounts concentrate on the business as a whole, aggregating revenues and costs from different operations.	Management accounts can focus on specific areas of an organisation's activities. Information may be produced to aid a decision rather than to be an end product of a decision.
Most financial accounting information is of a monetary nature.	Management accounts incorporate non-monetary measures. Management may need to know, for example, tonnes of aluminium produced, monthly machine hours, or miles travelled by sales representatives.
Financial accounts present an essentially historical picture of past operations.	Management accounts are both an historical record and a future planning tool.

4 Cost units and cost centres

Before we can go on to look at costs in detail in the rest of this Interactive Text, you need to understand a bit about the organisation of the cost accounting system.

4.1 Cost units

A **cost unit** is a unit of product which has a cost attached to it. The cost unit is the **basic control unit** for costing purposes.

A cost unit is not always a single item. It might be a batch of 1,000 if that is how the individual items are made. For example, a cost per 1,000 (or whatever) is often more meaningful information, especially if calculating a cost for a single item gives an amount that you cannot hold in your hand, like 0.003p. Examples of cost units are as follows.

- A batch of 1,000 pairs of shoes or 200 pens
- A passenger mile (for a bus company)
- A patient night (for a hospital)

4.2 Cost centres

Cost centres are the essential 'building blocks' of a costing system. They act as a collecting place for certain costs before they are analysed further.

There are a number of different types of cost centre, which include the following.

- A **department,** for example in a factory making cakes there could be a mixing department and a baking department.
- A **person,** for example the company solicitor may incur costs on books and stationery that are unique to his or her function.
- A **group of people,** for example the laboratory staff.
- An **item of equipment** such as a machine which incurs running and maintenance costs.

The number and types of cost centres that an organisation uses will depend on the structure of the organisation and on the type of product or service it produces.

Cost centres may vary in nature, but what they have in common is that they **incur costs**. It is therefore logical to **collect costs** initially under the headings of the various different cost centres that there may be in an organisation.

5 Cost Classification

Before any attempt is made to establish stock valuations and measure profits, to plan, to make decisions or exercise control (in other words, do any cost accounting), costs must be classified. Classification involves arranging costs into groupings of similar items in order to make stock valuation, profit measurement, planning, decision making and control easier.

5.1 Production costs

Let us suppose that you are holding a red pen. Look at your pen and consider what it consists of. There is probably a red plastic cap and a little red thing that fits into the end, and perhaps a yellow plastic sheath. There is an opaque plastic ink holder with red ink inside it. At the tip there is a gold plastic part holding a metal nib with a roller ball. How much do all these separate **materials** cost?

Now think about how the pen was manufactured. The manufacturer probably has machines to mould the plastic and do some of the assembly. How much does it cost, per batch of pens, to run the machines: to set them up so that they produce the right shape of moulded plastic? How much are the production line workers' wages per batch of pens? How much are all these separate **labour costs**?

Any of these separate production costs are known as **direct costs** because they can be traced directly to specific units of production.

5.2 Overheads

Overheads (or indirect costs) include costs that go into the making of the pen that you do not see when you dismantle it. You can touch the materials and you can appreciate that a combination of man and machine put them together. It is not so obvious that the manufacturer also has to do other things including the following.

- Lubricate machines and employ people to supervise the assembly staff
- Pay rent for the factory and for somewhere to keep the stock of materials
- Pay someone to buy materials, recruit labour and run the payroll
- Deliver the finished pens to the wholesaler
- Employ staff at head office to take orders and collect payments

Overheads are the biggest problem for cost accountants because it is not easy to tell by either looking at or measuring the product, what overheads went into getting it into the hands of the buyer. Overheads, or indirect costs, unlike direct costs, will not be identified with any single cost unit because they are **incurred for the benefit of all units rather than for any one specific unit.**

In this Interactive Text you will see how the cost accounting system tries to **apportion overheads (indirect costs) to each cost unit as fairly as possible.**

5.3 Prime cost

The cost of an item can be divided into the following cost elements.

- Materials
- Labour
- Expenses

Each element can be split into two, as follows.

Materials	=	Direct materials	+	Indirect materials
+		+		+
Labour	=	Direct labour	+	Indirect labour
+		+		+
Expenses	=	Direct expenses	+	Indirect expenses
Total cost	=	Direct cost	+	Overhead

Total direct cost is sometimes referred to as **prime cost.**

5.4 Fixed costs and variable costs

There is one other important way in which costs can be analysed and that is between fixed costs and variable costs.

- If you produce two identical pens you will use twice as many direct materials as you would if you only produced one pen. Direct materials are in this case a **variable cost**. They vary according to the volume of production.

- If you rent the factory that houses your pen-making machines you will pay the same amount of annual rent per annum whether you produce one pen or 10,000 pens. Factory rental is an indirect expense and it is **fixed** no matter what the volume of activity is.

DIRECT/INDIRECT COSTS

> **Costs are either direct or indirect, depending upon how easily they can be traced to a specific unit of product or service.**

VARIABLE/FIXED COSTS

> **Costs are either variable or fixed, depending upon whether they change in total when the volume of activity changes.**

6 Presentation of information to management

Information will usually be presented to management in the form of a **written report**. In small organisations it is possible, however, that information will be communicated less formally (orally or using informal reports/memos).

Throughout this Interactive Text, you will come across a number of techniques which are used to collect management information. Once it has been collected the information is usually analysed and reported back to management in the form of a **report**.

We will be studying written reports in detail in Chapter 22 of this Interactive Text. If you are not studying Units 6 and 7 together, it would be a good idea to have a look through this chapter **before** you complete your Unit 6 studies.

Key learning points

- The main uses of management information are as follows.
    - Planning
    - Control
    - Decision making

- **Planning** involves establishing a company's objectives and then developing strategies in order to achieve these objectives.

- An **objective** is the aim or goal of an organisation.

- A **strategy** is a possible course of action that might enable an organisation to achieve its objectives.

- The objectives of an organisation might include the following.
    - Maximise profits
    - Maximise shareholder value
    - Minimise costs
    - Maximise revenue
    - Increase market share

- **Control** is the action of monitoring something so as to keep it on course (eg variance analysis).

- **Decision making** involves making a choice between alternatives (based on information available to management).

- An organisation's **cost accounting system** is designed to record the organisation's costs and revenues.

- **Financial accounting systems** ensure that the assets and liabilities of a business are properly accounted for, and provide information about profits and so on to shareholders and to other interested parties.

- **Management accounting systems** provide information specifically for the use of managers within the organisation.

- The relationship between cost accounting and management accounting may be summarised as follows: **cost accounting provides a bank of data for the management accountant to use.**

- Costs can be divided into three elements, **materials, labour** and **expenses.**

- A **cost unit** is a unit of product or service which has costs attached to it.

- A **cost centre** is something that incurs costs. It may be a place, a person, a group of people or an item of equipment.

- Costs can be analysed in different ways. For example direct, indirect, fixed, variable. Total direct cost is sometimes referred to as **prime cost.**

- Data and information are usually presented to management in the form of a **report**.

1: INTRODUCTION TO RECORDING AND EVALUATING COSTS AND REVENUES

Quick quiz

1. A strategy is the aim or goal of an organisation.

    ☐ True

    ☐ False

2. Complete the following table.

Organisation	Objective
Profit making	
Non-profit making	

3. A fixed cost is a cost which tends to vary with the level of activity.

    ☐ True

    ☐ False

4. List six differences between financial accounts (FA) and management accounts (MA).

5. What is prime cost?

Answers to quick quiz

1. ☑ False.

    This is the definition of an **objective**. A strategy is a possible course of action that might enable an organisation to **achieve** its objectives.

2.
Organisation	Objective
Profit making	Maximise profits
Non-profit making	Provide goods and services

3. ☑ False.

    Fixed costs are unaffected by changes in the level of activity.

4. - FA = Performance over defined period
     MA = Planning, control and decision making aid

   - FA = Ltd companies (by law) must prepare
     MA = No legal requirement to prepare

- FA = Format of published accounts determined by Law/SSAPs/FRSs
  MA = Format entirely at management discretion

- FA = Concentrate on business as a whole
  MA = Can focus on specific areas of a business

- FA = Mostly of a monetary nature
  MA = Monetary and non-monetary nature

- FA = Historical picture of past operations
  MA = Historical report *and* future planning tool

5   Prime cost is the **total direct cost** of a product or service.

chapter 2

Materials

Contents

1 Introduction
2 Types of material
3 Buying materials
4 Valuing materials issues and stocks
5 Stock control
6 Reordering stock

Performance criteria

6.1.A Identify **direct costs** in accordance with the organisation's costing procedures
6.1.B Record and analyse information relating to direct costs
6.1.C Calculate direct costs in accordance with the organisation's policies and procedures
6.1.D Check cost information for **stocks** against usage and stock control practices
6.1.E Resolve or refer queries to the appropriate person

Range statement

6.1 **Direct costs:**
- Materials

6.1 **Stocks:**
- Raw materials
- Part-finished goods
- Finished goods

Knowledge and understanding

4   Recording of cost and revenue data in the accounting records
5   Methods of stock control and valuation including First In First Out, Last In First Out and Weighted Average Cost
19 Relationship between the materials costing system and the stock control system
27 The sources of information for revenue and costing data

1 Introduction

In the last chapter you learned about the various cost elements that go to make up the total cost of a product or service. In this chapter you will be going on to learn about the first cost element in detail: **materials.**

You will learn about how material stocks are **valued,** and how to maintain an effective **stock control system.**

2 Types of material

2.1 Raw materials

Raw materials are goods purchased for incorporation into products or services for sale.

Raw materials is a term which you are likely to come across often, both in your studies and your workplace. Examples of raw materials are as follows.

- Clay for making terracotta garden pots.
- Timber for making dining room tables.
- Paper for making books.

Activity 2.1

Without getting too technical, what are the main raw materials used in the manufacture of the following items?

(a) A car
(b) A box of breakfast cereal
(c) A house (just the basic structure)
(d) Your own organisation's products or services

Activity 2.2

How would you distinguish direct materials from indirect materials?

Activity 2.3

Classify the following as either direct or indirect materials.

- (a) The foil wrapping around Easter eggs
- (b) Paper used for the pages of a book
- (c) Lubricant used on sewing machines in a clothing factory
- (d) Plastic used to make audio cassette boxes
- (e) Shoe boxes

2.2 Work in progress

Work in progress is a term used to represent an intermediate stage between the manufacturer purchasing the materials that go to make up the finished product and the finished product. Work in progress is another name for **part-finished goods**.

Work in progress means that some work has been done on the materials purchased as part of the process of producing the finished product, but **the production process is not complete.** Examples of work in progress are as follows.

- Terracotta pots which have been shaped, but which have not yet been fired
- Tables which have been assembled, but which have not yet been polished

Work in progress must be subjected to further processing before it becomes **finished goods,** which are completed and ready for sale. Valuing work in progress is one of the most difficult tasks in cost accounting.

Activity 2.4

Distinguish between raw materials, work in progress and finished goods.

3 Buying materials

3.1 Purchasing procedures

All businesses have to buy materials of some sort, and this means that decisions have to be made and somebody has to be responsible for doing the **buying**. Large businesses have specialist **buying departments** managed by people who are very skilled at the job.

The following diagram shows the different purchasing procedures and the departments involved.

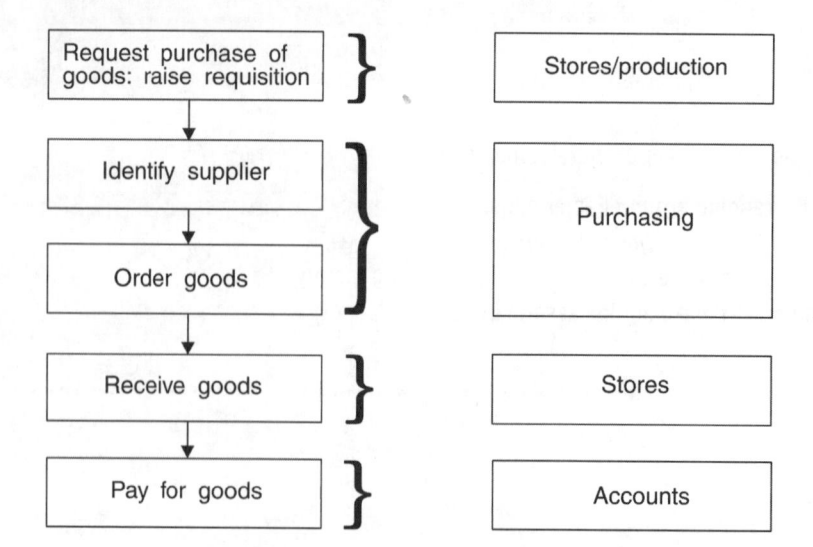

```
Request purchase of          Stores/production
goods: raise requisition
         ↓
   Identify supplier    ⎫
         ↓              ⎬    Purchasing
     Order goods        ⎭
         ↓
    Receive goods       }    Stores
         ↓
     Pay for goods      }    Accounts
```

3.2 Purchasing documentation

We shall describe a manual system that might be used in a fairly large organisation. In reality it is likely that much of the procedure would be computerised, but this does not alter the basic principles or information flows.

3.2.1 Purchase requisition

The first stage will be that the department requiring the goods will complete a **purchase requisition** asking the **purchasing department** to carry out the necessary transaction. An example is shown below.

```
                    PURCHASE REQUISITION   Req. No.

 Department _____           Date
 Suggested supplier:

                                       Requested by:
                                       Latest date required:

┌──────────┬────────────────────────────┬─────────────────────┐
│ Quantity │  Description and code no.  │   Estimated cost    │
│          │                            ├──────────┬──────────┤
│          │                            │   Unit   │    £     │
│          │                            │          │          │
│          │                            │          │          │
│          │                            │          │          │
│          │                            │          │          │
├──────────┴────────────────────────────┴──────────┴──────────┤
│ Authorised signature:                                       │
└─────────────────────────────────────────────────────────────┘
```

Note that the purchase requisition will usually need some form of **authorisation**, probably that of a senior person in the department requiring the goods **and** possibly also that of a senior person in the finance department if substantial expense is involved.

3.2.2 Order form

Once a **purchase requisition** is received in the purchasing department, the first task is to identify the most suitable **supplier**. Often the business will use a regular source of supply. The purchasing department may be aware of special offers or have details of new suppliers.

A **purchase order** is then completed by the purchasing department.

Purchase Order/Confirmation		Fenchurch Garden Centre Pickle Lane Westbridge Kent		
Our Order Ref:	Date			
To ⌈ *(Address)* ⌉ ⌊ ⌋		Please deliver to the above address Ordered by: Passed and checked by: Total Order Value £		
Quantity	Code No	Description	Unit cost £	Total £
		Subtotal		
		VAT (@ 17.5%)		
		Total		

Key

(a) Sent to the supplier.
(b) Legally binding document. Authorised personnel only should complete it.
(c) Provides a means of checking that the goods received are the same as those ordered.
(d) Copies sent to:

- The person who requisitioned the goods
- The stores department
- The accounts department

The **purchase order** is important because it provides a means by which the business can later **check that the goods received are the same as those ordered**.

3.2.3 Despatch note

Certain other documents may be completed before the goods are actually received. The supplier may acknowledge the order and perhaps indicate how long it is likely to take to be fulfilled. A **despatch note** may be sent to warn that the goods are on their way.

3.2.4 Delivery note

We now move to the stores department. When the goods are delivered, the goods inwards department will be presented with a **delivery note** or **advice note**. This is the supplier's document and a copy is signed by the person receiving the goods and this copy is returned to the supplier. If the actual goods cannot be inspected immediately, the delivery note should be signed **'subject to inspection'**.

3.2.5 Goods received note

Once the goods have been delivered they should be inspected and checked as soon as possible. A **goods received note (GRN)** will then be completed.

```
                                                    ACCOUNTS COPY
        ┌─────────────────────────────────────────────────────────┐
        │         GOODS RECEIVED NOTE  WAREHOUSE COPY             │
        │  DATE:  7 March 20X1   TIME:  2.00 pm      NO  5565     │
        │  ORDER NO: _____                      │
        │  SUPPLIER'S ADVICE NOTE NO: _____  WAREHOUSE A    │
        │  ┌──────────┬──────────┬─────────────────────────────┐  │
        │  │ QUANTITY │ CODE NO  │ DESCRIPTION                 │  │
        │  ├──────────┼──────────┼─────────────────────────────┤  │
        │  │    20    │  TP 400  │ Terracotta pots, medium     │  │
        │  │          │          │                             │  │
        │  └──────────┴──────────┴─────────────────────────────┘  │
        │   RECEIVED IN GOOD CONDITION:  L. W.     (INITIALS)     │
        └─────────────────────────────────────────────────────────┘
```

Key

(a) Copy of **goods received note** sent to purchasing department so that it can be matched with the purchase order.

(b) Copy of **goods received note** sent to accounts department so that it can be matched with the supplier's invoice.

The transaction ends with payment of the invoice (once any discrepancies have been sorted out).

Activity 2.5

Name four items that would be shown on a purchase order.

Helping hand. Thinking about the purpose of a purchase order will help you to reason through what details are required.

Activity 2.6

Draw a flow diagram illustrating the main documents involved in a materials purchase, from its initiation up until the time of delivery.

4 Valuing materials issues and stocks

When a stock item is issued from the stores to be used, say, in production, the cost accountant will record the **value of stock to be charged to the relevant cost centre**.

Example: Stock valuation

(a) Suppose, for example, that you have 50 litres of a chemical in stock. You buy 2,000 litres to allow for the next batch of production. Both the opening stock and the newly-purchased stock cost £2 per litre.

	Litres	£
Opening stock	50	100
Purchases	2,000	4,000
	2,050	4,100

(b) You actually use 1,600 litres, leaving you with 450 litres in stock. You know that each of the 1,600 litres used cost £2, as did each of the 450 litres remaining. There is no costing problem here.

(c) Now suppose that in the following month you decide to buy another 1,300 litres, but have to pay £2.10 per litre because you lose a 10p discount if buying under 1,500 litres.

	Litres	Cost per litre £	Total cost £
Opening stock	450	2.00	900
Purchases	1,300	2.10	2,730
	1,750		3,630

(d) For the next batch of production you use 1,600 litres, as before. What did the 1,600 litres used cost, and what value should you place on the 150 litres remaining in stock?

Solution

(a) If we could identify which litres were used there would be no problem. Some would cost £2 per litre but most would cost £2.10. It may not, however, be possible to identify litres used. For instance, the chemical may not be perishable, and new purchases may simply be mixed in with older stock in a central tank. There would thus be no way of knowing to which delivery the 1,600 litres used belonged. Even if the chemical were stored in tins with date stamps it would be a tedious and expensive chore to keep track of precisely which tins were used when.

(b) It may not therefore be possible or desirable to track the progress of each individual litre. However **we need to know the cost of the litres that we have used** so that we know how much to charge for the final product and so that we can compare this cost with the equivalent cost in earlier or future periods. We also **need to know the cost of closing stock** both because it will form part of the usage figure in the next period and for financial accounting purposes. Closing stock is often a significant figure in the financial statements and it appears in both the profit and loss account and the balance sheet.

(c) We therefore have to use a consistent method of pricing the litres which provides a reasonable approximation of the costs of the stock.

There are a number of different methods of valuing stock and the issues from stock.

- FIFO
- LIFO
- Weighted average cost

4.1 FIFO – First In First Out

This method values **issues at the prices of the oldest items in stock at the time the issues were made.** The remaining **stock will thus be valued at the price of the most recent purchases.** Say, for example ABC Ltd's stock consisted of four deliveries of raw material in the last month.

	Units		
1 September	1,000	at	£2.00
8 September	500	at	£2.50
15 September	500	at	£3.00
22 September	1,000	at	£3.50

If on 23 September 1,500 units were issued, 1,000 of these units would be priced at £2 (the cost of the 1,000 oldest units in stock), and 500 at £2.50 (the cost of the next oldest 500). 1,000 units of closing stock would be valued at £3.50 (the cost of the 1,000 most recent units received) and 500 units at £3.00 (the cost of the next most recent 500).

4.2 LIFO – Last In First Out

This method is the opposite of FIFO. **Issues will be valued at the prices of the most recent purchases**; hence **stock remaining will be valued at the cost of the oldest items.** In the example above it will be 1,000 units of **issues** which will be valued at £3.50, and the other 500 units issued will be valued at £3.00. 1,000 units of **closing stock** will be valued at £2.00, and 500 at £2.50.

4.3 Weighted average cost method

With this method we calculate an **average cost of all the units in stock whenever a new delivery is received.** Thus the individual price of the units issued *and* of the units in closing stock will be (22 September being the date of the last delivery) as follows.

$$\frac{\text{Total cost of units in stock at 22 September}}{\text{Units in stock at 22 September}}$$

The average price per unit will be $\dfrac{£8{,}250}{3{,}000} = £2.75$.

Example: FIFO, LIFO and Weighted average cost

Let's go back to the stock valuation example at the beginning of this section.

(a) **FIFO**

	Litres	Cost per litre £	Total cost £
Opening stock	450	2.00	900
Purchases	1,300	2.10	2,730
	1,750		3,630
Usage (oldest items first)	(450)	2.00	(900)
	1,300		2,730
Usage (1,600 – 450)	(1,150)	2.10	(2,415)
Closing stock	150		315

Total cost of usage is £900 + £2,415 = £3,315 and the value of closing stock is £315.

(b) **LIFO**

	Litres	Cost per litre £	Total cost £
Opening stock	450	2.00	900
Purchases	1,300	2.10	2,730
	1,750		3,630
Usage (most recent items first)	(1,300)	2.10	(2,730)
	450		900
Usage (1,600 – 1,300)	(300)	2.00	(600)
	150		300

Total cost of usage is £2,730 + £600 = £3,330 and the value of closing stock is £300.

(c) **Weighted average cost**

	Litres	Cost per litre £	Total cost £
Opening stock	450	2.000	900
Purchases	1,300	2.100	2,730
Stock at (£3,630/1,750)	1,750	2.074	3,630
Usage (at average price)	(1,600)	2.074	(3,318)
	150		312

Usage costs £3,318 under this method and closing stock is valued at £312.

For FIFO, LIFO and weighted average cost, note that the total of usage costs plus closing stock value is the same (£3,630) whichever method is used. In other words, **the total expenditure of £3,630 is simply split in different proportions between the usage cost for the period and the remaining stock value**. Note that there is no single correct method, each has its own advantages and disadvantages.

Activity 2.7

The following transactions took place during May. You are required to calculate the value of all issues and of closing stock using each of the following methods of valuation.

TRANSACTIONS DURING MAY

	Quantity Units	Unit cost £	Total cost £
Opening balance, 1 May	100	2.00	200
Receipts, 3 May	400	2.10	840
Issues, 4 May	200		
Receipts, 9 May	300	2.12	636
Issues, 11 May	400		
Receipts, 18 May	100	2.40	240
Issues, 20 May	100		
Closing balance, 31 May	200		
			1,916

Tasks

Calculate the value of all issues and of closing stock using each of the following methods of valuation.

(a) FIFO
(b) LIFO
(c) Weighted average cost

4.4 Advantages and disadvantages of the FIFO method

Advantages	Disadvantages
It is a logical pricing method which probably represents what is physically happening: in practice the oldest stock is likely to be used first.	FIFO can be cumbersome to operate because of the need to identify each batch of material separately.
It is easy to understand and explain to managers.	Managers may find it difficult to compare costs and make decisions when they are charged with varying prices for the same materials.
The closing stock value can be near to a valuation based on the cost of replacing the stock.	

4.5 Advantages and disadvantages of the LIFO method

Advantages	Disadvantages
Stocks are issued at a price which is close to current market value. This is not the case with FIFO when there is a high rate of inflation.	The method can be cumbersome to operate because it sometimes results in several batches being only part-used in the stock records before another batch is received.
Managers are continually aware of recent costs when making decisions, because the costs being charged to their department or products will be close to current costs.	LIFO is often the opposite to what is physically happening and can therefore be difficult to explain to managers.
	As with FIFO, decision making can be difficult because of the variations in prices.

4.6 Advantages and disadvantages of weighted average cost method

Advantages	Disadvantages
Fluctuations in prices are smoothed out, making it easier to use the data for decision making.	The resulting issue price is rarely an actual price that has been paid, and can run to several decimal places.
It is easier to administer than FIFO and LIFO, because there is no need to identify each batch separately.	Prices tend to lag a little behind current market values when there is rapid inflation.

Activity 2.8

(a) What is the main disadvantage of the FIFO method of stock valuation?
(b) What is the main advantage of the LIFO method?
(c) What is the main advantage and the main disadvantage of the weighted average cost method?

5 Stock control

Stock control is the regulation of stock levels, one aspect of which is putting a value to the amounts of stock issued and remaining. The stock control system can also be said to include ordering, purchasing and receiving goods and keeping track of them while they are in the warehouse.

The cost of purchasing stock is usually one of the largest costs faced by an organisation and, once obtained, stock has to be carefully controlled and checked.

5.1 Just-in-time

Some organisations operate a **just-in-time (JIT)** stock system. With a JIT system, supplies are ordered and delivered just as they are needed for production, and goods are manufactured just as they are needed for sales. **Stocks are therefore kept to a minimum,** and the system relies on **accurate forecasting** and **reliable suppliers.**

5.2 Buffer stock

Most organisations keep a certain amount of stock in reserve. This reserve of stock is known as **buffer stock.**

5.3 Reasons for holding stocks

- To ensure sufficient goods are available to meet expected demand
- To provide a buffer between processes
- To meet any future shortages
- To take advantage of bulk purchasing discounts
- To absorb seasonal fluctuations and any variations in usage and demand

5.4 Holding costs

If stocks are too high, **holding costs** will be incurred unnecessarily. Such costs occur for a number of reasons.

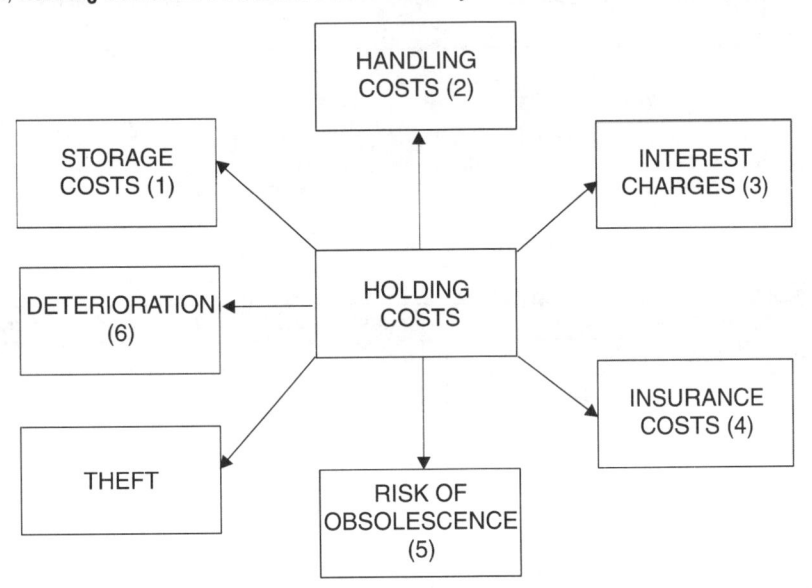

```
                    HANDLING
                    COSTS (2)
                        ↑
    STORAGE                         INTEREST
    COSTS (1) ←                  →  CHARGES (3)
                    HOLDING
                    COSTS
    DETERIORATION ←              →  INSURANCE
    (6)                             COSTS (4)
                        ↓
    THEFT ←         RISK OF
                    OBSOLESCENCE
                    (5)
```

Key

(1) Higher stock levels require more storage space
(2) Higher stock levels require extra staff to handle them
(3) Holding stocks ties up capital on which interest must be paid
(4) The larger the value of stocks, the greater the insurance premiums

(5) Stock may become out-of-date when held for long periods
(6) Stock may deteriorate if stored for long periods

5.5 Ordering costs

If stocks are kept low, small quantities of stock will have to be ordered more frequently. This increases the amount of **ordering costs**. Ordering costs include the following.

- **Clerical and administrative costs** associated with purchasing, accounting for and receiving goods.
- **Transport costs**
- **Production run costs,** for stock which is manufactured internally rather than purchased from external sources.

5.6 Recording stock levels

One of the objectives of storekeeping is to **maintain accurate records of current stock levels.** This involves the recording of stock movements (issues from and receipts into stores). The most common system for recording stock movements is the use of **bin cards** and **stores record cards.**

5.6.1 Bin cards

A **bin card** shows the level of stock of an item at a particular stores location. It is kept with the actual stock and is updated by the storekeeper as stocks are received and issued. A typical bin card is shown below.

```
                          BIN CARD

   Description..................        Bin No:..................
                                        Code No:.................
   Reorder Quantity............         Maximum:.................
                                        Minimum:.................
                                        Re-order Level:..........
```

Receipts			Issues			Balance	Remarks
Date	G.R.N No.	Quantity	Date	Req. No.	Quantity	Quantity	

Note that the bin card does not need to show any information about the cost of materials.

5.6.2 Stores record cards

Organisations will also maintain a **stores record card** for each stock item.

	STORES RECORD CARD										

Material: .... Maximum Quantity: ....
Code: .... Minimum Quantity: ....
                                                 Re-order Level: ....
                                                 Re-order Quantity: ....

Date	Receipts				Issues				Stock		
	G.R.N. No.	Quantity	Unit Price £	Amount £	Materials Req. No.	Quantity	Unit Price £	Amount £	Quantity	Unit Price £	Amount £

Details from **GRNs** and **materials requisition notes** (see later) are used to update **stores record cards**, which then provide a record of the **quantity** and **value** of each stock item in the stores. The stores record cards are normally kept in the cost department or in the stores office.

5.6.3 Stock control checks

The use of bin cards and stores record cards provides a **control check**. The balances on the bin cards in the stores can be compared with the balances on the stores record cards in the office.

5.6.4 Perpetual inventory system

The use of bin cards and stores record cards ensures that every issue and receipt of stock is recorded as it occurs so that there is a continuous clerical record of the balance of each item of stock. This is known as a **perpetual inventory system.**

5.7 Coding of materials

Each item held in stores must be **unambiguously identified** and this can best be done by numbering them with **stock codes**.

```
                    ADVANTAGES
                    OF CODING
                    MATERIALS
```

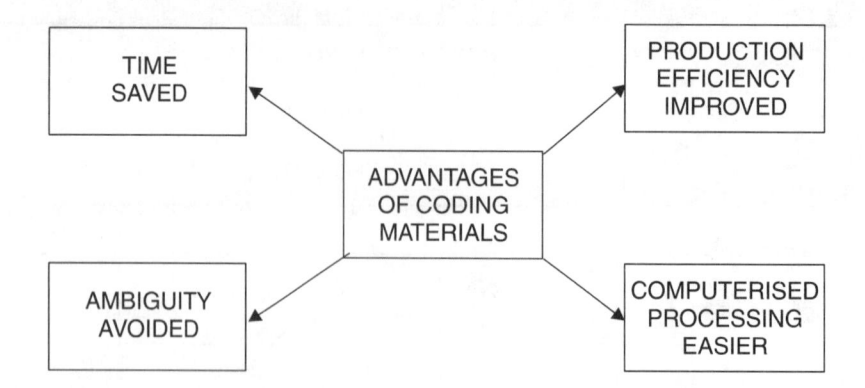

TIME SAVED → ADVANTAGES OF CODING MATERIALS → PRODUCTION EFFICIENCY IMPROVED

AMBIGUITY AVOIDED → ADVANTAGES OF CODING MATERIALS → COMPUTERISED PROCESSING EASIER

The digits in a code can stand for the type of stock, supplier, location and so forth. For example stock item A234/1279 might refer to the item of stock kept in row A, bay 2, bin 3, shelf 4. The item might be identified by the digits 12 and its supplier might be identified by the digits 79.

5.8 Issuing materials

Stocks are held so that they can be used to make products. Stocks are issued from stores to production in the first instance. This transaction will be initiated by the production department who will complete a **materials requisition note** and pass it to the warehouse.

5.8.1 Materials requisition note

```
                    MATERIALS REQUISITION NOTE
    Material Required for:                              No.
        (Job or Overhead Account)
    Department:                           Date:

    | Quantity | Description | Code No. | Weight | Price | Value £ | Notes |

    Supervisor signature:
```

Key

(a) The materials requisition note may also have a space for **the account code to be charged.**
(b) If the material is for a **specific job**, the **job number** will be included on the materials requisition note.
(c) The value of material issues will be based on either the FIFO, LIFO or weighted average cost method.

The stores department will locate the stock, withdraw the amount required and **update the bin card** as appropriate. The **stores record card** will also be updated.

Activity 2.9

An extract from the accounts code list of A Limited is as follows.

Cost centre codes		**Expenditure codes**	
Machining cost centre	100	Direct materials	100
Finishing cost centre	200	Indirect materials	200
Packing cost centre	300		
Maintenance cost centre	400		

Insert the correct account codes for the following materials issues from stores.

	Cost centre code no.	Expenditure code no.
Issue of packing materials to production	....	....
Issue of raw materials to machining centre	....	....
Issue of lubricating oils to maintenance	....	....
Issue of cleaning materials to finishing centre	....	....

Helping hand. The expenditure code will be 100, ie direct materials, if the materials are to become part of the finished product. If the materials cannot be traced directly to the finished product they should be coded as indirect materials.

5.8.2 Materials returned note

If the amount of materials required is overestimated the excess should be sent back to stores accompanied by a **materials returned note**. The form in our illustration is almost identical to a materials requisition note. In practice it would be wise to colour code the two documents (one white, one yellow, say) to prevent confusion.

MATERIALS RETURNED NOTE						
Material not needed for: (Job or Overhead Account) Department:					No. Date:	
Quantity	Description	Code No.	Weight	Price	Value £	Notes
Supervisor signature:						

5.8.3 Materials transfer note

There may be occasions when materials already issued but not required for one job can be used for another job in progress. In this case there is no point in returning the materials to the warehouse. Instead a **materials transfer note** can be raised indicating which job or cost centre is to be credited with the cost of material transferred, and which job or cost centre is to be debited. This prevents one job or cost centre being charged with too many materials and another with too little.

5.9 Stocktaking

Stocktaking involves **counting the physical stock on hand** at a certain date and then **checking this against the balance shown in the clerical records.** There are two methods of carrying out this process.

5.9.1 Periodic stocktaking

Periodic stocktaking is usually carried out annually and the objective is to count all items of stock on a specific date.

5.9.2 Continuous stocktaking

Continuous stocktaking involves counting and checking a number of stock items on a regular basis so that each item is checked **at least once a year**, and valuable items can be checked more frequently. This has a number of advantages over periodic stocktaking. It is less disruptive, less prone to error, and achieves greater control because discrepancies are identified earlier.

5.10 Stock discrepancies

There will be occasions when stock checks disclose **discrepancies between the physical amount of an item in stock and the amount shown in the stock records**. When this occurs, the cause of the discrepancy should be investigated, and appropriate action taken to ensure that it does not happen again.

5.10.1 Possible causes of discrepancies

- **Suppliers deliver a different quantity of goods than is shown on the goods received note (GRN).**
- **The quantity of stock issued to production is different from that shown on the materials requisition note.**
- **Excess stock is returned from production without documentation.**
- **Clerical errors may occur in the stock records.**
- **Breakages in stores may go unrecorded.**
- **Stock may be stolen.**

Activity 2.10

Give five reasons why stocktaking may identify discrepancies between the physical stock held and the balance shown on the stock records.

6 Reordering stock

6.1 Stock control levels

As noted earlier, the ideal is for businesses not to have any stocks on the premises **unless they are about to be used in production which can be sold immediately.** In practice many businesses would regard this approach as **too risky or impractical** because they are unable to predict either their own levels of demand or the reliability of their suppliers or both. They therefore set various **control levels**, the purpose of which is to ensure the following.

- The business **does not run out of stock** and suffer disruption to production as a result.
- The business **does not carry an excessive amount of stocks** which take up space, incur storage costs and possibly deteriorate with age.

Example: Stock control levels

(a) A new manufacturing business is being set up to make a single product, by moulding plastic. Jonathan, the manager, expects to make 10 units per day and has found that each unit will require 5 kg of plastic. He decides to obtain enough materials to last a week (5 days). How much should he order?

(b) This is not difficult. Jonathan should order 5 days × 10 units × 5 kg = 250 kg.

The materials are placed in the stores ready for the commencement of production on the following Monday.

(c) The following week everything goes as planned. The following Monday however, Jonathan realises that he has no materials left. (This is called a **'stock-out'**). He contacts a number of suppliers but to his dismay none can deliver in less than 2 days. There is therefore no production for the whole of Monday and Tuesday.

(d) Jonathan doesn't want this to happen again so he orders four weeks' worth of materials, even though this means increasing his overdraft at the bank by £4,000.

(e) The materials duly arrive on Wednesday morning but of the 1,000 kg delivered (20 × 10 × 5 = 1,000) Jonathan finds he only has room to store 500 kg. To accommodate the remainder he has to rent space in the factory next door at a cost of £200.

(f) Twenty days go by and production goes as planned. Jonathan doesn't want to get caught out again, so two days before he is due to run out of materials he places a fresh order, this time for only 500 kg.

(g) Unfortunately, this time the suppliers are unable to deliver in 2 days as promised, but take 4 days. Another 2 days' production is lost.

(h) As Jonathan's product establishes itself in the market, demand starts to increase. He starts to produce 15 units a day but again he is caught out because, obviously, this means that the materials are used up more quickly. He often runs out before the next delivery has arrived.

(i) So it goes on for the whole of Jonathan's first year in business. By the end of this time he works out that he has lost nearly three weeks' production due to materials shortages. In despair he contacts a management consultant for advice.

Solution

(a) Jonathan is told to calculate a number of figures from his records.

  (i) The maximum daily usage

  (ii) The maximum lead time. (**Lead time** is the time it takes between ordering stocks and having them delivered.)

  (iii) The average daily usage and average lead time

  (iv) The minimum daily usage and minimum lead time

  (v) The cost of holding one unit of stock for one year (holding cost)

  (vi) The cost of ordering a consignment of stock

  (vii) The annual demand for materials

(b) Jonathan has kept careful records and can easily calculate some of these figures.

Maximum usage	100 kg per day
Average usage	75 kg per day
Minimum usage	50 kg per day
Annual demand	19,500 kg (52 weeks × 5 days × 75 kg)
Maximum lead time	4 days
Average lead time	3 days
Minimum lead time	2 days

(c) The calculation of the **holding cost** is quite complicated. Jonathan has to work out a number of figures.

(i) Materials can only be bought in 5 kg boxes and therefore 'one unit' of stock is 5 kg, not 1 kg.

(ii) The total cost of holding one box in stock is made up of a number of separate costs.

- Interest paid on the money borrowed to buy one box
- Rental of the floor space taken up by one box
- The warehouse keeper's wages
- Administrative costs of taking deliveries, issuing materials, and keeping track of them
- The cost of insuring the stock

Eventually Jonathan works out that the figure is £0.62 per 'unit' of 5 kg. He is shocked by this and wonders whether he should order smaller quantities more frequently. (Fortunately for Jonathan, there is little risk of obsolescence or deterioration of boxes. Many organisations have to include the cost of obsolescence or deterioration in holding costs, however.)

(d) To calculate the **ordering costs** Jonathan has to take the following into account.

- The cost of stationery and postage
- The cost of phoning round to suppliers
- The time taken up by doing this

He is surprised to find that the figure works out to £19.87 per order. He wonders whether he should make fewer larger orders to reduce these costs.

(e) Now that Jonathan has these figures the consultant tells him how to calculate four **stock control levels**. These will help him to avoid running out of stock and to keep down the costs of holding and ordering stock.

(i) **Reorder level**.

Jonathan already realises that stocks have to be reordered before they run out completely. **This number tells him how low stocks can be allowed to fall before an order should be placed.** It assumes that maximum usage and maximum lead time, the two worst events from the point of view of stock control, coincide.

Reorder level = maximum usage × maximum lead time
Reorder level = 100 kg × 4 days
            = 400 kg

(ii) **Reorder quantity**

The **reorder quantity** is the quantity of stock which is to be re-ordered when stock reaches the reorder level.

Jonathan has never known what the best amount to order would be. He is beginning to understand that there must be some way **of juggling the costs of holding stock, the costs of ordering stock and the amount of stock needed** but he does not know how to work it out. His consultant fortunately does and she gives him the following formula.

The **economic order quantity (Q)**, or **EOQ** is the best amount to order and is calculated as follows.

$$Q = \sqrt{\frac{2cd}{h}}$$

where h is the cost of holding one unit of stock for one year
       c is the cost of ordering a consignment
       d is the annual demand

Remembering that a 'unit' of stock is 5 kg and therefore annual demand is 19,500 kg /5 kg = 3,900 units, we can calculate the order quantity as follows.

$$Q = \sqrt{\frac{2 \times 19.87 \times 3,900}{0.62}}$$

= 500 units (approximately)

= 2,500 kg (500 units × 5 kg)

(f) Jonathan is not entirely convinced by the EOQ calculation but promises to try it out since it seems like a reasonable amount to order. He then asks what the other two control levels are, since he seems to have all the information he needs already.

(g) The consultant points out that the calculations done so far don't allow for other **uncertain factors** like a severe shortage of supply or unexpected rises or falls in demand.

(h) As a precaution Jonathan needs a **minimum stock level** below which stocks should never be allowed to fall, and a **maximum stock level** above which stock should not be able to rise. There is a **risk of stock-outs** if stock falls below the minimum level and a **risk of stock being at a wasteful level** if above the maximum level.

Minimum stock level = reorder level – (average usage × average lead time)
Minimum stock level = 400 kg – (75 kg × 3 days)
                    = 175 kg

Maximum stock level = reorder level + reorder quantity –
                          (minimum usage × minimum lead time)
Maximum stock level = 400 kg + 2,500 kg – (50 kg × 2 days)
                    = 2,800 kg

(i) The maximum stock level and minimum stock level act as **management warnings levels**. If stock regularly reaches either of these levels, Jonathan will need to **review his reorder level and reorder**

quantity. It may be that the usage and delivery patterns are now different from those that were used to determine the various control levels.

6.2 Buffer stock

Jonathan is delighted that his stock is now well controlled, but to be on the safe side, he decides to hold a **buffer stock** in future. The buffer stock is to be equal to two days' average usage.

Buffer stock = 2 × 75 kg = 150 kg

This buffer stock will remain as a **permanent 'buffer'** against unexpected circumstances.

This permanent buffer stock means that Jonathan will need to reorder at a higher stock level, to ensure that the buffer stock always remains untouched. The new formula for the reorder level, **when a buffer stock exists**, will be

Reorder level = Buffer stock + (maximum usage × maximum lead time)
= 150 kg + (100 kg × 4 days)
= 550 kg

Activity 2.11

Watkins Ltd uses 4,000 kg of a raw material in a year. It costs £10 to hold 1 kg for one year, and the costs of ordering each consignment of raw materials are £200.

Watkins Ltd uses between 100 kg and 600 kg a month, and the company's suppliers can take between 1 and 3 months to deliver materials that have been ordered.

Task

Calculate the following.

(a) The reorder quantity
(b) The reorder level
(c) The maximum level of stock the company should hold

Activity 2.12

Complete the following stores record card to show the quantity and value of stock on 12 November.

Comment on any occasions when company stock control practices were not correctly observed.

STORES RECORD CARD

Material: A4 paper, white
Code: PWA4
Maximum Quantity: 140 boxes
Minimum Quantity: 40 boxes
Re-order Level: 60 boxes
Re-order Quantity: 80 boxes

Date	Receipts				Issues				Stock balance		
	Document number	Qty	Price £ per box	Total £	Document number	Qty	Price £ per box	Total £	Qty	Price £ per box	Total £
1/11									60	2.30	138.00
									20	2.32	46.40
									80		184.40
3/11					389	30	2.30	69.00	30	2.30	69.00
									20	2.32	46.40
									50		115.40
5/11	123	100	2.33								
8/11					397	40					
9/11					401	30					
12/11	137	80	2.35								

Key learning points

- **Raw materials** are goods purchased for incorporation into products or services for sale.
- **Work in progress** represents an intermediate stage between the manufacturer purchasing the materials that go to make up the finished product, and the finished product. It is another name for **part-finished goods**.
- A **finished good** is a product ready for sale or despatch.
- **FIFO** (First In First Out) prices materials issues at the prices of the oldest items in stock, and values closing stock at the value of the most recent purchases.
- **LIFO** (Last In First Out) prices materials issues at the prices of the most recent purchases, and values closing stock at the value of the oldest items.
- The **weighted average cost** method calculates an average cost of all stock items whenever a new delivery is received. The price for materials issues and for stock remaining after the issues will be the same.
- **Stock control** is the regulation of stock levels, which includes giving a value to the amounts of stock issued and remaining. Stock control also includes ordering, purchasing, receiving and storing goods.
- Materials held in stock are generally **coded** in order that each item is clearly identified.
- **Periodic stocktaking** is usually carried out annually, when all items of stock are counted on a specific date.
- **Continuous stocktaking** involves counting and checking a number of stock items on a regular basis so that each item is checked at least once a year.
- **Stock control levels** can be calculated in order to maintain stocks at the optimum level. The four critical control levels are as follows.
    - Reorder level
    - Reorder quantity
    - Minimum stock level
    - Maximum stock level
- The **economic order quantity** (Q) is the ordering quantity which minimises stock costs (holding costs and ordering costs). It is calculated as follows.

    $$Q = \sqrt{\frac{2cd}{h}}$$

    Where h is the cost of holding one unit of stock for one year
            c is the cost of ordering a consignment
            d is the annual demand

UNIT 6 RECORDING AND EVALUATING COSTS AND REVENUES

Quick quiz

1 What are raw materials?

2 Items which are ready for sale or despatch are known as work in progress.

   ☐ True

   ☐ False

3 List the five documents which you are likely to use when buying materials.

   (a) ....
   (b) ....
   (c) ....
   (d) ....
   (e) ....

4 The goods received note is matched with two other documents in the buying process. What are they?

5 How would you calculate the cost of a unit of material using the weighted average cost method?

   Weighted average cost $= \dfrac{A}{B}$

   where   A = ...
               B = ...

6 List three advantages of FIFO.

   (a) ....
   (b) ....
   (c) ....

7 Which purchasing documents are used to update the stores record card?

8 What are the two methods of stocktaking that are commonly used?

9 If the economic order quantity, $Q = \sqrt{\dfrac{2cd}{h}}$

   c = ...
   d = ...
   h = ...

10 Match up the following.

Reorder level		Maximum usage × maximum lead time
Minimum level	?	Reorder level – (average usage × average lead time)
Maximum level		Reorder level + reorder quantity – (minimum usage × minimum lead time)

Answers to quick quiz

1   Goods purchased for incorporation into products or services for sale.

2   ✓   False. Items which are ready for sale or despatch are known as finished goods.

3   (a)   Purchase requisition form
    (b)   Order form
    (c)   Despatch note
    (d)   Delivery note
    (e)   Goods received note (GRN)

4   The purchase order and the supplier's invoice.

5   A = Total cost of units in stock
    B = Number of units in stock

6   (a)   It is a logical pricing method
    (b)   It is easy to understand
    (c)   The closing stock can be near to a valuation based on the cost of replacing the stock

7   Goods received notes, materials requisition notes and materials returned notes.

8   Periodic stocktaking and continuous stocktaking.

9   c = cost of ordering a consignment
    d = annual demand
    h = cost of holding one unit of stock for one year

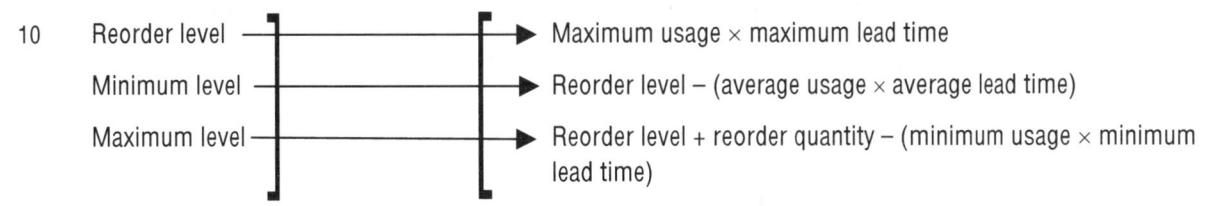

10 Reorder level ──────▶ Maximum usage × maximum lead time
    Minimum level ──────▶ Reorder level – (average usage × average lead time)
    Maximum level ──────▶ Reorder level + reorder quantity – (minimum usage × minimum lead time)

UNIT 6 RECORDING AND EVALUATING COSTS AND REVENUES

Activity checklist

This checklist shows which performance criteria, range statement or knowledge and understanding point is covered by each activity in this chapter. Tick off each activity as you complete it.

Activity

Activity		Description
2.1	☐	This activity deals with Range Statement 6.1: Raw materials
2.2	☐	This activity deals with Performance Criteria 6.1.A regarding the identification of direct costs
2.3	☐	This activity deals with Range Statement 6.1: Materials
2.4	☐	This activity deals with Range Statement 6.1: Stocks
2.5	☐	This activity deals with Knowledge and Understanding point 27 regarding the sources of information for revenue and costing data
2.6	☐	This activity deals with Knowledge and Understanding point 4 regarding the recording of revenue and costing data
2.7	☐	This activity deals with Performance Criteria 6.1.B, 6.1.C and 6.1.D regarding direct costs and stocks
2.8	☐	This activity deals with Knowledge and Understanding point 5 regarding methods of stock control and valuation
2.9	☐	This activity deals with Performance Criteria 6.1.A and 6.1.B regarding the identification, recording and analysis of direct costs
2.10	☐	This activity deals with Performance Criteria 6.1.D regarding stocks
2.11	☐	This activity deals with Performance Criteria 6.1.D regarding stocks
2.12	☐	This activity deals with Performance Criteria 6.1.B and 6.1.E regarding direct costs

chapter 3

Labour costs

Contents

1 Introduction
2 Determining labour costs
3 Recording labour costs
4 Overtime, bonuses and absences

Performance criteria

6.1.A Identify **direct costs** in accordance with the organisation's costing procedures
6.1.B Record and analyse information relating to direct costs
6.1.C Calculate direct costs in accordance with the organisation's policies and procedures
6.1.E Resolve or refer queries to the appropriate person
6.2.A Identify **overhead costs** in accordance with the organisation's procedures
6.2.D Record and analyse information relating to overhead costs in accordance with the organisation's procedures

Range statement

6.1 Direct costs:
- Direct labour costs

6.2 Overhead costs:
- Fixed
- Variable
- Semi-variable

Knowledge and understanding

4 Recording of cost and revenue data in the accounting records
6 Methods for and calculation of payments for labour
20 Relationship between the labour costing system and the payroll accounting system
27 The sources of information for revenue and costing data

1 Introduction

In this chapter you will be learning more about the second cost element we discussed in Chapter 1, labour.

You will be looking at a variety of aspects of **direct labour** and **indirect labour** and how labour costs are **identified, calculated, analysed and recorded**.

2 Determining labour costs

2.1 What are labour costs?

Labour costs include any or all of the following items.

- The gross amount of salary or wages paid to an employee
- Employer's National Insurance
- Amounts paid to recruit labour
- Amounts paid for staff welfare
- Training costs
- The costs of benefits such as company cars

The word labour is generally associated with strenuous physical effort but in the context of cost accounting it is not confined to manual work. **Labour costs** are the amounts paid to any employee, including supervisors, office staff and cleaning staff.

2.2 Determining labour costs

There are three ways in which labour costs can be determined.

- According to some prior agreement
- According to the amount of time worked
- According to the amount and/or quality of work done

Payment for most jobs is by a combination of the first two methods. There will be the following.

- A **basic wage** or **salary** which is agreed when the appointment is made.
- A **set number of hours** per week during which the employee is expected to be available for work.
- **Extra payments** for time worked over and above the set hours.
- **Deductions** for time when the employee is not available, beyond an agreed limit.

3 Recording labour costs

Records of labour costs fall into three categories.

- Records of agreed basic wages and salaries
- Records of time spent working
- Records of work done

In practice, timekeeping would probably be monitored by the production department or by the personnel department.

3.1 Attendance time

The bare minimum record of employees' time is a **simple attendance record** showing days absent because of holiday, sickness or other reason. Such a system is usually used when it is assumed that all of the employee's time is taken up doing one job and no further analysis is required.

The next step up is to have some **record of time of arrival, time of breaks and time of departure**. The simplest form is a **'signing-in' book** at the entrance to the building with, say, a page for each employee. Many employers use a **time recording clock** which stamps the time on a clock card inserted by the employee.

More modern systems involve the use of a plastic card like a credit card which is 'swiped' through a device which makes a **computer record** of the time of arrival and departure.

The next step is to analyse the hours spent at work according to what was done during those hours. Wages are calculated on the basis of the hours noted on the **attendance record.**

3.2 Detailed analysis of time: continuous production

Where **routine, repetitive work** is carried out it might not be practical to record the precise details. For example if a worker stands at a conveyor belt for seven hours the work can be measured by keeping a note of the number of units that pass through the employee's part of the process during that time. If a group of employees all contribute to the same process, the total units processed per period can be divided by the number of employees.

3.3 Detailed analysis of time: job costing

When the work is not of a repetitive nature the records required might be one or more of the following.

- Daily time sheets
- Weekly time sheets
- Job cards
- Route cards

3.3.1 Daily time sheets

These are filled in by the employee to indicate the **time spent on each job** (job code) or **area of work** (cost code).

UNIT 6 RECORDING AND EVALUATING COSTS AND REVENUES

```
Time Sheet No. ..................
Employee Name.............  Clock Code............  Dept..........
Date ..............................  Week No. ......................
```

Job No.	Start Time	Finish Time	Qty	Checker	Hrs	Rate	Extension

3.3.2 Weekly time sheets

These are similar to daily time sheets but are passed to the cost office at the end of the week.

WEEKLY TIME SHEET

NAME _____ Staff Number ☐☐☐☐☐ WEEK end date D D M M Y Y ☐☐☐☐☐☐

CLIENT or NON-CHARGEABLE TIME DESCRIPTION	HOURS WORKED Sat & Sun M T W T F	Total Hrs Incl O/T	O/T Hrs Incl	Client Number	Charge A/C Number	Hours to 2 Decimal Places

TOTAL   TOTAL

Signed _____ Authorised _____ Date _____

3.3.3 Job cards

Cards are prepared for each job (showing the work to be done and the expected time it should take) unlike time sheets which are made out for each employee. When an employee works on a job he or she records on the job card the time spent on that job.

```
┌─────────────────────────────────────────────────────────────────┐
│                           JOB CARD                              │
│                                                                 │
│  Department _____   Job no _____│
│  Date _____   Operation no _____│
│                                                                 │
│  Time allowance _____   Time started _____│
│                                     Time finished _____│
│                                     Hours on job _____│
│                                                                 │
│  Description of job         │  Hours  │  Rate  │  Cost          │
│                             │         │        │                │
│                             │         │        │                │
│                             │         │        │                │
│                             │         │        │                │
│                                                                 │
│  Employee no _____   Certified by _____ │
│  Signature _____                                    │
└─────────────────────────────────────────────────────────────────┘
```

3.3.4 Route cards

These are similar to job cards, except that they follow the job through the works and carry details of all operations to be carried out. They thus carry the cost of all operations involved in a job and are very useful for control purposes. **Production costs** are obtained from **time sheets/job cards/route cards.**

3.3.5 Salaried labour

You might think there is little point in salaried staff filling in a detailed timesheet about what they do every hour of the day, as their basic pay is a flat rate every month. In fact, in many organisations they are required to do so. There are a number of reasons for this.

- Such timesheets aid the creation of **management information** about product costs, and hence **profitability**.

- The timesheet information may have a direct impact on the **revenue the organisation receives.** For example a consultancy firm might charge their employees' time to clients. This means that if an employee spends an hour with a particular client, the client will be invoiced for one hour of the employee's time.

- Timesheets are used to record hours spent and so **support salaried staffs' claims for overtime payments**.

3.3.6 Idle time

There may be times when, through no fault of their own, employees cannot get on with their work. A machine may break down or there may simply be a temporary shortage of work. This is known as **idle time**

Idle time has a cost because employees will still be paid their basic wage or salary for these unproductive hours. Therefore there must be a record of idle time. This may simply comprise an entry on time sheets coded to 'idle time' generally. Alternatively a supervisor might enter the following details on separate **idle time record cards.**

- The time and duration of a stoppage
- The cause of the stoppage
- The employees made idle

Each stoppage should have a separate reference number which can be entered on time sheets or job cards as appropriate.

3.3.7 Payment by output

Piecework is a method of labour payment where workers are paid according to the amount of production completed.

The labour cost of work done by pieceworkers is determined from what is known as a **piecework ticket** or an **operation card**. The card records the total number of items (or **pieces**) produced and the number of rejects. Payment is only made for 'good' production.

OPERATION CARD				
Operator's Name		Total Batch Quantity		
Clock No		Start Time		
Pay week No .... Date		Stop Time		
Part No		Works Order No		
Operation		Special Instructions		
Quantity Produced	No Rejected	Good Production	Rate	£
Inspector		Operative		
Supervisor		Date		
PRODUCTION CANNOT BE CLAIMED WITHOUT A PROPERLY SIGNED CARD				

A **disadvantage of the piecework method** is that workers may be so concerned with the volume of output that they produce, that the **quality** of the goods might suffer.

Activity 3.1

(a) Walter Wally is chief foreman in one of Sleepy Jeans Ltd's factories which is working on about thirty different jobs at any one time. He spends most of his day on his feet, dealing with personnel and technical problems as and when they arise.

How might Walter's time be analysed?

(b) Peter Pratt is a cashier at Sleepy Jeans Ltd.

How might Peter's time be analysed?

3.4 Coding of job costs

In order to analyse labour costs effectively it is necessary to be able to link up different pieces of information in various ways. Organisations usually develop a series of codes for each of the following in order to make the analysis of labour costs more simple.

- **Employee number** (or team number)
- **Pay rate**, for example 'A' for £6 per hour, 'B' for £7 per hour
- **Department** and/or **location**
- **Job** or **batch number**
- **Client number**

Activity 3.2

Below are shown some extracts from the files of Sleepy Jeans Ltd.

Personnel files

	George	Paul	Ringo	John
Grade	A	B	C	D

Payroll - Master file

Grade	Basic rate per hour
A	£8.20
B	£7.40
C	£6.50
D	£5.30

Production report - labour

Job	Employee	Hours
249	George	14
249	Paul	49
250	George	2
250	John	107
250	Ringo	74

Task

You are required to calculate the labour cost of jobs 249 and 250.

4 Overtime, bonuses and absences

4.1 Overtime

One of the most common forms of **time work** is a **day-rate system**.

Wages (for a day-rate system) = Hours worked × rate of pay per hour

If an employee works for more hours than the basic daily requirement many organisations pay an extra amount, known as an **overtime payment.**

The overtime payment may simply be at the **basic rate**. If an employee earns £6 an hour he will be paid an extra £6 for every hour worked in addition to the basic hours.

Usually, however, overtime is paid at a **premium rate**. You will hear expressions like 'time and a third', 'time and a half' and so on. This means that the hourly rate for overtime hours is $(1 + 1/3)$ × basic rate or $(1 + 1/2)$ × basic rate.

Example: Overtime premium

Sleepy Jeans Ltd pays overtime at time and a quarter. Jo's basic hours are 9 am to 5 pm with an hour for lunch, but one particular Friday she worked until six o'clock. She is paid a basic wage of £6 per hour. How much did she earn on the Friday in question, and how much of this is overtime premium?

Solution

For costing purposes, the overtime premium must always be **identified separately** from the basic pay for the hours worked. Therefore the calculation is best presented as follows.

	£
Basic pay (8 × £6)	48.00
Overtime premium (1/4 × £6)	1.50
	49.50

4.1.1 Overtime premiums

The **overtime premium** in the example above is £1.50. This is an important point because overtime premium is usually treated as an **indirect cost**. This is quite reasonable if you think about it. If you and your colleague use identical calculators it is reasonable to suppose that they cost the same amount to produce. It might be that one was assembled at 10 o'clock in the morning and the other at 10 o'clock at night (ie during overtime hours), but this doesn't make the calculators different from each other. They should therefore have the same cost and so **most organisations treat overtime premium as an indirect cost or overhead** and do not allocate it to the products that happen to be manufactured outside basic hours.

There is one exception to this rule.

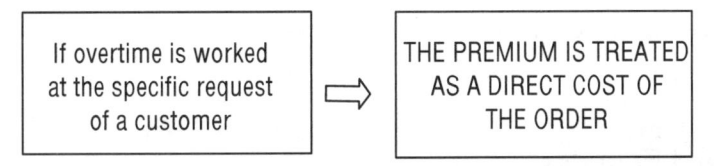

If overtime is worked at the specific request of a customer ⟹ THE PREMIUM IS TREATED AS A DIRECT COST OF THE ORDER

Activity 3.3

Peter works for Sleepy Jeans Ltd. Below is shown Peter's payslip for April. Peter spent the whole of April working on Job 472 without assistance. What is the direct labour cost of Job 472?

Employee: TORK, P Staff No: 017	Employer: SLEEPY JEANS LTD	
NI No: NA 123456C Tax Code: 344L Pay By: Cheque	Date: 30/4/X1 Tax Period: 1	
DESCRIPTION	AMOUNT	THIS YEAR
BASIC BONUS	1,327.42 145.83	
TOTAL PAY >>>	1,473.25	1,473.25
OTHER DEDUCTIONS INCOME TAX NATIONAL INSURANCE	282.41 93.44	282.41 93.44
NET PAY >>>	1,097.40	
OTHER ITEMS ADD EXPENSES REIMBURSED	301.28	
(HOL PAY ACCRUED 0.00) TOTAL NET PAY >>>	1,398.68	

Activity 3.4

Sleepy Jeans Ltd carries out a job for a customer that takes one employee, Dave, 50 hours in one week. The customer has asked that overtime is worked on the job in order that it may be completed as quickly as possible. Dave's basic hours are 9 am to 5 pm with an hour for lunch. He is paid a basic wage of £8 per hour and is paid overtime at time and a half. Two clerks in the accounts office are having a debate about how much of Dave's overtime premium should be charged to overheads. Jenny thinks it should be £60 and Mel says it should be £120.

Task

Try to resolve the dispute about the analysis of overtime premium.

4.2 Incentives and bonuses

Overtime premiums are paid to encourage staff to work longer hours than normal or to reward them for doing so. **Incentives and bonuses** are paid to encourage staff to work harder whatever the time of day.

Incentive schemes include the following.

- Piecework
- Time-saved bonus
- Group bonus scheme
- Profit-sharing scheme

4.2.1 Piecework

Pieceworking can be seen as an incentive scheme since the more output you produce the more you are paid. If you are paid 5p per unit produced and you want to earn £300 gross a week you know you have to produce 6,000 units that week (6,000 units × £0.05 = £300).

The system can be further refined by paying a different rate for different levels of production (**differential piecework**). For example the employer could pay 3p per unit for output of up to 3,500 a week, and 5p per unit for every unit over 3,500.

In practice, persons working on such schemes normally receive a **guaranteed minimum wage** because they may not be able to work due to problems outside their control.

Example: Piecework

An employee is paid £5 per piecework hour produced. In a 35 hour week he produces the following output.

	Piecework time allowed per unit
3 units of product A	2.5 hours
5 units of product B	8.0 hours

Task

Calculate the employee's pay for the week.

Solution

Piecework hours produced are calculated as follows.

Product A	3 × 2.5 hours	7.5 hours
Product B	5 × 8 hours	40.0 hours
Total piecework hours		47.5

Therefore employee's pay = 47.5 × £5 = £237.50 for the week.

Activity 3.5

Mr Shah works in one of Sleepy Jeans Ltd's factories. Using the information on piecework rates, complete the operation card shown below and calculate Mr Shah's gross wages for pay week number 17.

Number of units	Piecework rates
Up to 100 units a day	20p per unit on all units produced
101 to 120 units a day	30p per unit on all units produced
121 to 140 units a day	40p per unit on all units produced
Over 140 units a day	50p per unit on all units produced

OPERATION CARD				
Operator's Name Shah, L		Total Batch Quantity -		
Clock No 7142		Start Time -		
Pay week No 17 Date W/E XX/XX/XX		Stop Time -		
Part No 713/V		Works Order No 14 AB		
Operation Drilling		Special Instructions -		
Quantity Produced	No Rejected	Good Production	Rate	£
Monday 173	14			
Tuesday 131	2			
Wednesday 92	-			
Thursday 120	7			
Friday 145	5			
Inspector ND		Operative LS		
Supervisor AN		Date XX/XX/XX		
PRODUCTION CANNOT BE CLAIMED WITHOUT A PROPERLY SIGNED CARD				

4.2.2 Time-saved bonus

Suppose that a garage has calculated that it takes an average of 45 minutes for an engineer to perform an MOT test, but the job could be done competently in 30 minutes (ie the **standard time allowance** for an MOT is 30 minutes). It could encourage its engineers to do such work at the faster rate by paying **a bonus for every minute saved** on the job up to a maximum of 15 minutes.

The **standard time** allowed to produce a unit or complete a job is a measure of the **expected time** to produce a unit or complete a job.

Activity 3.6

Chris Steele works for Sleepy Jeans Ltd and is paid an hourly rate of £8 per hour. She is paid a bonus of 40% of any time saved against a standard allowance for work done. Last week she worked 35 hours and completed 90 units. The standard time allowed for one unit is 30 minutes.

Task

Calculate Chris's gross wages for last week.

4.2.3 Group bonus schemes

Sometimes it is not possible to measure individual effort because overall performance is not within any one person's control, for example a team of railway workers. In such cases, however, it is possible to measure **overall performance** of the team and **a bonus can therefore be paid to all those who contributed.**

Bonus payments are usually treated as indirect wages (or overhead).

4.2.4 Profit-sharing schemes

In a **profit-sharing scheme** employees receive **a certain proportion of their company's year-end profits.** The size of their bonus might also be related to the level of responsibility and length of service.

4.3 Absence from work

An employee may be absent from work for a variety of reasons, the most common are as follows.

- Holidays
- Sickness
- Maternity/paternity/adoption leave
- Training

The costs relating to absence through sickness, maternity/paternity/adoption and training are usually **treated as an overhead or indirect labour cost** rather than a direct cost of production.

Although some organisations treat holiday pay as an overhead, sometimes it is treated as a direct cost by charging an **inflated hourly rate.**

Time absent because of holidays is paid at the normal basic rate, as is absence on training courses as a rule. There are statutory minimum levels for maternity/paternity/adoption pay and sickness pay, but above these employers can be as generous (or otherwise) as they wish.

Activity 3.7

J Wain works for Sleepy Jeans Ltd and her latest time sheet and relevant information are shown below.

- J Wain is paid an hourly rate of £11 per hour.
- The first two digits of the code represent the cost centre to be charged.

    10   Finishing cost centre
    20   Packing cost centre
    30   Administration department
    40   Personnel department

- The last three digits of the code represent the expenditure code to be charged.

    100   Direct wages
    200   Indirect wages

- Administration, training and holiday time are classified as indirect time.
- Time spent on training courses is charged to the personnel department.
- Holiday pay is charged to the administration department.

Task

Use the information given to complete the time sheet and the accounts code boxes below.

WEEKLY TIME SHEET

Name: J. Wain
Staff number: 17254
Week ending: 091201

	M	T	W	T	F	TOTAL Hours	£	CODE
Direct time								
Finishing	5	4		1	3			
Packing				6	3			
Direct total	5	4		7	6			
Administration								
Budget meeting	2				1			
Total admin	2				1			
Training and courses								
First Aid course		3						
Total training		3						
Holidays, sickness								
Holiday			7					
Total leave			7					
TOTAL	7	7	7	7	7	35		

Signed: RS   Authorised: LW

Key learning points

- **Labour costs** can be determined according to some prior agreement, the amount of time worked or the quantity/quality of work done.

- **Labour attendance time** is recorded on an **attendance record** or a **clockcard**. The analysis of time worked may be recorded on the following.
  - Daily time sheets
  - Weekly time sheets
  - Job cards
  - Route cards

- **Idle time** may occur when employees are not able to get on with their work through no fault of their own. Idle time has a cost and must therefore be recorded.

- **Piecework** is a method of labour payment where workers are paid according to the amount of production completed.

- The labour cost of work done by **pieceworkers** is recorded on a **piecework ticket/ operation card.**

- There are four main types of **incentive scheme**.
  - Piecework
  - Time-saved bonus
  - Group bonus scheme
  - Profit-sharing scheme

- If employees work more than their basic hours, many employers pay overtime. Usually, overtime is paid at a **premium rate.**

- **Overtime premium** is usually treated as an **indirect cost.** However, if overtime is worked at the specific request of a customer, the premium is a direct cost of the customer's job/order.

Quick quiz

1. What are the three basic ways of determining labour costs?

2. Which two documents can be used to record attendance time?

    (a) ....

    (b) ....

3. What is idle time? Give two examples of why it may occur.

4. What is overtime premium?

5. Tick the relevant box to indicate whether each of the following elements of labour cost would be treated as direct or indirect. All of the payments are made to, or on behalf of, **direct employees**.

		Direct labour cost	Indirect labour cost
(a)	Overtime premium paid:		
	(i) due to a temporary backlog in production		
	(ii) at the specific request of a customer		
(b)	Shift premium paid		
(c)	Bonuses paid		
(d)	Basic pay for overtime hours		
(e)	Sick pay		
(f)	Pay for diverted hours, spent cleaning machines		

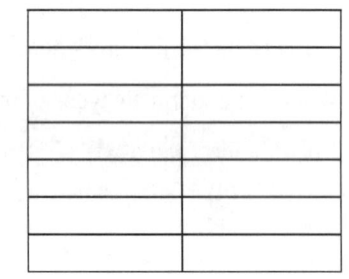

6. List four types of incentive scheme.

7. Match the descriptions of remuneration schemes to the graphs below.

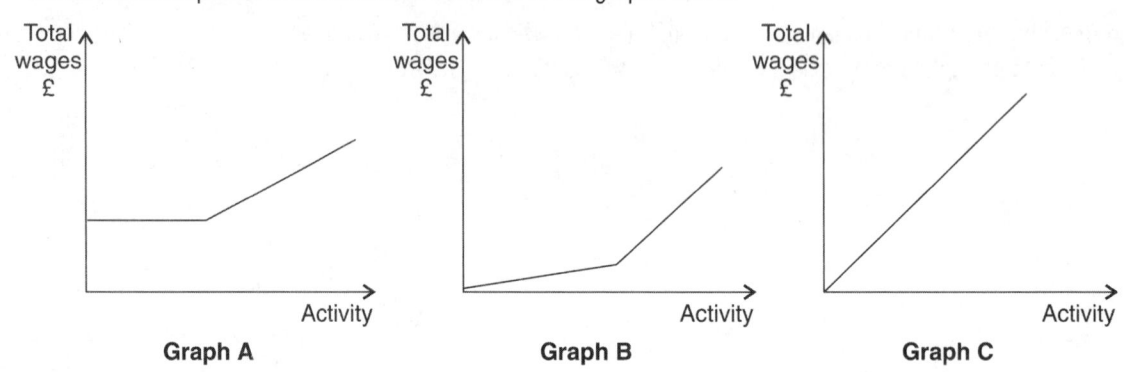

   Graph A   Graph B   Graph C

   Descriptions

   (a) A basic hourly rate is paid for hours worked, with an overtime premium payable for hours worked in excess of 35 per week.

   (b) A straight piece rate scheme is operated.

   (c) A straight piece rate scheme is operated, with a minimum guaranteed weekly wage.

Answers to quick quiz

1 Agreed basic wages and salaries, time spent, work done.

2 (a) Record of attendance
  (b) Clockcard

3 Time during which employees are being paid, but cannot get on with their work (though it is not their fault). It may occur when a machine breaks down or when there is a temporary shortage of work.

4 The extra amount paid, above the basic rate, for working overtime.

5

		Direct labour cost	Indirect labour cost
(a) Overtime premium paid:			
(i) due to a temporary backlog in production			✓
(ii) at the specific request of a customer		✓	
(b) Shift premium paid			✓
(c) Bonuses paid			✓
(d) Basic pay for overtime hours		✓	
(e) Sick pay			✓
(f) Pay for diverted hours, spent cleaning machines			✓

Explanations

(a) (i) **Indirect**. It would be 'unfair' to charge the items produced in overtime hours with the premium, just because they happen to be worked on during a direct employee's overtime hours.

   (ii) **Direct**. This overtime premium can be specifically identified with the customer's order.

(b) **Indirect**. This is usually treated as an indirect labour cost, again because it would be 'unfair' to charge the extra payment to items that happen to be produced during a shift where a premium is paid.

(c) **Indirect**. Unless the bonus payment can be traced to a specific cost unit, in which case it would be a direct cost of that unit.

(d) **Direct**. The basic pay for direct employees' overtime hours is a direct cost.

(e) **Indirect**. Direct employees' sick pay cannot be traced to a specific cost unit.

(f) **Indirect**. Diverted hours are those spent by direct employees doing indirect tasks, such as cleaning machines or counting stock.

6 (a) Piecework
  (b) Time-saved bonus
  (c) Group bonus scheme
  (d) Profit-sharing scheme

7 (a) Graph B
  (b) Graph C
  (c) Graph A

UNIT 6 RECORDING AND EVALUATING COSTS AND REVENUES

Activity checklist

This checklist shows which performance criteria, range statement or knowledge and understanding point is covered by each activity in this chapter. Tick off each activity as you complete it.

Activity

3.1	☐	This activity deals with Performance Criteria 6.1.B regarding the recording and analysis of information relating to direct costs
3.2	☐	This activity deals with Performance Criteria 6.1.C regarding the calculation of direct costs
3.3	☐	This activity deals with Performance Criteria 6.1.A regarding the identification of direct costs
3.4	☐	This activity deals with Performance Criteria 6.1.A and 6.1.E regarding the identification of direct costs and the resolution of queries
3.5	☐	This activity deals with Performance Criteria 6.1.C regarding the calculation of direct costs
3.6	☐	This activity deals with Performance Criteria 6.1.C regarding the calculation of direct costs
3.7	☐	This activity deals with Performance Criteria 6.1.B and 6.2.D regarding the recording and analysis of information relating to direct costs and overhead costs

chapter 4

Expenses

Contents

1. Introduction
2. Revenue and capital expenditure
3. Types of expense
4. Depreciation and obsolescence
5. Recording and coding expenses

Performance criteria

6.2.A Identify **overhead costs** in accordance with the organisation's procedures

6.2.D Record and analyse information relating to overhead costs in accordance with the organisation's procedures

6.2.F Review methods of allocation, apportionment and absorption at regular intervals in discussions with senior staff and ensure agreed changes to methods are implemented

6.2.G Consult staff working in operational departments to resolve any queries in overhead cost data

Range statement

Overhead costs:
- Fixed
- Variable
- Semi-variable

Knowledge and understanding

- 4 Recording of cost and revenue data in the accounting records
- 7 Procedures and documentation relating to expenses
- 8 Bases of allocating and apportioning indirect costs to responsibility centres: direct and step down methods
- 21 Relationship between the accounting system and the expenses costing system
- 27 The sources of information for revenue and costing data

1 Introduction

We have now looked at materials costs and labour costs in some detail in Chapters 2 and 3. Any other costs that might be incurred by an organisation are generally known as **expenses**. In this chapter we will be going on to look at a variety of **direct expenses** and **indirect expenses**.

2 Revenue and capital expenditure

2.1 Classification of expenses

Like materials and labour costs, expenses can also be divided into different categories. One such classification of expenses is as either **revenue expenditure** or as **capital expenditure.**

2.1.1 Capital expenditure

- **Capital expenditure** is expenditure which results in the acquisition of fixed assets.
- **Fixed assets** are assets which are acquired to provide benefits in more than one accounting period and are not intended to be resold in the normal course of trade.

Capital expenditure is not charged to the profit and loss account as an expense. Instead a **depreciation charge** is charged to the profit and loss account in order to write off the capital expenditure over a period of time. The depreciation charge is therefore an expense in the profit and loss account, so that the cost of the asset is spread over the years which benefit from its use.

Example: Depreciation charges

If an asset is bought for £20,000 and it is expected to last for 5 years and have no value at the end of that time, then for five years, £4,000 (£20,000 ÷ 5 years) will be charged as a **depreciation expense** to the profit and loss account.

2.1.2 Revenue expenditure

Revenue expenditure is expenditure which is incurred for one of the following reasons.

- For the purpose of the trade of the business, including administration expenses, selling and distribution expenses and finance charges.
- In order to maintain the existing earning capacity of fixed assets.

Revenue expenditure is charged to the profit and loss account in the period to which it relates.

2.2 Revenue and capital expenditure compared

Let us look at an example which should help you to distinguish between **revenue expenses** and **capital expenses**.

Example: Revenue items and capital items

Suppose that Bevan Ltd purchases a building for £30,000. A few years later it adds an extension to the building at a cost of £10,000. The building needs to have a few broken windows mended, its floors polished, and some missing roof tiles replaced. These cleaning and maintenance jobs cost £900.

Which items of expenditure are revenue expenditure and which are capital expenditure?

Solution

The original purchase cost (£30,000) and the cost of the extension (£10,000) are **capital expenditure** because they are incurred to acquire and then improve a fixed asset. The other costs of £900 are **revenue expenditure** because they are maintaining the existing earning capacity of the building.

The capital expenditure would be shared over several years' profit and loss accounts via a **depreciation expense**. The revenue expenditure would be charged as an **expense in the profit and loss account of the year it is incurred**.

2.3 Revenue and capital expenditure and costing

Revenue expenditure is of more relevance to the costing of products than capital expenditure. Capital expenditure is only of relevance when it is turned into revenue expenditure in the form of a **depreciation expense**.

2.4 Direct expenses and indirect expenses

A second major distinction that must be made is between **direct** and **indirect** expenses.

2.4.1 Direct expenses

Direct expenses are any expenses which are incurred on a specific product or service other than direct material cost and direct wages.

Direct expenses are charged to the product or service as part of the **prime cost** or **total direct cost**. Examples of direct expenses are as follows.

- The cost of **special** designs, drawings or layouts for a particular job
- The **hire of tools** or equipment for a particular job
- **Royalties** payable for each unit produced, for use of a copyright design

Direct expenses are also referred to as **chargeable expenses.**

2.4.2 Indirect expenses

Indirect expenses are expenses which cannot be identified in full with a specific item that is being costed. They are also known as overheads and are studied in detail in the next chapter.

Activity 4.1

The following information relates to Derbyshire Ltd.

State whether each of the following items should be classified as 'capital' or 'revenue' expenditure.

(a) Purchase of freehold premises

(b) Annual depreciation of freehold premises

(c) Solicitors' fees in connection with the purchase of freehold premises

(d) Costs of adding extra storage capacity to a mainframe computer used by the business

(e) Computer repairs and maintenance costs

(f) Cost of new machinery

(g) Customs duty charged on the machinery when imported into the country

(h) 'Carriage' costs of transporting the new machinery from the supplier's factory to the premises of the business purchasing the machinery

(i) Cost of installing the new machinery in the premises of the business

(j) Wages of the machine operators

3 Types of expense

Revenue expenditure other than materials and labour costs can arise for a number of different reasons.

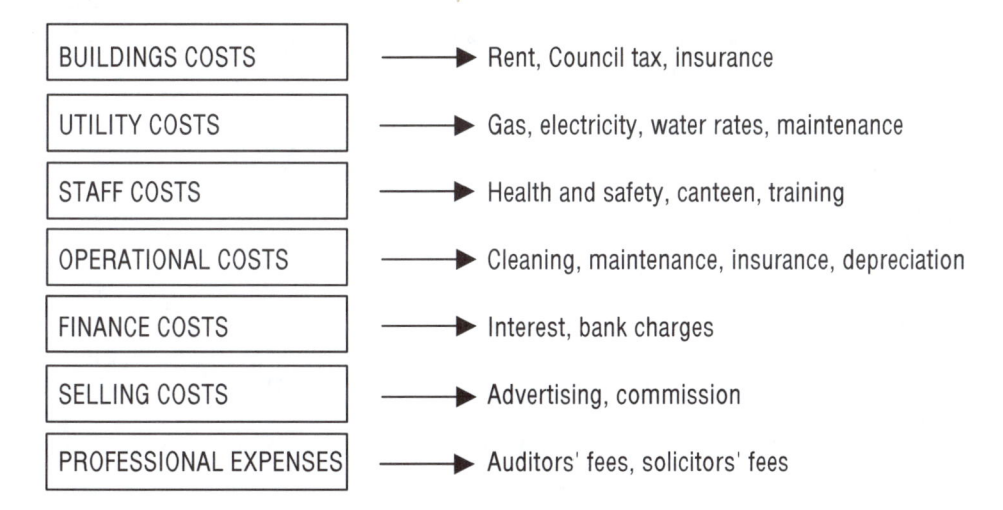

BUILDINGS COSTS	→ Rent, Council tax, insurance
UTILITY COSTS	→ Gas, electricity, water rates, maintenance
STAFF COSTS	→ Health and safety, canteen, training
OPERATIONAL COSTS	→ Cleaning, maintenance, insurance, depreciation
FINANCE COSTS	→ Interest, bank charges
SELLING COSTS	→ Advertising, commission
PROFESSIONAL EXPENSES	→ Auditors' fees, solicitors' fees

4 Depreciation and obsolescence

4.1 Depreciation

We have already described depreciation as a method of writing off capital expenditure.

There are two principal methods of depreciating a fixed asset, the **straight line method** and the **reducing balance method**.

- The **straight line method** charges an equal amount of depreciation each period.
- The **reducing balance method** charges the largest amount of depreciation at the beginning of an asset's life. As the asset grows older the amount charged each period gets steadily smaller.

Example: Depreciation methods

Derbyshire Ltd purchased two fixed assets for £8,000 each. They will have no value after four years. One is depreciated over four years using the straight line method and the other is depreciated at the rate of 25% per annum on the reducing balance. What is the book value of each asset after four years and how much per year is charged to the profit and loss account as depreciation expense?

Solution

	Asset A		Asset B	
	Balance sheet	Profit and loss account	Balance sheet	Profit and loss account
	£	£	£	£
Capital cost	8,000		8,000	
Year 1 depreciation charge	(2,000)	2,000	(2,000)	2,000
c/f	6,000		6,000	
Year 2 depreciation charge	(2,000)	2,000	(1,500)	1,500
c/f	4,000		4,500	
Year 3 depreciation charge	(2,000)	2,000	(1,125)	1,125
c/f	2,000		3,375	
Year 4 depreciation charge	(2,000)	2,000	(844)	844
c/f	Nil		2,531	

The profit and loss account charge for asset A is calculated by dividing the £8,000 capital cost by four. For asset B it is calculated by taking 25% of the opening balance each year.

In order to decide which method is most appropriate we need to think a little more about why we are depreciating the asset at all.

4.2 The objectives of depreciation accounting

4.2.1 Objective 1

If an asset is purchased for £8,000 at the beginning of the year and sold for £6,000 at the end of the year then it is reasonable to conclude that the cost of owning the asset for a year is £2,000 (£8,000 – £6,000). This £2,000 is in addition to the costs of using the asset, like fuel and repairs costs.

If the business had not owned the asset it would not have been able to make its product or provide its service. It is therefore reasonable that the £2,000 cost should be recorded and charged as a cost of the product or service.

The first objective of depreciation accounting is therefore **to find some way of calculating this cost of ownership.**

4.2.2 Objective 2

Consider, however, the use of a machine that is constructed to do a specific job for a specific firm. It may last 20 years and yet be of no use to anybody else at any time in which case its resale value would be nil on the same day that it was bought. It is, however, hardly fair to charge the whole cost of the machine to the first product that it makes, or even to the first year's production. Very probably the products it is making in year 19 will be just as well made as the products made in year 1.

The second objective of depreciation accounting is therefore **to spread out the capital cost of the asset over as long a period as the asset is used.** In the example given there is a good case for spreading this cost in equal proportions over the whole 20 years.

4.2.3 Which method of depreciation accounting is best?

The answer to the question 'which method is best?' therefore depends upon the following.

- The asset in question
- The way it is used
- The length of time it is used
- The length of time it is useful in the light of changes in products, production methods and technology

4.3 Depreciation in practice

This sounds as if there are a lot of things to take into account, but in practice you may find that the method most often used is the **straight line method** because it is simple and gives a reasonable approximation.

Typical depreciation rates under the **straight line method** are as follows.

- Freehold land — Not depreciated
- Freehold buildings — 2% per annum (50 years)
- Leasehold buildings — Over the period of the lease
- Plant and machinery — 10% per annum (10 years)
- Motor vehicles — 25% per annum (4 years)

Note that these are not rules. Businesses can choose whatever method or rate they think is most appropriate.

Sometimes you may encounter depreciation methods that try to measure the fall in value or the cost of use more accurately, for example, the **machine-hour method**.

Example: The machine-hour method

A machine costing £100,000 was purchased by Derbyshire Ltd in 20X3 and it is estimated that it will be sold for £5,000 at the end of its useful life. Experience has shown that such machines can run for approximately 10,000 hours before they wear out. What is the depreciation charge for the first year if the machine was used for 1,500 hours during the year?

Solution

The **machine-hour rate** is calculated as follows.

$$\text{Depreciation per machine hour} = \frac{\text{Cost} - \text{residual value}}{\text{Useful life}}$$

$$\frac{£(100,000 - 5,000)}{10,000 \text{ hours}} = £9.50 \text{ per machine hour}$$

The depreciation charge for the first year is therefore

1,500 hours × £9.50 = £14,250

4.4 Obsolescence

Obsolescence is the loss in value of an asset because it has been superseded, for example due to the development of a technically superior asset or changes in market conditions.

As the loss in value is due to quite another reason than the **wear and tear** associated with depreciation and because obsolescence may be rapid and difficult to forecast, it is not normal practice to make regular charges relating to obsolescence. Instead, **the loss resulting from the obsolescence should be charged as an expense direct to the costing profit and loss account when it arises.**

Activity 4.2

Derbyshire Ltd purchased a leather stamping machine last year. At the end of its first year of use the meter on the machine read 9728. It cost £4,000 and the suppliers are willing to buy it back for 20% of its cost at any time so that it can be used for parts. The sales literature claimed that it was capable of producing at least 100,000 stampings.

Task

What question will you need to ask the operational department concerned in order to determine whether the depreciation charge for the machine is a direct expense or an indirect expense?

Activity 4.3

Derbyshire Ltd purchased a machine three years ago for £75,000. Due to a change in government regulations, the component the machine produces can only be used for a further two years. At the end of two years, however, the machine can be sold for scrap for £5,000.

Task

Calculate the depreciation charge for the five years the machine is owned using both the straight line method and a rate of 42% per annum on the reducing balance.

5 Recording and coding expenses

In this chapter we are going to deal only with the initial stages of recording expenses. Much more detail will be found in the next chapter which explains how overhead costs are attributed to the total costs of individual units of product or service.

5.1 Direct expenses

Direct expenses (such as plant hire for a **specific** job or a solicitor's fees for drawing up a contract to provide a **specific** service) can simply be **coded to the appropriate job or client** when the invoice arrives. The expense would be recorded together with other direct costs against the relevant job or client numbers.

5.2 Indirect expenses

Indirect expenses **cannot be charged directly** to a **specific** cost unit. Instead a process of **allocation and apportionment** is necessary.

Allocation is the process by which whole cost items are charged direct to a cost unit or cost centre.

Indirect expenses are initially allocated where possible to the appropriate **cost centres**.

Cost centre type	Examples	
	Production	Service
Location	Finishing department	Hotel restaurant
Function	Sales department	Accounts department
Activity	Painting	Invoicing
Item of equipment	Spray-gun	Computer

The decision as to which cost centre is the appropriate one for an expense depends upon the type of expense. Some expenses will be **solely related to production** or to **administration** or to **selling and distribution** and can easily be **allocated** to the appropriate cost centre.

Other costs, however, will be shared between these various functions and so such costs cannot be allocated directly to one particular cost centre. Cost centres therefore have to be established for the **initial allocation** of such shared expenses. Examples of shared expenses include: rent, rates, heating and lighting, buildings maintenance and so on.

Example: Overhead allocation

The coding, analysis and recording of indirect expenses and other overheads at the initial stage may be demonstrated by the following example.

The weekly costs of Departments A and B include the following.

Wages of supervisor of Department A	£1,000
Wages of supervisor of Department B	£1,200
Indirect materials consumed in Department A	£400
Rent of premises shared by Departments A and B	£1,500

The cost accounting system includes the following cost centres.

Code
101   Department A
102   Department B
201   Rent

Show the cost centres to which the costs will be initially coded.

Solution

(a)

	£	Code
Wages of supervisor of Department A	1,000	101
Wages of supervisor of Department B	1,200	102
Indirect materials consumed in Department A	400	101
Rent of premises shared by Departments A and B	1,500	201

(b) You may think that this is so obvious as not to be worth explaining. You will certainly not be surprised to be told that the next stage is to **share the rent paid between the two departments.** Why, you might ask, do we not split the cost of rent straightaway and not bother with cost centre 201?

(c) To answer this question consider the following extract from the cost accounts several months after the previous example. Cost centre 201 is no longer used because nobody could see the point of it.

	Cost centre 101 £	Cost centre 102 £
Wages	1,172.36	1,415.00
Materials	73.92	169.75
Rent	638.25	1,086.75

You have just received a memo telling you that starting from this month (to which the above figures relate), Department A is to pay 25% of the total rent for the premises shared with Department B and Department B is to be split into two departments, with the new department (C) paying 37% of the remaining rent charge. The manager of Department B is standing over you asking you how much the department's new monthly rent charge will be.

(d) The answer is £815.06. More importantly the first thing you have to do to calculate the answer is to recreate the total cost information that used to be allocated to cost centre 201. This is not very difficult in the present example, but imagine that there were ten cost centres sharing premises and the cost information was recorded in a bulky ledger. Do you think it would have been easy to spot that the monthly rent had increased to £1,725?

5.3 Documentation

There are several ways in which this initial allocation could be documented. A common method is to put a stamp on the invoice itself with boxes to fill in, as appropriate. Suppose that Department C is given the code number 103. The rent invoice would be coded as follows.

%	Account codes no.	£	p
25.00	101	431	25
47.25	102	815	06
27.75	103	478	69
	.		
TOTAL	201	1725	00

Approved		Date	
Authorised		Date	
Posted		Date	

The dividing up of the total cost into portions to share it over the relevant cost centres is called **apportionment**. This process will be described in more detail in the next chapter.

5.4 Apportionment and responsibility accounting

The apportionment of costs raises another important question. It is unlikely that the managers of departments A, B and C have any **control** over the amount of rent that is paid for the building. They need to be **made aware that their part of the building is not free** but they are not **responsible** for the cost. The person responsible for controlling the amount of a cost such as this is more likely to be a separate manager, who looks after the interests of all of the company's buildings.

If cost centre 201 is maintained it can therefore be used to collect all the costs that are the **responsibility of the premises manager.** This approach is known as **responsibility accounting** and such cost centres can be called **responsibility centres**.

Activity 4.4

Derbyshire Ltd's accounts are prepared by Beancounters, a firm of accountants. Listed below are fifteen entries in the cash book of Beancounters. You are required to code the invoices according to the sort of expense you think has been incurred.

Nominal codes *Nominal account*

0010 Advertising
0020 Bank charges
0030 Books and publications
0040 Cleaning
0050 Computer supplies
0060 Heat and light
0070 Motor expenses

UNIT 6 RECORDING AND EVALUATING COSTS AND REVENUES

Nominal codes	Nominal account
0080	Motor vehicles
0090	Office equipment
0100	Printing, postage and stationery
0110	Rates
0120	Rent
0130	Repairs and maintenance
0140	Staff training
0150	Staff welfare
0160	Subscriptions
0170	Telephone
0180	Temporary staff
0190	Travel

Invoice received from	£	Code
Strange (Properties) Ltd	4,000.00	
Yorkshire Electricity plc	1,598.27	
Dudley Stationery Ltd	275.24	
Dora David (cleaner)	125.00	
BPP Publishing Ltd	358.00	
AAT	1,580.00	
British Telecom	1,431.89	
Kall Kwik (Stationers)	312.50	
Interest to 31.3.X3	2,649.33	
L & W Office Equipment	24.66	
Avis	153.72	
Federal Express	32.00	
Starriers Garage Ltd	79.80	

Activity 4.5

Beancounters is divided into three departments: audit, business services and tax. Which of the expenses listed in Activity 4.4 do you think are chargeable in total directly to individual clients, which are chargeable in total directly to departments and which cannot be split except by some method of apportionment?

Helping hand. There is no definitive answer to this activity, but take a few minutes to give it some thought. If you consider that you need more information, think about the queries that you would raise and who you would ask for the information.

We shall look at the coding of costs and revenues in more detail when we study Chapter 8 *Recording costs and revenues*.

Key learning points

- **Capital expenditure** is expenditure which results in the acquisition of fixed assets. Fixed assets are assets acquired to provide benefits in more than one accounting period. Capital expenditure is charged as an **expense** to the profit and loss account via a depreciation charge over a period of time.

- **Revenue expenditure** is expenditure which is incurred for the purpose of the trade of the business, or in order to maintain the existing earning capacity of fixed assets. It is charged as an **expense** to the profit and loss account in the period to which it relates.

- There are two principal methods of depreciating an asset, the **straight-line** method and the **reducing balance** method.

- **Obsolescence** is the loss in value of an asset because it has been superseded.

- **Direct expenses** are recorded by coding them to the appropriate job or client.

- **Indirect expenses** are initially **allocated** to appropriate cost centres and then spread out or **apportioned** to the cost centres that have benefited from the expense.

- In **responsibility accounting,** cost centres collect the costs that are the responsibility of the cost centre manager, and hence may be known as **responsibility centres.**

Quick quiz

1   Capital expenditure is charged to the profit and loss account at the end of an accounting period.

　　☐ True

　　☐ False

2   What is revenue expenditure?

3   The two main methods of depreciating an asset are:

　　(a)   ……………………………………………..

　　(b)   ……………………………………………..

4   When an asset loses value because it has been superseded due to the development of a technically superior asset, this is known as ☐

5   The process by which whole cost items are charged direct to a cost unit or cost centre is known as:

　　A   Expenditure
　　B   Depreciation
　　C   Allocation
　　D   Obsolescence

6   What is responsibility accounting?

Answers to quick quiz

1   ✓ False

2   Revenue expenditure is expenditure incurred for the purpose of the trade of the business, or in order to maintain the existing earning capacity of fixed assets. It is charged as an expense in the period to which it relates.

3   (a)   Straight line method
　　(b)   Reducing balance method

4   Obsolescence

5   C   Allocation is the process by which whole cost items are charged direct to a cost unit or cost centre.

6   When cost centre managers have responsibility for controlling the amount of the cost collected within certain cost centres, such cost centres are called responsibility centres.

Activity checklist

This checklist shows which performance criteria, range statement or knowledge and understanding point is covered by each activity in this chapter. Tick off each activity as you complete it.

Activity

4.1	☐	This activity deals with Performance Criteria 6.2.A regarding the identification of overhead costs
4.2	☐	This activity deals with Performance Criteria 6.2.G regarding the consultation of staff working in operational departments
4.3	☐	This activity deals with Performance Criteria 6.2.D regarding the recording and analysis of information relating to overhead costs
4.4	☐	This activity deals with Performance Criteria 6.2.B and 6.2.D regarding overhead allocation
4.5	☐	This activity deals with Performance Criteria 6.2.F and 6.2.G regarding allocation and apportionment.

chapter 5

Overheads and absorption costing

Contents

1. Introduction
2. What are overheads?
3. What is absorption costing?
4. Overhead apportionment – Stage 1
5. Overhead apportionment – Stage 2
6. Overhead absorption
7. Single factory-wide absorption rates and separate departmental absorption rates
8. Over and under absorption

Performance criteria

- 6.2.A Identify **overhead costs** in accordance with the organisation's procedures
- 6.2.B Attribute overhead costs to production and service cost centres in accordance with agreed **bases of allocation and apportionment**
- 6.2.C Calculate overhead absorption rates in accordance with agreed **bases of absorption**
- 6.2.D Record and analyse information relating to overhead costs in accordance with the organisation's procedures
- 6.2.E Make adjustments for under and over recovered overhead costs in accordance with established procedures
- 6.2.F Review methods of allocation, apportionment and absorption at regular intervals in discussions with senior staff and ensure agreed changes to methods are implemented
- 6.2.G Consult staff working in operational departments to resolve any queries in overhead cost data

Range statement

Overhead costs:
- Fixed
- Variable
- Semi-variable

Bases of allocation and apportionment:
- Direct methods
- Step down methods

Bases of absorption:
- Labour hour methods
- Machine hour methods

Knowledge and understanding

4   Recording of cost and revenue data in the accounting records
8   Bases of allocating and apportioning indirect costs to responsibility centres: direct and step down methods
10 The arbitrary nature of overhead apportionments
11 Bases of absorption
23 Absorption costing
27 The sources of information for revenue and costing data

1 Introduction

Now that we have completed our detailed study of direct materials, direct labour and direct expenses, we can move on to look in more depth at **indirect costs,** or **overheads**. Overheads may be dealt with in a number of different ways. In this chapter we will be looking at **traditional absorption costing**. The only other method that you need to have knowledge of is **marginal costing**. We will be looking at marginal costing in detail in the next chapter.

2 What are overheads?

2.1 General overheads

An **overhead** is the cost incurred in the course of making a product, providing a service or running a department, but which cannot be traced directly and in full to the product, service or department.

Overheads are the total of the following.

- Indirect materials
- Indirect labour
- Indirect expenses

(Note that in the previous chapter we were looking at **expenses**, and whether they were direct or indirect.)

One common way of categorising overheads is as follows.

- Production overhead
- Administration overhead
- Selling overhead
- Distribution overhead

2.2 Production overhead

Production (or factory) overhead includes all indirect material costs, indirect wages and indirect expenses incurred in the factory.

- **Indirect materials** eg cleaning materials and maintenance materials
- **Indirect wages**, eg salaries of supervisors
- **Indirect expenses** eg rent of the factory and depreciation of machinery

2.3 Administration overhead

Administration overhead is all indirect material costs, wages and expenses incurred in the direction, control and administration of an organisation.

- **Depreciation** of office equipment
- **Office salaries**, including salaries of secretaries and accountants
- Rent, rates, insurance, lighting, cleaning and heating of **general offices**

2.4 Selling overhead

Selling overhead is all indirect material costs, wages and expenses incurred in promoting sales and retaining customers.

- **Printing** and **stationery**, such as catalogues and price lists
- **Salaries** and **commission** of sales representatives and sales department staff
- **Advertising** and **sales promotion**, market research
- Rent and insurance of **sales offices**, bad debts and collection charges

2.5 Distribution overhead

Distribution overhead is all indirect material costs, wages and expenses incurred in making the packed product ready for despatch and delivering it to the customer.

- Cost of packing cases.
- Wages of packers, drivers and despatch clerks.
- Freight and insurance charges, depreciation of delivery vehicles.

3 What is absorption costing?

3.1 The objective of absorption costing

The objective of absorption costing is to include in the total cost of a product or service an appropriate share of the organisation's total overhead. By an appropriate share we mean an amount that reflects the amount of time and effort that has gone into producing the unit of product or service.

If an organisation had only one production department and produced identical units then the total overheads would be divided among the total units produced. Life is, of course, never that simple. **Absorption costing is a method of sharing overheads between a number of different products or services on a fair basis.**

3.2 Absorption costing procedures

The three steps involved in calculating the costs of overheads to be charged to cost units are

- Allocation
- Apportionment
- Absorption

Allocation is the process of assigning whole items of cost to cost centres. We studied the process of allocation in the previous chapter.

We shall now begin our study of absorption costing by looking at the first stage of **overhead apportionment**.

Activity 5.1

(a) What is absorption costing?
(b) What are the three stages of absorption costing?

4 Overhead apportionment – Stage 1

Apportionment is a procedure whereby indirect costs (overheads) are spread fairly between cost centres.

4.1 Sharing out common costs

Overhead apportionment follows on from overhead allocation. The first stage of overhead apportionment is to **identify all overhead costs** as production, administration, selling and distribution overhead. This means that the shared costs (such as rent and rates, heat and light and so on) initially allocated to a single cost centre must now be **shared out** between the other (functional) cost centres.

4.2 Bases of apportionment

It is important that overhead costs are shared out on a **fair basis** using appropriate bases of apportionment. The bases of apportionment for the most usual cases are given below.

Overhead	Basis of apportionment
Rent, rates, heating and light, repairs and depreciation of buildings	Floor area occupied by each cost centre
Depreciation, insurance of equipment	Cost or book value of equipment
Personnel office, canteen, welfare, wages and cost office, first aid	Number of employees, or labour hours worked in each cost centre
Heating, lighting (see above)	Volume of space occupied by each cost centre

Don't forget that some overhead costs can be **allocated directly** to the user cost centre without having to be apportioned. For example indirect wages can be directly allocated because they relate solely to an individual cost centre.

Example: Bases of apportionment

Bravo Ltd incurred the following overhead costs.

	£
Depreciation of factory	1,000
Factory repairs and maintenance	600
Factory office costs (treat as production overhead)	1,500
Depreciation of equipment	800
Insurance of equipment	200
Heating	390
Lighting	100
Canteen	900
	5,490

Information relating to the production and service departments in the factory is as follows.

	Department			
	Production A	Production B	Service X	Service Y
Floor space (m^2)	1,200	1,600	800	400
Volume (m^3)	3,000	6,000	2,400	1,600
Number of employees	30	30	15	15
Book value of equipment	£30,000	£20,000	£10,000	£20,000

On what bases should the overhead costs be apportioned between the four departments? How much overhead would be apportioned to each department?

Solution

Item of cost	Basis of apportionment	Total cost £	A £	B £	X £	Y £
				To Department		
Factory depreciation	floor area	1,000	300	400	200	100
Factory repairs	floor area	600	180	240	120	60
Factory office	no. of employees	1,500	500	500	250	250
Equipment depn	book value	800	300	200	100	200
Equipment insurance	book value	200	75	50	25	50
Heating	volume	390	90	180	72	48
Lighting	floor area	100	30	40	20	10
Canteen	no. of employees	900	300	300	150	150
Total		5,490	1,775	1,910	937	868

Workings

Factory depreciation

Total floor space = $(1,200 + 1,600 + 800 + 400) m^2$
= $4,000 m^2$

Factory depreciation is apportioned to the different departments as follows.

Production department A = $\frac{1,200}{4,000} \times £1,000 = £300$

Production department B = $\frac{1,600}{4,000} \times £1,000 = £400$

Service department X = $\frac{800}{4,000} \times £1,000 = £200$

Service department Y = $\frac{400}{4,000} \times £1,000 = £100$

The same method can be applied in order to calculate the apportionments of the other overheads.

Activity 5.2

Baldwin's Ltd is preparing its production overhead budgets. Cost centre expenses and related information have been budgeted as follows.

	Total £	Machine shop A £	Machine shop B £	Assembly £	Canteen £	Maintenance £
Indirect wages	78,560	8,586	9,190	15,674	29,650	15,460
Consumable materials (inc. maintenance)	16,900	6,400	8,700	1,200	600	-
Rent and rates	16,700					
Buildings insurance	2,400					
Power	8,600					
Heat and light	3,400					
Depreciation of machinery	40,200					
Value of machinery	402,000	201,000	179,000	22,000	-	-
Other information:						
Power usage – technical estimates (%)	100	55	40	3	-	2
Direct labour (hours)	35,000	8,000	6,200	20,800	-	-
Machine usage (hours)	25,200	7,200	18,000	-	-	-
Area (square metres)	45,000	10,000	12,000	15,000	6,000	2,000

Task

Calculate the overheads to be apportioned to the five cost centres.

5 Overhead apportionment – Stage 2

5.1 Reapportionment of service cost centre costs

The second stage of overhead apportionment concerns the treatment of service cost centres.

A factory is usually divided into **several production cost centres** and also **many service cost centres**. Service cost centres might include the **stores** or the **canteen**.

Only the production cost centres are directly involved in the manufacture of the units. In order to be able to **add production overheads to unit costs**, it is necessary to have all the overheads charged to the **production cost centres only**.

The next stage in absorption costing is therefore to **apportion the overheads of service cost centres to the production cost centres**. This is sometimes called **reapportionment**.

5.2 Methods of reapportionment

The reapportionment of service cost centre costs can be done by a number of methods. You only need to know about the following two methods.

- Direct method of reapportionment
- Step down method of reapportionment

Whichever method of reapportionment is used, **the basis of apportionment must be fair**. A different apportionment basis may be applied for each service cost centre. This is demonstrated in the following table.

Service cost centre	Possible basis of apportionment
Stores	Number or cost value of material requisitions
Maintenance	Hours of maintenance work done for each cost centre
Production planning	Direct labour hours worked in each production cost centre

5.3 Direct method of reapportionment

The **direct method of reapportionment** involves apportioning the costs of each service cost centre **to production cost centres only**.

This method is most easily explained by working through the following example.

Example: Direct method of reapportionment

Baldwin's Ltd incurred the following overhead costs.

	Production departments		Stores department	Maintenance department
	P	Q		
	£	£	£	£
Allocated costs	6,000	4,000	1,000	2,000
Apportioned costs	2,000	1,000	1,000	500
	8,000	5,000	2,000	2,500

Production department P requisitioned materials to the value of £12,000. Department Q requisitioned £8,000 of materials. The maintenance department provided 500 hours of work for department P and 750 hours for department Q.

Task

Calculate the total production overhead costs of Departments P and Q.

Solution

Service department	Basis of apportionment	Total cost £	Dept P £	Dept Q £
Stores	Value of requisitions (W1)	2,000	1,200	800
Maintenance	Maintenance hours (W2)	2,500	1,000	1,500
		4,500	2,200	2,300
Previously allocated and apportioned costs		13,000	8,000	5,000
Total overhead		17,500	10,200	7,300

Workings

(1) **Stores department overheads**

These are reapportioned as follows.

Total value of materials requisitioned = £12,000 + £8,000
= £20,000

Reapportioned to Department P = $\dfrac{£12,000}{£20,000} \times £2,000 = £1,200$

Reapportioned to Department Q = $\dfrac{£8,000}{£20,000} \times £2,000 = £800$

(2) **Maintenance department overheads**

These are reapportioned as follows.

Total hours worked = 500 + 750 = 1,250 hours

Reapportioned to Department P = $\dfrac{500}{1,250} \times £2,500 = £1,000$

Reapportioned to Department Q = $\dfrac{750}{1,250} \times £2,500 = £1,500$

The total overhead has now been shared, on a fair basis, between the two production departments.

Activity 5.3

The following information also relates to Baldwin's Ltd.

	Total £	Machine shop A £	Machine shop B £	Assembly £	Canteen £	Maintenance £
Indirect wages	78,560	8,586	9,190	15,674	29,650	15,460
Consumable materials	16,900	6,400	8,700	1,200	600	
Rent and rates	16,700	3,711	4,453	5,567	2,227	742
Insurance	2,400	533	640	800	320	107
Power	8,600	4,730	3,440	258		172
Heat and light	3,400	756	907	1,133	453	151
Depreciation	40,200	20,100	17,900	2,200	–	–
	166,760	44,816	45,230	26,832	33,250	16,632

Other information:

	Total	Machine shop A	Machine shop B	Assembly	Canteen	Maintenance
Power usage – technical estimates (%)	100	55	40	3	–	2
Direct labour (hours)	35,000	8,000	6,200	20,800	–	–
Machine usage (hours)	25,200	7,200	18,000	–	–	–
Area (square metres)	45,000	10,000	12,000	15,000	6,000	2,000

Task

Using the bases which you consider to be the most appropriate, calculate overhead totals for Baldwin's Ltd's three production departments, Machine Shop A, Machine Shop B and Assembly.

5.4 Step down method of reapportionment

This method works as follows.

Step 1 Reapportion one of the service cost centre's overheads to all of the other centres which make use of its services (production and service).

Step 2 Reapportion the overheads of the remaining service cost centre to the production departments only. The other service cost centre is ignored.

Example: Step down method of reapportionment

A company has two production departments and two service departments (stores and maintenance). The following information about activity in a recent costing period is available.

	Production departments		Stores department	Maintenance department
	1	2		
Overhead costs	£10,030	£8,970	£10,000	£8,000
Value of material requisitions	£30,000	£50,000	–	£20,000
Maintenance hours used	8,000	1,000	1,000	–

The stores and maintenance departments do work for each other as shown in the table below

	Production departments		Stores department	Maintenance department
	1	2		
Stores work done (100%)	30%	50%	–	20%
Maintenance work done (100%)	80%	10%	10%	–

Task

Using the information given above, apportion the service department overhead costs using the step down method of apportionment, **starting with the stores department**.

Solution

	Production departments		Stores department	Maintenance department
	1	2		
	£	£	£	£
Overhead costs	10,030	8,970	10,000	8,000
Apportion stores (30%/50%/20%)	3,000	5,000	(10,000)	2,000
				10,000
Apportion maintenance ($^8/_9$/$^1/_9$)	8,889	1,111	–	(10,000)
	21,919	15,081	–	–

If the first apportionment had been the maintenance department, then the overheads of £8,000 would have been apportioned as follows.

	Production departments		Stores department	Maintenance department
	1	2		
	£	£	£	£
Overhead costs	10,030	8,970	10,000	8,000
Apportion maintenance (80%/10%/10%)	6,400	800	800	(8,000)
			10,800	–
Apportion stores ($^3/_8$/$^5/_8$)	4,050	6,750	(10,800)	
	20,480	16,520	–	–

Note. Notice how the final results differ, depending upon whether the stores department or the maintenance department is apportioned first.

Activity 5.4

Elm Ltd has two service departments serving two production departments. Overhead costs apportioned to each department are as follows.

Production 1	Production 2	Service 1	Service 2
£	£	£	£
97,428	84,947	9,384	15,823

Service 1 department is expected to work a total of 40,000 hours for the other departments, divided as follows.

	Hours
Production 1	20,000
Production 2	15,000
Service 2	5,000

Service 2 department is expected to work a total of 12,000 hours for the other departments, divided as follows.

	Hours
Production 1	3,000
Production 2	8,000
Service 1	1,000

Task

The finance director has asked you to reapportion the costs of the two service departments using the direct method of apportionment.

Activity 5.5

When you show the finance director how you have reapportioned the costs of the two service departments, he says 'Did I say that we used the direct method? Well, I meant to say the step down method.'

Task

Prove to the finance director that you know how to use the step down method. (**Note.** Apportion the overheads of service department 1 first.)

6 Overhead absorption

6.1 Overhead absorption rate

Overhead absorption is the process whereby overhead costs allocated and apportioned to production cost centres are added to unit, job or batch costs. Overhead absorption is sometimes called **overhead recovery**.

Having allocated and apportioned all overheads, the next stage in the costing treatment of overheads is to add them to, or **absorb them into, cost units.**

Overheads are usually added to cost units using a **predetermined overhead absorption rate**, which is calculated using figures from the budget.

An overhead absorption rate for the forthcoming accounting period is calculated and used as follows.

Step 1 **Estimate the overhead** likely to be incurred during the coming period.

Step 2 **Estimate the activity level for the period.** This could be **total hours, units, or direct costs** or whatever measure of activity upon which the overhead absorption rates are to be based.

Step 3 **Divide the estimated overhead by the budgeted activity level.** This produces the predetermined overhead absorption rate.

Step 4 **Absorb** or **recover** the overhead into the cost unit by applying the calculated absorption rate.

Example: Overhead absorption rates

Channel Ltd makes two products, the Jersey and the Guernsey. Jerseys take 2 labour hours each to make and Guernseys take 5 labour hours.

Task

Calculate the overhead cost per unit for Jerseys and Guernseys respectively if overheads are absorbed on the basis of labour hours.

Solution

Step 1 Estimate the overhead likely to be incurred during the coming period

Channel Ltd estimates that the total overhead will be £50,000

Step 2 Estimate the activity level for the period

Channel Ltd estimates that a total of 100,000 direct labour hours will be worked

Step 3 Divide the estimated overhead by the budgeted activity level

$$\text{Overhead absorption rate} = \frac{£50,000}{100,000\,\text{hrs}} = £0.50 \text{ per direct labour hour}$$

Step 4 Absorb the overhead into the cost unit by applying the calculated absorption rate

	Jersey	Guernsey
Labour hours per unit	2	5
Absorption rate per labour hour	£0.50	£0.50
Overhead absorbed per unit	£1	£2.50

6.2 Possible bases of absorption

The most common absorption bases (or **'overhead recovery rates'**) are as follows.

- A rate per machine hour
- A rate per direct labour hour
- A percentage of direct labour cost
- A percentage of direct materials cost
- A percentage of total direct cost (prime cost)
- A rate per unit
- A percentage of factory cost (for administration overhead)
- A percentage of sales value or factory cost (for selling and distribution overhead)

The most appropriate basis for production overhead depends largely on the organisation concerned. As with apportionment it is a matter of being fair.

Many factories tend to use the **direct labour hour rate** or **machine hour rate** in preference to a rate based on a percentage of direct materials cost, wages or prime cost.

A **machine hour rate** would be used in departments where production is controlled or dictated by machines. A **direct labour hour basis** is more appropriate in a labour intensive environment.

Example: Bases of absorption

The budgeted production overheads and other budget data of Bases Ltd are as follows.

	Production dept X	Production dept Y
Budget		
Production overhead cost	£36,000	£5,000
Direct materials cost	£32,000	
Direct labour cost	£40,000	
Machine hours	10,000	
Direct labour hours	18,000	
Units of production		1,000

What would the absorption rate be for each department using the various bases of apportionment?

Solution

(a) **Department X**

(i) Rate per machine hour $\dfrac{£36,000}{10,000 \text{ hrs}}$ = £3.60 per machine hour

(ii) Rate per direct labour hour $\dfrac{£36,000}{18,000 \text{ hrs}}$ = £2 per direct labour hour

(iii) % of direct labour cost $\dfrac{£36,000}{£40,000} \times 100\%$ = 90%

(iv) % of direct materials cost $\dfrac{£36,000}{£32,000} \times 100\%$ = 112.5%

(v) % of total direct cost $\dfrac{£36,000}{£72,000} \times 100\%$ = 50%

(b) For **department Y** the absorption rate will be based on units of output.

$\dfrac{£5,000}{1,000 \text{ units}}$ = £5 per unit produced

Activity 5.6

(a) If production overheads in total are expected to be £108,000 and direct labour hours are planned to be 90,000 hours costing £5 per hour, what is the overhead absorption rate per direct labour hour?

(b) If production overheads in total are expected to be £720,000 and direct machine hours are planned to be 50,000 hours, what is the overhead absorption rate per direct machine hour?

6.3 The arbitrary nature of absorption costing

It should be obvious to you that, even if a company is trying to be 'fair', there is a great **lack of precision** about the way an absorption base is chosen.

This arbitrariness is one of the main criticisms of absorption costing, and if absorption costing is to be used then it is important that **the methods used are kept under regular review.** Changes in working conditions should, if necessary, lead to changes in the way in which work is accounted for.

For example, a **labour intensive department** may become **mechanised**. If a direct labour hour rate of absorption had been used previous to the mechanisation, it would probably now be more appropriate to change to the use of a machine hour rate.

7 Single factory-wide absorption rates and separate departmental absorption rates

7.1 Single factory-wide absorption rates

A **single factory-wide overhead absorption rate** is an absorption rate used throughout a factory for all jobs and units of output irrespective of the department in which they were produced. It is sometimes called a **blanket overhead absorption rate.**

Consider a factory in which total overheads were £500,000 and there were 250,000 machine hours, during a period. We could calculate a **single factory-wide overhead absorption rate** of £2 per machine hour (£500,000 ÷ 250,000). This would mean that all jobs passing through the factory would be **charged at the same rate** of £2 per machine hour.

The factory may have a number of departments undertaking different activities and jobs may not spend an equal amount of time in each department. In this situation the use of a **single factory-wide overhead absorption rate** is not really appropriate.

The main argument against the use of single factory-wide overhead absorption rates is the fact that **some products will absorb a higher overhead charge than is fair. Other products will absorb less overhead cost than is fair.**

If different departments use separate absorption rates **appropriate to the department's activity**, overheads should be charged to products on a **fairer basis** than when blanket overhead absorption rates are used. The overhead charged to products should then be **representative of the costs of the efforts and resources put into making them.**

7.2 Separate departmental absorption rates

Gibson Ltd has two production departments, for which the following budgeted information is available.

	Department Alpha	Department Beta	Total
Estimated overheads	£360,000	£200,000	£560,000
Estimated direct labour hours	200,000	40,000	240,000

If a single factory-wide overhead absorption rate per direct labour hour is applied, the factory-wide rate of overhead recovery would be:

$$\frac{£560,000}{240,000 \text{ hrs}} = £2.33 \text{ per direct labour hour}$$

If separate departmental overhead absorption rates are applied, these would be:

Department Alpha $= \dfrac{£360,000}{200,000 \text{ hours}}$ **Department Beta** $= \dfrac{£200,000}{40,000 \text{ hours}}$

$= £1.80$ per direct labour hour $= £5$ per direct labour hour

Department Beta has a higher overhead absorption rate per hour worked.

Activity 5.7

Le Toast Ltd make two types of toaster. One model is for domestic use selling for £400 and the other for industrial applications selling for £500. Unit costs are as follows.

	Domestic £	Industrial £
Direct materials	28	40
Direct labour	180	80
Direct expenses	40	200

Direct labour is paid at the rate of £10 per hour. Direct expenses comprise machine running costs and these are incurred at the rate of £8 per machine hour.

Production overheads in the coming year are expected to be £1,040,000. Planned production volume is 20,000 units of each product.

Task

Calculate the production overhead absorption rate and the total (direct and indirect) production cost per unit of each product if a single factory-wide overhead absorption rate per direct labour hour is used.

Helping hand. Use the information about labour cost per unit to derive the number of labour hours per unit, and hence the total forecast labour hours.

8 Over and under absorption

8.1 Predetermined recovery rates

It was stated earlier that the usual method of accounting for overheads is to add overhead costs on the basis of a **predetermined recovery rate**. This rate is a sort of **expected cost** since it is based on figures representing what is supposed to happen (that is, figures from the budget). Using the **predetermined overhead absorption rate**, the actual cost of production can be established as follows.

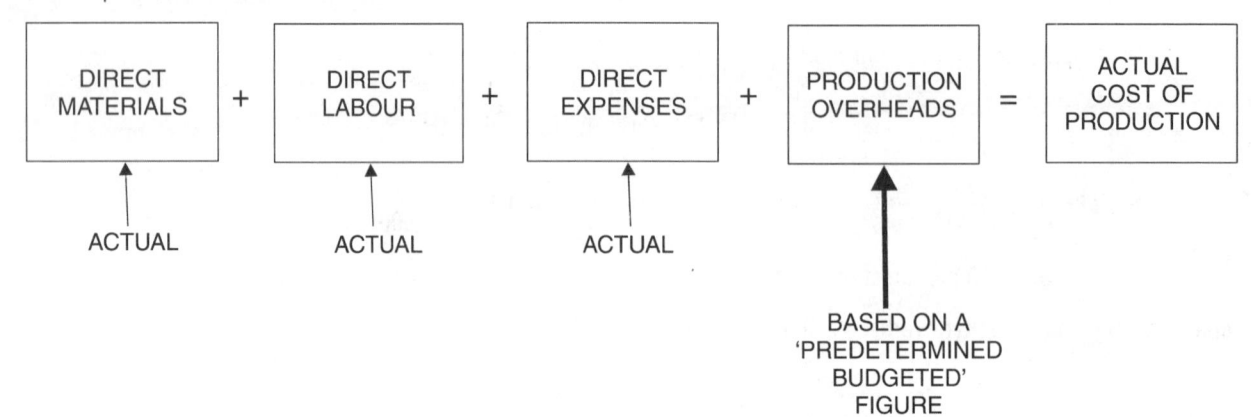

DIRECT MATERIALS (ACTUAL) + DIRECT LABOUR (ACTUAL) + DIRECT EXPENSES (ACTUAL) + PRODUCTION OVERHEADS (BASED ON A 'PREDETERMINED BUDGETED' FIGURE) = ACTUAL COST OF PRODUCTION

Many students become seriously confused about what can appear to be a very unusual method of costing (**actual cost** of production including a figure based on the **budget**). Study the following example. It will help to clarify this tricky point.

Example: Using the predetermined recovery rate

Fred Ltd budgeted to make 100 units of product called Ashley at a cost of £3 per unit in direct materials and £4 per unit in direct labour. The sales price would be £12 per unit, and production overheads were budgeted to amount to £200. A unit basis of overhead recovery is in operation. During the period 120 units were actually produced and sold (for £12 each) and the actual cost of direct materials was £380 and of direct labour, £450. Overheads incurred came to £210.

Task

Calculate the cost of sales and profit for product Ashley. Ignore administration, selling and distribution overheads.

Solution

The cost of production is the actual direct cost plus the cost of overheads, **absorbed at a predetermined rate** as established in the budget.

Overhead recovery rate = $\dfrac{£200}{100 \text{ units}}$ = £2 per unit produced.

The actual cost of sales of product Ashley is calculated as follows.

	£
Direct materials (actual)	380
Direct labour (actual)	450
Overheads absorbed (120 units × £2)	240
Full cost of sales	1,070
Sales value (120 units × £12)	1,440
Profit	370

8.2 Under/over absorption of overheads

You may already have noticed in the example above that **the actual overheads incurred, £210, are not the same as the overheads absorbed** (or included) into the cost of production. It is the overheads absorbed (£240) that will be debited to the profit and loss account. At the end of the accounting period an adjustment will need to be made in order to reflect the actual overheads of £210 that were incurred.

The discrepancy between actual overheads incurred, and the overheads absorbed is the **under absorption** or **over absorption** of overhead. This under/over absorption is an inevitable feature of absorption costing.

8.3 Why does under or over absorption occur?

The overhead absorption rate is predetermined from estimates of overhead cost and the expected volume of activity. It is quite likely, therefore, that either one or both of the estimates will not agree with what actually occurs. When this happens, under or over absorption of overheads will arise.

Example: Under/over absorption of overheads

The estimated overhead in a production department is £80,000 and the estimated activity is 40,000 direct labour hours. The overhead recovery rate (using a direct labour hour basis) would be £2 per direct labour hour (£80,000 ÷ 40,000 direct labour hours).

Actual overheads in the period are, say £84,000 and 45,000 direct labour hours are worked.

	£
Overhead incurred (actual)	84,000
Overhead absorbed (45,000 × £2)	90,000
Over absorption of overhead	6,000

In this example, the cost of units produced has been charged with £6,000 more than was actually spent. An adjustment to reconcile the overheads charged to the actual overhead is necessary and the over-absorbed overhead will be **written off as a credit in the profit and loss account** at the end of the accounting period.

Example: More under/over absorption of overheads

Uttoxeter Ltd has a budgeted production overhead of £50,000 and a budgeted activity of 25,000 direct labour hours and therefore a recovery rate of £2 per direct labour hour (£50,000 ÷ 25,000 direct labour hours). Calculate the under-/over-absorbed overhead, and explain the reasons for the under/over absorption, in the following circumstances.

(a) Actual overheads cost £47,000 and 25,000 direct labour hours are worked.
(b) Actual overheads cost £50,000 and 21,500 direct labour hours are worked.
(c) Actual overheads cost £47,000 and 21,500 direct labour hours are worked.

Solution

(a)
	£
Actual overhead	47,000
Absorbed overhead (25,000 × £2)	50,000
Over-absorbed overhead	3,000

Here there is **over absorption** because although the actual and estimated direct labour hours are the same, actual overheads cost *less* than expected and so too much overhead has been charged against profit.

(b)
	£
Actual overhead	50,000
Absorbed overhead (21,500 × £2)	43,000
Under-absorbed overhead	7,000

Here there is **under absorption** because although estimated and actual overhead costs were the same, fewer direct labour hours were worked than expected and hence insufficient overheads have been charged against profit.

(c)
	£
Actual overhead	47,000
Absorbed overhead (21,500 × £2)	43,000
Under-absorbed overhead	4,000

The reason for the net **under absorption** is a combination of the reasons in (a) and (b).

Activity 5.8

The actual total production overhead expenditure of Nuthatch Ltd, was £176,533. Its actual activity, and the predetermined overhead absorption rates were as follows.

	Machine shop A	Machine shop B	Assembly
Direct labour hours	8,200	6,500	21,900
Machine usage hours	7,300	18,700	-
Predetermined overhead absorption rates	£7.94 per machine hr	£3.50 per machine hr	£2.24 per direct labour hr

Task

Calculate the under or over absorption of overheads.

The following equation should help you to calculate the under/over absorption of overheads quickly and easily.

ACTUAL OVERHEADS – ABSORBED OVERHEADS = POSITIVE / NEGATIVE VALUE

- If the result is NEGATIVE (N), there is OVER ABSORPTION (O)
- If the result is POSITIVE (P), there is UNDER ABSORPTION (U)

Remember **NOPU!**

Key learning points

- **Overhead** is part of the cost incurred in the course of making a product, providing a service or running a department, which cannot be traced directly and in full to the product, service or department.

- The four main types of overhead are **production, administration, selling** and **distribution**.

- The objective of absorption costing is to include in the total cost of a product or service an appropriate share of the organisation's total overhead.

- **Allocation, apportionment** and **absorption** are the three steps of calculating the costs of overheads to be charged to manufactured output.

- **Apportionment** is a procedure whereby indirect costs (overheads) are spread fairly between cost centres.

- The **first stage of apportionment** is the **sharing out of common costs** using appropriate bases of apportionment.

- The **second stage of apportionment** is the apportionment of the service cost centre overheads to the production cost centres. This is sometimes called **reapportionment**.

- Service cost centre costs may be apportioned to production cost centres by the **direct method,** or the **step down method.**

- Overhead absorption is the process whereby costs of cost centres are added to unit, job or batch costs. Overhead absorption is sometimes called **overhead recovery.**

- **Predetermined overhead absorption** rates are calculated using budgeted figures. **Direct machine hour rates** are appropriate where production is controlled or dictated by machines. A **direct labour hour rate is** more appropriate in a labour intensive environment.

- There is a lack of precision about the way an absorption basis is chosen – the **arbitrary nature** of absorption costing is one of its main criticisms.

- The actual cost of production is made up of the following.
    - Direct materials
    - Direct labour
    - Direct expenses
    - Overheads (based on the predetermined overhead absorption rate)

- **A single factory-wide overhead absorption rate** (or **blanket overhead absorption rate**) is an absorption rate used throughout a factory for all jobs and units of output irrespective of the department in which they were produced. Sometimes it might be more appropriate to calculate **separate departmental absorption rates**.

- **Under** or **over absorption** of overheads occurs because the predetermined overhead absorption rates are based on forecasts (estimates).

- If actual overheads are greater than absorbed overheads, then overheads are **under absorbed**.

- If actual overheads are less than absorbed overheads, then overheads are **over absorbed**.

- The **NOPU** rule should help you to calculate under/over absorption of overheads quickly and easily.

    ACTUAL OVERHEADS – ABSORBED OVERHEADS = POSITIVE / NEGATIVE VALUE

    - If the result is NEGATIVE (N), there is OVER ABSORPTION (O)
    - If the result is POSITIVE (P), there is UNDER ABSORPTION (U)

Quick quiz

1. What is allocation?

2. Match the following overheads with the most appropriate basis of apportionment.

   Overhead

   (a) Depreciation of equipment
   (b) Heat and light costs
   (c) Canteen
   (d) Insurance of equipment

   Basis of apportionment

   (1) Direct machine hours
   (2) Number of employees
   (3) Book value of equipment
   (4) Floor area

3. Which of the following departments are directly involved in production?

Department	Involved in production (✓)
Finished goods warehouse	
Canteen	
Machining department	
Offices	
Assembly department	

4. In relation to calculating total absorption cost, label the following descriptions in the correct order as Steps 1 – 5.

   Description   **Step**

   A   Apportion overhead costs between departments
   B   Establish the overhead absorption rate
   C   Choose fair methods of apportionment
   D   Apply the overhead absorption rate to products
   E   Reapportion service department costs

5. How do the direct and step down methods of service cost centre apportionment differ?

6. A direct labour hour basis of overhead absorption is most appropriate in which of the following environments?

   A   Machine-intensive
   B   Labour-intensive
   C   When all units produced are identical
   D   None of the above

7. Does over absorption occur when absorbed overheads are greater than or less than actual overheads?

   ☐ Greater than

   ☐ Less than

8   Bridge Ltd has a budgeted production overhead of £214,981 and a budgeted activity of 35,950 hours of direct labour. Before settling on these estimates the company's accountant had a number of other possibilities for each figure, as shown below. Determine (preferably by inspection rather than full calculation) whether overheads will be over or under absorbed in each case if the alternatives turn out to be the actual figures.

		Over or under absorption
(a)	$\dfrac{£215,892}{35,950}$	
(b)	$\dfrac{£214,981}{36,005}$	
(c)	$\dfrac{£213,894}{36,271}$	
(d)	$\dfrac{£215,602}{35,440}$	

Answers to quick quiz

1   The process whereby whole cost items are charged direct to a cost unit or cost centre.

2   (a)   (3)
    (b)   (4)
    (c)   (2)
    (d)   (3)

3

Department	Involved in production (✓)
Finished goods warehouse	
Canteen	
Machining department	✓
Offices	
Assembly department	✓

4   A = 2
    B = 4
    C = 1
    D = 5
    E = 3

5   The **direct method** is generally used when inter-service department work is not taken into account, ie the costs of each service cost centre are apportioned to production cost centres only.

The step down method involves the following.

- Apportioning one of the service cost centre's overheads to the cost centres using its services (production and service).
- Apportioning the overheads of the remaining service cost centre to the **production departments only.**

6   B

7   [✓]   Greater than

8   **Helping hand.** You could try to answer this activity by considering how the value of a simple fraction like 4 divided by 2 would increase or decrease as the value of the denominator or numerator varied. Remember that if the actual rate is more than the estimated rate there will be under absorption and vice versa.

   (a)   Under (because actual production overheads are higher than estimated).
   (b)   Over (because actual hours are higher than estimated).
   (c)   Over (because actual production overheads are lower than estimated and actual hours are higher).
   (d)   Under (because actual hours are lower than estimated and actual hours are higher).

   Helping hand. If you find it difficult to do this by inspection, there is nothing wrong with calculating the estimated rate (£214,981 ÷ 35,950 hours = £5.98) and then the actual rate in each case (£6.00; £5.97; £5.90; £6.08), but having done this make sure that you can explain in non-numerical terms what has happened. For example, in (c) lower overheads and a higher number of active hours have led to over absorption.

Activity checklist

This checklist shows which performance criteria, range statement or knowledge and understanding point is covered by each activity in this chapter. Tick off each activity as you complete it.

Activity

5.1	☐	This activity deals with Knowledge and Understanding point 23 regarding absorption costing
5.2	☐	This activity deals with Performance Criteria 6.2.A and 6.2.D regarding the identification, recording and analysis of overhead costs
5.3	☐	This activity deals with Performance Criteria 6.2.B regarding bases of allocation and apportionment
5.4	☐	This activity deals with Performance Criteria 6.2.B regarding bases of allocation and apportionment
5.5	☐	This activity deals with Performance Criteria 6.2.B and 6.2.F regarding bases of allocation and apportionment
5.6	☐	This activity deals with Performance Criteria 6.2.C regarding bases of absorption
5.7	☐	This activity deals with Performance Criteria 6.2.C regarding overhead absorption rates
5.8	☐	This activity deals with Performance Criteria 6.2.E regarding under and over recovered overhead costs

Note. There is no specific activity covering Performance Criteria 6.2.G since it is assumed that competence in Performance criteria 6.2.A – F will automatically lead to competence in Performance criteria 6.2.G.

chapter 6

Marginal costing and absorption costing

Contents

1. Introduction
2. Marginal cost and marginal costing
3. The principles of marginal costing
4. Marginal costing and absorption costing and the calculation of profit
5. Reconciling the profit figures given by the two methods
6. Marginal costing versus absorption costing – which is better?

Knowledge and understanding

9   Marginal versus absorption costing for costing and reporting purposes
22   Marginal costing

1 Introduction

This chapter looks at one of the other methods of dealing with overheads, that of **marginal costing**.

Marginal costing treats all fixed costs as **period costs**, whereas **absorption costing** recognises fixed production costs as part of the cost of a unit of output and hence as **product costs**.

Each costing method produces a different profit figure because of the differences in stock valuations. We will be looking at this particular point in detail.

2 Marginal cost and marginal costing

2.1 Marginal costing

Marginal costing is an alternative method of costing to absorption costing. In marginal costing, **only variable costs are charged as a cost of sale** and a **contribution** is calculated.

Contribution is the difference between sales value and the marginal cost of sales.

Contribution is of fundamental importance in marginal costing, and the term 'contribution' is really short for 'contribution towards covering fixed overheads and making a profit'.

- Closing stocks of work in progress or finished goods are valued at marginal (variable) production cost.
- Fixed costs are treated as a period cost, and are charged in full to the profit and loss account of the accounting period in which they are incurred.

2.2 Marginal cost

Marginal cost is the cost of a unit of a product or service which would be avoided if that unit were not produced or provided.

The marginal production cost per unit of an item usually consists of the following.

- Direct materials
- Direct labour
- Variable production overheads

The **marginal cost of sales** usually consists of the marginal cost of production adjusted for stock movements plus the variable selling costs, which would include items such as sales commission, and possibly some variable distribution costs.

3 The principles of marginal costing

3.1 Principle 1

Period fixed costs are the same, for any volume of sales and production (provided that the level of activity is within the 'relevant range'). Therefore, by selling an extra item of product or service the following will happen.

- Revenue will increase by the sales value of the item sold.
- Costs will increase by the variable cost per unit.
- Profit will increase by the amount of contribution earned from the extra item.

3.2 Principle 2

If the volume of sales falls by one item, the profit will fall by the amount of contribution earned from the item.

3.3 Principle 3

Profit measurement should therefore be based on an analysis of total contribution. Since fixed costs relate to a period of time, and do not change with increases or decreases in sales volume, it is misleading to charge units of sale with a share of fixed costs. Absorption costing is therefore misleading, and it is more appropriate to deduct the fixed costs from the total contribution for the period to derive a profit figure.

3.4 Principle 4

When a unit of product is made, the extra costs incurred in its manufacture are the **variable production costs**. Fixed costs are unaffected, and no extra fixed costs are incurred when output is increased. It is therefore argued that **the valuation of closing stocks should be at variable production cost** (direct materials, direct labour, direct expenses and variable production overhead) because these are the only costs properly attributable to the product.

Example: Marginal costing principles

Bain Painkillers Ltd makes a drug called 'Relief', which has a variable production cost of £6 per unit and a sales price of £10 per unit. At the beginning of June, there were no opening stocks and production during the month was 20,000 units. Fixed costs for the month were £45,000 (production, administration, sales and distribution). There were no variable marketing costs.

Tasks

Calculate the contribution and profit for June, using marginal costing principles, if sales were as follows.

(a) 10,000 Reliefs
(b) 15,000 Reliefs
(c) 20,000 Reliefs

Solution

The first stage in the profit calculation must be to identify the variable cost of sales, and then the contribution. Fixed costs are deducted from the total contribution to derive the profit. All closing stocks are valued at marginal production cost (£6 per unit).

	10,000 Reliefs £	10,000 Reliefs £	15,000 Reliefs £	15,000 Reliefs £	20,000 Reliefs £	20,000 Reliefs £
Sales (at £10)		100,000		150,000		200,000
Opening stock	0		0		0	
Variable production cost	120,000		120,000		120,000	
	120,000		120,000		120,000	
Less value of closing stock (at marginal cost)	60,000		30,000		–	
Variable cost of sales		60,000		90,000		120,000
Contribution		40,000		60,000		80,000
Less fixed costs		45,000		45,000		45,000
Profit/(loss)		(5,000)		15,000		35,000
Profit/(loss) per unit		£(0.50)		£1.00		£1.75
Contribution per unit		£4.00		£4.00		£4.00

The conclusions which may be drawn from this example are as follows.

(a) The **profit per unit varies** at differing levels of sales, because the average fixed overhead cost per unit changes with the volume of output and sales.

(b) The **contribution per unit is constant** at all levels of output and sales. Total contribution, which is the contribution per unit multiplied by the number of units sold, increases in direct proportion to the volume of sales.

(c) Since the **contribution per unit does not change**, the most effective way of calculating the expected profit at any level of output and sales would be as follows.

Step 1 Calculate the total contribution.
Step 2 Deduct fixed costs as a period charge in order to find the profit.

(d) In our example the expected profit from the sale of 17,000 Reliefs would be as follows.

	£
Total contribution (17,000 × £4)	68,000
Less fixed costs	45,000
Profit	23,000

Activity 6.1

Denver Ltd makes two products, the Cloud and the Sky. Information relating to each of these products for August is as follows.

	Cloud	Sky
Opening stock	nil	nil
Production (units)	15,000	6,000
Sales (units)	10,000	5,000
Sales price per unit	£20	£30
Unit costs	£	£
Direct materials	8	14
Direct labour	4	2
Variable production overhead	2	1
Variable sales overhead	2	3

Fixed costs for the month	£
Production costs	40,000
Administration costs	15,000
Sales and distribution costs	25,000

Tasks

(a) Using marginal costing principles, calculate the profit for August.

(b) Calculate the profit if sales had been 15,000 units of Cloud and 6,000 units of Sky.

3.5 Profit or contribution information

The main advantage of **contribution information** is that it allows an easy calculation of profit if sales increase or decrease from a certain level.

By comparing total contribution with fixed overheads, it is possible to determine whether profits or losses will be made at certain sales levels.

Profit information, on the other hand, does not lend itself to easy manipulation but note how easy it was to calculate profits using contribution information in Activity 6.1.

4 Marginal costing and absorption costing and the calculation of profit

Marginal costing as a cost accounting system is significantly different from absorption costing. It is an **alternative** method of accounting for costs and profit, which rejects the principles of absorbing fixed overheads into unit costs.

4.1 Marginal costing – calculation of profit

- Closing stocks are valued at marginal production cost.
- Fixed costs are charged in full against the profit of the period in which they are incurred.

4.2 Absorption costing – calculation of profit

- Closing stocks are valued at full production cost, and include a share of fixed production costs.
- This means that the cost of sales in a period will include some fixed overhead incurred in a previous period (in opening stock values) and will exclude some fixed overhead incurred in the current period but carried forward in closing stock values as a charge to a subsequent accounting period.

Example: Marginal and absorption costing compared

Look back at the information contained in Activity 6.1. Suppose that the budgeted production for August was 15,000 units of Cloud and 6,000 units of Sky, and production overhead is absorbed on the basis of budgeted direct labour costs.

Tasks

Calculate the absorption costing profit if production was as budgeted, and sales were as follows.

(a) 10,000 units of Cloud and 5,000 units of Sky
(b) 15,000 units of Cloud and 6,000 units of Sky

Administration, sales and distribution costs should be charged as a period cost against profit.

Solution

Budgeted production overhead is calculated as follows.

		£
Fixed		40,000
Variable:	Clouds (15,000 × £2)	30,000
	Skys (6,000 × £1)	6,000
Total		76,000

The production overhead absorption rate would be calculated as follows.

$$\frac{\text{Budgeted production overhead}}{\text{Budget direct labour cost}} = \frac{£76,000}{(15,000 \times £4) + (6,000 \times £2)} \times 100\%$$

$$= \frac{£76,000}{£(60,000 + 12,000)} \times 100\%$$

$$= \frac{£76,000}{£72,000} \times 100\%$$

$$= 105.56\% \text{ of direct labour cost}$$

(a) If sales are 10,000 units of Cloud and 5,000 units of Sky, profit would be as follows.

	Absorption costing		
	Cloud £	Sky £	Total £
Costs of production			
Direct materials	120,000	84,000	204,000
Direct labour	60,000	12,000	72,000
Overhead (105.56% of labour)	63,333	12,667	76,000
	243,333	108,667	352,000
Less closing stocks	(1/3) 81,111	(1/6) 18,111	99,222
Production cost of sales	162,222	90,556	252,778
Administration costs			15,000
Sales and distribution costs			
Variable			35,000
Fixed			25,000
Total cost of sales			327,778
Sales	200,000	150,000	350,000
Profit			22,222

Note. There is no under/over absorption of overhead, since actual production is the same as budgeted production.

The profit derived using absorption costing techniques is different from the profit (£10,000) using marginal costing techniques at this volume of sales (see Activity 6.1).

(b) If production and sales are exactly the same, (15,000 units of Cloud and 6,000 units of Sky) profit would be £40,000.

	£
Sales (300,000 + 180,000)	480,000
Cost of sales (352,000* + 15,000 + 48,000 + 25,000)	440,000
Profit	40,000

* No closing stock if sales and production are equal.

This is the same as the profit calculated by marginal costing techniques in Activity 6.1.

4.3 Marginal versus absorption

- In **marginal costing**, it is necessary to identify the following. — Variable costs / Contribution / Fixed costs

- In **absorption costing** it is not necessary to distinguish variable costs from fixed costs.

- Marginal costing and absorption costing are different techniques for assessing profit in a period.
- If there are changes in stocks during a period, so that opening stock volumes are different to closing stock volumes, marginal costing and absorption costing give different results for profit obtained.

UNIT 6 RECORDING AND EVALUATING COSTS AND REVENUES

- If the opening and closing stock volumes are the same, marginal costing and absorption costing will give the same profit figure. This is because the total cost of sales during the period would be the same, no matter how calculated.

4.4 The long-run effect on profit

In the long run, total profit for a company will be the same whether marginal costing or absorption costing is used. Different accounting conventions merely affect the profit of individual accounting periods.

Example: Comparison of total profits

To illustrate this point, let us suppose that a company makes and sells a single product. At the beginning of period 1, there are no opening stocks of the product, for which the variable production cost is £4 per unit and the sales price is £6 per unit. Fixed costs are £2,000 per period, of which £1,500 are fixed production costs.

	Period 1	Period 2
Sales	1,200 units	1,800 units
Production	1,500 units	1,500 units

Tasks

Determine the profit in each period using the following methods of costing.

(a) Absorption costing. Assume normal output is 1,500 units per period.
(b) Marginal costing.

Solution

It is important to notice that although production and sales volumes in each period are different (and therefore the profit for each period by absorption costing will be different from the profit by marginal costing), over the full period, total production equals total sales volume. The total cost of sales is the same, and therefore the profit is the same by either method of accounting.

(a) **Absorption costing:** the absorption rate for fixed production overhead is

$$\frac{£1,500}{1,500 \text{ units}} = £1 \text{ per unit}$$

Total unit cost for stock valuation = £4 + £1 = £5

	Period 1		Period 2		Total	
	£	£	£	£	£	£
Sales		7,200		10,800		18,000
Production costs						
Variable	6,000		6,000		12,000	
Fixed	1,500		1,500		3,000	
	7,500		7,500		15,000	
Add opening stock b/f	–		1,500			
	7,500		9,000			
Less closing stock c/f (300 × £5)	1,500		–		–	
Production cost of sales	6,000		9,000		15,000	
Other costs	500		500		1,000	
Total cost of sales		6,500		9,500		16,000
Profit		700		1,300		2,000

(b) **Marginal costing**

	Period 1		Period 2		Total	
	£	£	£	£	£	£
Sales		7,200		10,800		18,000
Variable production cost	6,000		6,000		12,000	
Add opening stock b/f	–		1,200			
	6,000		7,200			
Less closing stock c/f (300 × £4)	1,200		–		–	
Variable production cost of sales		4,800		7,200		12,000
Contribution		2,400		3,600		6,000
Fixed costs		2,000		2,000		4,000
Profit		400		1,600		2,000

Notes:

(a) The total profit over the two periods is the same for each method of costing, but the profit in each period is different.

(b) In absorption costing, fixed production overhead of £300 is carried forward from period 1 into period 2 in stock values, and becomes a charge to profit in period 2. In marginal costing all fixed costs are charged in the period they are incurred, therefore the profit in period 1 is £300 lower and in period 2 is £300 higher than the absorption costing profit.

5 Reconciling the profit figures given by the two methods

The difference in profits reported under the two costing systems is due to the different stock valuation methods used.

If stock levels increase between the beginning and end of a period, absorption costing will report the higher profit. This is because some of the fixed production overhead incurred during the period will be carried forward in closing stock (which reduces cost of sales) to be set against sales revenue in the following period instead of being written off in full against profit in the period concerned.

If stock levels decrease, absorption costing will report the lower profit because as well as the fixed overhead incurred, fixed production overhead which had been carried forward in opening stock is released and is also included in cost of sales.

Example: Reconciling profits

The profits reported under absorption costing and marginal costing for period 1 in Example: Comparison of Total profits, would be reconciled as follows.

	£
Marginal costing profit	400
Adjust for fixed overhead in stock:	
Stock increase of 300 units × £1 per unit	300
Absorption costing profit	700

If you have trouble reconciling the different profits reported under absorption costing and marginal costing, remember the following formula.

Marginal costing profit	X
Increase/(decrease) in stock units × fixed production overhead absorption rate per unit	Y
Absorption costing profit	Z

Activity 6.2

The overhead absorption rate for product X is £10 per machine hour. Each unit of product X requires five machine hours. Stock of product X on 1.1.X1 was 150 units and on 31.12.X1 it was 100 units. What is the difference in profit between results reported using absorption costing and results reported using marginal costing?

- A The absorption costing profit would be £2,500 less
- B The absorption costing profit would be £2,500 greater
- C The absorption costing profit would be £5,000 less
- D The absorption costing profit would be £5,000 greater

Activity 6.3

When opening stocks were 8,500 litres and closing stocks 6,750 litres, a company reported a profit of £62,100 using marginal costing.

Assuming that the fixed overhead absorption rate was £3 per litre, what would be the profit using absorption costing?

    A £41,850   B £56,850   C £67,350   D £82,350

6 Marginal costing versus absorption costing – which is better?

There are arguments in favour of each costing method.

6.1 Arguments in favour of absorption costing

- Fixed production costs are incurred in order to make output and it is therefore 'fair' to charge all output with a share of these costs.

- Closing stock will be valued using the principles required by SSAP 9 for the financial accounting valuation of stocks.

- When calculating the contribution of various products made by a company, it may not be clear whether the contribution earned by each product is enough to cover fixed costs. By charging fixed overhead to a product we can decide whether it is profitable or not.

- Where stock building is necessary fixed costs should be included in stock valuations otherwise a series of losses will be shown in earlier periods, to be offset eventually by excessive profits when the goods are sold.

6.2 Arguments in favour of marginal costing

- It is simple to operate.

- There are no apportionments (frequently done on an arbitrary basis) of fixed costs.

- Fixed costs will be the same regardless of the volume of output. It makes sense, therefore, to charge them in full as a cost to the period.

- The cost to produce an extra unit is the variable production cost. It is realistic to value closing stock items at this directly attributable cost.

- As we have seen, the size of total contribution varies directly with sales volume at a constant rate per unit. For management purposes, better information about expected profit is obtained from the use of variable costs and contribution in the accounting system.

- It is also argued that absorption costing gives managers the wrong signals. Goods are produced, not to meet market demand, but to absorb allocated overheads. Production in excess of demand in fact increases the overheads (for example warehousing) the organisation must bear.

- Under or over absorption of overheads is avoided.

UNIT 6 RECORDING AND EVALUATING COSTS AND REVENUES

Key learning points

- ☑ **Absorption costing** is most often used for routine profit reporting and must be used for financial accounting purposes. **Marginal costing** provides better management information for planning and decision making.

- ☑ **Marginal cost** is the variable cost of one unit of product or service.

- ☑ **Contribution** is an important measure in marginal costing, and it is calculated as the difference between sales value and marginal or variable cost.

- ☑ **In marginal costing, fixed production costs are treated as period costs** and are written off as they are incurred.

- ☑ **In absorption costing, fixed production costs are absorbed into the cost of units** and are carried forward in stock to be charged against sales for the next period. Stock values using absorption costing are therefore greater than those calculated using marginal costing.

- ☑ **Reported profit figures** using marginal costing or absorption costing will differ if there is any change in the level of stocks in the period. If production is equal to sales, there will be no difference in calculated profits using these costing methods.

- ☑ If stock levels **increase** during a period, absorption costing will report a **higher** profit than marginal costing.

- ☑ If stock levels **decrease** during a period, absorption costing will report a **lower** profit than marginal costing.

- ☑ There are a number of arguments in favour of each of the costing systems.

- ☑ The distinction between marginal costing and absorption costing is very important and it is vital that you understand the differences between the two systems.

Quick quiz

1. What is marginal costing?

2. What is a period cost in marginal costing?

3. Sales value – marginal cost of sales = ...

4. Marginal costing and absorption costing are different techniques for assessing profit in a period. If there are changes in stock during a period, marginal costing and absorption costing will report different profits.

    Which of the following statements are true?

    I   If stock levels increase, marginal costing will report the higher profit.

    II   If stock levels decrease, marginal costing will report the lower profit.

    III   If stock levels decrease, marginal costing will report the higher profit.

    IV   If the opening and closing stock volumes are the same, marginal costing and absorption costing will report the same profit figure.

    A   All of the above
    B   I, II and IV
    C   I and IV
    D   III and IV

5. Which of the following are arguments in favour of marginal costing? Tick as appropriate.

    | | (a) | Closing stock is valued in accordance with SSAP 9. |
    | | (b) | It is simple to operate. |
    | | (c) | There is no under or over absorption of overheads. |
    | | (d) | Fixed costs are the same regardless of activity levels. |
    | | (e) | The information from this costing method may be used for decision making. |

Answers to quick quiz

1. Marginal costing is an alternative method of costing to absorption costing. In marginal costing, only variable costs are charged as a cost of sale and a contribution is calculated (sales revenue – variable cost of sales).

2. A fixed cost

3. Contribution

4. D

UNIT 6 RECORDING AND EVALUATING COSTS AND REVENUES

5 ☐ (a)
  ✓ (b)
  ✓ (c)
  ✓ (d)
  ✓ (e)

Activity checklist

This checklist shows which performance criteria, range statement or knowledge and understanding point is covered by each activity in this chapter. Tick off each activity as you complete it.

Activity

6.1	☐	This activity deals with Knowledge and Understanding point 22 regarding marginal costing
6.2	☐	This activity deals with Knowledge and Understanding point 9 regarding marginal versus absorption costing
6.3	☐	This activity deals with Knowledge and Understanding point 9 regarding marginal versus absorption costing

chapter 7

Cost behaviour

Contents

1 Introduction
2 General principles of cost behaviour
3 Cost behaviour patterns
4 Cost behaviour and levels of activity
5 Determination of fixed and variable elements: the high-low technique

Knowledge and understanding

13 Analysis of the effect of changing activity levels on unit costs
15 The identification of fixed, variable and semi-variable costs and their use in cost recording, cost reporting and cost analysis
24 Cost behaviour
27 The sources of information for revenue and costing data

1 Introduction

In Chapter 1 of this Interactive Text you saw that costs could be analysed according to whether they were **fixed** or **variable.** In this chapter we will be looking further at this sort of analysis of costs: the analysis according to the way costs behave in relation to the **level of activity.**

We can demonstrate the ways in which costs behave by drawing graphs. This chapter aims to examine the different ways in which costs behave (this is known as **cost behaviour** analysis) and to demonstrate this behaviour graphically.

2 General principles of cost behaviour

2.1 Cost behaviour

The general rule is that **variable costs vary directly with changes in activity levels,** whereas **fixed costs do not vary directly with changes in activity levels.**

Cost behaviour is the way in which costs are affected by changes in the volume of output (level of activity).

2.2 Level of activity

The **level of activity** refers to the amount of work done, or the number of events that have occurred.

Depending on circumstances, the level of activity may be measured in a number of different ways including the following.

- The volume of production
- The number or value of items sold
- The number of invoices issued
- The number of units of electricity consumed

For our purposes in this chapter, the level of activity for measuring cost will generally be taken to be the volume of production.

2.3 Basic principles of cost behaviour

The basic principle of cost behaviour is that **as the level of activity rises, costs will usually rise**. It will cost more to produce 2,000 units of output than it will cost to produce 1,000 units; it will usually cost more to make five telephone calls than to make one call and so on.

3 Cost behaviour patterns

3.1 Fixed costs

A fixed cost is a cost which tends to be unaffected by increases or decreases in the volume of output. Fixed costs are a **period charge**, in that they relate to a span of time. As the time span increases, so too will the fixed costs (which are sometimes referred to as **period costs** for this reason).

3.1.1 Graph of fixed cost

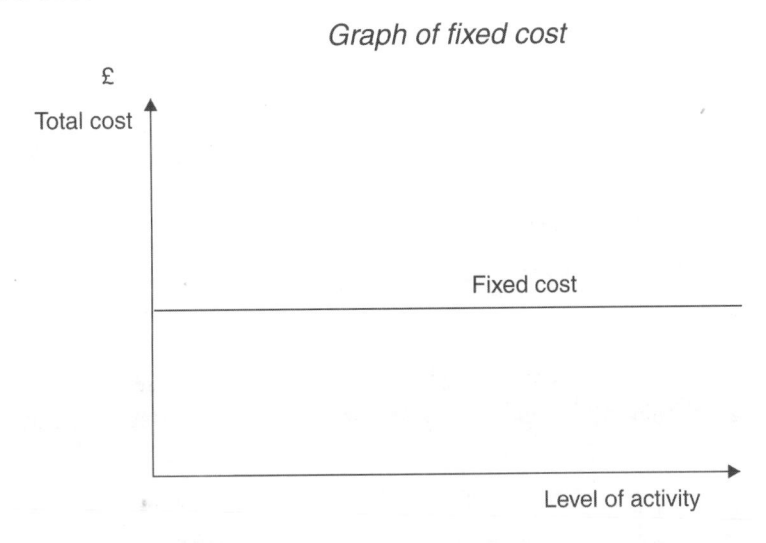

Graph of fixed cost

3.1.2 Examples of fixed costs

- The salary of the managing director (per month or per annum)
- The rent of a single factory building (per month or per annum)
- Straight line depreciation of a single machine (per month or per annum)

3.2 Step costs

Many items of cost are a **fixed cost in nature within certain levels of activity.** For example the depreciation of a machine may be fixed if production remains below 1,000 units per month, but if production exceeds 1,000 units, a second machine may be required, and the cost of depreciation (on two machines) would go up a step.

3.2.1 Graph of a step cost

Graph of step cost

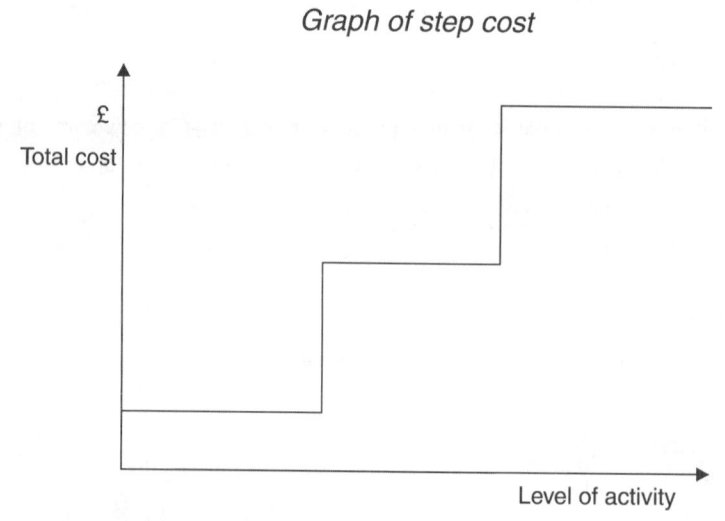

A step cost is sometimes called a **stepped-fixed cost**.

3.2.2 Examples of step costs

- **Rent**, where accommodation needs increase as output levels increase.
- **Basic wages**. As output rises, more employees with a fixed wage (direct workers, supervisors) are required.

3.3 Variable costs

A variable cost is a cost which tends to **vary directly with the volume of output.** The variable cost per unit is the **same amount for each unit produced** whereas **total** variable cost increases as volume of output increases.

3.3.1 Graph of variable cost

Graph of variable cost

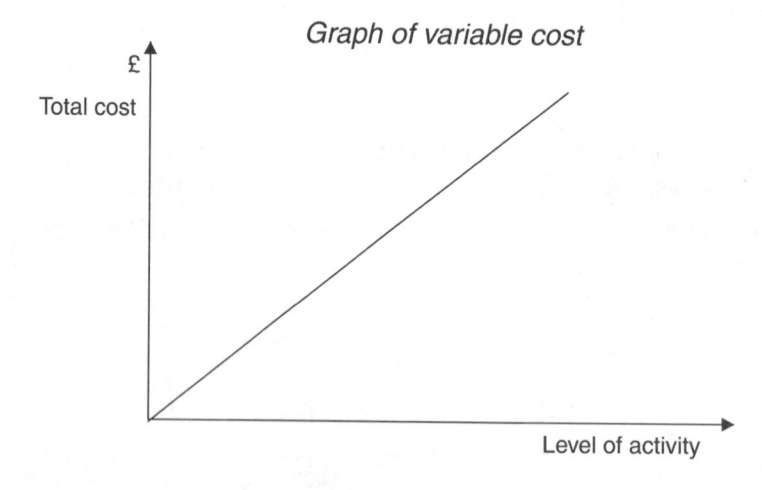

3.3.2 Examples of variable costs

- The most important variable cost is the cost of **raw materials** (where there is no discount for bulk purchasing. Bulk purchase discounts reduce the cost of purchases).
- Sales commission is variable in relation to the volume or value of sales.

3.4 Semi-variable costs (or mixed costs or semi-fixed costs)

These are cost items which are **part fixed** and **part variable**, and are therefore partly affected by changes in the level of activity.

3.4.1 Graph of semi-variable cost

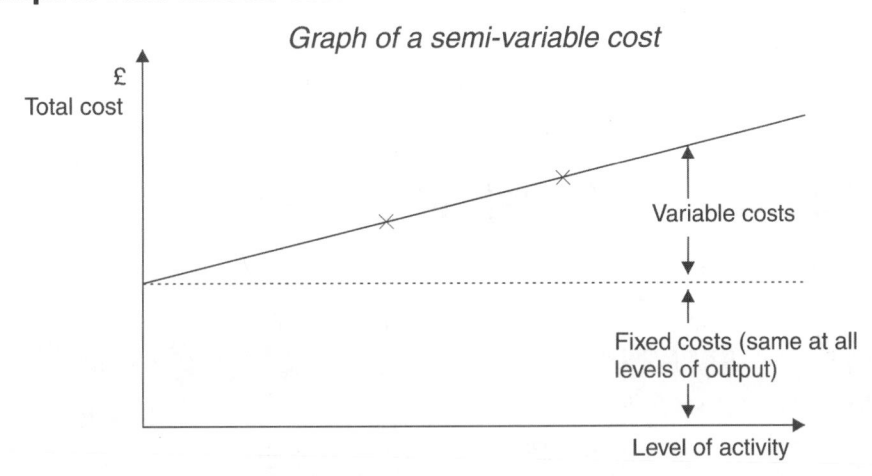

Graph of a semi-variable cost

3.4.2 Examples of semi-variable costs

- Electricity bills
- Gas bills

Both of these costs usually include a standing basic charge plus a variable charge per unit of consumption.

Activity 7.1

Are the following likely to be fixed, variable or semi-variable costs?

(a) Telephone bill
(b) Annual salary of the chief accountant
(c) The accounting technician's annual membership fee to AAT (paid by the company)
(d) Cost of materials used to pack 20 units of product X into a box
(e) Wages of warehouse staff, paid on an hourly basis

Activity 7.2

Draw graphs to illustrate the following cost behaviour patterns.

- (a) Variable cost
- (b) Fixed cost
- (c) Step cost

4 Cost behaviour and levels of activity

The following example highlights how and why costs may be analysed into fixed, variable and step cost items. Make sure that you study it carefully and that you have a clear understanding of the cost behaviour principles involved.

Example: Cost behaviour and levels of activity

Brandy Snap Ltd has a fleet of company cars for sales representatives. Running costs have been estimated as follows.

- (a) Cars cost £12,000 when new, and have a guaranteed trade-in value of £6,000 at the end of two years. Depreciation is charged on a straight-line basis.
- (b) Petrol and oil cost 15 pence per mile.
- (c) Tyres cost £300 per set to replace; replacement occurs after 30,000 miles.
- (d) Routine maintenance costs £200 per car (on average) in the first year and £450 in the second year.
- (e) Repairs average £400 per car over two years and are thought to vary with mileage. The average car travels 25,000 miles per annum.
- (f) Tax, insurance, membership of motoring organisations and so on cost £400 per annum per car.

Task

Calculate the average cost per annum of cars which travel 20,000 miles per annum and 30,000 miles per annum.

Solution

Costs may be analysed into fixed, variable and step cost items, a step cost being a cost which is fixed in nature but only within certain levels of activity.

(a) **Fixed costs**

	£ per annum
Depreciation £(12,000 – 6,000) ÷ 2	3,000
Routine maintenance £(200 + 450) ÷ 2	325
Tax, insurance etc	400
	3,725

(b) **Variable costs**

	Pence per mile
Petrol and oil	15.0
Repairs (£400 ÷ 50,000 miles)	0.8
	15.8

(c) Step costs are tyre replacement costs, which are £300 at the end of every 30,000 miles.

    (i) If the car travels less than or exactly 30,000 miles in two years, the tyres will not be changed. Average cost of tyres per annum = £0.

    (ii) If a car travels more than 30,000 miles and up to (and including) 60,000 miles in two years, there will be one change of tyres in the period. Average cost of tyres per annum = £150 (£300 ÷ 2).

    (iii) If a car exceeds 60,000 miles in two years (up to 90,000 miles) there will be two tyre changes. Average cost of tyres per annum = £300. (£600 ÷ 2).

The estimated costs per annum of cars travelling 20,000 miles per annum and 30,000 miles per annum would therefore be as follows.

	20,000 miles per annum £	30,000 miles per annum £
Fixed costs	3,725	3,725
Variable costs (15.8p per mile)	3,160	4,740
Tyres	150	150
Cost per annum	7,035	8,615
Cost per mile	£0.35	£0.29

Notice that the cost per mile is lower if more miles are travelled in a year. This is because the **fixed element** of the various costs is **spread over a greater number of miles.**

5 Determination of fixed and variable elements: the high-low technique

We have seen that a semi-variable cost has a **basic fixed cost element,** and a variable cost element which **depends on the level of activity.** But how can we identify how much of the cost is fixed, and how much is variable?

There are several methods for identifying the fixed and variable elements of semi-variable costs. Each method is only an estimate, and each will produce different results. One of the principal methods is the **high-low technique.**

5.1 High-low technique

Step 1   **Select the highest and lowest activity level**

    Review records of costs in previous periods. Select the following.

- The period with the highest activity level
- The period with the lowest activity level

UNIT 6 RECORDING AND EVALUATING COSTS AND REVENUES

Step 2 **Determine the costs and units at each activity level**

- Total cost at high activity level
- Total cost at low activity level
- Total units at high activity level
- Total units at low activity level

Step 3 **Calculate the variable cost per unit**

$$\frac{\text{Total cost at high activity level} - \text{total cost at low activity level}}{\text{Total units at high activity level} - \text{total units at low activity level}}$$

This will be the variable cost per unit, since the change in costs at the two activity levels must be due to a change in variable costs.

Step 4 **Determine the fixed cost**

Fixed cost = (Total cost at high activity level) − (total units at high activity level × variable cost per unit)

Example: The high-low technique

Brandy Snap Ltd has recorded the following total costs during the last five years.

Year	Output volume Units	Total cost £
20X3	65,000	145,000
20X4	80,000	160,000
20X5	90,000	170,000
20X6	60,000	140,000
20X7	75,000	155,000

Task

Calculate the total cost that should be expected in 20X8 if output is 85,000 units.

Solution

Step 1 **Select the highest and lowest activity level**

- Period with highest activity = 20X5
- Period with lowest activity = 20X6

Step 2 **Determine the costs and units at each activity level**

- Total cost at high activity level = £170,000
- Total cost at low activity level = £140,000
- Total units at high activity level = 90,000
- Total units at low activity level = 60,000

Step 3 Calculate the variable cost per unit

Variable cost per unit (V) is calculated as follows.

$$\frac{\text{Total cost at high activity level} - \text{total cost at low activity level}}{\text{Total units at high activity level} - \text{total units at low activity level}}$$

$$= \frac{£170,000 - £140,000}{90,000 - 60,000} = \frac{£30,000}{30,000} = £1 \text{ per unit}$$

Step 4 Determine the fixed cost

Fixed costs (F) are calculated as follows.

F = (Total cost at high activity level) − (total units at high activity level × variable cost per unit)
= £170,000 − (90,000 × £1)
= £170,000 − £90,000
= £80,000

Therefore the expected costs in 20X8 for output of 85,000 units are as follows.

		£
Variable costs (V) =	85,000 × £1 =	85,000
Fixed costs (F) =		80,000
		165,000

Activity 7.3

The costs of operating the Maintenance department of a computer manufacturer, Port and Lemon Ltd, for the last four months have been as follows.

Month	Output volume units	Total cost £
1	7,000	110,000
2	8,000	115,000
3	7,700	111,000
4	6,000	97,000

Task

What costs should be expected in month 5 when output is expected to be 7,500 units?

UNIT 6 RECORDING AND EVALUATING COSTS AND REVENUES

Key learning points

- **Cost behaviour patterns** demonstrate the way in which costs are affected by changes in the level of activity.
- Costs which are affected by the level of activity are **variable costs**.
- Costs which are not affected by the level of activity are **fixed costs** or **period costs**.
- **Step costs** are costs which are fixed in nature within certain levels of activity.
- **Semi-variable** (mixed costs/semi-fixed costs) are partly fixed and partly variable, and therefore only partly affected by changes in activity levels.
- The level of activity is the amount of work done or the number of events that have occurred.
- The **high-low technique** is used to estimate the fixed and variable elements of semi-variable costs.

Quick quiz

1. Cost behaviour is ....

2. The basic principle of cost behaviour is that as the level of activity rises, costs will usually rise/fall.

3. Fill in the gaps for each of the graph titles below.

   (a)

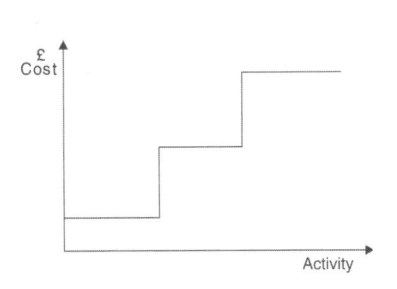

   Graph of a .... cost

   Example:

   (b)

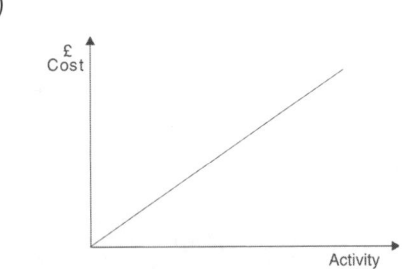

   Graph of a .... cost

   Example:

   (c)

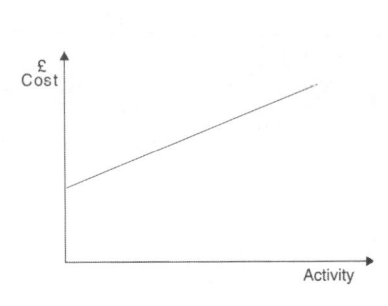

   Graph of a .... cost

   Example:

   (d)

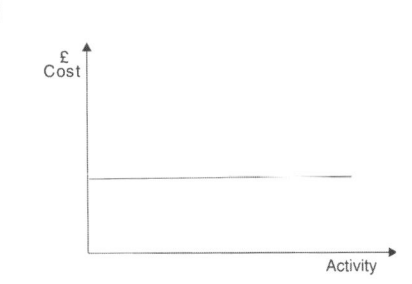

   Graph of a .... cost

   Example:

4   The costs of operating the canteen at 'Eat a lot Company' for the past three months are as follows.

Month	Cost £	Employees
1	72,500	1,250
2	75,000	1,300
3	68,750	1,175

Variable cost (per employee per month) =

Fixed cost per month =

Answers to quick quiz

1   The variability of **input** costs with activity undertaken.

2   Rise

3   (a)   Step cost. Example: rent, supervisors' salaries
    (b)   Variable cost. Example: raw materials, direct labour
    (c)   Semi-variable cost. Example: electricity, telephone
    (d)   Fixed cost. Example: rent, depreciation (straight-line)

4   Variable cost = £50 per employee per month
    Fixed costs = £10,000 per month

	Activity	Cost £
High	1,300	75,000
Low	1,175	68,750
	125	6,250

Variable cost per employee = £6,250/125 = £50

For 1,175 employees, total cost = £68,750

Total cost   = variable cost + fixed cost
£68,750   = (1,175 × £50) + fixed cost
∴ Fixed cost   = £68,750 − £58,750
                  = £10,000

Activity checklist

This checklist shows which performance criteria, range statement or knowledge and understanding point is covered by each activity in this chapter. Tick off each activity as you complete it.

Activity

7.1	☐	This activity deals with Knowledge and Understanding point 15 regarding fixed, variable and semi-variable costs
7.2	☐	This activity deals with Knowledge and Understanding point 24 regarding cost behaviour
7.3	☐	This activity deals with Knowledge and Understanding, point 13 regarding changing activity levels

chapter 8

Recording costs and revenues

Contents

1 Introduction
2 Ledger accounting and control accounts
3 Cost bookkeeping systems
4 Coding costs and revenues

Knowledge and understanding

3 Maintaining an appropriate cost accounting system
4 Recording of cost and revenue data in the accounting records
19 Relationship between the materials costing system and the stock control system
20 Relationship between the labour costing system and the payroll accounting system
21 Relationship between the accounting system and the expenses costing system

1 Introduction

You should now have a good idea of the way that the materials, labour and overhead costs of an item are determined. Now it is time to see how the costs and revenues are recorded **in total** in the **cost bookkeeping system.**

2 Ledger accounting and control accounts

2.1 Ledger accounting

The cost records we have described so far in this Interactive Text are adequate for individual products or jobs. However, unless records of **totals** are maintained (in control accounts) and checks of these records are made, there is no way of knowing whether all the costs that should have been recorded really have been recorded. The solution to this problem is **to link the cost records to the cash and credit transactions that are summarised in the nominal ledger.**

2.1.1 Control accounts

A **control account** is an account which records total cost. In contrast, individual ledger accounts record individual debits and credits.

2.2 Materials

First, let's look at how a single purchase of materials works through into the final accounts. The relevant double entries are as follows.

			£	£
(a)	DEBIT	Materials	X	
	CREDIT	Cash		X

Being the buying of materials which are put into raw materials stock

(b)	DEBIT	Work in progress	X	
	CREDIT	Materials stock		X

Being the issue of materials to production for use in work in progress

(c)	DEBIT	Finished goods	X	
	CREDIT	Work in progress		X

Being the transfer of units that are now finished to finished goods stock

(d)	DEBIT	Cost of sales	X	
	CREDIT	Finished goods		X

Being the taking of units out of finished goods stock and selling them

(e)	DEBIT	Profit and loss account	X	
	CREDIT	Cost of sales		X

Being the closing off of ledger accounts and the drawing up of financial statements. This entry would only be made at the end of a period.

2.2.1 Materials control account

A materials control account (or **stores control account**) records the total cost of invoices received for each type of material purchased. It also records the total cost of each type of material issued to various departments.

Example: Materials costing system

Tobias Ltd begins trading with £200 cash. £200 is initially spent on timber to make garden furniture. £100 worth of timber is left in store, while the other £100 is worked on to make garden chairs and tables. Before long, £50 worth of timber has been converted into garden furniture and this furniture is sold for £150.

Task

Show how these events and transactions will be reflected in the accounts.

Solution

CASH ACCOUNT

	£		£
Cash – opening balance	200	Purchase of materials	200
Sale of finished goods-sales	150	Closing balance	150
	350		350

MATERIALS ACCOUNT

	£		£
Cash purchase	200	Transfer to WIP	100
		Closing balance	100
	200		200

WORK IN PROGRESS ACCOUNT

	£		£
Transfer from materials	100	Transfer to finished goods	50
		Closing balance	50
	100		100

FINISHED GOODS ACCOUNT

	£		£
Transfer from WIP	50	Transfer to cost of sales	50
	50		50

COST OF SALES ACCOUNT

	£		£
Transfer from finished goods	50	Shown in profit and loss account	50
	50		50

SALES ACCOUNT

	£		£
Shown in profit and loss account	150	Cash	150
	150		150

TOBIAS LTD

PROFIT AND LOSS ACCOUNT

	£
Sales	150
Cost of sales	50
Profit	100

2.3 Labour costs

2.3.1 Wages control account

A **wages control account** records the total cost of the payroll (plus Employer's National Insurance Contributions) and the total cost of direct and indirect labour.

We will use an example to review briefly the principal bookkeeping entries for labour costs.

Example: Labour costing system

The following details were extracted from a weekly payroll for 500 employees at a factory in St Lucia.

Analysis of gross wages

	Direct workers £	Indirect workers £	Total £
Ordinary time	36,000	22,000	58,000
Overtime: basic wage	8,700	5,430	14,130
premium	4,350	2,715	7,065
Shift allowance	3,465	1,830	5,295
Sick pay	950	500	1,450
Idle time	3,200	–	3,200
Total gross wages	56,665	32,475	89,140
Net wages paid to employees	£45,605	£24,220	£69,825

Task

Prepare the wages control account for the week.

Solution

The wages control account acts as a sort of **collecting place** for net wages paid and deductions made from gross pay. The gross pay is then analysed between **direct** and **indirect wages**.

Step 1   Determine direct costs ⟶ DR WORK IN PROGRESS A/C

Step 2   Determine indirect costs ⟶ DR PRODUCTION OVERHEAD A/C

Direct wages

	£
Ordinary time – direct workers	36,000
Overtime (basic wage) – direct workers	8,700
	44,700

Indirect wages

	£
Ordinary time – indirect workers	22,000
Overtime (basic wage) – indirect workers	5,430
	27,430

The net wages paid are debited to the control account, and the balance then represents the deductions which have been made for income tax, national insurance, and so on.

WAGES CONTROL ACCOUNT

	£		£
Bank: net wages paid	69,825	Work in progress: direct labour	44,700
Deductions control accounts*		Production overhead control:	
(£89,140 – £69,825)	19,315	indirect labour	27,430
		Overtime premium	7,065
		Shift allowance	5,295
		Sick pay	1,450
		Idle time	3,200
	89,140		89,140

* In practice there would be a separate deductions control account for each type of deduction made (for example, PAYE and National Insurance).

2.4 Overheads

2.4.1 Under-/over-absorbed overhead

When an absorption costing system is in use, we know that the amount of overhead included in the cost of an item is **absorbed at a predetermined rate.** The entries made in the cash book and the nominal ledger, however, are the **actual amounts**.

As we saw in an earlier chapter, it is highly unlikely that the actual amount and the predetermined amount will be the same. The difference is called **under- or over-absorbed overhead**. To deal with this in the cost accounting books we need to have an account to collect under- or over-absorbed amounts for each type of overhead.

2.4.2 Production overhead control account

A **production overhead control account** is a total record of actual expenditure incurred and the amount absorbed into individual units/jobs/batches.

Example: Overheads costing system

Gnocci Ltd absorbs production overheads at the rate of £0.50 per operating hour and administration overheads at 20% of the production cost of sales. Actual data for one month was as follows.

Administration overheads	£32,000
Production overheads	£46,500
Operating hours	90,000
Production cost of sales	£180,000

What entries need to be made for overheads in the ledgers?

Solution

PRODUCTION OVERHEAD CONTROL ACCOUNT

	£		£
Cash	46,500	Absorbed into WIP	
		(90,000 × £0.50)	45,000
		Under-absorbed overhead	1,500
	46,500		46,500

ADMINISTRATION OVERHEAD CONTROL ACCOUNT

	£		£
Cash	32,000	To cost of sales (£180,000 × 0.2)	36,000
Over-absorbed overhead	4,000		
	36,000		36,000

UNDER-/OVER-ABSORBED OVERHEAD ACCOUNT

	£		£
Production overhead	1,500	Administration overhead	4,000
Balance to profit and loss a/c	2,500		
	4,000		4,000

Less production overhead has been absorbed than has been spent so there is **under-absorbed production overhead of £1,500**. More administration overhead has been absorbed (into cost of sales, note, not into WIP) and so there is **over-absorbed administration overhead of £4,000**. The net over-absorbed overhead of £2,500 is a **credit in the profit and loss account**.

Activity 8.1

PO Ltd absorbs production overheads using a direct labour hour rate. Data for last period are as follows.

Production overheads incurred – paid through bank account	£125,478
Depreciation of production machinery	£4,100
Direct labour hours worked	27,000
Production overhead absorption rate per direct labour hour	£5

Task

Prepare the production overhead control account for the period.

3 Cost bookkeeping systems

There are two types of cost bookkeeping system, the **interlocking** and the **integrated**. Interlocking systems require **separate ledgers** to be kept for the cost accounting function and the financial accounting function, which means that the cost accounting profit and financial accounting profit have to be **reconciled**. Integrated systems, on the other hand, **combine the two functions in one set of ledger accounts.**

Modern cost accounting systems (computerised) integrate cost accounting information and financial accounting information and are known as **integrated systems.** You are much more likely to deal with integrated systems, and this is the system we shall be looking at in detail.

An **integrated system** is a system where the cost accounting function and the financial accounting function are combined in one system of ledger accounts.

Example: Recording costs and revenues

In the absence of the accountant you have been asked to prepare a month's cost accounts for Ashbourne Ltd, a company which operates a costing system which is fully **integrated** with the financial accounts. The accounting technician has provided you with the following information.

(a) **Balances at beginning of month**

	£
Stores ledger control account	24,175
Work in progress control account	19,210
Finished goods control account	34,164
Creditors control account	15,187

(b) **Information relating to events during the month**

	£
Materials purchased on credit	76,150
Materials issued from stores to production	29,630
Gross wages paid: direct workers	15,236
indirect workers	9,462
Payments to creditors	58,320
Selling and distribution overheads incurred	5,240
Other production overheads incurred but not yet paid for	16,300
Sales	75,400
Cost of finished goods sold	59,830
Cost of goods completed and transferred into finished goods store during the month	62,130

(c) The production overhead absorption rate is 150% of direct wages.

Task

Prepare the following accounts for the month.

Stores ledger control account
Work in progress control account
Finished goods control account
Production overhead control account
Creditors control account
Profit and loss account

Solution

STORES LEDGER CONTROL ACCOUNT

	£		£
Opening balance b/f	24,175	Work in progress control	
Creditors control		(materials issued)	29,630
(materials purchased)	76,150	Closing stock c/f	70,695
	100,325		100,325

WORK IN PROGRESS CONTROL ACCOUNT

	£		£
Opening balance b/f	19,210	Finished goods control	
Stores ledger account		(cost of goods transferred)	62,130
(materials issued)	29,630	Closing stock c/f	24,800
Wages control			
(direct wages)	15,236		
Production overhead control			
(overhead absorbed			
15,236 × 150%)	22,854		
	86,930		86,930

FINISHED GOODS CONTROL ACCOUNT

	£		£
Opening balance b/f	34,164	Profit and loss account	
Work in progress control		(cost of sales)	59,830
(cost of goods completed)	62,130	Closing stock c/f	36,464
	96,294		96,294

PRODUCTION OVERHEAD CONTROL ACCOUNT

	£		£
Wages control (indirect	9,462	Work in progress control	
workers wages)		(overheads absorbed)	22,854
Creditors control (other		Profit and loss account (under-	
overheads incurred)	16,300	absorbed overhead) (bal.)	2,908
	25,762		25,762

CREDITORS CONTROL ACCOUNT

	£		£
Cash account (payments)	58,320	Opening balance b/f	15,187
Creditors c/f	49,317	Stores ledger control	
		(materials purchased)	76,150
		Production overhead control	
		(other overheads)	16,300
	107,637		107,637

PROFIT AND LOSS ACCOUNT

	£		£
Finished goods control		Sales	75,400
(cost of goods sold)	59,830		
Gross profit c/f	15,570		
	75,400		75,400
Selling and distribution		Gross profit b/f	15,570
overheads	5,240		
Production overhead control			
(under-absorbed overhead)	2,908		
Net profit c/f	7,422		
	15,570		15,570

Activity 8.2

The following data relate to the materials control account of Dollar Ltd for the month of April.

	£
Opening stock	18,500
Closing stock	16,100
Deliveries from suppliers	142,000
Returns to suppliers	2,300
Cost of indirect materials issued	25,200

Tasks

(a) Calculate the value of the issue of direct materials during April.
(b) State the double entry to record the issue of direct materials in the cost accounts.

Activity 8.3

What would be the double entry to record the following events in a cost accounting system?

(a) Materials costing £10,000 are purchased on credit and put into stock.
(b) Finished units costed at £50,000 are made available for sale.
(c) Materials valued at £5,000 are issued to the administration department.
(d) Indirect production wages of £20,000 are charged to the production department.

4 Coding costs and revenues

4.1 Codes

In many organisations, cost and revenue items are **coded** before they are included in the accounting records. Coded means giving something a **code**. We had a brief look at coding in Chapter 4 when we studied **expenses**. We are now going to look at coding in more detail

4.1.1 SOS!

You have probably all heard of the international code-signal of extreme distress (or help): **SOS**. SOS is a code for 'help'. Businesses also make use of codes in order to make life easier and more organised in the accounts department!

4.1.2 Computerised coding

Most organisations use computers to record their accounting transactions because they have the following advantages.

- They record and retrieve information quickly and easily
- They are automatically accurate and have built in checking facilities
- They can file a large amount of information in a small space
- They are capable of sorting information in many different ways

Some information must be separately identifiable in order to meet other regulatory requirements (for example **VAT**) or specific accounting requirements (for example, depreciation on fixed assets).

Some computer systems are able to sort information from transaction processing into the correct categories for both financial and management accounting purposes. This avoids the need to enter data more than once.

4.2 Types of code

When data is entered into an accounting system, each item is coded with a specific **code** from a list of accounts. Codes can be **alphabetical** and/or **numerical**.

The length and complexity of a coding system will depend upon the needs and complexity of the organisation.

4.2.1 Numeric codes

For financial accounting purposes it is common to use **numeric codes** which correspond to the different areas of the balance sheet and profit and loss account.

Example: numeric codes

Type of account	Code range
Fixed asset	1000 – 1999
Current asset	2000 – 2999
Current liability	3000 – 3999
Revenue	4000 – 4999
Long-term liability	5000 – 5999
Capital	6000 – 6999

Within each section, the codes can be broken down into smaller sections:

Type of account	Code range
Fixtures and fittings	1000 – 1099
Land and buildings	1100 – 1199
Plant and machinery	1200 – 1299
Motor vehicles	1300 – 1399

and so on. Gaps between the numbers used give scope for breaking the categories down further (for example there could be a separate account for each building) and for adding new categories if necessary.

Some types of account require **more detail**. For example, each customer needs a separate account, although in the balance sheet the total 'debtors' will be shown. Suppliers (trade creditors) also need an account each and a total for the balance sheet.

4.2.2 Alphabetical codes

Alphabetical codes, using part of the company or person's name, are common but, because names can be duplicated, an additional code may be necessary.

Example: Alphabetical codes

Customer	Code
J Miller Ltd	MIL 010
M Miller	MIL 015
A Milton	MIL 025

Some computer systems save time for operators by offering a **'menu'** of accounts when part of the name is typed in.

4.2.3 Stock codes

Some codes can help users to **recognise the items** they describe. For example, a shoe shop could code their stock by type of shoe, colour, size, style and male or female. A pair of women's red sandals, size 5, style 19 could then become:

Shoe type	Colour	Size	Style	Male/Female
SA	R	5	19	F
BO	B	8	11	M

and the second item would be men's brown boots, size 8, style 11.

4.2.4 Coding VAT

Don't forget that the cost to the company will be the **net** cost and **VAT** will be coded to the **VAT account** to be set off against **VAT on sales**. Coding the net cost will depend on the firm's **policy** for dealing with a particular product or job.

4.2.5 Coding income

Coding structures can also be used to break down various types of **income**. Sales revenue for example can be broken down by different products or geographical areas. If a business charges VAT on sales that it makes, only the **net income** will be coded to the revenue account. The VAT element of any sales will be separately coded to the **VAT account**.

Activity 8.4

Here is a summary of the net value of sales invoices for the month of September and an extract from the coding list of a company that sells cosmetics worldwide. Can you apply the right codes to each invoice?

Invoice No	Net sales value £	Country
8730	10,360.00	Canada
8731	12,750.73	Australia
8732	5,640.39	Spain
8733	15,530.10	Northern Ireland
8734	3,765.75	South Africa
8735	8,970.22	Kenya
8736	11,820.45	Italy
8737	7,640.00	France
8738	9,560.60	Australia
8739	16,750.85	Germany

Sales revenue codes: R100 – R199

Code	Area	Country
R110	Area 1	UK
R120	Area 2	North America
R130	Area 3	South America
R140	Area 4	Europe
R150	Area 5	Africa
R160	Area 6	Australia

Helping hand. If you are not sure whether the countries listed are in a particular area of the world – find yourself an atlas and look them up.

Key learning points

- A **control account** is an account which records total cost, unlike an individual ledger account which records individual debits and credits.

- The **wages control account** acts as a collecting place for wages before they are analysed into work in progress and production overhead control accounts.

- The **production overhead control account** acts as a collecting place for production overheads before they are absorbed into work in progress.

- Production overhead is absorbed into work in progress using the **predetermined overhead absorption rate.**

- Any balance remaining on the production overhead control account at the end of the period represents the **overhead under or over absorbed** during the period.

- There are two main types of cost bookkeeping system, **interlocking systems** and **integrated systems.**

- An **integrated system** is one in which the cost accounting function and the financial accounting function are combined in one system of ledger accounts.

- In many organisations costs and revenues are **coded** before they are included in the accounting records. A **code** is a system of words, letters, figures or symbols used to represent others.

- In an assessment, be prepared to complete partially completed cost accounts, and always make sure that your debits equal your credits!

8: RECORDING COSTS AND REVENUES

Quick quiz

1. What is a control account?
2. What is the double entry for indirect materials issued to production?
3. What does it mean if the debit total on the production overhead control account is higher than the credit total?
4. GF Ltd bought £100,000 worth of materials and issued £75,000 to production. Which of the following entries represents the correct bookkeeping treatment? (Select three options.)

☐	Dr	Raw materials	£75,000
☐	Dr	Raw materials	£100,000
☐	Cr	Work-in-progress	£75,000
☐	Cr	Raw materials	£75,000
☐	Cr	Raw materials	£100,000
☐	Dr	Work-in-progress	£75,000
☐	Dr	Work-in-progress	£100,000

5. **Extract from code list**

    Telephone expenses 5500-5599
    5510 General administration
    5530 Sales and marketing
    5570 Manufacturing

    Telephone numbers and locations

    020 7668 9923 Managing director
    020 7668 9871 Marketing manager
    020 7668 9398 Factory floor
    020 7668 9879 Accounts office
    0879 6534 Salesperson's mobile

    Which lines would you charge to which code?

Answers to quick quiz

1. An account which records total cost, as opposed to individual costs (which are recorded in individual ledger accounts).
2. Debit Production overhead control account; Credit Materials stock account
3. Production overhead is under absorbed.
4.
✓	Dr	Raw materials	£100,000
✓	Cr	Raw materials	£75,000
✓	Dr	Work in progress	£75,000

Costs incurred are debited to the materials account, and those issued as direct materials to production are credited to the materials account and subsequently debited to the work-in-progress account.

5 Telephone numbers and locations

		Code
020 7668 9923	Managing director	5510
020 7668 9871	Marketing manager	5530
020 7668 9398	Factory floor	5570
020 7668 9879	Accounts office	5510
0879 6534	Salesperson's mobile	5530

Activity checklist

This checklist shows which performance criteria, range statement or knowledge and understanding point is covered by each activity in this chapter. Tick off each activity as you complete it.

Activity

8.1	☐	This activity deals with Knowledge and Understanding point 21 regarding the expenses costing system
8.2	☐	This activity deals with Knowledge and Understanding point 19 regarding the materials costing system and the stock control system
8.3	☐	This activity deals with Knowledge and Understanding points 19 and 20 regarding the materials costing system and the labour costing system
8.4	☐	This activity deals with Knowledge and Understanding point 4 regarding the recording of cost and revenue data in the accounting records

chapter 9

Costing Systems

Contents

1. Introduction
2. Job costing
3. Batch costing
4. Unit costing
5. Service costing

Knowledge and understanding

12   Calculation of product and service cost
26   Costing systems appropriate to the organisation: job, batch, unit and process costing systems

1 Introduction

In this chapter we will be looking at four important costing systems.

- Job costing
- Batch costing
- Unit costing
- Service costing

In the next chapter we will be looking at another important system, that of **process costing**.

A **costing system** is a system of collecting costs which is designed to suit the way that goods are processed or manufactured or the way that services are provided.

Each organisation's costing system will have unique features but **costing systems of organisation's in the same line of business will have common aspects.** On the other hand, organisations involved in completely different activities, such as hospitals and car part manufacturers, will each use very different costing systems.

2 Job costing

2.1 Aim of job costing

The aim of **job costing** is simply to collect the cost information shown below.

	£
Direct materials	X
Direct labour	X
Direct expenses	X
Direct cost	X
Production overhead	X
Total production cost	X
Administration overhead	X
Selling overhead	X
Cost of sales	X

To the final figure is added a profit **'mark-up'** and the total is the selling price of the job.

In other words, all we are doing is looking at one way of putting together the pieces of information that we have studied separately so far.

2.2 What is a job?

A **job** is a cost unit which consists of a single order or contract.

With other methods of costing it is usual to **produce for stock**. Management therefore decide in advance how many units of each type, size, colour, quality and so on will be produced during the coming period. These decisions will all be taken without taking into account the identity of the individual customers who will eventually buy the products.

In job costing on the other hand, production is usually carried out in accordance with the **special requirements** of each customer. It is therefore usual for each job to **differ in one or more respects from every other job**, which means that a separate record must be maintained to show the details of a particular job.

The work relating to a job is usually carried out within a factory or workshop and moves through processes and operations as a **continuously identifiable unit**.

2.3 Procedure for the performance of jobs

The normal procedure in jobbing concerns involves the following.

- The prospective customer approaches the supplier and indicates the **requirements** of the job.

- A responsible official sees the prospective customer and agrees the **precise details of the items** to be supplied, for example the quantity, quality and colour of the goods, the date of delivery and any special requirements.

- The estimating department of the organisation then prepares an **estimate** for the job. The total of these items will represent the **quoted selling price**.

- At the appropriate time, the job will be **'loaded'** on to the factory floor. This means that as soon as all materials, labour and equipment are available and subject to the scheduling of other orders, the job will be started.

2.4 Collection of job costs

Each job will be given a **number** to identify it. A separate record must be maintained to show the details of individual jobs. The process of collecting job costs may be outlined as follows.

- **Materials requisitions are sent to stores.**

- **The materials requisition note will be used to cost the materials issued to the job** concerned, and this cost may then be recorded on a **job cost sheet**.

- **The job ticket is passed to the worker who is to perform the first operation.**

- When the job is completed by the worker who performs the final operation, the **job ticket is sent to the cost office**, where the time spent will be costed and recorded on the job cost sheet.

- The **relevant costs** of materials issued, direct labour performed and direct expenses incurred as recorded on the job cost sheet **are charged to the job account** in the work in progress ledger.

- **The job account is debited with the job's share of the factory overhead**, based on the absorption rate(s) in operation.

- **On completion of the job**, the job account is charged with the appropriate administration, selling and distribution overhead, after which the **total cost of the job can be ascertained**.

- The difference between the agreed selling price and the total actual cost will be the supplier's profit (or loss).

2.5 Job account

Here is a proforma job account, which will be one of the accounts in the work in progress control account.

JOB ACCOUNT

	£		£
Materials issued	X	Finished jobs	X
Direct labour	X		
Direct expenses	X		
Production overhead at predetermined rate	X		
Other overheads	X		
	X		X

2.6 Job cost sheet (or card)

When jobs are completed, **job cost sheets** are transferred from the **work in progress** category to **finished goods**. When delivery is made to the customer, the costs become a **cost of sale**.

Example: Job cost sheet

JOB COST CARD																
Customer	Mr J White				Customer's Order No.							Job No.	B641			
Job Description	Repair damage to offside front door											Vehicle make	Peugot 205 GTE			
Estimate Ref.	2599				Invoice No.							Vehicle reg. no.	G 614 SOX			
Quoted price	£338.68				Invoice price	£355.05						Date to collect	14.6.X0			

Material						Labour								Overheads			
Date	Req. No.	Qty.	Price	Cost £	p	Date	Employee	Cost Ctre	Hrs.	Rate	Bonus	Cost £	p	Hrs	OAR	Cost £	p
12.6	36815	1	75.49	75	49	12.6	018	B	1.98	6.50	-	12	87	7.9	2.50	19	75
12.6	36816	1	33.19	33	19	13.6	018	B	5.92	6.50	-	38	48				
12.6	36842	5	6.01	30	05						13.65	13	65				
13.6	36881	5	3.99	19	95												
Total C/F				158	68	Total C/F						65	00	Total C/F		19	75

Expenses						Job Cost Summary	Actual		Estimate	
Date	Ref.	Description	Cost £	p			£	p	£	p
12.6	-	N. Jolley Panel-beating	50	-		Direct Materials B/F	158	68	158	68
						Direct Expenses B/F	50	00		
						Direct Labour B/F	65	00	180	00
						Direct Cost	273	68		
						Overheads B/F	19	75		
							293	43		
						Admin overhead (add 10%)	29	34		
						= Total Cost	322	77	338	68
						Invoice Price	355	05		
Total C/F			50	-		Job Profit/Loss	32	28		

Comments

Job Cost Card Completed by _____

2.7 Job costing and computerisation

Job cost cards exist in **manual** systems, but it is increasingly likely that in large organisations the job costing system will be **computerised**, using accounting software specifically designed to deal with job costing requirements.

Job costing systems may also be used to control the costs of **internal service departments**, eg the maintenance department.

Example: Job costing

Pansy Ltd is a company that carries out jobbing work. One of the jobs carried out in May was job 2409, to which the following information relates.

Direct material Y:	400 kilos were issued from stores at a cost of £5 per kilo.
Direct material Z:	800 kilos were issued from stores at a cost of £6 per kilo. 60 kilos were returned to stores.
Department P:	300 labour hours were worked, of which 100 hours were overtime.
Department Q:	200 labour hours were worked, of which 100 hours were overtime.

Overtime work is not normal in Department P, where basic pay is £6 per hour plus an overtime premium of £1 per hour. Overtime work was done in Department Q in May because of a request by the customer of another job to complete his job quickly. Basic pay in Department Q is £8 per hour and overtime premium is £1.50 per hour. Overhead is absorbed at the rate of £3 per direct labour hour in both departments.

Tasks

(a) Calculate the direct materials cost of job 2409
(b) Calculate the direct labour cost of job 2409
(c) Calculate the full production cost of job 2409 using absorption costing

Solution

(a)
	£
Direct material Y (400 kilos × £5)	2,000
Direct material Z (800 – 60 kilos × £6)	4,440
Total direct material cost	6,440

(b)
	£
Department P (300 hours × £6)	1,800
Department Q (200 hours × £8)	1,600
Total direct labour cost	3,400

Overtime premium will be charged to overhead in the case of Department P, and to the job of the customer who asked for overtime to be worked in the case of Department Q.

		£
(c)	Direct material cost	6,440
	Direct labour cost	3,400
	Production overhead (500 hours × £3)	1,500
		11,340

Activity 9.1

A curtain-making business manufactures quality curtains to customers' orders. It has three production departments (X, Y and Z) which have overhead absorption rates (per direct labour hour) of £12.86, £12.40 and £14.03 respectively.

Two pairs of curtains are to be manufactured for customers. Direct costs are as follows.

	Job TN8	Job KT2
Direct material	£154	£108
Direct labour	20 hours dept X	16 hours dept X
	12 hours dept Y	10 hours dept Y
	10 hours dept Z	14 hours dept Z

Labour rates are as follows: £3.80(X); £3.50 (Y); £3.40 (Z)

The firm quotes prices to customers that reflect a required profit of 25% on selling price.

Task

Calculate the total cost and selling price of each job.

3 Batch costing

A **batch** is a cost unit which consists of a separate, readily identifiable group of product units which maintains its separate identity throughout the production process.

The procedures for **costing batches** are very similar to those for costing jobs.

- The batch is treated as a **job** during production and the costs are collected as described earlier in this chapter.
- Once the batch has been completed, the **cost per unit** can be calculated as the total batch cost divided by the number of units in the batch.

Example: Batch costing

A company manufactures model cars to order and has the following budgeted overheads for the year, based on normal activity levels.

Department	Budgeted overheads £	Budgeted activity
Welding	6,000	1,500 labour hours
Assembly	10,000	1,000 labour hours

Selling and administrative overheads are 20% of production cost. An order for 250 model cars type XJS1, made as Batch 8638, incurred the following costs.

Materials £12,000
Labour 100 hours welding shop at £8/hour
200 hours assembly shop at £9/hour

£500 was paid for the hire of special X-ray equipment for testing the welds.

Task

Calculate the cost per unit for Batch 8638.

Solution

The first step is to calculate the overhead absorption rate for the production departments.

$$\text{Welding} = \frac{£6,000}{1,500} = £4 \text{ per labour hour}$$

$$\text{Assembly} = \frac{£10,000}{1,000} = £10 \text{ per labour hour}$$

Total cost – Batch no 8638

	£	£
Direct material		12,000
Direct expense		500
Direct labour 100 × £8 =	800	
200 × £9 =	1,800	
		2,600
Prime cost		15,100
Overheads 100 × 4 =	400	
200 × 10 =	2,000	
		2,400
Production cost		17,500
Selling and administrative cost (20% of production cost)		3,500
Total cost		21,000

$$\text{Cost per unit} = \frac{£21,000}{250} = £84$$

Activity 9.2

Lyfsa Kitchen Units Ltd crafts two different sizes of standard unit and a DIY all-purpose unit for filling up awkward spaces. The units are built to order in batches of around 250 (although the number varies according to the quality of wood purchased), and each batch is sold to NGJ Furniture Warehouses Ltd.

The costs incurred in May were as follows.

	Big unit	Little unit	All-purpose
Direct materials purchased	£5,240	£6,710	£3,820
Direct labour			
Skilled (hours)	1,580	1,700	160
Semi-skilled (hours)	3,160	1,900	300
Direct expenses	£1,180	£1,700	£250
Selling price of batch	£48,980	£43,125	£25,660
Completed at 31 May	100%	80%	25%

The following information is available.

All direct materials for the completion of the batches have been recorded. Skilled labour is paid £9 per hour, semi-skilled £7 per hour. Administration expenses total £4,400 per month and are to be allocated to the batches on the basis of direct labour hours. Direct labour costs, direct expenses and administration expenses will increase in proportion to the total labour hours required to complete the little units and the all-purpose units. On completion of the work the practice of the manufacturer is to divide the calculated profit on each batch 20% to staff as a bonus, 80% to the company. Losses are absorbed 100% by the company.

Tasks

(a) Calculate the profit or loss made by the company on big units.
(b) Project the profit or loss likely to be made by the company on little units and all-purpose units.

4 Unit costing

With batch costing and job costing, each cost unit is separately identifiable. The costs incurred could be traced to each table or to each batch of pens.

Some organisations may produce goods or services as a continuous stream of identical units which are not separately identifiable for costing purposes. For example:

- A sauce manufacturer produces a continuous stream of identical bottles of sauce.
- A fast food restaurant serves a continuous supply of packets of chips with meals.

In these types of environment the costing system averages the costs incurred over all of the units of output in a period.

$$\text{Cost per unit} = \frac{\text{total cost for period}}{\text{number of units of output in the period}}$$

Activity 9.3

Which method of costing (job, batch or unit costing) would be most appropriate for these businesses?

- A baker
- A transport company
- A plumber
- An accountancy firm
- A paint manufacturer

We will go on to study a unit costing system known as process costing in detail in the next chapter.

5 Service costing

Service costing is a method of accounting for services or functions, eg canteens, maintenance, personnel. These may be referred to as service centres, service departments or service functions.

5.1 What are service organisations?

Service organisations **do not make or sell tangible goods**. Profit-seeking service organisations include accountancy firms, law firms, transport companies, banks and hotels. Almost all not-for-profit organisations – hospitals, schools, libraries and so on – are also service organisations.

Service costing differs from the other costing methods in the following ways.

- In general, with service costing, the cost of direct materials consumed will be relatively small compared to the labour, direct expenses and overheads cost.
- Indirect costs tend to represent a higher proportion of total cost compared with product costing.
- The output of most service organisations is often intangible and it is therefore difficult to establish a measurable unit cost.

5.2 Characteristics of services

- **Intangibility**
- **Simultaneity**
- **Perishability**
- **Heterogeneity**

Consider the service of providing a haircut.

- A haircut is **intangible** in itself, and the performance of the service comprises many other intangible factors, like the music in the salon, the personality of the hairdresser, the quality of the coffee.

- The production and consumption of a haircut are **simultaneous,** and therefore it cannot be inspected for quality in advance, nor can it be returned if it is not what was required.

- Haircuts are **perishable,** that is, they cannot be stored. You cannot buy them in bulk, and the hairdresser cannot do them in advance and keep them stocked away in case of heavy demand. The incidence of work in progress in service organisations is less frequent than in other types of organisation.

- A haircut is **heterogeneous** and so the exact service received will vary each time: not only will two hairdressers cut hair differently, but a hairdresser will not consistently deliver the same standard of haircut.

5.3 Unit cost measures

A particular problem with service costing is the difficulty in defining a realistic cost unit that represents a suitable measure of the service provided. Frequently, a **composite cost unit** may be deemed more appropriate if the service is a function of two activity variables. Hotels, for example, may use the **'occupied bed-night'** as an appropriate unit for cost ascertainment and control.

Typical cost units used by companies operating in a service industry are shown below.

Service	Cost unit
Road, rail and air transport services	Passenger-kilometre, tonne-kilometre
Hotels	Occupied bed-night
Education	Full-time student
Hospitals	Patient-day
Catering establishments	Meal served

Each organisation will need to ascertain the cost unit most appropriate to its activities. If a number of organisations within an industry use a common cost unit, valuable **comparisons** can be made between similar establishments. This is particularly applicable to hospitals, educational establishments and local authorities.

5.4 Calculation of cost per service unit

$$\text{Cost per service unit} = \frac{\text{Total costs for period}}{\text{Number of service units in the period}}$$

The calculation of cost per service unit is best explained by means of an example.

Example: Cost per service unit

Carry Ltd operates a small fleet of delivery vehicles. Expected costs and activity details are as follows.

Loading	1 hour per tonne loaded
Loading costs:	
Labour (casual)	£6 per hour
Equipment depreciation	£80 per week
Supervision	£80 per week
Drivers' wages (fixed)	£100 per driver per week
Petrol	10p per kilometre
Repairs	5p per kilometre
Depreciation	£80 per week per vehicle
Supervision	£120 per week
Other general expenses (fixed)	£200 per week

There are two drivers and two vehicles in the fleet.

During a slack week, only six journeys were made.

Journey	Tonnes carried (one way)	One-way distance of journey Kilometres
1	5	100
2	8	20
3	2	60
4	4	50
5	6	200
6	5	300

Task

Calculate the expected average full cost per tonne/kilometre for the week.

Solution

Variable costs

Journey	1	2	3	4	5	6
	£	£	£	£	£	£
Loading labour	30	48	12	24	36	30
Petrol (both ways)	20	4	12	10	40	60
Repairs (both ways)	10	2	6	5	20	30
	60	54	30	39	96	120

Total costs

	£
Variable costs (total for journeys 1 to 6)	399
Loading equipment depreciation	80
Loading supervision	80
Drivers' wages	200
Vehicles depreciation	160
Drivers' supervision	120
Other costs	200
	1,239

Journey	Tonnes	One-way distance Kilometres	Tonne-kilometres
1	5	100	500
2	8	20	160
3	2	60	120
4	4	50	200
5	6	200	1,200
6	5	300	1,500
			3,680

Cost per tonne-kilometre = $\dfrac{£1,239}{3,680}$ = £0.337

Note that the large element of fixed costs may distort this measure but that a variable cost per tonne-kilometre of £399/3,680 = £0.108 may be useful for budgetary planning and control.

Activity 9.4

(a) Which of the following would be appropriate cost units for a passenger coach company?

    (i) Vehicle cost per passenger-kilometre
    (ii) Fuel cost for each vehicle per kilometre
    (iii) Fixed cost per kilometre

    A (i) only   B (i) and (ii) only   C (i) and (iii) only   D All of them

(b) The following information is available for the Whiteley Hotel for the latest thirty day period.

Number of rooms available per night	40
Percentage occupancy achieved	65%
Room servicing cost incurred	£3,900

The room servicing cost per occupied room-night last period, to the nearest penny, was:

    A £3.25   B £5.00   C £97.50   D £150.00

Key learning points

- **Job costing** is the costing method used where each cost unit is separately identifiable.
- Each job is given a **number** to distinguish it from other jobs.
- Costs for each job are collected on a **job cost sheet** or **job card.**
- Material costs for each job are determined from **materials requisition notes**.
- Labour times on each job are recorded on a **job ticket**, which is then costed and recorded on the job cost sheet.
- **Overhead** is absorbed into the cost of jobs using the predetermined overhead absorption rates.
- An **internal job costing system** can be used for costing the work of service departments.
- In an assessment, you may be asked to determine the amount of profit to be added to a job cost. Remember that profit may be expressed either as a percentage of job cost (such as 25% (25/100) mark up) or as a percentage of price (such as 20% (25/125) margin).
- **Batch costing** is similar to job costing in that each batch of similar articles is separately identifiable. The **cost per unit** manufactured in a batch is the total batch cost divided by the number of units in the batch.
- **Unit costing systems** average the costs incurred in a period over all of the units of output in a period.

    $$\text{Cost per unit} = \frac{\text{Total cost for a period}}{\text{Number of units of output in the period}}$$

- **Service costing** can be used by companies operating in a service industry or by companies wishing to establish the cost of services carried out by different departments.
- Characteristics of services
    - Intangibility
    - Simultaneity
    - Perishability
    - Heterogeneity
- If a service is a function of two activity variables, a **composite cost unit** might be appropriate.

    $$\text{Cost per service unit} = \frac{\text{Total costs for a period}}{\text{Number of service units in the period}}$$

Quick quiz

1. Which of the following are not characteristics of job costing?

   I   Customer driven production
   II Complete production possible within a single accounting period
   III Homogeneous products

   A I and II only
   B I and III only
   C II and III only
   D III only

2. The cost of a job is £100,000

   (a) If profit is 25% of the job cost, the price of the job = £..................
   (b) If there is a 25% margin, the price of the job = £.....................

3. How would you calculate the cost per unit of a completed batch?

4. Match up the following services with their typical cost units

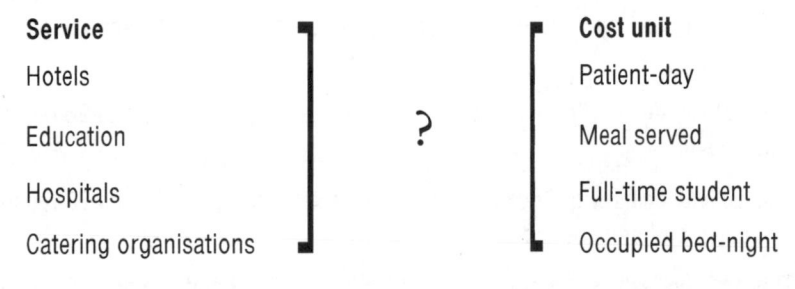

Service		Cost unit
Hotels		Patient-day
Education	?	Meal served
Hospitals		Full-time student
Catering organisations		Occupied bed-night

5. Cost per service unit = ─────────────

Answers to quick quiz

1. D

2. (a) £100,000 + (25% × £100,000) = £100,000 + £25,000 = £125,000

   (b) Profit is 25 per cent of the selling price, therefore selling price should be written as 100%:

	%
Selling price	100
Profit	25
Cost	75

   ∴ Price = £100,000 × 100/75 = £133,333.

3. $$\frac{\text{Total batch cost}}{\text{Number of units in the batch}}$$

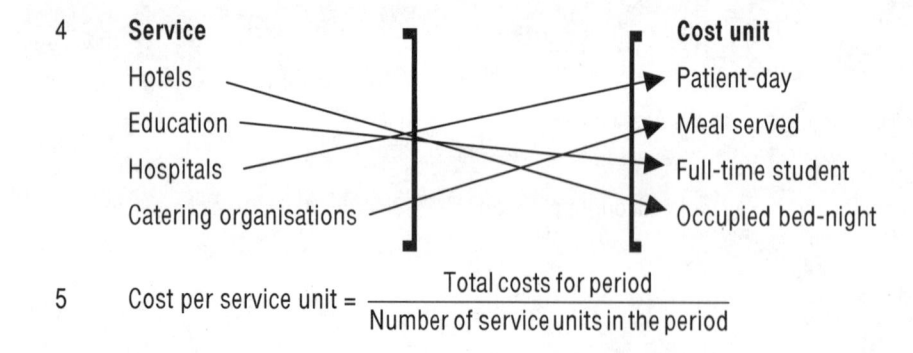

4 **Service**   **Cost unit**
   Hotels   Patient-day
   Education   Meal served
   Hospitals   Full-time student
   Catering organisations   Occupied bed-night

Matching: Hotels → Occupied bed-night; Education → Full-time student; Hospitals → Patient-day; Catering organisations → Meal served

5 Cost per service unit = $\dfrac{\text{Total costs for period}}{\text{Number of service units in the period}}$

Activity checklist

This checklist shows which performance criteria, range statement or knowledge and understanding point is covered by each activity in this chapter. Tick off each activity as you complete it.

Activity

9.1	☐	This activity deals with Knowledge and Understanding points 12 and 26 regarding job costing
9.2	☐	This activity deals with Knowledge and Understanding points 12 and 26 regarding batch costing
9.3	☐	This activity deals with Knowledge and Understanding points 12 and 26 regarding job, batch and unit costing
9.4	☐	This activity deals with Knowledge and Understanding points 12 and 26 regarding service costing

chapter 10

Process costing

Contents

1. Introduction
2. Features of process costing
3. Basics of process costing
4. Losses and gains
5. Accounting for scrap
6. Closing work in progress

Knowledge and understanding

12   Calculation of product and service cost

26   Costing systems appropriate to the organisation: job, batch, unit and process costing systems

1 Introduction

We have now looked at four cost accounting methods that apply to **specific orders**: **job costing**, **batch costing**, **unit costing** and **service costing**. In this chapter we will consider another costing method, **process costing**. Process costing is applied when output consists of a continuous stream of **identical units**. We will begin from basics and look at how to account for the most simple of processes. We will then move on to how to account for any **losses** which might occur, as well as what to do with any **scrapped units** which are sold. Next we will consider how to deal with **closing work in progress** before examining situations involving closing work in progress and losses.

2 Features of process costing

Process costing is a costing method used where it is not possible to identify separate units of production, usually because of the continuous nature of the production processes involved.

It is common to identify process costing with **continuous production** such as the following.

- Oil refining
- The manufacture of soap
- Paint manufacture
- Food and drink manufacture

Features of process costing.

- The continuous nature of production in process costing means that it is not possible to calculate the cost per unit of output or the cost per unit of closing stock.
- There is often a **loss in process** due to spoilage, wastage, evaporation and so on.
- The **output** of one process becomes the **input** to the next until the finished product is made in the final process.
- Output from production may be a single product, but there may also be one or more **by-products** and/or **joint products**.

3 Basics of process costing

3.1 Basic techniques

Before tackling the more complex areas of process costing, we will begin by looking at a very simple process costing example which will illustrate the basic techniques which we will build upon in the remainder of this chapter.

Example: Basics of process costing

Suppose that Royal Oak Ltd make coloured terracotta pots. Production of the pots involves two processes, shaping and colouring. During the year to 31 March 20X3, 1,000,000 units of material worth £500,000 were input to the first process, shaping. Direct labour costs of £200,000 and production overhead costs of £200,000 were also incurred in connection with the shaping process. There were no opening or closing stocks in the shaping department. The process account for shaping for the year ended 31 March 20X3 is as follows.

Process 1

PROCESS 1 (SHAPING) ACCOUNT

	Units	£		Units	£
Direct materials	1,000,000	500,000	Output to Process 2	1,000,000	900,000
Direct labour		200,000			
Production overheads		200,000			
	1,000,000	900,000		1,000,000	900,000

You will see that a **process account** is nothing more than a **ledger account** with debit and credit entries although it does have an additional column on both the debit and credit sides showing **quantity**. When preparing process accounts, perhaps as part of your workings, you are advised to include these memorandum quantity columns and to balance them off (ie ensure they total to the same amount on both sides) **before** attempting to complete the monetary value columns since they will help you to check that you have missed nothing out. This becomes increasingly important as more complications are introduced into questions.

Process 2

When using process costing, if a series of separate processes is needed to manufacture the finished product, the **output of one process becomes the input to the next until the final output is made in the final process**. In our example, all output from shaping was transferred to the second process, colouring, during the year to 31 March 20X3. Additional material costing £300,000 was input to the colouring process. Direct labour costs of £150,000 and production overhead costs of £150,000 were also incurred. There were no opening or closing stocks in the colouring department. The process account for colouring for the year ended 31 March 20X3 is as follows.

PROCESS 2 (COLOURING) ACCOUNT

	Units	£		Units	£
Materials from process 1	1,000,000	900,000	Output to finished		
Added materials		300,000	goods	1,000,000	1,500,000
Direct labour		150,000			
Production overhead		150,000			
	1,000,000	1,500,000		1,000,000	1,500,000

Added materials, labour and overhead in Process 2 are usually **added gradually** throughout the process. Materials from Process 1, in contrast, will often be **introduced in full at the start of the second process**.

3.2 Cost per unit

The main aim of process costing is to calculate a cost per unit that gives completed units and closing stocks a value.

$$\text{Cost per unit} = \frac{\text{Costs incurred}}{\text{Expected output}}$$

Example: Cost per unit

We can calculate a cost per unit for the earlier example (Royal Oak Ltd) as follows.

$$\text{Cost per unit} = \frac{\text{Costs incurred}}{\text{Expected output}}$$

$$\text{Process 1 cost per unit} = \frac{£900,000}{1,000,000 \text{ units}}$$

$$= £0.90 \text{ per unit}$$

$$\text{Process 2 cost per unit} = \frac{£1,500,000}{1,000,000 \text{ units}}$$

$$= £1.50 \text{ per unit}$$

Activity 10.1

During a period, 50,000 units of material were input to Process 1 at the production plant of Jingles Ltd. The following costs were incurred.

Materials	£100,000
Direct labour	£200,000
Production overhead	£100,000

50,000 units were completed in Process 1 and transferred to Process 2. There were no opening or closing work in progress stocks.

Task

Calculate the cost per unit of Process 1 output.

3.3 Framework for dealing with process costing

Process costing is centred around **four key steps**. The exact work done at each step will depend on the circumstances of the question, but the approach can always be used. Don't worry about the terms used. We will be looking at their meaning as we work through the chapter.

Step 1. Determine output and losses

- Determine expected output.
- Calculate normal loss and abnormal loss and gain.
- Calculate equivalent units if there is closing work in progress.

Step 2. Calculate cost per unit of output, losses and WIP

Calculate cost per unit or cost per equivalent unit.

Step 3. Calculate total cost of output, losses and WIP

In some examples this will be straightforward. In cases where there is work in progress, a **statement of evaluation** will have to be prepared.

Step 4. Complete accounts

- Complete the process account.
- Write up the other accounts required by the question.

4 Losses and gains

During a production process, a loss may occur due to wastage, spoilage, evaporation, and so on.

- **Normal loss** is the loss expected during a process. It is not given a cost.
- **Abnormal loss** is the extra loss resulting when actual loss is greater than normal or expected loss, and it is given a cost.
- **Abnormal gain** is the gain resulting when actual loss is less than the normal or expected loss, and it is given a 'negative cost'.

Since **normal loss is not given a cost**, the cost of producing these units is borne by the 'good' units of output.

Abnormal loss and gain units are valued at the same unit rate as 'good' units. Abnormal events do not therefore affect the cost of good production. Their costs are **analysed separately** in an **abnormal loss or abnormal gain account**.

Example: Normal loss

Suppose 2,000 units are input to a process. Normal loss is 5% of input and there are no opening or closing stocks.

Task

Calculate the normal loss.

Solution

Normal loss = 5% × 2,000 units
            = 100 units

Example: Abnormal loss

Suppose 2,000 units are input to a process. Normal loss is 5% of input and there are no opening and closing stocks. Actual output was 1,800 units.

Task

Calculate the abnormal loss.

Solution

Normal loss = 5% × 2,000 units
= 100 units

Actual loss = 2,000 – 1,800
= 200 units

∴ Abnormal loss = Actual loss – normal loss
= 200 units – 100 units
= 100 units

Example: Abnormal gain

Suppose 2,000 units are input to a process. Normal loss is 5% of input and there are no opening or closing stocks. Actual output was 1,950 units.

Task

Calculate the abnormal gain.

Solution

Normal loss = 5% × 2,000 units
= 100 units

Actual loss = 2,000 units – 1,950 units
= 50 units

Abnormal gain = Actual loss – normal loss
= 50 units – 100 units
= 50 units

Activity 10.2

Jingles Ltd operates a single manufacturing process, and during March the following processing took place.

Opening stock	nil	Closing stock	nil
Units introduced	1,000 units	Output	900 units
Costs incurred	£4,500	Loss	100 units

Tasks

Determine the cost of output in the following circumstances.

(a) Expected or normal loss is 10% of input.
(b) There is no expected loss, so that the entire loss of 100 units was unexpected.

Example: Losses and gains

Suppose 1,000 units at a cost of £4,500 are input to a process. Normal loss is 10% and there are no opening or closing stocks.

Tasks

(a) Complete the process account and the abnormal loss/gain account if actual output was 860 units (so that actual loss is 140 units).

(b) Complete the process account and the abnormal loss/gain account if actual output was 920 units (so that actual loss is 80 units).

Solution

Before we demonstrate the use of the 'four-step framework' we will summarise the way that the losses are dealt with.

- Normal loss is given no share of cost.
- The cost of output is therefore based on the **expected** units of output, which in our example amount to 90% of 1,000 = 900 units.
- **Abnormal loss** is given a cost, which is written off to the profit and loss account via an abnormal loss/gain account.
- **Abnormal gain** is treated in the same way, except that being a gain rather than a loss, it appears as a **debit** entry in the process account (whereas a loss appears as a **credit** entry in this account).

(a) **Output is 860 units**

Step 1. Determine output and losses

If actual output is 860 units and the actual loss is 140 units:

	Units
Actual loss	140
Normal loss (10% of 1,000)	100
Abnormal loss	40

Step 2. Calculate cost per unit of output and losses

The cost per unit of output and the cost per unit of abnormal loss are based on **expected** output.

$$\frac{\text{Costs incurred}}{\text{Expected output}} = \frac{£4,500}{900 \text{ units}} = £5 \text{ per unit}$$

Step 3. Calculate total cost of output and losses

Normal loss is not assigned any cost.

	£
Cost of output (860 × £5)	4,300
Normal loss	0
Abnormal loss (40 × £5)	200
	4,500

Step 4. Complete accounts

PROCESS ACCOUNT

	Units	£		Units	£
Cost incurred	1,000	4,500	Normal loss	100	0
			Output (finished goods a/c)	860	(× £5) 4,300
			Abnormal loss	40	(× £5) 200
	1,000	4,500		1,000	4,500

ABNORMAL LOSS/GAIN ACCOUNT

	Units	£		Units	£
Process a/c	40	200	Profit and loss a/c	40	200

(b) **Output is 920 units**

Step 1. Determine output and losses

If actual output is 920 units and the actual loss is 80 units:

	Units
Actual loss	80
Normal loss (10% of 1,000)	100
Abnormal gain	20

Step 2. Calculate cost per unit of output and losses

The cost per unit of output and the cost per unit of abnormal gain are based on **expected** output.

$$\frac{\text{Costs incurred}}{\text{Expected output}} = \frac{£4,500}{900 \text{ units}} = £5 \text{ per unit}$$

(Whether there is abnormal loss or gain does not affect the valuation of units of output. The figure of £5 per unit is exactly the same as in the previous paragraph, when there were 40 units of abnormal loss.)

Step 3. Calculate total cost of output and losses

	£
Cost of output (920 × £5)	4,600
Normal loss	0
Abnormal gain (20 × £5)	(100)
	4,500

Step 4. Complete accounts

PROCESS ACCOUNT

	Units	£		Units	£
Cost incurred	1,000	4,500	Normal loss	100	0
Abnormal gain a/c	20	(× £5) 100	Output (finished goods a/c)	920	(× £5) 4,600
	1,020	4,600		1,020	4,600

ABNORMAL LOSS/GAIN

	Units	£		Units	£
Profit and loss a/c	20	100	Process a/c	20	100

If there is a closing balance in the abnormal loss or gain account when the profit for the period is calculated, this balance is taken to the profit and loss account: an **abnormal gain** will be a **credit** to profit and loss and an **abnormal loss** will be a **debit** to profit and loss.

Activity 10.3

During period 3, costs of input to a process were £29,070. Input was 1,000 units, output was 850 units and normal loss is 10% of input.

During the next period, period 4, costs of input were again £29,070. Input was again 1,000 units, but output was 950 units.

There were no units of opening or closing stock.

Task

Prepare the process account and the abnormal loss or gain account for each period.

5 Accounting for scrap

Loss may have a scrap value. The following basic rules are applied in accounting for this value in the process accounts.

(a) **Revenue from scrap** is treated, not as an addition to sales revenue, but as a **reduction in costs**.

(b) The scrap value of **normal loss** is therefore used to reduce the material costs of the process.

  DEBIT   Scrap account
  CREDIT Process account

  with the scrap value of the normal loss.

(c) The scrap value of **abnormal loss** is used to reduce the cost of abnormal loss.

  DEBIT   Scrap account
  CREDIT Abnormal loss account

  with the scrap value of abnormal loss, which therefore reduces the write-off of cost to the profit and loss account at the end of the period.

(d) The scrap value of **abnormal gain** arises because the actual units sold as scrap will be less than the scrap value of normal loss. Because there are fewer units of scrap than expected, there will be less revenue from scrap as a direct consequence of the abnormal gain. The abnormal gain account should therefore be debited with the scrap value.

DEBIT   Abnormal gain account

CREDIT   Scrap account

with the scrap value of abnormal gain.

(e) The **scrap account** is completed by recording the **actual cash received** from the sale of scrap.

DEBIT   Cash received

CREDIT   Scrap account

with the cash received from the sale of the actual scrap.

The same basic principle therefore applies that only **normal losses** should affect the cost of the good output. The scrap value of **normal loss only** is credited to the process account. The scrap values of abnormal losses and gains are analysed separately in the abnormal loss or gain account.

Example: Scrap and abnormal loss or gain

A factory has two production processes. Normal loss in each process is 10% of input and scrapped units sell for £0.50 each from process 1 and £3 each from process 2. Relevant information for costing purposes relating to period 5 is as follows.

	Process 1	Process 2
Direct materials added:		
units	2,000	1,250
cost	£8,100	£1,900
Direct labour	£4,000	£10,000
Production overhead	150% of direct labour cost	120% of direct labour cost
Output to process 2/finished goods	1,750 units	2,800 units
Actual production overhead	£17,800	

Task

Prepare the accounts for process 1, process 2, scrap, abnormal loss or gain and production overhead.

Solution

Step 1. Determine output and losses

	Process 1	Process 2
	Units	Units
Output	1,750	2,800
Normal loss (10% of input)	200	300
Abnormal loss	50	–
Abnormal gain	–	(100)
	2,000	3,000*

* 1,750 units from Process 1 + 1,250 units input to process.

Step 2. Calculate cost per unit of output and losses

		Process 1 £		Process 2 £
Cost of input				
– material		8,100		1,900
– from Process 1		–	(1,750 × £10)	17,500
– labour		4,000		10,000
– overhead	(150% × £4,000)	6,000	(120% × £10,000)	12,000
		18,100		41,400
less: scrap value of **normal loss**	(200 × £0.50)	(100)	(300 × £3)	(900)
		18,000		40,500

	Process 1	Process 2
Expected output		
90% of 2,000	1,800	
90% of 3,000		2,700
Cost per unit		
£18,000 ÷ 1,800	£10	
£40,500 ÷ 2,700		£15

Step 3. Calculate total cost of output and losses

	Process 1 £		Process 2 £
Output (1,750 × £10)	17,500	(2,800 × £15)	42,000
Normal loss (200 × £0.50)*	100	(300 × £3)*	900
Abnormal loss (50 × £10)	500		–
	18,100		42,900
Abnormal gain	–	(100 × £15)	(1,500)
	18,100		41,400

* Remember that normal loss is valued at scrap value only.

Step 4. Complete accounts

PROCESS 1 ACCOUNT

	Units	£		Units	£
Direct material	2,000	8,100	Scrap a/c (normal loss)	200	100
Direct labour		4,000	Process 2 a/c	1,750	17,500
Production overhead a/c		6,000	Abnormal loss a/c	50	500
	2,000	18,100		2,000	18,100

PROCESS 2 ACCOUNT

	Units	£		Units	£
Direct materials					
From process 1	1,750	17,500	Scrap a/c (normal loss)	300	900
Added materials	1,250	1,900	Finished goods a/c	2,800	42,000
Direct labour		10,000			
Production overhead		12,000			
	3,000	41,400			
Abnormal gain	100	1,500			
	3,100	42,900		3,100	42,900

ABNORMAL LOSS ACCOUNT

	£		£
Process 1 (50 units)	500	Scrap a/c: sale of scrap of extra loss (50 units)	25
		Profit and loss a/c	475
	500		500

ABNORMAL GAIN ACCOUNT

	£		£
Scrap a/c (loss of scrap revenue due to abnormal gain, 100 units × £3)	300	Process 2 abnormal gain (100 units)	1,500
Profit and loss a/c	1,200		
	1,500		1,500

SCRAP ACCOUNT

	£		£
Scrap value of normal loss		Cash a/c – cash received	
Process 1 (200 units)	100	Loss in process 1 (250 units)	125
Process 2 (300 units)	900	Loss in process 2 (200 units)	600
Abnormal loss a/c (process 1)	25	Abnormal gain a/c (process 2)	300
	1,025		1,025

PRODUCTION OVERHEAD ACCOUNT

	£		£
Overhead incurred	17,800	Process 1 a/c	6,000
Over-absorbed overhead a/c (or P & L a/c)	200	Process 2 a/c	12,000
	18,000		18,000

Activity 10.4

Parks Ltd operates a processing operation involving two stages, the output of process 1 being passed to process 2. The process costs for period 3 were as follows.

Process 1
Material	3,000 kg at £0.25 per kg
Labour	£120

Process 2
Material	2,000 kg at £0.40 per kg
Labour	£84

General overhead for period 3 amounted to £357 and is absorbed into process costs at a rate of 375% of direct labour costs in process 1 and 496% of direct labour costs in process 2.

The normal output of process 1 is 80% of input and of process 2, 90% of input. Waste matter from process 1 is sold for £0.20 per kg and that from process 2 for £0.30 per kg.

The output for period 3 was as follows.

Process 1	2,300 kgs
Process 2	4,000 kgs

There was no stock of work in progress at either the beginning or the end of the period and it may be assumed that all available waste matter had been sold at the prices indicated.

Tasks

Prepare the following accounts.

(a) Process 1 account
(b) Process 2 account
(c) Finished stock account
(d) Scrap account
(e) Abnormal loss and gain account

6 Closing work in progress

In the examples we have looked at so far we have assumed that opening and closing stocks of work in process have been nil. We must now look at more realistic examples and consider how to allocate the costs incurred in a period between completed output (ie finished units) and partly completed closing stock.

Some examples will help to illustrate the problem, and the techniques used to share out (apportion) costs between finished output and closing work in progress.

Example: Valuation of closing stock

Trotter Ltd is a manufacturer of processed goods. In one process, there was no opening stock, but 5,000 units of input were introduced to the process during the month, and the following costs were incurred.

	£
Direct materials	16,560
Direct labour	7,360
Production overhead	5,520
	29,440

Of the 5,000 units introduced, 4,000 were completely finished during the month and transferred to the next process. Closing stock of 1,000 units was only 60% complete with respect to materials and conversion costs.

Solution

(a) The problem in this example is to **divide the costs of production** (£29,440) between the finished output of 4,000 units and the closing stock of 1,000 units.

(b) To apportion costs fairly and proportionately, units of production must be converted into the equivalent of completed units, ie into **equivalent units of production**.

Equivalent units are notional whole units which represent incomplete work, and which are used to apportion costs between work in process and completed output.

Step 1. Determine output

For this step in our framework we need to prepare a statement of equivalent units.

STATEMENT OF EQUIVALENT UNITS

	Total units	Completion	Equivalent units
Fully worked units	4,000	100%	4,000
Closing stock	1,000	60%	600
	5,000		4,600

Step 2. Calculate cost per unit of output, and WIP

For this step in our framework we need to prepare a statement of costs per equivalent unit because equivalent units are the basis for apportioning costs.

STATEMENT OF COSTS PER EQUIVALENT UNIT

$$\frac{\text{Total cost}}{\text{Equivalent units}} = \frac{£29,440}{4,600}$$

Cost per equivalent unit   £6.40

Step 3. Calculate total cost of output and WIP

For this stage in our framework a statement of evaluation may now be prepared, to show how the costs should be apportioned between finished output and closing stock.

STATEMENT OF EVALUATION

	Equivalent units	Cost per equivalent unit	Valuation £
Fully worked units	4,000	£6.40	25,600
Closing stock	600	£6.40	3,840
	4,600		29,440

Step 4. Complete accounts

The process account would be shown as follows.

PROCESS ACCOUNT

		Units	£		Units	£
(Stores a/c)	Direct materials	5,000	16,560	Output to next process	4,000	25,600
(Wages a/c)	Direct labour		7,360	Closing stock c/f	1,000	3,840
(O'hd a/c)	Production o'hd		5,520			
		5,000	29,440		5,000	29,440

When preparing a process 'T' account, it might help to make the entries as follows.

(a) **Enter the units first.** The units columns are simply memorandum columns, but they help you to make sure that there are no units unaccounted for (for example as loss).

(b) **Enter the costs of materials, labour and overheads next.** These should be given to you.

(c) **Enter your valuation of finished output and closing stock next.** The value of the credit entries should, of course, equal the value of the debit entries.

Activity 10.5

A liquid chemical compound is manufactured as a result of two processes.

Details for the second process – Process Y – for the month of December are as follows:

Opening work in process	Nil
Materials transferred from Process X	50,000 litres valued at £47,500
Labour cost	500 hours paid at £6.00 per hour
Overheads	50.83% of labour cost
Output transferred to finished goods	41,000 litres
Closing work in process	4,500 litres

Quality control checks at the end of the process of manufacture normally lead to a rejection rate of 5%.

Closing work in process is 100% complete for material content, and 50% complete for both labour and overheads.

Task

Prepare the process Y account for December.

Clearly show your workings.

6.1 Different rates of input

In many industries, materials, labour and overhead may be added at **different rates** during the course of production.

(a) Output from a previous process (for example the output from process 1 to process 2) may be introduced into the subsequent process all at once, so that closing stock is 100% complete in respect of these materials.

(b) Further materials may be **added gradually** during the process, so that closing stock is only **partially complete** in respect of these added materials.

(c) Labour and overhead may be 'added' at yet another different rate. When production overhead is absorbed on a labour hour basis, however, we should expect the degree of completion on overhead to be the same as the degree of completion on labour.

When this situation occurs, equivalent units, and a cost per equivalent unit, should be **calculated separately for each type of material, and also for conversion costs**.

Example: Equivalent units and different degrees of completion

Suppose that Shaker Ltd is a manufacturer of processed goods, and that results in process 2 for a period were as follows.

Opening stock	nil
Material input from process 1	4,000 units
Costs of input:	£
material from process 1	6,000
added materials in process 2	1,080
conversion costs	1,720

Output is transferred into the next process, process 3. No losses occur in the process.

Closing work in process amounted to 800 units, complete as to:

process 1 material	100%
added materials	50%
conversion costs	30%

Task

Prepare the process 2 account for the period.

Solution

Step 1. Determine output and losses

STATEMENT OF EQUIVALENT UNITS (OF PRODUCTION IN THE PERIOD)

Input Units	Output	Total Units	Equivalent units of production					
			Process 1 material		Added materials		Labour and overhead	
			Units	%	Units	%	Units	%
4,000	Completed production	3,200	3,200	100	3,200	100	3,200	100
	Closing stock	800	800	100	400	50	240	30
4,000		4,000	4,000		3,600		3,440	

Step 2. Calculate cost per unit of output and WIP

STATEMENT OF COST (PER EQUIVALENT UNIT)

Input	Cost £	Equivalent production in units	Cost per unit £
Process 1 material	6,000	4,000	1.50
Added materials	1,080	3,600	0.30
Labour and overhead	1,720	3,440	0.50
	8,800		2.30

Step 3. Calculate total cost of output and WIP

STATEMENT OF EVALUATION (OF FINISHED WORK AND CLOSING STOCKS)

Production	Cost element	Number of equivalent units	Cost per equivalent unit £	Total £	Cost £
Completed production		3,200	2.30		7,360
Closing stock:	process 1 material	800	1.50	1,200	
	added material	400	0.30	120	
	labour and overhead	240	0.50	120	
					1,440
					8,800

Step 4. Complete accounts

PROCESS 2 ACCOUNT

	Units	£		Units	£
Process 1 material	4,000	6,000	Process 3 a/c (finished output)	3,200	7,360
Added material		1,080			
Conversion costs		1,720	Closing stock c/f	800	1,440
	4,000	8,800		4,000	8,800

Activity 10.6

Prepare a process account from the following information.

Opening stock	Nil
Input units	10,000 at a cost of £5,150
Labour cost	£2,700
Normal loss	5% of input
Scrap value of units of loss	£1 per unit
Output to finished goods	8,000 units
Closing stock	1,000 units
Completion of closing stock	80% for material
	50% for labour

10: PROCESS COSTING

Key learning points

- ☑ **Process costing** is a costing method used where it is not possible to identify separate units of production usually because of the continuous nature of the production processes involved.

- ☑ The main aim of process costing is to calculate a **cost per unit** that gives completed units and closing stocks a value.

    $$\text{Cost per unit} = \frac{\text{Costs incurred}}{\text{Expected output}}$$

- ☑ Use our suggested four-step approach when dealing with process costing questions.

    Step 1. Determine output and losses
    Step 2. Calculate cost per unit of output, losses and WIP
    Step 3. Calculate total cost of output, losses and WIP
    Step 4. Complete accounts

- ☑ Losses may occur during a process for a number of reasons, including the following.
    - Wastage
    - Spoilage
    - Evaporation

- ☑ **Normal loss** is the loss expected during a process and it is not given a cost. If it has a scrap value then it is valued at this amount.

- ☑ **Abnormal loss** is the extra loss resulting when actual loss is greater than normal or expected loss and it is given a cost.

- ☑ **Abnormal gain** is the gain resulting when actual loss is less than the normal or expected loss, and it is given a 'negative cost'.

- ☑ Loss may have a **scrap value**. Revenue from scrap is treated as a reduction in costs.

- ☑ It is conventional for the **scrap value of normal loss to be deducted from the cost of materials** before a cost per equivalent unit is calculated.

- ☑ When units are partly completed at the end of a period (ie when there is **closing work in progress**) it is necessary to calculate the **equivalent units of production** in order to determine the cost of a completed unit.

- ☑ The costs of labour and overhead are sometimes referred to as **conversion costs.**

- ☑ In many processes materials, labour and overhead may be added at different rates during the course of production. When this situation occurs, equivalent units, and a cost per equivalent unit, should be **calculated separately for each type of material, and also for conversion costs.**

UNIT 6 RECORDING AND EVALUATING COSTS AND REVENUES

Quick quiz

1. Define process costing.

2. Process costing is centred around four key steps.

   Step 1. ....

   Step 2. ....

   Step 3. ....

   Step 4. ....

3. Abnormal gains result when actual loss is less than normal or expected loss.

   ☐ True

   ☐ False

4. Normal loss (no scrap value) ⎤   ⎡ Same value as good output (positive cost)

   Abnormal loss   ⎬   ?   ⎨ No value

   Abnormal gain   ⎦   ⎣ Same value as good output (negative cost)

5. How is revenue from normal scrap treated?

   A   As an addition to sales revenue
   B   As a reduction in costs of processing
   C   As a bonus to employees
   D   All of the above

6. When there is closing WIP at the end of a process, what is the first step in the four-step approach to process costing questions and why must it be done?

Answers to quick quiz

1. **Process costing** is a costing method used where it is not possible to identify separate units of production, or jobs, usually because of the continuous nature of the production processes involved.

2. **Step 1.** Determine output and losses
   Step 2. Calculate cost per unit of output, losses and WIP
   Step 3. Calculate total cost of output, losses and WIP
   Step 4. Complete accounts

3. ☑ True

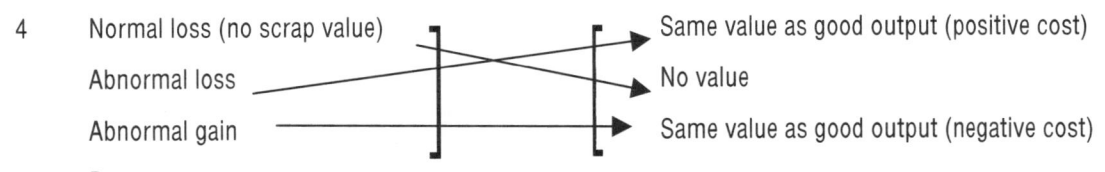

4   Normal loss (no scrap value) — Same value as good output (positive cost)

    Abnormal loss — No value

    Abnormal gain — Same value as good output (negative cost)

5   B

6   **Step 1.** It is necessary to calculate the equivalent units of production (by drawing up a statement of equivalent units). Equivalent units of production are notional whole units which represent incomplete work and which are used to apportion costs between work in progress and completed output.

Activity checklist

This checklist shows which performance criteria, range statement or knowledge and understanding point is covered by each activity in this chapter. Tick off each activity as you complete it.

Activity

10.1	☐	This activity deals with Knowledge and Understanding points 12 and 26 regarding process costing
10.2	☐	This activity deals with Knowledge and Understanding points 12 and 26 regarding process costing
10.3	☐	This activity deals with Knowledge and Understanding points 12 and 26 regarding process costing
10.4	☐	This activity deals with Knowledge and Understanding points 12 and 26 regarding process costing
10.5	☐	This activity deals with Knowledge and Understanding points 12 and 26 regarding process costing
10.6	☐	This activity deals with Knowledge and Understanding points 12 and 26 regarding process costing

chapter 11

Short term decisions

Contents

1. Introduction
2. Cost-volume-profit analysis
3. Breakeven point and profit volume ratio
4. Margin of safety
5. Target profit
6. Charts
7. Limiting factors
8. Writing reports

Performance criteria

- 6.3.A Identify information relevant to estimating current and future revenues and costs
- 6.3.B Prepare **estimates** of future income and costs
- 6.3.C Calculate the effects of variations in capacity on product costs
- 6.3.D Analyse critical factors affecting costs and revenues using appropriate accounting techniques and draw clear conclusions from the analysis
- 6.3.E State any assumptions used when evaluating future costs and revenues
- 6.3.F Identify and evaluate options and solutions for their contribution to organisational goals
- 6.3.G **Present** recommendations to appropriate people in a clear and concise way and supported by a clear rationale

Range statement

Estimates: short term decisions

- Break-even analysis
- Margin of safety
- Target profit
- Profit volume ratio
- Limiting factors

Methods of presentation:

- Verbal presentation
- Written reports

Knowledge and understanding

13 Analysis of the effect of changing activity levels on unit costs
14 Methods of presenting information in written reports
15 The identification of fixed, variable and semi-variable costs and their use in cost recording, cost reporting and cost analysis
16 Cost-volume-profit analysis
17 The identification of limiting factors
22 Marginal costing
24 Cost behaviour

1 Introduction

You should by now realise that as an accounting technician you need estimates of **fixed** and **variable costs**, and **revenues**, at various output levels. You must also be fully aware of **cost behaviour** because, in order to be able to estimate costs, you must know what a particular cost will do given particular conditions.

An understanding of cost behaviour is not all that you may need to have, however. The application of **cost-volume-profit analysis**, which is based on the cost behaviour principles and marginal costing ideas, is sometimes necessary so that the appropriate decision-making information can be provided. As you may have guessed, this chapter is going to look at that very topic, **cost-volume-profit analysis** (also known as **breakeven analysis).**

2 Cost-volume-profit analysis

Cost-volume-profit (CVP) analysis is the study of the interrelationships between costs, volume and profit at various levels of activity. It is also known as **breakeven analysis.**

The management of an organisation usually wishes to know the profit likely to be made if the budgeted production and sales for the year are achieved. Management may also be interested to know the following when making short term decisions.

- Breakeven point
- Margin of safety
- Target profits
- Profit volume ratio
- The existence of limiting factors

Don't worry if all of these terms are new to you – we shall be studying each one of them in detail as we progress through this chapter.

3 Breakeven point and profit volume ratio

3.1 Breakeven point

The breakeven point is the activity level at which neither a profit nor a loss is made.

The breakeven point (BEP) can be calculated arithmetically as follows.

$$\text{Breakeven point} = \frac{\text{Total fixed costs} = \text{Contribution required to break even}}{\text{Contribution per unit}}$$

= Number of units of sale required to break even.

You will remember that **contribution** = selling price – variable costs.

The contribution required to breakeven is equal to the total fixed costs.

Example: Breakeven point

The following information relates to Product G which is manufactured by Darling Ltd.

Expected sales revenue	10,000 units at £8 = £80,000
Variable cost	£5 per unit
Fixed costs	£21,000

Task

Calculate the breakeven point.

Solution

The contribution per unit is £(8–5)	=	£3
Contribution required to break even	=	fixed costs = £21,000
Breakeven point (BEP)	=	21,000 ÷ 3
	=	7,000 units
In revenue, BEP	=	(7,000 × £8) = £56,000

Sales revenue above £56,000 will result in profit of £3 per unit of additional sales and sales revenue below £56,000 will mean a loss of £3 per unit for each unit by which sales fall short of 7,000 units. In other words, profit will increase or decrease by the amount of contribution per unit.

	7,000 units	7,001 units
	£	£
Revenue	56,000	56,008
Less variable costs	35,000	35,005
Contribution	21,000	21,003
Less fixed costs	21,000	21,000
Profit	0 (= breakeven)	3

3.2 Profit volume (P/V) ratio

An alternative way of calculating the breakeven point to give an answer in terms of sales revenue is as follows.

$$\frac{\text{Required contribution} = \text{Fixed costs}}{\text{P/V ratio}} = \textbf{Sales revenue at breakeven point}$$

The **profit volume** or **P/V ratio** is also sometimes called a C/S (contribution/sales) ratio.

The profit volume ratio is a measure of how much contribution is earned from each £1 of sales.

Profit volume ratio = $\dfrac{\text{Contribution}}{\text{Sales}} \times 100\%$

Example: Profit volume ratio

We can use the data relating to Product G which is manufactured by Darling Ltd, to calculate the profit volume ratio.

Solution

Contribution = Selling price – variable costs
 = £8 – £5
 = £3

Profit volume ratio = $\dfrac{\text{Contribution}}{\text{Sales}} \times 100\%$

= $\dfrac{£3}{£8} \times 100\%$

= 37.5%

A profit volume ratio of 37.5% means that for every £1 of sales, a contribution of 37.5p is earned.

Example: Sales revenue at breakeven point

Returning to Darling Ltd, we can calculate the sales revenue at breakeven point for Product G, as follows.

If sales revenue at breakeven point = $\dfrac{\text{Required contribution}}{\text{P/V ratio}}$

We know required contribution = fixed costs
 = £21,000

Profit volume ratio (as calculated earlier) = 37.5%

∴ Sales revenue at breakeven point for product G = $\dfrac{£21,000}{37.5\%}$
 = £56,000

At a price of £8 per unit this represents 7,000 units of sales.

Activity 11.1

The P/V ratio of product W is 20%. IB Ltd, the manufacturer of product W, wishes to make a contribution of £50,000 towards fixed costs. How many units of product W must be sold if the selling price is £10 per unit?

4 Margin of safety

The **margin of safety** is the difference in units between the budgeted sales volume and the breakeven sales volume and it is sometimes expressed as a percentage of the budgeted sales volume.

The margin of safety may also be expressed as the difference between the budgeted sales revenue and breakeven sales revenue, expressed as a percentage of the budgeted sales revenue.

The margin of safety can be calculated arithmetically as follows.

Margin of safety = Budgeted sales volume (or revenue) – breakeven sales volume (or revenue)

As a percentage of budgeted sales volume (or revenue): $= \dfrac{\text{Margin of safety}}{\text{Budgeted sales volume (or revenue)}} \times 100\%$

Example: Margin of safety

Darling Ltd also makes and sells Product J which has a variable cost of £30 per unit and which sells for £40 per unit. Budgeted fixed costs are £70,000 and budgeted sales are 8,000 units.

Tasks

Calculate the breakeven point and the margin of safety.

Solution

Breakeven point $= \dfrac{\text{Total fixed costs}}{\text{Contribution per unit}}$

$= \dfrac{£70,000}{£(40-30)}$

= 7,000 units

Margin of safety = Budgeted sales volume – breakeven sales volume
= 8,000 – 7,000 units
= 1,000 units

which may also be expressed as $\dfrac{\text{Margin of safety}}{\text{Budgeted sales volume}} \times 100\%$

$$\dfrac{1,000 \text{ units}}{8,000 \text{ units}} \times 100\%$$

$$= 12\tfrac{1}{2}\% \text{ of budgeted sales volume}$$

The margin of safety indicates to management that actual sales can fall short of budget by 1,000 units or 12½% before the breakeven point is reached and no profit at all is made.

Activity 11.2

Happy Days Ltd makes and sells Product Rio which has a variable cost of £90 per unit and which sells for £120 per unit. Budgeted fixed costs are £210,000 and budgeted sales are 9,000 units.

Tasks

Calculate the breakeven point and the margin of safety (both in terms of sales volume and as a percentage of budgeted sales volume).

5 Target profit

5.1 Breakeven arithmetic

At the **breakeven point**, sales revenue equals total costs and there is no profit.

$$S = V + F$$

where S = Sales revenue
  V = Total variable costs
  F = Total fixed costs

Subtracting V from each side of the equation, we get:

  S − V = F, that is, **total contribution = fixed costs**

Example: Breakeven arithmetic

Darling Ltd also makes Product BC which has a variable cost of £7 per unit.

Fixed costs are £63,000 per annum.

Task

Calculate the required selling price per unit for Product BC if the company wishes to break even with a sales volume of 12,000 units per annum.

Solution

Contribution required to break even (= Fixed costs)	=	£63,000
Volume of sales	=	12,000 units

			£
Required contribution per unit (S – V)	=	£63,000 ÷ 12,000 =	5.25
Variable cost per unit (V)	=		7.00
Required sales price per unit (S)	=		12.25

5.2 Target profit

A similar formula may be applied where a company wishes to achieve a certain profit during a period. To achieve this profit, sales must cover all costs and leave the required profit.

The **target profit** is achieved when: S = V + F + P,
where P = required profit

Subtracting V from each side of the equation, we get:

S – V = F + P, so
Total contribution required = F + P

Example: Target profit

Darling Ltd also makes and sells Product H, for which variable costs per unit are as follows.

	£
Direct materials	10
Direct labour	8
Variable production overhead	6
	24

The sales price is £30 per unit, and fixed costs per annum are £68,000. The company wishes to make a profit of £16,000 per annum.

Task

Calculate the sales required to achieve this profit.

Solution

Required contribution = fixed costs + profit = £68,000 + £16,000 = £84,000

Required sales can be calculated in one of two ways.

(a) $\dfrac{\text{Required contribution}}{\text{Contribution per unit}} = \dfrac{£84,000}{£(30-24)} = $ 14,000 units, or £420,000 (14,000 × £30) in revenue

(b) $\dfrac{\text{Required contribution}}{\text{P/V ratio}} = \dfrac{£84,000}{20\%\,*} = $ £420,000 of revenue, or 14,000 units (£420,000 ÷ £30).

* P/V ratio = $\dfrac{£30 - £24}{£30} = \dfrac{£6}{£30} = 0.2 = 20\%$.

Activity 11.3

Seven League Boots Ltd wishes to sell 14,000 units of its product, which has a variable cost of £15 per unit to make and sell. Fixed costs are £47,000 and the required profit is £23,000.

Task

Calculate the required sales price per unit.

Activity 11.4

Betty Battle Ltd manufactures a product which has a selling price of £20 and a variable cost of £10 per unit. The company incurs annual fixed costs of £29,000. Annual sales demand is 9,000 units.

New production methods are under consideration, which would cause a £1,000 increase in fixed costs and a reduction in variable cost to £9 per unit. The new production methods would result in a superior product and would enable sales to be increased to 9,750 units per annum at a price of £21 each.

If the change in production methods were to take place, the breakeven output level would be:

A   400 units higher
B   400 units lower
C   100 units higher
D   100 units lower

6 Charts

6.1 Breakeven charts

The breakeven point can also be determined graphically using a breakeven chart. This is a chart which shows approximate levels of profit or loss at different sales volume levels within a limited range.

6.1.1 Axes

A breakeven chart has the following axes.

- A **horizontal** axis showing **sales/output** (in value or units)
- A **vertical axis** showing £ for **sales revenues** and **costs**

6.1.2 Lines

The following lines are drawn on the breakeven chart.

The **sales line**
- Starts at the origin
- Ends at the point representing expected sales

The **fixed costs line**
- Runs parallel to the horizontal axis
- Meets the vertical axis at total fixed costs value

The **total costs line**
- Starts where the fixed costs line meets the vertical axis
- Ends at the point which represents anticipated sales on the horizontal axis and total costs of anticipated sales on the vertical axis

Breakeven point = **intersection** of the **sales line** and the **total costs line**.

Margin of safety = distance between the **breakeven point** and the **expected (or budgeted) sales**, in units.

Example: Breakeven chart

The budgeted maximum capacity of one of Darling Ltd's factories is 120,000 units. The fixed overheads amount to £40,000 and the variable costs are 50p per unit. The sales price is £1 per unit, at which price the factory is operating at maximum capacity.

Task

Draw a breakeven chart showing the current breakeven point and profit earned up to the present maximum capacity.

Solution

We begin by calculating the profit at the budgeted annual output.

	£
Sales (120,000 units)	120,000
Variable costs	60,000
Contribution	60,000
Fixed costs	40,000
Profit	20,000

The chart is drawn as follows.

(a) The **vertical axis** represents **money** (costs and revenue) and the **horizontal axis** represents the **level of activity** (production and sales).

(b) The fixed costs are represented by a **straight line parallel to the horizontal axis** (in our example, at £40,000).

(c) The **variable costs** are added 'on top of' fixed costs, to give **total costs**. It is assumed that fixed costs are the same in total and variable costs are the same per unit at all levels of output.

The line of costs is therefore a straight line and only two points need to be plotted and joined up. Perhaps the two most convenient points to plot are total costs at zero output, and total costs at the budgeted output and sales.

- At zero output, costs are equal to the amount of fixed costs only, £40,000, since there are no variable costs.
- At the budgeted output of 120,000 units, costs are £100,000.

	£
Fixed costs	40,000
Variable costs (120,000 × 50p)	60,000
Total costs	100,000

(d) The sales line is also drawn by plotting two points and joining them up.

- At zero sales, revenue is nil.
- At the budgeted output and sales of 120,000 units, revenue is £120,000 (120,000 × £1).

11: SHORT TERM DECISIONS

Breakeven chart

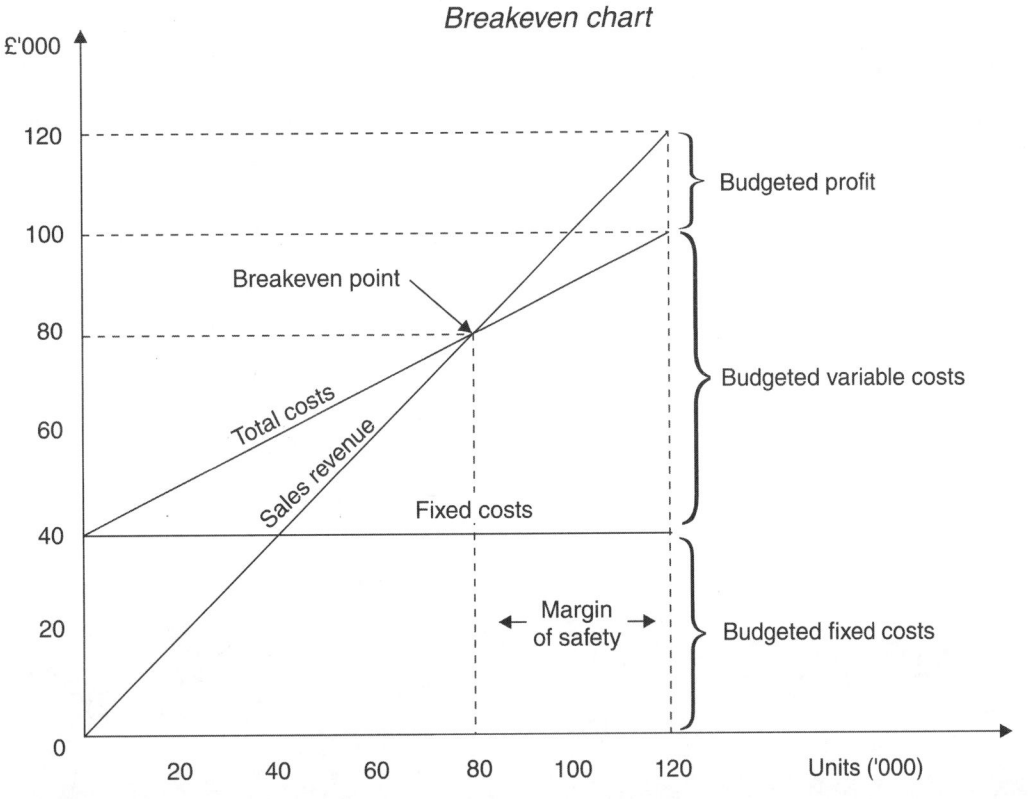

[Breakeven chart showing £'000 on y-axis (0 to 120) and Units ('000) on x-axis (0 to 120+). Lines plotted: Total costs, Sales revenue, Fixed costs (horizontal at 40). Breakeven point marked at 80,000 units / £80,000. Right side brackets indicate: Budgeted profit, Budgeted variable costs, Budgeted fixed costs. Margin of safety shown between 80 and 120 units.]

The breakeven point is where total costs are matched exactly by total revenue. From the chart, this can be seen to occur at output and sales of 80,000 units, when revenue and costs are both £80,000. This breakeven point can be proved mathematically as follows.

$$\frac{\text{Required contribution (= fixed costs)}}{\text{Contribution per unit}} = \frac{£40,000}{50\text{p per unit}} = 80,000 \text{ units}$$

The margin of safety can be seen on the chart as the difference between the budgeted level of activity and the breakeven level.

6.2 Contribution (or contribution breakeven) chart

A contribution breakeven chart is very similar to a breakeven chart. The main difference is that the fixed costs line is not plotted on a contribution breakeven chart. Instead, a variable costs line is plotted.

Example: Contribution breakeven chart

If we return to our example in Section 6.1, the contribution breakeven chart for Darling Ltd would be drawn as follows.

Contribution chart

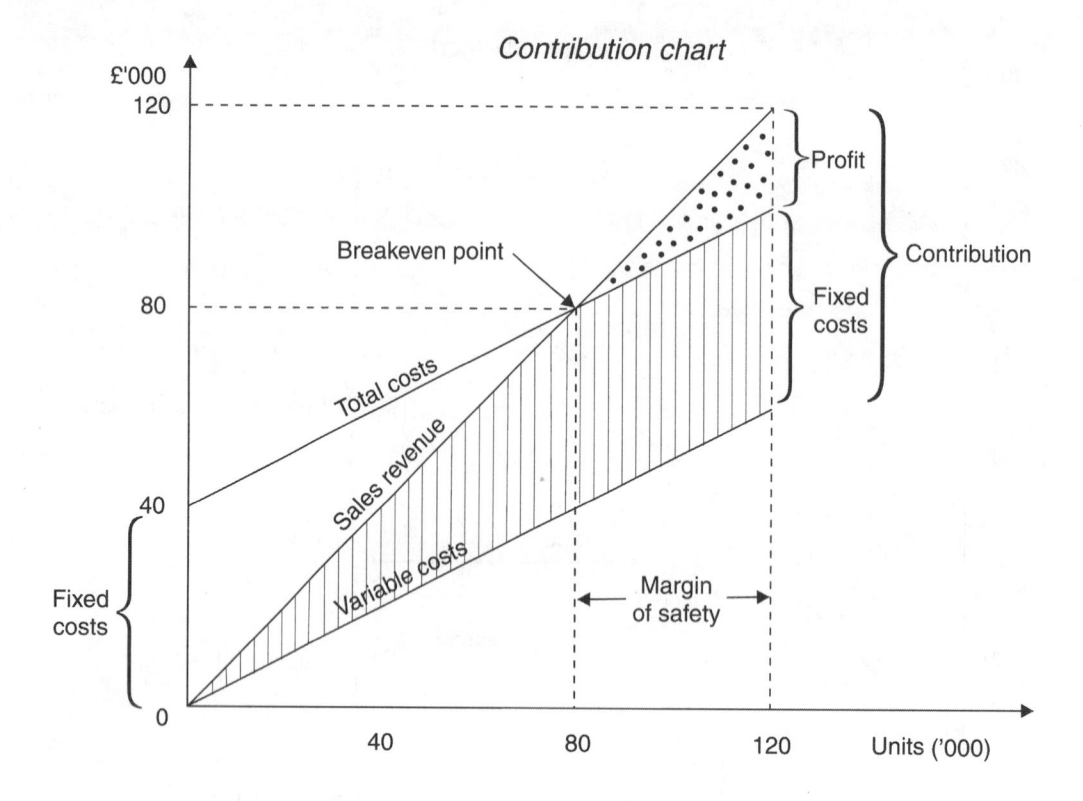

A number of important points are highlighted on the contribution breakeven chart.

- Breakeven point (where contribution = fixed costs)
- Contribution at different levels of production (shaded plus dotted area)
- Fixed costs (area between total costs line and variable costs line)
- Margin of safety
- Profit at different levels of production (dotted area)

The main advantage of the contribution breakeven chart is that contribution can be identified more easily.

6.3 The profit volume (P/V) chart

The **profit volume (P/V) chart** is a variation of the breakeven chart which illustrates the profit or loss at different levels of activity.

Example: Profit volume chart

Returning to Darling Ltd, at sales of 120,000 units, total contribution will be 120,000 × £(1 – 0.5) = £60,000 and total profit will be £20,000.

The profit volume chart for Darling Ltd is drawn as follows.

Step 1. Plot sales at 120,000 units against profit of £20,000

Step 2. Plot sales at zero units against fixed costs of £40,000
Step 3. Join these two points – the point where this line crosses the horizontal-axis is the **breakeven point**

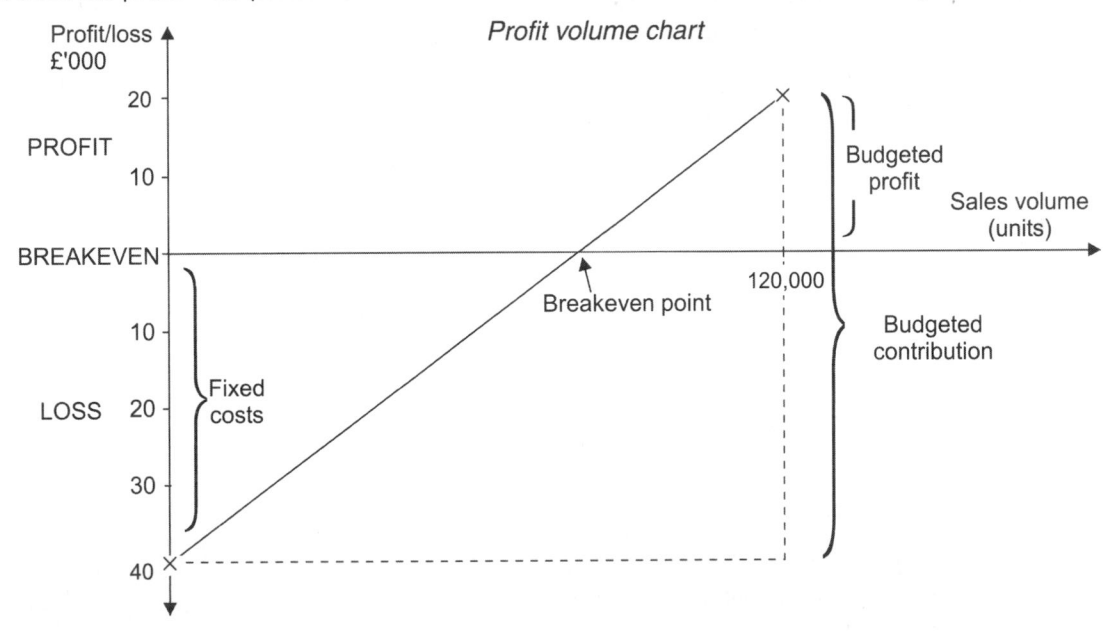

Profit volume chart

[Profit/volume chart showing Profit/loss (£'000) on vertical axis ranging from -40 (loss) to +20 (profit), and Sales volume (units) on horizontal axis. A line starts at -40,000 (fixed costs) and rises through the breakeven point to +20,000 at 120,000 units. Budgeted profit and budgeted contribution are indicated on the right side.]

The P/V chart shows clearly the effect of any changes in selling price, variable cost, fixed cost and sales demand on the **profit** and **breakeven point.**

Note that the examiner has said that he will not expect you to draw any of these charts in an examination. However, you must make sure that you appreciate how to draw them as they are fundamental to your understanding of CVP analysis.

7 Limiting factors

One of the more common short term decision making problems managers might be faced with is a situation where there are not enough resources to meet the potential sales demand of all products. When this happens a decision must be made about what mix of products to produce, using the available resources as effectively as possible.

A **limiting factor** is a factor which limits the activities of a business.

A **limiting factor** could be sales if there is a limit to sales demand but any one of the organisation's resources (labour, materials and so on) may be insufficient to meet the level of production demanded.

Example: Limiting factors

Suppose Darling Ltd makes a single product which it sells for £40. The variable costs per unit of the product are as follows.

	£
Direct materials: 6 kg at £2 per kg	12
Direct labour: 2 hours at £6 per hour	12
	24

The fixed costs for the period under consideration are £100,000.

Tasks

(a) If the availability of direct materials is limited to 60,000 kg, how many units of the product should Darling Ltd produce and what will be the profit for the period?

(b) If the availability of direct labour is limited to 40,000 hours, how many units of the product should Darling Ltd produce and what will be the profit for the period?

Solution

(a) **Limiting factor – direct materials**

$$\text{Darling Ltd can produce} = \frac{60,000 \text{ kg}}{6 \text{ kg per unit}}$$

$$= 10,000 \text{ units}$$

Profit statement

	£
Sales revenue (10,000 × £40)	400,000
Variable costs (10,000 × £24)	240,000
Contribution	160,000
Fixed costs	100,000
Profit for period	60,000

(b) **Limiting factor – direct labour**

$$\text{Darling Ltd can produce} = \frac{40,000 \text{ hours}}{2 \text{ hours per unit}}$$

$$= 20,000 \text{ units}$$

Profit statement

	£
Sales revenue (20,000 × £40)	800,000
Variable costs (20,000 × £24)	480,000
Contribution	320,000
Fixed costs	100,000
Profit for period	220,000

7.1 Profit maximisation and limiting factors

It is assumed in limiting factor analysis that management wishes to maximise profit and that **profit will be maximised when contribution is maximised** (given no change in the fixed cost expenditure incurred). In other words, **marginal costing ideas are applied**.

Contribution will be maximised by earning the biggest possible contribution from each unit of limiting factor. For example if grade A labour is the limiting factor, contribution will be maximised by earning the biggest contribution from each hour of grade A labour worked.

11: SHORT TERM DECISIONS

The **limiting factor decision** therefore involves the determination of the contribution earned by each different product from each unit of the limiting factor.

The **optimal production** plan can be determined by following this five-step approach.

Step 1. Identify the limiting factor
Step 2. Calculate contribution per unit for each product
Step 3. Calculate contribution from each product per unit of limiting factor
Step 4. Rank products (make product with highest contribution per unit of limiting factor first)
Step 5. Make products in rank order until scarce resource is used up **(optimal production plan)**

Example: Profit maximisation and limiting factors

Suppose Darling Ltd makes two products, the Ay and the Be. Unit variable costs are as follows.

	Ay £	Be £
Direct materials	1	3
Direct labour (£3 per hour)	6	3
Variable overhead	1	1
	8	7

The sales price per unit is £14 per Ay and £11 per Be. During July the available direct labour is limited to 8,000 hours. Sales demand in July is expected to be 3,000 units for Ays and 5,000 units for Bes.

Task

Determine the profit-maximising production mix, assuming that monthly fixed costs are £20,000, and that there are no opening stocks of finished goods and work in progress.

Solution

Confirm that the limiting factor is something other than sales demand.

	Ay	Be	Total
Labour hours per unit	2 hrs	1 hr	
Sales demand	3,000 units	5,000 units	
Labour hours needed	6,000 hrs	5,000 hrs	11,000 hrs
Labour hours available			8,000 hrs
Shortfall			3,000 hrs

Labour is the limiting factor on production.

UNIT 6 RECORDING AND EVALUATING COSTS AND REVENUES

Identify the contribution earned by each product per unit of limiting factor, that is per labour hour worked.

	Ay £	Be £
Sales price	14	11
Variable cost	8	7
Unit contribution	6	4
Labour hours per unit	2 hrs	1 hr
Contribution per labour hour (= unit of limiting factor)	£3	£4

Although Ays have a higher unit contribution than Bes, two Bes can be made in the time it takes to make one Ay. Because labour is in short supply it is more profitable to make Bes than Ays.

Determine the **optimum production plan**. Sufficient Bes will be made to meet the full sales demand, and the remaining labour hours available will then be used to make Ays.

(a)

Product	Demand Units	Hours required	Hours available	Priority of manufacture
Bes	5,000	5,000	5,000	1st
Ays	3,000	6,000	3,000 (bal)	2nd
		11,000	8,000	

(b)

Product	Units	Hours needed	Contribution per unit £	Total £
Bes	5,000	5,000	4	20,000
Ays	1,500	3,000	6	9,000
		8,000		29,000
Less fixed costs				20,000
Profit				9,000

Note the following points.

- Unit contribution is **not** the correct way to decide priorities.

- Labour hours are the scarce resource, and therefore contribution **per labour hour** is the correct way to decide priorities.

- The Be earns £4 contribution per labour hour, and the Ay earns £3 contribution per labour hour. Bes therefore make more profitable use of the scarce resource, and should be manufactured first.

Activity 11.5

LF Ltd makes a single product for which the standard cost details are as follows.

	£ per unit
Direct material (£3 per kg)	12
Direct labour (£8 per hour)	72
Production overhead	18
Total production cost	102

Demand for next period will be 20,000 units. No stocks are held and only 75,000 kg of material and 190,000 hours of labour will be available. What will be the limiting factor next period?

A   Material only
B   Labour only
C   Material and labour
D   There will be no limiting factor next period

8 Writing reports

This chapter has looked at cost-volume-profit analysis and a number of related techniques that are used in short term decision making.

- Breakeven point
- Profit volume ratio
- Margin of safety
- Target profit
- Limiting factors
- Breakeven, contribution breakeven and profit volume charts

If you are required to report on short term decisions in an exam or an assessment, you should bear the following points in mind.

- Any detailed cost-volume-profit analysis calculations should be included in an appendix at the end of your report.

- Any conclusions that are made at the end of your report should be justified by the detailed calculations included in your appendix.

- Make sure that any cost-volume-profit analysis charts included in your report are drawn neatly and accurately. Always use a ruler, label your axes and use an appropriate scale.

We will be looking in detail at report writing later on in Chapter 22 of this Interactive Text.

Key learning points

- **Cost-volume-profit (CVP) analysis** is the study of the interrelationships between costs, volume and profits at various levels of activity. It is also known as **breakeven analysis.**

- **Breakeven point** = **Number of units of sale** required to breakeven

  $$= \frac{\text{Fixed costs}}{\text{Contribution per unit}} = \frac{\text{Contribution required to break even}}{\text{Contribution per unit}}$$

- The **profit volume ratio** is a measure of how much contribution is earned from each £1 of sales.

- **Breakeven point** = **Sales revenue** required to break even

  $$= \frac{\text{Contribution required to break even}}{\text{P/V ratio}} = \frac{\text{Fixed costs}}{\text{P/V ratio}}$$

- The **margin of safety** is the difference in units between the **budgeted sales volume** and the **breakeven sales volume.** It is sometimes expressed as a percentage of the budgeted sales volume.

- Alternatively, the **margin of safety** can be measured as the difference between the **budgeted sales revenue** and the **breakeven sales revenue**, expressed as a percentage of the budgeted sales revenue.

- At the **breakeven point**, sales revenue = total costs and there is no profit. At the breakeven point **total contribution = fixed costs.**

- The **target profit** is achieved when S = V + F + P. Therefore the **total contribution required** for a target profit = **fixed costs + required profit.**

- The breakeven point can also be determined graphically using a **breakeven chart** or a **contribution breakeven chart**.

- Breakeven charts show the fixed cost and total cost lines, whereas the contribution breakeven chart shows the variable cost and total costs lines.

- The **profit volume (PV) chart** is a variation of the breakeven chart which illustrates the profit or loss at different levels of activity.

- A **limiting factor** is a factor which limits the activities of a business.

- It is assumed in **limiting factor analysis** that management wishes to maximise profits and that **profits will be maximised when contribution is maximised.**

- Follow this five-step approach if you need to determine an **optimum production plan**

    Step 1. Identify the limiting factor
    Step 2. Calculate contribution per unit for each product
    Step 3. Calculate contribution from each product per unit of limiting factor
    Step 4. Rank products (make product with highest contribution per unit of limiting factor first)
    Step 5. Make products in rank order until scarce resource is used up **(optimal production plan)**

- Remember that you can pick up easy marks in an examination or an assessment for drawing graphs neatly and accurately. Always use a ruler, label your axes and use an appropriate scale.

Quick quiz

1. What does cost-volume-profit analysis study?

2. Use the following to make up three formulae which can be used to calculate the breakeven point.

   | Contribution per unit |
   | Contribution per unit |
   | Fixed costs |
   | Fixed costs |
   | Contribution required to breakeven |
   | Contribution required to breakeven |
   | P/V ratio |
   | P/V ratio |

   (a) Breakeven point (sales units) = _____

   or _____

   (b) Breakeven point (sales revenue) = _____

   or _____

3. The profit volume ratio is a measure of how much profit is earned from each £1 of sales.

   ☐ True

   ☐ False

4. The **margin of safety** is the difference in units between the budgeted sales volume and the breakeven sales volume. How is it sometimes expressed?

5. Profits are maximised at the breakeven point.

   ☐ True

   ☐ False

6. At the breakeven point, total contribution = ...

7. The total contribution required for a **target profit** = ...

8   Breakeven charts show approximate levels of profit or loss at different sales volume levels within a limited range. Which of the following are true?

   I   The sales line starts at the origin
   II   The fixed costs line runs parallel to the vertical axis
   III Breakeven charts have a horizontal axis showing the sales/output (in value or units)
   IV   Breakeven charts have a vertical axis showing £ for revenues and costs
   V   The breakeven point is the intersection of the sales line and the fixed cost line

   A   I and II
   B   I and III
   C   I, III and IV
   D   I, III, IV, and V

9   On a breakeven chart, the distance between the breakeven point and the expected (or budgeted) sales, in units, indicates the ………………………………. .

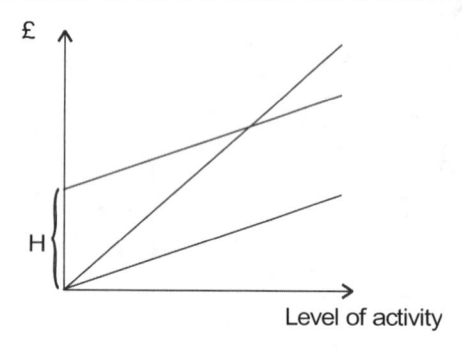

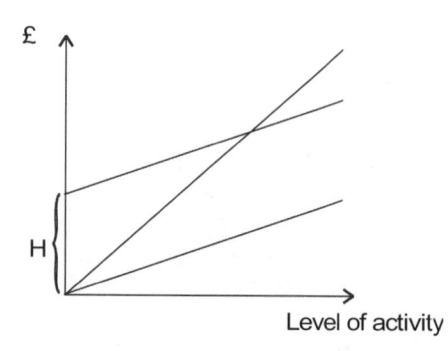

10 H on the graph above indicates the value of

   A   Contribution
   B   Fixed cost
   C   Sales value
   D   Variable cost

11 A limiting factor is a factor which …………………………………………………………..

Answers to quick quiz

1. The interrelationship between **costs, volume** and **profits** of a product at various activity levels.

2. (a) Breakeven point (sales units) = $\dfrac{\text{Fixed costs}}{\text{Contribution per unit}}$

    or $\dfrac{\text{Contribution required to breakeven}}{\text{Contribution per unit}}$

    (b) Breakeven point (sales revenue) = $\dfrac{\text{Fixed costs}}{\text{P/V ratio}}$

    or $\dfrac{\text{Contribution required to breakeven}}{\text{P/V ratio}}$

3. ✓ False.

    The P/V ratio is a measure of how much **contribution** is earned from each £1 of sales.

4. As a **percentage** of the budgeted sales volume.

5. ✓ False.

    At the breakeven point there is no profit.

6. At the breakeven point, total contribution = fixed costs

7. Fixed costs + required profit

8. C

9. Margin of safety

10. B The distance H is the total cost at zero activity, ie the fixed cost. **Option A**, contribution, is the distance between the sales line and the variable cost line, which are the two lines that pass through the origin. Sales value (**option C**) is represented by the steepest of the two lines passing through the origin. Variable cost (**option D**) is represented by the less steep of the two lines passing through the origin.

11. A limiting factor is a factor which **limits the organisation's activities**

Activity checklist

This checklist shows which performance criteria, range statement or knowledge and understanding point is covered by each activity in this chapter. Tick off each activity as you complete it.

Activity

11.1	☐	This activity deals with Knowledge and Understanding point 16 regarding cost-volume-profit analysis and breakeven point and P/V ratio
11.2	☐	This activity deals with Knowledge and Understanding point 16 regarding cost-volume-profit analysis and breakeven point and margin of safety
11.3	☐	This activity deals with Knowledge and Understanding point 16 regarding cost-volume-profit analysis and target profit
11.4	☐	This activity deals with Knowledge and Understanding point 13 regarding the analysis of the effect of changing activity levels on unit costs and breakeven points
11.5	☐	This activity deals with Knowledge and Understanding point 17 regarding the identification of limiting factors

chapter 12

Long term decisions

Contents

1. Introduction
2. Interest
3. The principles of discounted cash flow
4. Annuities and perpetuities
5. Project appraisal – discounted cash flow methods
6. Project appraisal – payback method
7. Writing reports

Performance criteria

- 6.3.A Identify information relevant to estimating current and future revenues and costs
- 6.3.B Prepare **estimates** of future income and costs
- 6.3.C Calculate the effects of variations in capacity on product costs
- 6.3.D Analyse critical factors affecting costs and revenues using appropriate accounting techniques and draw clear conclusions from the analysis
- 6.3.E State any assumptions used when evaluating future costs and revenues
- 6.3.F Identify and evaluate options and solutions for their contribution to organisational goals
- 6.3.G **Present** recommendations to appropriate people in a clear and concise way and supported by a clear rationale

Range statement
Estimates: long term decisions
- Project appraisal using payback and discounted cash flow methods

Methods of presentation:
- Verbal presentation
- Written reports

Knowledge and understanding

18 Methods of project appraisal: payback and discounted cash flow methods (NPV and IRR)
25 The principles of discounted cash flow

1 Introduction

Long term decisions generally involve looking at the options available when a company (or an individual) puts money into an investment.

If a company invests in a project, it will expect some sort of financial return (or more money) at some point in the future. If the project runs for a number of years then whether or not to invest in the project will involve taking a long term decision.

One of the things companies will need to consider when investing in long term projects is the **time value of money**.

Think about the following question.

'If I have £5 in my pocket **now**, how much will it be worth in four years' time?'

This is a difficult question to answer, but we will be looking at ways in which companies use the concept of the **time value of money** when they are appraising projects and making long term decisions.

2 Interest

2.1 Simple interest

- **Interest** is the amount of money which an investment earns over time.
- **Simple interest** is interest which is earned in equal amounts every year (or month) and which is a given proportion of the original investment (the principal).

If a sum of money is invested for a period of time, then the amount of simple interest which accrues is equal to the number of periods × the interest rate × the amount invested. We can write this as a formula.

The formula for **simple interest** is as follows.

$S = P + nrP$

where P = the original sum invested
         r = the interest rate (expressed as a proportion, so 10% = 0.1)
         n = the number of periods (normally years)
         S = the sum invested after n periods, consisting of the original capital (P) plus interest earned (future value)

Example: Simple interest

Fred invests £1,000 at 10% simple interest per annum.

Task

Calculate how much Fred will have after five years.

Solution

Using the formula $S = P + nrP$

where $P = £1,000$
$r = 10\%$
$n = 5$

$\therefore S = £1,000 + (5 \times 0.1 \times £1,000) = £1,500$

2.2 Compound interest

Interest is normally calculated by means of **compounding**.

If a sum of money is invested at a fixed rate of interest and the interest is added to the original sum of money, then the **interest earned in earlier periods will also earn interest in later periods**.

Example: Compound interest

Suppose that Fred invests £2,000 at 10% interest per annum. After one year, the original principal plus interest will amount to £2,200.

	£
Original investment	2,000
Interest in the first year (10%)	200
Total investment at the end of one year	2,200

(a) **After two years** the total investment will be £2,420.

	£
Investment at end of one year	2,200
Interest in the second year (10%)	220
Total investment at the end of two years	2,420

The second year interest of £220 represents 10% of the original investment, and 10% of the interest earned in the first year.

(b) Similarly, **after three years**, the total investment will be £2,662.

	£
Investment at the end of two years	2,420
Interest in the third year (10%)	242
Total investment at the end of three years	2,662

Instead of performing the calculations shown above, we could have used the following formula.

The basic formula for **compound interest** is $S = P(1 + r)^n$

where P = the original sum invested
  r = the interest rate, expressed as a proportion (so 5% = 0.05)
  n = the number of periods (normally years)
  S = the sum invested after n periods (future value)

Using the formula for compound interest, $S = P(1 + r)^n$

where P = £2,000
  r = 10% = 0.1
  n = 3

  S = £2,000 × 1.10^3
   = £2,000 × 1.331
   = £2,662.

The interest earned over three years is £662, which is the same answer that was calculated in the example above.

Today's date is 31 May 20X3. Note the following timings of cash flows.

- Time 0 = now (31 May 20X3)
- Time 1 = one year's time (31 May 20X4)
- Time 2 = two year's time (31 May 20X5)

Activity 12.1

If Fred invests £5,000 now (28 February 20X3) how much will his investment be worth:

(a) on 28 February 20X6, if the interest rate is 20% per annum?
(b) on 28 February 20X7, if the interest rate is 15% per annum?
(c) on 28 February 20X6, if the interest rate is 6% per annum?

3 The principles of discounted cash flow

The basic principle of **discounting** is that if we wish to have £S in n years' time, we need to invest a certain sum *now* (year 0) at an interest rate of r% in order to obtain the required sum of money in the future. In day-to-day terms, we could say that if we wish to have £1,000 in five years' time, how much would we need to invest **now** at an interest rate of 4%?

Example: Principles of discounted cash flow

If we wish to have £14,641 in four years' time, how much money would we need to invest now at 10% interest per annum?

Using our compounding formula, $S = P(1 + r)^n$

where P = the original sum invested
       r = 10% = 0.1
       n = 4
       S = £14,641

$£14,641 = P(1 + 0.1)^4$

$£14,641 = P \times 1.4641$

$\therefore P = \dfrac{£14,641}{1.4641} = £10,000$

£10,000 now, with the capacity to earn a return of 10% per annum, is the equivalent in value of £14,641 after four years. We can therefore say that **£10,000 is the present value of £14,641 at year 4, at an interest rate of 10%**.

3.1 Present values

The term **'present value'** simply means the amount of money which must be invested now for n years at an interest rate of r%, to earn a given future sum of money at the time it will be due.

The **discounting formula** is

$P = S \times \dfrac{1}{(1+r)^n}$

where S is the sum to be received after n time periods
       P is the present value (PV) of that sum
       r is the rate of return, expressed as a proportion
       n is the number of time periods (usually years).

The rate r is sometimes called the cost of capital.

Note that this equation is just a rearrangement of the compounding formula.

Example: Present values

(a) Calculate the present value of £60,000 received at the end of year 6, if interest rates are 15% per annum.
(b) Calculate the present value of £100,000 received at the end of year 5, if interest rates are 6% per annum.

Solution

The discounting formula, $X = P \times \dfrac{1}{(1+r)^n}$ is required.

(a) $S = £60,000$
$n = 6$
$r = 0.15$

$PV = 60,000 \times \dfrac{1}{1.15^6}$

$= 60,000 \times 0.432$
$= £25,920$

(b) $S = £100,000$
$n = 5$
$r = 0.06$

$PV = 100,000 \times \dfrac{1}{1.06^5}$

$= 100,000 \times 0.747$
$= £74,700$

3.1.1 Present value tables

Now that you understand the principles of discounting and you are able to calculate present values, you will be happy to hear that you do not need to remember the formula for discounting. This is because the present value tables at the end of this Interactive Text have already calculated all of the discount factors that you will ever need for Unit 6.

Refer to the **present value tables** on page 525.

The use of present value tables is best explained by means of an example.

Example: Present value tables

(a) Using tables, calculate the present value of £60,000 at year 6, if interest rates are 15% per annum.
(b) Using tables, calculate the present value of £100,000 at year 5, if interest rates are 6% per annum.

Solution

(a) Looking at the present value tables at the back of this Interactive Text, look along the row n = 6 (year 6) and down column r = 15% (interest rates are 15% per annum). The required discount rate is 0.432.

The present value of £60,000 at year 6, when interest rates are 15% is therefore:

£60,000 × 0.432 = £25,920

(b) Looking at the present value tables at the back of this Interactive Text, look along the row n = 5 (year 5) and down column r = 6% (interest rates are 6% per annum). The required discount rate is 0.747.

The present value of £100,000 at year 5, when interest rates are 6% is therefore:

£100,000 × 0.747 = £74,700

Do either of these present values look familiar? Well, both of them should be as they are the same present values that we calculated in the previous example using the discounting formula!

Activity 12.2

Today's date is 30 April 20X3. If Fred wishes to have £16,000 saved by 30 April 20X8, how much should he invest if interest rates are 5%? Use the present value tables at the back of this Interactive Text.

4 Annuities and perpetuities

4.1 Annuities

An **annuity** is a constant sum of money received or paid each year for a given number of years. For example, the present value of a three year annuity of £100 which begins in one year's time when interest rates are 5% is calculated as follows.

Time	Cash flow £	Discount factor 5%	Present value £
1	100	0.952	95.20
2	100	0.907	90.70
3	100	0.864	86.40
			272.30

There is a rather long and complicated formula which can be used to calculate the present value of an annuity. Fortunately there are also **annuity tables** which calculate all of the **annuity factors** that you might ever need for Unit 6.

In order to calculate the present value of a constant sum of money, we can multiply the annual cash flow by the sum of the discount factors for the relevant years. These total factors are known as **cumulative present value factors or annuity factors.**

Present value of an annuity = Annuity × annuity factor

Example: Annuity tables

What is the annuity factor (cumulative present value factor) of £1 per annum for five years at 11% interest.

Solution

Refer to the annuity tables on page 526 at the back of this Interactive Text.

Read across to the column headed 11% (r = 11%) and down to period 5 (n = 5). The annuity factor = 3.696

Now look back at the present value tables on page ??? and look in the column n = 11%. The cumulative present value rates for n = 1 to 5 = 0.901 + 0.812 + 0.731 + 0.659 + 0.593 = 3.696. Can you see now why these annuity tables are also called cumulative present value tables?

Example: Present value of an annuity

Fred has to make an annual payment of £1,000 to a car hire company on 30 June 20X3 each year until 30 June 20X8.

Task

Calculate the present value of Fred's total payments if today's date is 1 July 20X2. Use a discount rate of 7%.

Solution

The first payment will be in one year's time ie time 1.

There will be six annual payments.

Annuity factor (where n = 6, r = 7%) = 4.767

Present value of payments = £1,000 × annuity factor
= £1,000 × 4.767
= £4,767

4.2 Perpetuities

A **perpetuity** is an annuity which lasts forever.

The present value of a perpetuity = $\dfrac{\text{annuity}}{\text{interest rate *}}$

*expressed as a proportion eg 20% = 0.2

Example: A perpetuity

Fred is to receive £35,000 per annum in perpetuity starting in one year's time. If the annual rate of interest is 9% what is the present value of this perpetuity?

Solution

$$PV = \frac{\text{annuity}}{\text{interest rate}}$$

$$\therefore PV = \frac{£35,000}{0.09}$$

$$= £388,889$$

5 Project appraisal - discounted cash flow methods

Discounted cash flow methods can be used to appraise projects.

Discounted cash flow (DCF) involves the application of discounting arithmetic to the estimated future cash flows (receipts and expenditures) from a project in order to decide whether the project is expected to earn a satisfactory rate of return.

The two main discounted cash flow methods are as follows.

- The net present value (NPV) method
- The internal rate of return (IRR) method

5.1 The net present value (NPV) method

The **net present value (NPV) method** calculates the present values of all items of income and expenditure related to an investment at a given rate of return, and then calculates a net total. If it is positive, the investment is considered to be acceptable. If it is negative, the investment is considered to be unacceptable.

Example: The net present value of a project

Dog Ltd is considering whether to spend £5,000 on an item of equipment which will last for two years. The 'cash profits', ie the excess of income over cash expenditure, from the equipment would be £3,000 in the first year and £4,000 in the second year.

Task

Calculate the net present value of the investment in the equipment at a discount rate of 15%.

Solution

In this example, an outlay of £5,000 now promises a return of £3,000 **during** the first year and £4,000 **during** the second year. It is a convention in DCF, however, that cash flows spread over a year are assumed to occur **at the end of the year**, so that the cash flows of the project are as follows.

	£
Year 0 (now)	(5,000)
Year 1 (at the end of the year)	3,000
Year 2 (at the end of the year)	4,000

A net present value statement is drawn up as follows.

Year	Cash flow	Discount factor	Present value
	£	15%	£
0	(5,000)	1.000	(5,000)
1	3,000	0.870	2,610
2	4,000	0.756	3,024
		Net present value	+ 634

The project has a positive net present value, so it is acceptable.

5.2 The timing of cash flows

Note that annuity tables and the formulae both assume that the first payment or receipt is a year from now. **Always check examination and assessment questions for when the first payment falls**.

For example, if there are five equal annual payments starting now, and the interest rate is 8%, we should use a factor of 1 (for today's payment) + 3.312 (for the other four payments) = 4.312.

Activity 12.3

A company is wondering whether to spend £18,000 on an item of equipment, in order to obtain cash profits as follows.

Year	£
1	6,000
2	8,000
3	5,000
4	1,000

The company requires a return of 10% per annum.

Task

Use the net present value method to assess whether the project to invest in the equipment is viable.

Activity 12.4

Daisy Ltd is considering whether to make an investment costing £28,000 which would earn £8,000 cash per annum (starting in one year's time) for five years.

Task

What is the net present value of the investment at a cost of capital of 11%?

Activity 12.5

Mostly Ltd is considering a project which would cost £50,000 now and yield £9,000 per annum every year in perpetuity, starting a year from now. The cost of capital is 15%.

Task

Calculate the net present value of the project.

5.3 The internal rate of return (IRR) method

The **internal rate of return (IRR) method** of evaluating investments is an alternative to the NPV method. The NPV method of discounted cash flow determines whether an investment earns a **positive or a negative NPV when discounted at a given rate of interest**. If the NPV is zero (that is, the present values of costs and benefits are equal) the return from the project would be exactly the rate used for discounting.

The **IRR method of discounted cash flow** is a method which determines the rate of interest (the internal rate of return) at which the NPV is zero. The internal rate of return is therefore the rate of return on an investment.

The IRR method will indicate that a project is viable **if the IRR exceeds the minimum acceptable rate of return**. Thus if the company expects a minimum return of, say, 15%, a project would be viable if its IRR is more than 15%.

Note. The examiner has stated that tasks which require the computation of a project's internal rate of return will not be set but students should be aware of its meaning.

6 Project appraisal – payback method

6.1 What is the payback period?

The **payback period** is the time that is required for the total of the cash inflows of a capital investment project to equal the total of the cash outflows.

Before the payback period can be calculated, management must have details of the following.

- The initial cash outflow for the project under consideration
- Estimates of any future cash inflows or savings

Example: Payback method

Ruby Ltd is considering a new project which will require an initial investment £60,000. The estimated profits before depreciation are as follows.

Year	Estimated profits before depreciation £
1	20,000
2	30,000
3	40,000
4	50,000
5	60,000

The payback period is calculated by considering the cumulative estimated profits before depreciation.

Year	Estimated profits before depreciation £	Cumulative estimated profits before depreciation £
1	20,000	20,000
2	30,000	50,000
3	40,000	90,000
4	50,000	140,000
5	60,000	200,000

Initially, it appears that the initial investment of £60,000 is paid back in year 3. If the cash flows accrue evenly throughout the year, we can calculate the payback period as follows.

At the end of year 2, £50,000 of the cash invested has been 'paid back'.

At the end of year 3, £90,000 of the cash invested has been 'paid back'.

The point at which the £60,000 investment has been 'paid back' is actually:

2 years + (£10,000/£40,000 × 12 months) = 2 years and 3 months

If, on the other hand, the cash flows are received at the end of the year then the payback period would be 3 years.

6.2 Using the payback period to appraise projects

There are two ways in which the payback period can be used to appraise projects.

- If two or more projects are under consideration, the usual decision is to accept the project with the **shortest payback period.**

- If the management of a company have a **payback period limit**, then only projects with payback periods which are less than this limit would be considered for investment.

Example: Project appraisal – payback method

Suppose Ruby Ltd has a payback period limit of two years, and is considering investing in one of the following projects, both of which require an initial investment of £400,000. Cashflows accrue evenly throughout the year.

	Project A		Project B
Year	Cash inflow	Year	Cash inflow
	£		£
1	100,000	1	200,000
2	200,000	2	180,000
3	100,000	3	120,000
4	150,000	4	100,000
5	150,000	5	100,000

Task

Which project is acceptable from the point of view of the payback period?

Solution

Firstly, we need to calculate the payback periods for Projects A and B.

Project A

Year	Cash inflow	Cumulative cash inflow
	£	£
1	100,000	100,000
2	200,000	300,000
3	100,000	400,000
4	150,000	550,000
5	150,000	700,000

Project A has a payback period of 3 years.

Project B

Year	Cash inflow	Cumulative cash inflow
	£	£
1	200,000	200,000
2	180,000	380,000
3	120,000	500,000
4	100,000	600,000
5	100,000	700,000

Project B has a payback period of between 2 and 3 years.

Payback period = 2 years + (£20,000/£120,000 × 12 months)
= 2 years + 2 months

Since Ruby Ltd has a payback period limit of two years, neither project should be invested in (as both payback periods are greater than two years). If, however, Ruby Ltd did not have a payback limit, it should invest in Project B because it has the shorter payback period of the two projects.

Activity 12.6

A business is considering investing in one of the following projects on 1 April 20X3. The initial investment and estimated cash inflows are as follows.

	Project X £	Project Y £
Initial investment on 1 April 20X3	250,000	300,000
Cash inflow on 31 March 20X4	50,000	50,000
Cash inflow on 31 March 20X5	150,000	180,000
Cash inflow on 31 March 20X6	150,000	280,000
Cash inflow on 31 March 20X7	70,000	25,000
Cash inflow on 31 March 20X8	130,000	30,000

The business has a payback period limit of three years and will not invest in projects which have a payback period greater than this.

Cash inflows are spread evenly throughout the year

Task

From the point of view of the payback period, identify which project the business should invest in and explain your answer.

Payback is often used as an initial step in appraising a project. However, a project should not be evaluated on the basis of payback alone. If a project passes the 'payback test' ie if it has a payback period that is less than the payback period limit of the company then it should be evaluated further with a more sophisticated project appraisal technique (such as the NPV or IRR methods studied earlier in this chapter).

6.3 Advantages of the payback method

- It is a useful initial screening device
- Payback calculations are quick and simple
- It is easily understood by management

6.4 Disadvantages of the payback method

- It ignores the time value of money (unlike NPV/IRR methods)
- It ignores the timing of cash flows
- It is unable to distinguish between projects with the same payback period

7 Writing reports

This chapter has looked at project appraisal and a number of different methods that can be used in long term decision making.

- Payback method
- Net present value method
- Internal rate of return method

If you are required to report on long term decisions in an assessment or an exam, you should bear the following points in mind.

- Any detailed project appraisal calculations should be included in an appendix at the end of your report.

- Any conclusions that you make regarding the decision to invest in a project (or otherwise) should be detailed in your report and justified by the detailed calculations in your appendix.

Key learning points

- **Long term investments** include the purchase of buildings, machinery and equipment. Management will need to have estimates of the initial investment and future costs and revenues of a project in order to make any **long term decisions**.

- **Interest** is the amount of money which an investment earns over time. **Simple interest** is interest which is earned in equal amounts every year. If interest earned also earns interest itself in later periods, this is known as **compound interest**.

- The basic principle of **discounting** involves calculating the **present value** of an investment (ie the value of an investment **today** at time 0).

- The term **present value** means the amount of money which must be invested now (for a number of years) in order to earn a future sum (at a given rate of interest).

- **Discounted cash flow** involves discounting future cash flows from a project in order to decide whether the project will earn a satisfactory rate of return.

- An **annuity** is a constant sum of money received or paid each year for a given number of years.

- **Present value of an annuity** = annuity × annuity factor.

- **A perpetuity** is an annuity which lasts forever.

- **Present value of a perpetuity** = $\dfrac{\text{annuity}}{\text{interest rate}}$

- The two main **discounted cash flow methods** are as follows.
  - The net present value (NPV) method
  - The internal rate of return (IRR) method

- The **NPV method** works out the present values of an investment's cash inflows and outflows at a given rate of return and then calculates a net total. If an investment has a positive NPV then it is acceptable. An investment with a negative NPV should be rejected.

- The **IRR method** determines the rate of interest (internal rate of return) at which the NPV = 0. The internal rate of return is therefore the rate of return on an investment.

- Present value tables and annuity tables assume that the first payment or receipt is a **year from now.** Always check examination/assessment questions carefully to see when the first payment falls.

- The **payback period** is the time that is required for the cash inflows from a capital investment project to equal the cash outflows.

- The **payback method** can be used to appraise projects in two ways.
  - If two or more projects are under consideration, the usual decision is to accept the project with the **shortest payback period.**
  - If the management of a company have a **payback period limit**, then only projects which are less than this limit would be considered for investment.

- Unlike the NPV and IRR methods, the payback method does not use discounted cashflow techniques.

12: LONG TERM DECISIONS

Quick quiz

1. What does the term present value mean?

2. The discounting formula is $P = S \times \dfrac{1}{(1+r)^n}$

    Where

    S =
    P =
    r =
    n =

    (a) the rate of return (as a proportion)
    (b) the sum to be received after n time periods
    (c) the PV of that sum
    (d) the number of time periods

3. An annuity is a sum of money received every year.

    ☐ True

    ☐ False

4. What is a perpetuity?

5. What is the formula for the present value of a perpetuity?

6. What are the two usual methods of capital expenditure appraisal using discounted cash flow methods?

7. What is the payback period?

Answers to quick quiz

1. The amount of money which must be invested now for n years at an interest rate of r% to give a future sum of money at the time it will be due.

2. S = (b)
   P = (c)
   r = (a)
   n = (d)

3. ✓ False

    It is a **constant** sum of money **received** or **paid** each year for a **given number** of years.

4. An annuity which lasts forever.

5. $PV = \dfrac{\text{annuity}}{\text{interest rate}}$

6 The net present value (NPV) method
   The Internal rate of return (IRR) method

7 The payback period is the time that is required for the cash inflows of a capital investment project to equal the cash outflows.

Activity checklist

This checklist shows which performance criteria, range statement or knowledge and understanding point is covered by each activity in this chapter. Tick off each activity as you complete it.

Activity

12.1	☐	This activity deals with Knowledge and Understanding point 25 regarding the principles of discounted cash flow
12.2	☐	This activity deals with Knowledge and Understanding point 25 regarding the principles of discounted cash flow
12.3	☐	This activity deals with Knowledge and Understanding point 18 regarding the NPV method of project appraisal
12.4	☐	This activity deals with Knowledge and Understanding point 18 regarding the NPV method of project appraisal
12.5	☐	This activity deals with Knowledge and Understanding point 18 regarding the NPV method of project appraisal
12.6	☐	This activity deals with Knowledge and Understanding point 18 regarding the payback method of project appraisal

UNIT 7

Preparing reports and returns

chapter 13

The organisation, accounting and reporting

Contents

1. Introduction
2. Organisations and their structure
3. Accounting practices in different parts of the organisation
4. Internal and external reports

Knowledge and understanding

15. How the accounting systems of an organisation are affected by its organisational structure, its administrative systems and procedures and the nature of its business transactions
16. The purpose and structure of reporting systems within the organisation
17. Background understanding that a variety of outside agencies may require reports and returns from organisations and that these requirements must be built into administrative and accounting systems and procedures
18. Background understanding that recording and accounting practices may vary between organisations and different parts of organisations

1 Introduction

Welcome to the AAT's Intermediate Unit 7 – **Preparing Reports and Returns**, and in particular to this introductory chapter – **The organisation, accounting and reporting**.

In this chapter we shall be looking at the different kinds of **organisation** that there are and how they might be **structured**. We will then go on to look at how an organisation's accounting system is affected by the nature of its business transactions and the sort of business it is.

At the Foundation Stage you saw how information can be **recorded** in **ledgers** and various **books of account**. At the end of this chapter we shall go on to look at how the information recorded by an organisation can be reported in the form of **internal** and **external** reports.

2 Organisations and their structure

2.1 Organisations

There are many different kinds of organisation.

- Aircraft manufacturer
- Bank
- Government department
- Hospital
- Corner shop

It is possible to distinguish organisations from each other in a number of ways.

- By type of activity
- By size of business
- Profit orientated or non-profit orientated
- Legal status and ownership

2.1.1 By type of activity

Here are some examples.

- Retailers (eg greengrocer, supermarket chain)
- Manufacturers (eg of painkillers, ballbearings, cars)
- Service organisations (eg restaurants, schools)
- Contractors (eg building power stations)

2.1.2 By size of business

A large supermarket is likely to have more in common with another large organisation than with a small grocer's shop.

2.1.3 Profit orientated or non-profit orientated

An organisation in existence to make a profit seeks to maximise the difference between what it receives in revenue, and what it pays out in expenses. The **surplus**, or **profit**, is distributed to the owners to do with as they please. A charity, on the other hand, is a non-profit making organisation. Public sector organisations are funded from general taxation to provide services, not, generally speaking, to make a profit.

2.1.4 Legal status and ownership.

- The business affairs of **sole traders** are not distinguished from their personal affairs in the eyes of the law.
- A **partnership** is an agreement (normally documented) between two or more individuals, but the partners are still personally liable for the debts of the business.
- A **limited company**, on the other hand, is a **separate legal personality** in the eyes of the law, and is a **separate legal entity** from its owners (shareholders). A UK limited company can be identified by the words Limited or Public Limited Company.
- Some organisations (eg hospitals) are owned and funded by central or local government. These are **public sector organisations**.
- **Unincorporated associations**, such as sports clubs and societies are very common. They are not separate legal bodies from the members who make them up even though that membership is always changing. They are managed by **committees**.
- **Charities** are registered with the Charity Commissioners and have trustees.

2.2 Organisation structure

Organisations are often so large that there have be **formal** and **defined relationships** between the persons within the organisation. This is because of the following reasons.

- There is a large number of **tasks** that have to be done. These tasks have to be coordinated in some way.
- There is often a large number of **people** who have to be coordinated and motivated.

Many large organisations have a **person** or **committee** at the head who is responsible, ultimately, for the **direction** the organisation takes.

- An individual might be called **Chief Executive**, or **Managing Director**.
- A committee might be called a **Board of Directors** or an **Executive Committee**.

In a large organisation, the Board's decisions will 'cascade' down for detailed implementation, and **information** about performance will rise up. Each person at the top will have a number of people reporting to him or her, and these other people will also have their own **subordinates**. This is known as **management hierarchy**.

An organisation which manufactures a range of cars and buses which are both manufactured and sold in Europe and Asia could be organised in a number of different ways.

- Geographically
- Product-divisional basis
- Functional basis
- Matrix basis

2.2.1 Geographically

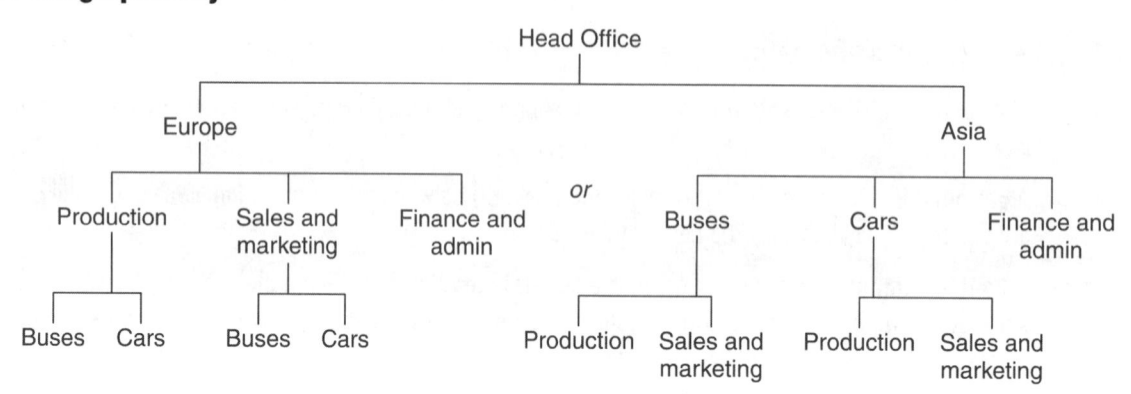

```
                          Head Office
              ┌───────────────┴───────────────┐
           Europe              or            Asia
      ┌──────┼──────┐                  ┌──────┼──────┐
  Production  Sales and  Finance and  Buses   Cars  Finance and
              marketing    admin                      admin
   ┌──┴──┐    ┌──┴──┐                  ┌──┴──┐  ┌──┴──┐
 Buses Cars Buses Cars              Production Sales Production Sales
                                              and             and
                                           marketing       marketing
```

In this **geographical organisation structure** the responsibility for all the activities of the company is divided on an **area basis**. The manager for Asia is in charge of producing and selling products in that area.

2.2.2 Product-divisional basis

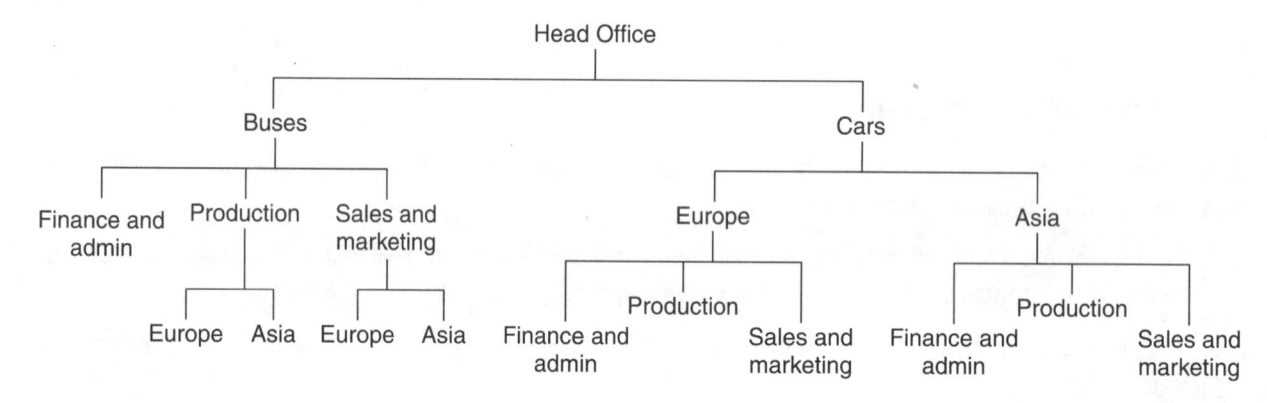

```
                          Head Office
              ┌───────────────┴───────────────┐
            Buses                            Cars
      ┌──────┼──────┐                  ┌──────┴──────┐
 Finance and Production Sales and    Europe          Asia
   admin                marketing  ┌────┴────┐   ┌────┴────┐
            ┌──┴──┐   ┌──┴──┐  Production  Sales  Production  Sales
         Europe Asia Europe Asia Finance and  and  Finance and  and
                                   admin   marketing  admin  marketing
```

In this **product-division structure** the responsibility for buses worldwide, and cars worldwide, are each given to one individual.

2.2.3 Functional basis

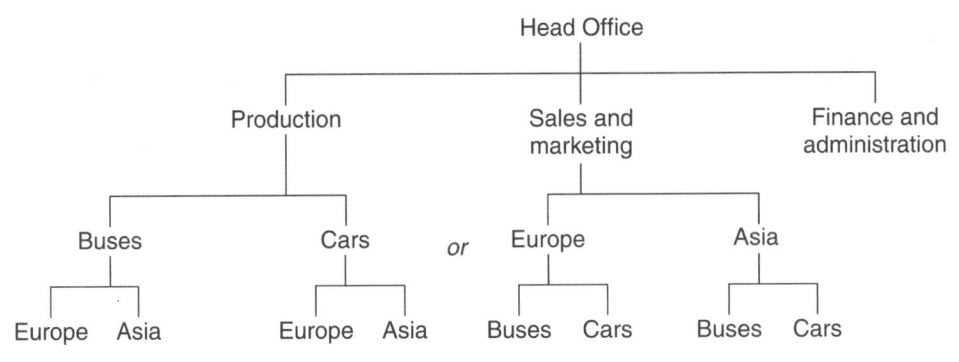

```
                        Head Office
          ┌──────────────┼──────────────┐
      Production      Sales and      Finance and
                      marketing      administration
       ┌──┴──┐          ┌──┴──┐
     Buses  Cars   or  Europe  Asia
     ┌┴┐    ┌┴┐         ┌┴┐    ┌┴┐
  Europe Asia Europe Asia Buses Cars Buses Cars
```

In this **functional organisation structure**, worldwide control of production is vested in one person, as is the case with sales and marketing.

2.2.4 Matrix basis

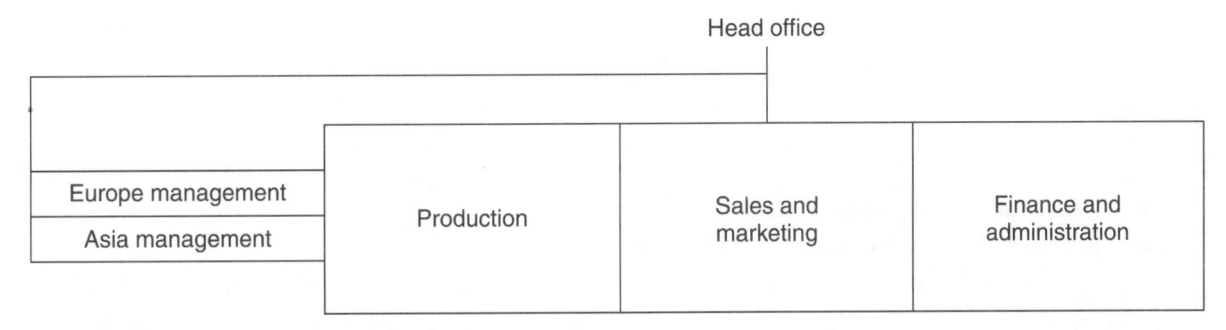

	Production	Sales and marketing	Finance and administration
Europe management			
Asia management			

(Head office above)

In a **matrix organisation structure**, somebody involved in production in Europe has to report equally to the European manager and to the production manager.

3 Accounting practices in different parts of the organisation

3.1 Accounting practices

An organisation's accounting systems are affected by the **nature of its business transactions** and the **sort of business** it is.

- Size
- Type of organisation
- Organisation structure

3.1.1 Size

A small business like a greengrocer will have a simple, **cash-based accounting system**, where the main accounting record will probably be the till roll. A large retail business, such as a chain of supermarkets, will have more complex **accounting systems** which use advanced computer technology.

3.1.2 Type of organisation

- A **service business** might need to record the time employees take on particular jobs (time sheets).
- A **public sector organisation**, such as a government department, may be more concerned with the monitoring of expenditure against performance targets than with recording revenue.
- A **manufacturing company** will account both for unit sales and revenue, but needs to keep track of costs for decision making purposes and so on.

3.1.3 Organisation structure

Accounting information can influence the **structure** of the organisation, as the way in which accounting information is collected and **summarised** will reflect the reporting structure of the organisation.

Accounting procedures therefore relate to the following.

- Collecting and **recording** accounting data.
- Providing and **reporting** accounting information.

3.2 Accounting procedures and geographical structure

An organisation's **geographical structure** must be taken into account.

- It might be **dispersed** over several different countries in the world.
- It might also be very **decentralised** in each country.

There are a number of ways in which the accounting procedures will be specifically affected by geography.

- Different currencies
- Different legal and accounting requirements
- Different ways of doing business
- Political, economic, social and technological factors

3.3 Accounting procedures and product information

Information is sometimes reported on a **product basis**.

This involves both **recording** and **reporting issues**. The resulting information is grouped in a particular way to highlight revenue earned and costs incurred by a particular product.

Recording accounting information relating to revenue is usually easy. An individual product has a selling price, and it is relatively simple to record unit sales.

Costs are more problematic. Electricity expenses can be incurred making a number of products but it is difficult to track these costs to individual products.

Cost information is necessary for **decision making** in any organisation.

3.4 Accounting procedures and business functions

3.4.1 Business functions

For convenience, we can identify the following functions.

- Sales and marketing
- Production
- Finance and administration

The function of **sales and marketing** includes the following.

- Sales order processing
- Distribution
- Invoicing
- Credit control
- Management of debtors
- Market research
- Advertising
- Public relations

The function of **production** includes the following.

- Purchasing
- Control of raw materials and finished goods stocks
- Costing
- Capital equipment purchasing

The function of **finance and administration** includes the following.

- Accounting function
- Treasury functions
- Credit control
- The management of debtors and creditors
- Personnel management

3.4.2 Accounting procedures

Accounting activities in an organisation relate to both the **recording** of information and the **reporting** of information.

- **Recording transactions data** is necessary so that all revenues, expenses, assets and liabilities are captured by the accounting system.
- **Reporting information** is necessary to make more use of this basic data.

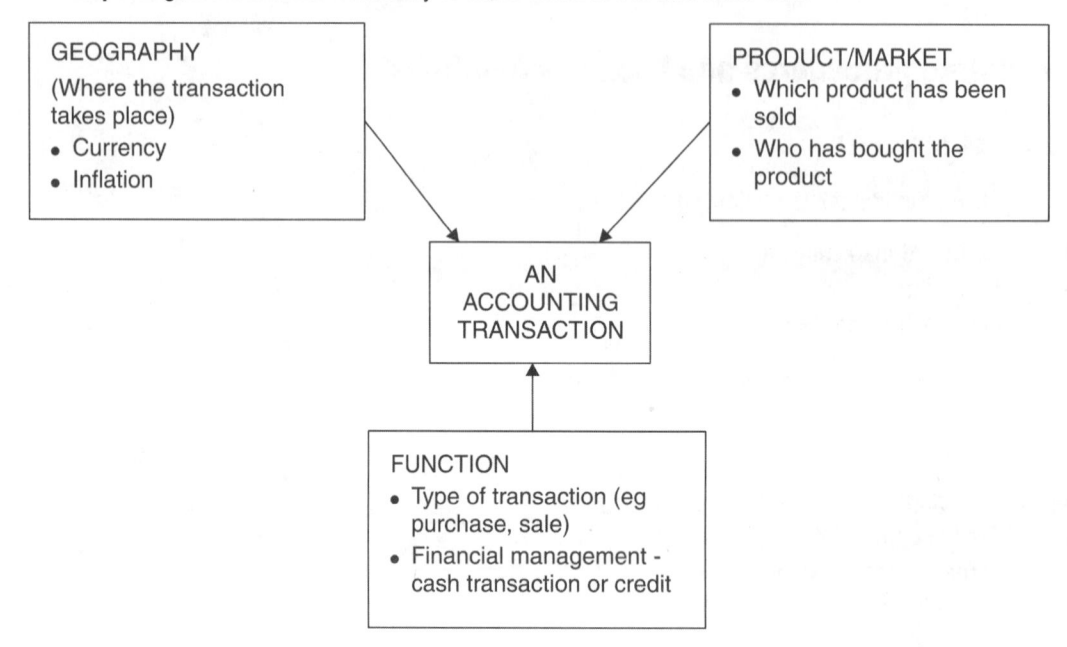

```
┌─────────────────────────┐                    ┌─────────────────────────┐
│ GEOGRAPHY               │                    │ PRODUCT/MARKET          │
│ (Where the transaction  │                    │ • Which product has     │
│  takes place)           │                    │   been sold             │
│ • Currency              │                    │ • Who has bought the    │
│ • Inflation             │                    │   product               │
└─────────────────────────┘                    └─────────────────────────┘
              ↘                                    ↙
                    ┌──────────────────┐
                    │ AN               │
                    │ ACCOUNTING       │
                    │ TRANSACTION      │
                    └──────────────────┘
                              ↑
                    ┌──────────────────────────┐
                    │ FUNCTION                 │
                    │ • Type of transaction    │
                    │   (eg purchase, sale)    │
                    │ • Financial management - │
                    │   cash transaction or    │
                    │   credit                 │
                    └──────────────────────────┘
```

4 Internal and external reports

4.1 Recording information

At the Foundation stage, the basic documentation for an accounting system was covered (eg invoices, credit notes and timesheets) in the course of learning about credit transactions, cash transactions and payroll transactions. This is how an organisation **records information**.

Once information has been recorded in the ledgers, it needs to be **reported.**

4.2 Reporting information

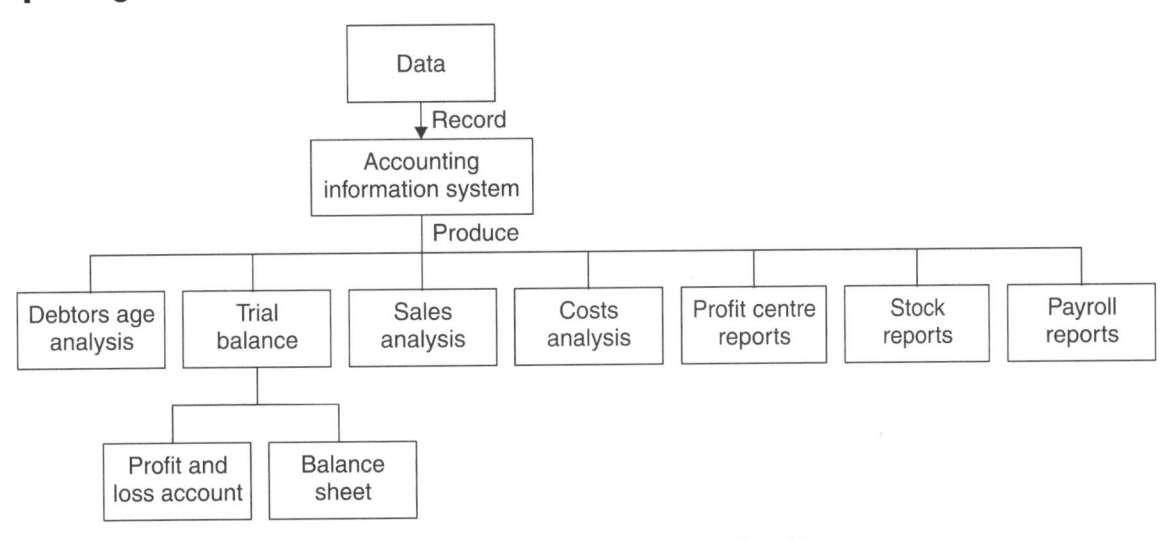

```
                    Data
                     │
                     ↓ Record
          Accounting information system
                     │
                     │ Produce
    ┌────────┬───────┬───────┬───────┬───────┬────────┐
 Debtors   Trial    Sales   Costs   Profit   Stock   Payroll
  age     balance  analysis analysis centre  reports reports
 analysis                           reports
            │
        ┌───┴───┐
     Profit   Balance
     and loss  sheet
     account
```

The basic accounting information is generally **collected**, **summarised**, and **analysed** into reports.

4.2.1 Reports produced by an organisation's accounting information systems

- Debtors age analysis
- Trial balance
- Balance sheet
- Profit and loss account
- Payroll summary

You have probably come across most of these reports either at work or in your Unit 5: **Maintaining Financial Information and Preparing Accounts** studies.

4.2.2 Reports for external agencies

There are also a number of reports which must be prepared for **external agencies**

- PAYE/National Insurance returns for the **Inland Revenue**
- VAT returns to HM **Customs and Excise**
- Limited companies must prepare **financial statements** for submission to shareholders
- Cash flow statements to **banks** or **building societies**

The requirements of these reports can sometimes be quite onerous, especially as the consequences for filling them in wrongly can be severe. (For example, there are heavy penalties for errors in VAT returns.)

If these reporting requirements are complex, it is unlikely that they will be built into the accounting system. **Information of a non-accounting nature** is often required to complete the report.

The problems of reporting to external agencies can be summarised as follows.

- **Identifying the data** as it falls from the transaction itself into the accounting system
- **Tagging the data** as it flows round the accounting system
- **Pulling this data** out of the accounting system, with other data of the same type
- **Aggregating, analysing** and **rearranging the data** in a format suitable for the report

Accounting systems which take into account these external reporting requirements when information is collected are very advantageous.

4.3 Designing an accounting system

When an accounting system is designed, a number of the following options might be taken.

- **Ledger accounts** can be set up for those assets, liabilities and items of income and expenditure which need to be reported.

- **Memorandum accounts** can be established to record this information specifically (for example, the memorandum sales ledger details individual debtor accounts).

- An **appropriate coding system** can be devised, especially in a computerised system, so that the relevant data can be easily extracted from the accounting records.

13: THE ORGANISATION, ACCOUNTING AND REPORTING

Key learning points

- ☑ The many different kinds of organisation may be classified as follows.
    - By type of activity
    - By size of business
    - Profit orientated or non-profit orientated
    - Legal status and ownership

- ☑ Large organisations are headed by a **person** or **committee** who is responsible for the **direction** that an organisation takes. This responsibility might lie with one of the following.
    - Chief Executive
    - Managing Director
    - Board of directors
    - Executive committee

- ☑ Organisations may be structured **geographically**, on a **product-divisional basis**, on a **functional basis**, or on a **matrix basis**.

- ☑ An organisation's accounting systems are affected by the following factors.
    - The size of the business
    - The type of organisation
    - The organisation structure

- ☑ The accounting procedures of an organisation will be specifically affected by geography in the following ways.
    - Different currencies
    - Different legal and accounting requirements
    - Different ways of doing business
    - Political, economic, social and technological factors

- ☑ The following main business functions may be identified within an organisation.
    - Sales and marketing
    - Production
    - Finance and administration

- ☑ Accounting activities in an organisation relate to both the **recording** of information and the **reporting** of information.

- ☑ Reports may be **internal** or **external**.

- ☑ When completing skills based assessments, always make sure that you think about your own organisation and its accounting and reporting systems. Any day-to-day experience that you are able to draw upon will be invaluable.

Quick quiz

1. How are sole traders, partnerships and limited companies distinguished from each other?
2. List eight functions of the sales and marketing department.
3. List four reports which are produced by an organisation's accounting information system.
4. What are the main returns submitted to the following external agencies.

    (a) Inland Revenue
    (b) HM Customs & Excise
    (c) Shareholders

5. What report might a bank wish to see on a regular basis if a business has borrowed a significant amount of money from the bank? Why?
6. What are the main problems associated with reporting to external agencies?

Answers to quick quiz

1. In the eyes of the law: the business affairs of sole traders are not distinguished from their personal affairs; partners in a partnership are personally liable for the debts of a business; and a limited company is a separate legal personality.

2.
    (a) Sales order processing
    (b) Distribution
    (c) Invoicing
    (d) Credit control
    (e) Debtor management
    (f) Market research
    (g) Advertising
    (h) Public relations

3.
    (a) Debtors age analysis
    (b) Balance sheet
    (c) Profit and loss account
    (d) Payroll summary

4.
    (a) PAYE/NI deductions
    (b) Value Added Tax
    (c) Financial statements (annual)

5. Cash flow statements – in order to see proof that the business is generating enough cash to repay the interest on its loan.

6.
    (a) Identifying the data in the first place
    (b) Tagging the data as it flows round the accounting system
    (c) Pulling the data out of the accounting system
    (d) Aggregating, analysing and rearranging the data in a format suitable for the report

chapter 14

Business and accounting information

Contents

1. Introduction
2. Business information
3. Accountants as information providers
4. Management information systems
5. The qualities of accounting information

Knowledge and understanding

3   Main types of outside organisations requiring reports and returns: regulatory; grant awarding; information collecting; trade associations

1 Introduction

In Chapter 13 we had a look at the following areas.

- Organisations and their structure
- Accounting practices in different parts of the organisation
- Internal and external reports

In this chapter we are going to look at **Business and accounting information**, and in particular

- What information is
- Qualities of good information
- Financial accounting and management accounting information
- Qualities of accounting information

The main thing to remember about using **business information** to prepare **internal** or **external reports** is that the information must be **relevant**.

2 Business information

2.1 Identifying the information you need

When you are preparing reports internally for your organisation or externally for outside agencies, you need to **identify the information which is relevant** to what you are doing.

The ways in which information is **presented** and the ways people **select** information can have important implications for which pieces of information they use.

For example, the information that you need in order to be competent in Unit 7 is contained in this Interactive Text. It is up to you how you use the information.

2.2 The purpose of the information

You need to be sure of the **purpose** to which the information will be put. The purpose of the information contained in this Interactive Text is to enable you to gain competence in **Preparing Reports and Returns**.

2.2.1 Internal reports

Your manager or supervisor may be required to make **reports and returns of various kinds**. Some reports and returns may be required by parts of the organisation for which your manager works. The chief purpose of these **internal reports** and returns is **to help in making business decisions**.

2.2.2 External reports

Other reports and returns are required by **external agencies** or **organisations**. VAT returns are an example which we have already mentioned. **Grant application forms** are another example.

From the point of view of you and your manager or supervisor, the purpose of **collecting** together and **presenting** the information needed by the external organisations is mainly to **comply with the requirements of that organisation, with regulations or with the law**.

2.3 Information and data

Information means 'telling' it also means 'what is told' – items of knowledge, news or whatever.

Data are the raw materials (facts, figures etc) which become **information**, when they are processed so as to have meaning for the person who receives them, leading to action or a decision of some kind.

2.3.1 Processing data

The processing of data may involve the following.

- Classifying
- Selecting
- Sorting
- Analysing
- Calculating
- Communicating

For example, train departure times are **data**: a schedule which groups those times according to destination and lists them in order of departure is **information** for a potential passenger on one of the trains.

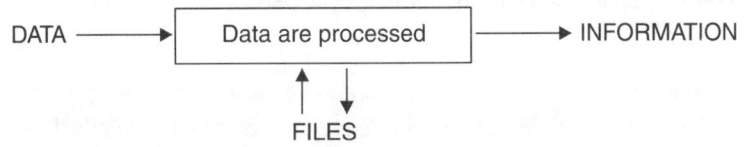

```
DATA  ──────▶  Data are processed  ──────▶  INFORMATION
                      ▲   ▼
                     FILES
```
(Files are used to provide data for processing and to store data/information after processing)

2.4 Characteristics of good information

Whether information is quantitative or qualitative, it should have the following characteristics.

- It should be **relevant** for its purpose.
- It should be **complete** for its purpose.
- It should be sufficiently **accurate** for its purpose.
- It should be **clear** to the user.
- The user should have **confidence** in it.

- It should be **communicated** to the right person.
- It should not be excessive – its **volume** should be manageable.
- It should be **timely** – ie communicated at the most appropriate time.
- It should be communicated by an appropriate **channel** of communication.
- It should be provided at a **cost** which is less than the value of its benefits.

2.5 Business information

Business information is any information which relates to the organisation and activities of one or more businesses.

The above definition includes the following.

- Information about 'business' in general.
- Information generated by and about each organisation.

2.5.1 Demand for information

There is a **constant demand** for information within an organisation, and also from outside. **Internal demand** comes from every member of the organisation.

The main types of information required in preparing **periodic performance reports** for management are information about **past trends** and **current operations** and information about **performance**.

2.5.2 Quantity and quality of financial information

The **quantity** and **quality** of financial information provided to managers depend on their level in the organisation's structure.

- **Strategic information** is needed by **senior managers** who are involved in setting objectives for the organisation as a whole.
- **Tactical information** will be needed by **middle managers** who are looking to ensure that the organisation's existing resources and structure are used efficiently and effectively.
- **Operational information. 'Front-line' managers** such as works supervisors and shift managers require information on the day-to-day operations of the organisation.

The main types of external organisation requiring reports and returns are as follows.

- Information collecting agencies
- Regulatory bodies
- Grant awarding agencies

2.5.3 Internal sources of business information

A lot of data is gathered by an organisation in the course of its business. It will appear on the various documents used by the organisation such as the following.

- Invoices
- Orders
- Delivery notes
- Job cards

This gathering of data involves **formal systems** for collecting and measuring data. Procedures must therefore be established for the following.

- What data is collected
- How frequently data is collected
- Who collects the data
- How the data is collected
- How the data is processed/filed/communicated as information

There will also be methods of **informal communication** between managers and staff (by word-of-mouth, at meetings, by telephone).

2.5.4 External sources of business information

If information is obtained from outside the organisation the following individuals might be involved.

- The tax or legal expert
- The market research manager
- The secretary who has to make travel arrangements

It might also be **informal.**

Informal gathering of information from outside sources goes on all the time because the employees of an organisation learn what is going on in the world around them – from **newspapers**, **television**, **experience** or **other people**. Organisations can also 'tap into' data banks compiled by other organisations for example the Office for National Statistics or the DTI (Department of trade and Industry).

Various publications can be helpful in identifying trends and setting standards for example, **trade journals** and **magazines**.

Alternatively, a business can employ a **research organisation** such as MORI or Gallup to carry out an investigation into market trends or other matters of interest.

The **Internet** is now a very useful source of information as well. We will look in detail at other sources of statistical information in Chapter 15.

3 Accountants as information providers

3.1 Financial accounting

Financial accounting consists of a mixture of **keeping data records** and **providing information**. The functions of the financial accountant include **communicating information**.

Financial accounting is also concerned with operational matters.

- Receiving and paying cash
- Borrowing and repaying loans
- Granting credit to customers
- Chasing late payers in the debt collection process

Financial accounting is largely a process of keeping data records and providing information.

3.2 Cost and management accounting

Cost and management accounting is concerned entirely with providing information in the form of periodic performance reports or special 'one-off' reports.

Examples of cost and management accounting information are as follows.

- Information about product costs and profitability
- Information about departmental costs and profitability
- Cost information to help with pricing decisions
- Budgets and standard costs
- Actual performance and variances between actual and budget
- Information to help with the evaluation of one-off decisions

3.3 Communication

Management accountants communicate mainly with **other managers**. Financial accountants provide information about the organisation to the **'outside world'**. Users of accounting information who are not part of the organisation's management are as follows.

- Equity investors (ie shareholders)
- Loan creditors (such as debenture holders, banks)
- Employees
- Financial analysts and advisers
- Business contacts – notably customers and trade creditors and suppliers
- Government
- The general public

4 Management information systems

4.1 Users of accounting information

Among the users of information are other managers, who need **tactical information** to help them to plan and control the resources of the organisation in the most **effective** and **efficient** way, so that an organisation can achieve its **objectives**.

4.2 Information systems

A **management information system (MIS)** is a collective term for the hardware and software used to drive a database system with the outputs, both to screen and print, being designed to provide easily assimilated information for management.

The accountant provides information to others, in **reports** and **statements**, and **communication**, of course, is the process of providing information to others.

There are several large, distinct management information systems within an organisation. These are as follows.

- The **financial information system**, with which we are mainly concerned in this Interactive Text
- The **logistics information system** (concerned with the physical flow of goods through production and to the customer)
- The **personnel information system** (concerned with employees and employee records)

Accounting information is used by managers throughout an organisation, and accountants are important providers of management information. **An organisation's accounting systems are therefore at the core of its MIS.**

4.3 Communicating information

Information can be communicated in the following ways.

- Visually
- Verbally
- Electronically (by computer system)

It may be helpful to think of a **formal accounting information system** as taking the form of a series of **reports** and **accounting statements** such as the following.

- Cost statements
- Product profit statements
- Budgets
- Standard cost statements
- Operating statements, comparing actual results against budget
- Forecast profit and cost statements
- Job cost estimates

4.3.1 Annual report and accounts

Financial accounting information is extracted from the financial accounting records, and results (for companies) are published in the **annual report and accounts**, which is produced for shareholders. In the case of large companies, a copy of the report and accounts must be filed with the **Registrar of Companies**, and so the financial accounting information is made available to a wider public.

Some **external information** user groups, such as the **Inland Revenue** and banks as lenders, have access to more detailed information about business organisations than that provided in the annual report and accounts prepared by the financial accountant.

Some companies provide reports for the benefit of employees. These **employee reports** are often a simplified version of the **annual report and accounts** and expressed in terms that all employees can understand. They are designed to show employees how well or how badly the organisation has been performing.

5 The qualities of accounting information

5.1 The quality of information

For accounting reports to have value, **they must act as a spur to management**. Managers should take planning or control decisions to earn favourable reports (or avoid bad ones). When significant adverse reports occur, managers must investigate them with a view to **taking control action**.

Reports will not provide an impetus for management action unless the information contained in them possesses **certain qualities**. We discussed qualities of good information in general earlier in this chapter. These qualities or attributes are explained with particular reference to accounting information in the following paragraphs.

5.2 The quality of communication

The quality of communication is important because of the following reasons.

- People need to know what is expected of them
- People need to know how they are doing

Good quality information about targets and plans, and reliable feedback of actual results, are essential for this planning and control cycle to work properly.

5.3 The Corporate Report

The Corporate Report is a publication which argued that companies do not provide enough information about themselves. It listed the following desirable qualities of accounting reports.

- Relevant
- Understandable
- Reliable
- Complete
- Objective
- Timely
- Comparable

These qualities are appropriate both to **internal** and **external information**.

5.3.1 Objective

Accounting reports should be **objective**. For example, a variance statement will indicate differences between actual costs and budgeted costs, and any variances that exceed a certain amount (eg 10% of budget). However, managers responsible for planning or control decisions must decide whether these reported variances are too high or not.

5.3.2 Comparable

Accounting information, especially information about return on investment, costs and profits, should enable users to make **suitable comparisons**.

- Comparing actual costs against budget
- Comparing actual return on capital employed (ROCE) against target
- Comparing the actual return from an investment against the forecast
- Comparing one company's profits and earnings per share against another's

For information to provide **comparability**, it ought to be prepared on a consistent basis – this is one of the reasons for having Accounting Standards. Return on capital employed (ROCE) is a performance measure to which we shall return to later on in this Interactive Text.

Key learning points

- ☑ The demand for business information comes from **within the organisation**, from **external organisations** and from **individuals** on a personal level.

- ☑ In a business environment, reports and returns may need to be presented to other parts of the organisation or to external organisations. We need to **identify**, **collate** and **present** the information in a way which best fits the purpose of the report or return.

- ☑ When preparing both internal and external reports, you must identify the **relevant information**.

- ☑ **Information** means 'telling' or 'what is told'.

- ☑ **Data** are the raw materials which become information when they are processed.

- ☑ Good information has the following qualities.

  - Relevance
  - Completeness
  - Accuracy
  - Clarity
  - Confidence
  - Communication
  - Appropriate volume
  - Timeliness
  - Channel of communication
  - Cost less than value of information

- ☑ Business information sources may be **internal** or **external**.

- ☑ **Financial accounting** is largely a process of keeping data records and providing information. **Cost and management accounting** is concerned entirely with providing information in the form of periodic performance reports or special 'one-off' reports.

- ☑ A **management information system (MIS)** is a collective term for the hardware and software used to drive a database system with the outputs, both to screen and print, being designed to provide easily assimilated information for management.

- ☑ The purpose of **financial accounting information** is to help external users to assess management performance and the prospects of the organisation.

- ☑ In an assessment, be prepared to compare the results of one organisation with those of another organisation in the same industry. Alternatively, you may be asked to extract accounting information (such as gross profit, net profit, current assets, current liabilities and so on) and use it to complete an **interfirm comparison form**. Such a form may include information relating to the industry best or industry average – all that you need to do is insert the relevant information into the appropriate space.

Quick quiz

1. What tasks might be involved in the processing of data?
2. What are the main types of financial information provided to managers?
3. Who are the main users of accounting information who are not part of the organisation's management?
4. What are the main distinct management information systems within an organisation?
5. How might information be communicated?
6. For whom is the annual report and accounts of an organisation produced?
7. One of the desirable characteristics of accounting reports is that they must be comparable. Give four examples of suitable comparisons.

Answers to quick quiz

1. Classifying, selecting, sorting, analysing, calculating and communicating.

2. (a) Strategic
   (b) Tactical
   (c) Operational

3. (a) Shareholders
   (b) Loan creditors
   (c) Employees
   (d) Customers
   (e) Government
   (f) General public

4. Financial, logistics and personnel information systems.

5. Visually, verbally or electronically.

6. Primarily for the shareholders of the company.

7. - Actual cost against budget
   - Actual return on capital employed (ROCE) against target, (or last year's ROCE)
   - Forecast return from an investment against the target
   - Profits of one company against the profits of another

chapter 15

Statistical information

Contents

1. Introduction
2. Using statistics
3. Populations and types of data
4. Sources of statistical data
5. Government statistical publications in the UK

Knowledge and understanding

1. Main sources of relevant government statistics

1 Introduction

We are going to start this chapter by thinking about what the term **statistics** means.

Statistics or quantitative data is the name given to data in the form of figures.

In a business environment, all sorts of **quantitative data** may be available to a manager or supervisor, for example on production levels, costs or sales.

On their own, the numbers are unlikely to mean very much. How can a manager make sense of the numbers? This depends partly on the purpose for which the information is needed.

The word **'statistics'** covers the following.

- Collecting data
- Presenting the data in a useful form
- Interpreting the data

Knowledge of statistical techniques is important to you not just because you can use these techniques to **present** information in reports and returns. It is also important because you will often need to **interpret** information which uses statistical techniques.

2 Using statistics

Statistics should be compiled only if they have a **purpose**. If they are not going to be used for anything, then there is no point in having them.

- The **purpose** of having particular statistics ought to be established.
- A **statistical measure** should be selected which achieves this purpose.

Example: Using statistics

Can you identify the errors in the following statements?

(a) 30% of students taking accountancy examinations pass. 60% of law students pass solicitors' examinations. Clearly, there are more qualified solicitors than qualified accountants.

(b) 30,000 French citizens can speak Russian, and 60,000 Russians can speak French. Clearly, French is more widely spoken in Russia than Russian in France.

Solution

(a) This statement shows how percentages without actual total figures can be misleading. If 10,000 accountancy students take examinations each year and just 2,000 law students take solicitors' examinations, the actual numbers becoming qualified each year would be 3,000 accountants and 1,200 lawyers: more accountants than lawyers, not the other way round.

(b) This statement shows how total figures without averages or percentages can be misleading. If the 30,000 French citizens speaking Russian come from a population of 50,000,000, whereas the 60,000 Russians speaking French come from a population of 200,000,000 we could argue that since a **larger proportion** of French citizens speak Russian than Russians speak French, Russian is more widely spoken in France than French in Russia.

Activity 15.1

Comment on the following statements.

(a) Sales of footwear are up on last year, but not as much as clothing.
(b) Turnover of company X has increased by 150% in the past two years.

3 Populations and types of data

3.1 Defining the population

A **statistical survey** is a survey which involves collecting statistics to help answer a question.

Consider a cat food manufacturer who wants to find out what proportion of cat owners use his particular brand. You might think that the first step to take in conducting such a survey is to **collect data,** that is, to ask people what they feed their cats.

There are quite a few things to think about before asking people what they feed their cats, otherwise a survey can go wrong from the start. If a survey does start off on the wrong track, the data subsequently collected and the conclusions subsequently drawn will be **useless**.

Example: Defining the population

A famous example of this occurred years ago in the United States, when an organisation was asked to conduct an **opinion poll** (which is a form of statistical survey) on whether the next president was likely to be Democrat or Republican.

The survey was carried out, but in the wrong way. The surveyors **telephoned** people, and far more Republicans than Democrats had telephones. The survey was useless, because it **had not been planned properly**.

The reason why the opinion poll turned out so badly, was that the **population** for the survey had not been defined properly. The opinion poll should have used the population 'all Americans of voting age', whereas it actually used the population 'all Americans with a telephone'.

Similarly, in the cat food example, the **population** is 'all people who look after cats', not 'all people who feed their cats tinned food'. (This population will be too small, as some cats are fed fresh or dried food.)

In statistics, the word **population** refers to the entire collection of items being considered.

3.2 Attributes and variables

The data gathered for a particular purpose may be of several types. The first major distinction is between **attributes** and **variables**.

- An **attribute** is something an object has either got or not got. It cannot be measured.
- A **variable** is something which can be measured.

Example: Attributes and variables

For example, an individual is either male or female. There is no measure of **how** male or **how** female somebody is: the sex of a person is an **attribute**. The height of a person can be measured according to some scale (such as centimetres), the height of a person is therefore a **variable**.

3.3 Discrete and continuous variables

Variables can be further classified as **discrete** or **continuous**.

- **Discrete variables** are variables which can only take specific values. The range of possible values is split into a series of steps. For example, the number of goals scored by a football team may be 0, 1, 2 or 3 but it cannot be 1.2 or 2.1.
- **Continuous variables** are variables which may take on any value. They are measured rather than counted. For example, it may be considered sufficient to measure the heights of a number of people to the nearest cm but there is no reason why the measurements should not be made to the nearest 0.001 cm.

Activity 15.2

Look through the following list of surveys and decide whether each is collecting data on **attributes**, **discrete variables** or **continuous variables**.

(a) A survey of statistics text books, to determine how many diagrams they contain.
(b) A survey of cans on a supermarket shelf, to determine whether or not each has a price sticker on it.
(c) A survey of athletes, to find out how long they take to run a mile.
(d) A survey of the results of an examination, to determine what percentage marks the students obtained.
(e) A survey of the heights of telegraph poles in England, to find out if there is any variation across the country.

3.4 Primary data and secondary data

The data used in a statistical survey, whether variables or attributes, can be either **primary data** or **secondary data**.

- **Primary data** are data collected especially for the purpose of whatever survey is being conducted. **Raw data** are primary data which have not been processed at all, but are still just (for example) a list of numbers.
- **Secondary data** are data which have already been collected elsewhere, for some other purpose, but which can be used or adapted for the survey being conducted.

3.4.1 Advantages of using primary data

Advantages of using primary data include the following.

- The investigator knows where the data came from
- The investigator knows the circumstances under which the data were collected
- The investigator knows any limitations in the data

3.4.2 Disadvantages of using secondary data

Disadvantages of secondary data include the following.

- The investigator may not know of any limitations in the data
- The data may not be entirely suitable for the purpose they are being used for

Secondary data are sometimes used despite their inadequacies, simply because they are **available cheaply**, whereas the extra cost of collecting primary data would far outweigh their extra value.

4 Sources of statistical data

4.1 Primary data

Primary data have to be gathered from a **source**. Methods of collecting primary data include the following.

- Personal investigation
- Teams of investigators
- Questionnaires

4.1.1 Personal investigation

Personal investigation involves the investigator collecting all the data himself, for example by interviewing people.

4.1.2 Disadvantages of personal investigation

This method of collecting data has the following **disadvantages**.

- It is time consuming
- It is expensive
- It is limited to the amount of data a single person can collect

4.1.3 Advantages of personal investigation

Personal investigation has the **advantage** that the data collected are likely to be **accurate** and **complete**, because the investigator knows exactly what he wants and how to get it. He is not relying on other people to do the survey work.

4.1.4 Teams of investigators

A survey could be carried out by a **team of investigators** who collect data separately and then pool their results.

A team of investigators can cover a larger field than a single investigator but will still be **expensive**. The members of the team must be carefully briefed to ensure that the data they collect are **satisfactory**. This method is sometimes called **delegated personal investigation**.

4.1.5 Questionnaires

With a **questionnaire**, the questions which need to be answered for the survey are listed and are either sent to a number of people (so that they can fill in their answers and send the questionnaires back) or used by investigators to interview people (perhaps by approaching people in the street and asking them the questions).

4.2 Secondary data

Secondary data are data that were originally collected as primary data for one purpose, or for general use, but are now being used for another purpose.

For example, the government collects data to help with making decisions about running the country, and makes these data available to the public.

Examples of secondary data are as follows.

- Published statistics
- Historical records

4.2.1 Published statistics

For example, the UK Government publishes statistics through the Office for National Statistics (ONS). The European Union and the United Nations also publish statistics. So do various newspapers and accountancy bodies.

4.2.2 Historical records

The type of historical record used for a survey obviously depends on what survey is being carried out. An accountant producing an estimate of future company sales might use historical records of past sales.

4.3 Sources of published statistics

The range of published economic, business and accounting data is very wide. The **main sources** of **relevant government statistics** form a part of the knowledge and understanding which you are expected to have for Unit 7.

All published statistics are a source of **secondary data**. Care must be taken in using them, since they may not be obtained or classified in precisely the same way as primary data which is collected **specifically** for the purpose of a statistical survey.

Despite the general shortcomings of secondary data, there are many circumstances in which published statistics can be of great value.

4.4 The Office for National Statistics and other bodies

In April 1996 the Office for National Statistics (ONS) was set up, as the **independent government agency** responsible for compiling, analysing and disseminating many of the UK's economic, social and demographic statistics.

The ONS is responsible to the Chancellor of the Exchequer and we shall be looking at it in more detail in the next section of this chapter.

The **European Union** (formerly the European Community) has a Statistical Office which gathers statistics from each of the member countries. This produces several statistical publications, including *Basic Statistics of the Community*.

The **United Nations** also publishes some statistics on the world economy (for example the *Statistical Yearbook*), and a *Yearbook of Labour Statistics* is published by the International Labour Organisation.

5 Government statistical publications in the UK

5.1 Governments

In the United Kingdom, official statistics supplied by the **Office for National Statistics** include the following.

- The *Annual Abstract of Statistics*
- The *Monthly Digest*
- *Financial Statistics*
- *Economic Trends* and *Regional Trends*
- The *United Kingdom National Accounts* (The *Blue Book*)
- The *United Kingdom Balance of Payments* (The *Pink Book*)
- *Social Trends*

5.1.1 The Annual Abstract of Statistics

This is a general reference book for the United Kingdom which includes data on climate, population, social services, justice and crime, education, defence, manufacturing and agricultural production.

The *Monthly Digest* is an **abbreviated version** of the *Annual Abstract of Statistics*.

5.1.2 Financial Statistics

This is a monthly compilation of financial data. It includes statistics on Government income, expenditure and borrowing, financial institutions, companies, the overseas sector, the money supply, exchange rates, interest rates and share prices.

5.1.3 Economic Trends and Regional Trends

These publications **indicate trends** using tables, maps and charts.

5.1.4 The United Kingdom National Accounts (The Blue Book)

This is an essential source of data on the following.

- Gross national product
- Gross national income
- Gross national expenditure

This publication gives a clear indication of how the nation makes and spends its money.

5.1.5 The United Kingdom Balance of Payments (The Pink Book)

This is an annual publication which gives data on the inflows and outflows of private capital in the United Kingdom.

5.1.6 Social Trends

This is an annual publication which provides data on the population, income, householders, families and many other aspects of British life and work.

5.2 Government departments

Monthly statistics are also published by many government departments.

5.2.1 The Department of Employment Gazette

For example, the Department of Employment in Britain publishes *The Department of Employment Gazette* which gives details on statistics relating to employment, including the following.

- Retail prices
- Employment
- Unemployment
- Unfilled job vacancies

We shall be looking at retail prices in more detail when we study changing price levels in Chapter 19.

5.2.2 British business

The Department of Trade and Industry in Britain publishes *British Business* on a weekly basis. It includes data on production, prices and trade.

5.2.3 Population data

Population data is also published by many governments and includes data such as the following.

- Population numbers
- Births
- Deaths
- Marriages

In Britain, the government carries out a full **census** of the whole population every ten years, the results of which are published.

5.2.4 The Bank of England Quarterly Bulletin

The *Bank of England Quarterly Bulletin* is a quarterly bulletin which includes data on the following.

- Banks in the UK
- The money supply
- Government borrowing and financial transactions.

Activity 15.3

Identify which of the following are secondary data sources.

I   *Economic Trends* (published by the Office for National Statistics).
II   The *Monthly Digest of Statistics* (published by the Office for National Statistics).
III Data collected for an attitude survey by means of personal interviews.
IV   Historical records of sales revenues to be used to prepare current forecasts.

A   I and II only
B   I, II and III only
C   I, II and IV only
D   I, II, III and IV

Activity 15.4

The *Annual Abstract of Statistics* includes long-term analyses of statistics for which more detailed analyses are available elsewhere.

In which publications would you find detailed short-term statistics covering the following?

(a) The level of unemployment.

(b) Trends in road transport.

(c) UK imports and exports.

(d) Geographical distribution of the resident population.

Key learning points

- ☑ **Statistics** is the name given to data in the form of figures, and covers the following.
    - Collecting data
    - Presenting data in a useful form
    - Interpreting the data

- ☑ A **statistical survey** is a survey which involves collecting statistics in order to answer a question.

- ☑ In statistics, the word **population** refers to the entire collection of items being considered.

- ☑ An **attribute** is something an object has either got or not got – it cannot be measured. A **variable** is something which can be measured, and may be either **discrete** (ie it can only take specific values) or **continuous** (ie it may take on any value).

- ☑ Data may be either **primary** (collected specifically for the purpose) or **secondary** (collected elsewhere for some other purpose).

- ☑ Primary data may be collected as follows.
    - Personal investigation
    - Teams of investigators
    - Questionnaires

- ☑ All **published statistics** are a source of secondary data. Examples include the following.
    - The *Monthly Digest*
    - The *Annual Abstract of Statistics*
    - *Economic Trends*
    - *Financial Statistics*
    - The *Department of Employment Gazette*
    - The *Bank of England Quarterly Bulletin*

- ☑ **Accuracy is more important than speed.** Make sure that you do not rush through the tasks to be completed in your assessment – take time to read through the instructions and the situation carefully before you make a start on the tasks. You will then have a better chance of completing your assessment as accurately as possible.

UNIT 7 PREPARING REPORTS AND RETURNS

Quick quiz

1   What does statistics cover?

2   Are the following discrete or continuous variables? (Tick as appropriate)

		Discrete	Continuous
(a)	The number of cars in a family		
(b)	The height of pupils in a class		
(c)	The temperature on Easter day last year		
(d)	The number of pupils in a class		

3   What is the main advantage of using primary data?

4   Why are secondary data sometimes used instead of collecting primary data?

5   Who are the main publishers of secondary data?

6   Where might you find information about wage rates in Britain?

    A   *Economic Trends*
    B   The *Department of Employment Gazette*
    C   *Financial Statistics*
    D   *Wage Rates Weekly*

Answer to quick quiz

1   **Collecting** data, **presenting** them in a useful form and **interpreting** them.

2

		Discrete	Continuous
(a)	The number of cars in a family	✓	
(b)	The height of pupils in a class		✓
(c)	The temperature on Easter day last year		✓
(d)	The number of pupils in a class	✓	

3   The collector knows where the data came from, the circumstances under which they were collected and any limitations or inadequacies in the data.

4   Because they are available cheaply.

5 (a) The UK Government (Office for National Statistics)
  (b) The European Union
  (c) The United Nations
  (d) The Department of Education and Employment
  (e) The Bank of England

6 B The *Department of Employment Gazette* (published by the Office for National Statistics) contains information about wage rates in Britain.

Activity checklist

This checklist shows which performance criteria, range statement or knowledge and understanding point is covered by each activity in this chapter. Tick off each activity as you complete it.

Activity

15.1 ☐ This activity deals with Knowledge and Understanding point 1 regarding the main sources of relevant government statistics

15.2 ☐ This activity deals with Knowledge and Understanding point 1 regarding the main sources of relevant government statistics

15.3 ☐ This activity deals with Knowledge and Understanding point 1 regarding the main sources of relevant government statistics

15.4 ☐ This activity deals with Knowledge and Understanding point 1 regarding the main sources of relevant government statistics

chapter 16

Presenting information: tables and charts

Contents

1 Introduction
2 Tables
3 Frequency distributions
4 Charts
5 Pie charts
6 Bar charts
7 Histograms
8 Frequency polygons

Knowledge and understanding

13 Tabulation of accounting and other quantitative information using spreadsheets
14 Methods of presenting information: written reports; diagrammatic; tabular

1 Introduction

In Chapter 15, we looked at **statistical information** including **populations** and **types of data** and **sources of statistical data.**

Once we have collected our data, what do we do with it? It is likely that we will want to **present** the data in a form which will allow us to understand it more easily.

In this chapter, we are going to be looking at the different ways of presenting data using the following.

- Tables
- Charts

Let's begin by looking at one of the most basic ways of summarising data, the preparation of a **table**.

2 Tables

2.1 Tabulation

Raw data (for example, the list of results from a survey, or a list of accounting balances) need to be summarised and analysed, to give them meaning. **Tabulation** of data summarises and analyses data to give them meaning.

Tabulation means putting data into tables. A table is a matrix of data in rows and columns, with the rows and the columns having titles.

Since a table is **two-dimensional**, it can only show two variables.

Example: Table

Resources for production

	Product items				
	Alpha	*Beta*	*Gamma*	*Delta*	*Total*
	£	£	£	£	£
Resources					
Direct material Alpha	X	X	X	X	X
Direct material Beta	X	X	X	X	X
Direct labour grade skilled	X	X	X	X	X
Direct labour grade semi-skilled	X	X	X	X	X
Supervision	X	X	X	X	X
Machine time	X	X	X	X	X
Total	X	X	X	X	X

You need to recognise what the **two dimensions** should represent before you can tabulate data. Start by preparing **rows** and **columns** with suitable **titles**, and then insert the data into the appropriate places in the table.

2.2 Guidelines for tabulation

The table in the example above illustrates certain guidelines which you should apply when presenting data in tabular form. These are as follows.

- The table should be given a **clear title**.
- All columns should be **clearly labelled**.
- Where appropriate, there should be **clear sub-totals**.
- A **total column** may be presented (usually the right-hand column).
- A **total figure** is often advisable at the bottom of each column of figures.
- Information presented should be easy to read.

Example: Tabulation of data

The total number of employees in a certain trading company is 1,000. They are employed in three departments: production, administration and sales. 600 people are employed in the production department and 300 in administration. There are 110 males under 21 in employment, 110 females under 21, and 290 females aged 21 years and over. The remaining employees are males aged 21 and over.

In the production department there are 350 males aged 21 and over, 150 females aged 21 and over and 50 males under 21, whilst in the administration department there are 100 males aged 21 and over, 110 females aged 21 and over and 50 males aged under 21.

Draw up a table to show all the details of employment in the company and its departments and provide suitable secondary statistics to describe the distribution of people in departments.

Solution

(a) The **basic table** required has as its two dimensions:

Departments
Age/gender analysis

(b) **Secondary statistics** (not the same thing as secondary data) are supporting figures that are supplementary to the main items of data, and which clarify the main data. A major example of secondary statistics is **percentages**. In this example, we could show either of the following.

 (i) The percentage of the total work force in each department belonging to each age/gender group
 (ii) The percentage of the total of each age/gender group employed in each department

(c) In this example, we have selected (i). Either (i) or (ii) could be suitable, depending on the purposes for which the data are being collected and presented.

(d) **Analysis of employees**

	Department							
	Production		Administration		Sales		Total	
	No	%	No	%	No	%	No	%
Males 21 yrs +	350	58.4	100	33.3	** 40	40.0	* 490	49.0
Females 21 yrs +	150	25.0	110	36.7	** 30	30.0	290	29.0
Subtotals 21 yrs +	500	83.4	210	70.0	70	70.0	780	78.0
Males under 21	* 50	8.3	50	16.7	** 10	10.0	110	11.0
Females under 21	50	8.3	* 40	13.3	** 20	20.0	110	11.0
Subtotals under 21	100	16.6	90	30.0	30	30.0	220	22.0
Total	600	100.0	300	100.0	100	100.0	1,000	100.0

* Balancing figure to make up the column total
** Balancing figure then needed to make up the row total

2.3 Significant digits and decimal places

Sometimes a decimal number has too many digits in it for practical use. This problem can be overcome by **rounding** the decimal number to a **specific number of significant digits** using the following rule.

IF THE FIRST DIGIT TO BE DISCARDED IS GREATER THAN OR EQUAL TO FIVE, THEN ADD ONE TO THE PREVIOUS DIGIT. OTHERWISE THE PREVIOUS DIGIT IS UNCHANGED.

Example: Significant digits

(a) 187.392 correct to five significant digits is 187.39.
Discarding a 2 causes nothing to be added to the 9.

(b) 187.392 correct to four significant digits is 187.4.
Discarding the 9 causes one to be added to the 3.

(c) 187.392 correct to three significant digits is 187.
Discarding a 3 causes nothing to be added to the 7.

You may be asked to make calculations correct to a certain number of **decimal places** and this is also done by applying the rule above.

Example: Decimal places

(a) 49.28723 correct to four decimal places is 49.2872.
Discarding a 3 causes nothing to be added to the 2.

(b) 49.28723 correct to three decimal places is 49.287.
Discarding a 2 causes nothing to be added to the 7.

(c) 49.28723 correct to two decimal places is 49.29.
Discarding the 7 causes one to be added to the 8.

(d) 49.28723 correct to one decimal place is 49.3.
Discarding the 8 causes one to be added to the 2.

(e) 49.28723 correct to two significant digits is 49.
Discarding a 2 causes nothing to be added to the 9.

Activity 16.1

What is £482,365.15 to the nearest:

(i)	£1	
(ii)	£100	
(iii)	£1,000	
(iv)	£10,000	

2.4 Rounding errors

Rounding errors may become apparent when, for example, a percentage column does not add up to 100%. When figures in a table are rounded and then added up, the effect of rounding will depend on the method of rounding used.

To avoid bias, any rounding should be to the **nearest unit** and the potential size of errors should be kept to a tolerable level by rounding to a small enough unit (for example to the nearest £10, rather than to the nearest £1,000).

2.5 Tally marks

Tally marks are another simple way of presenting data. If we measured the number of jobs completed by each employee during one week, the data could be collected and presented as follows.

Employee	Jobs completed	
Lynn	ℍℍ ////	= 9
Fred	ℍℍ ℍℍ ////	= 14
Stuart	ℍℍ //	= 7
Davina	///	= 3

Make sure that you can **present data** in a **tabulated form**, and then **extract** and **interpret** the **key information**.

Activity 16.2

By 2003, Mill Stream Ltd had been in business for ten years. It now employs 20,770 people, of whom the largest group (36%) were sales staff, the next largest group (21%) were buyers and the third largest group (18%) were administrative staff. Other groups of employees made up the rest of the staff.

Things had been very different when the company first began operations in 1994. Then, it had just 4,200 employees, of whom the 1,260 buyers were the biggest group; there were 1,176 sales staff and just 840 administrative staff.

By 1997, the company had nearly doubled in size, employing 7,650 people, of whom 2,448 were buyers, 2,372 were sales staff and 1,607 were administrators.

By 2000, the company employed 12,740 people, and the growth in numbers had been most noticeable amongst sales staff, of whom there were 4,840. There were 3,185 buyers. Administrative staff had increased substantially in number to 2,550.

The company's managing director has been very pleased with the growth in business over the past nine years, but has tried to limit the growth in the numbers of staff who are not sales staff, buyers or administrative staff.

Tasks

Present the given information in tabular form.

3 Frequency distributions

3.1 Frequency distributions

If a large number of measurements of a particular variable is taken (for example the number of units produced per employee per week) some values may occur more than once. A **frequency distribution** is obtained by recording the number of times each value occurs.

Example: Frequency distribution

(a) The output in units of 20 employees during one week was as follows.

65	71	68	70
69	70	69	68
70	69	67	67
72	74	73	69
71	70	71	70

(b) If the number of occurrences is placed against each output quantity, a **frequency distribution** is produced.

Output of employees in one week in units

Output Units	Number of employees (frequency)
65	1
66	0
67	2
68	2
69	4
70	5
71	3
72	1
73	1
74	1
	20

(c) The number of employees corresponding to a particular volume of output is called a **frequency**. When the data are arranged in this way it is immediately obvious that 69 and 70 units are the **most common volumes** of output per employee per week.

3.2 Grouped frequency distributions

It is often convenient to **group frequencies** together into **bands** or **classes**. For example, suppose that the units of output produced by each of 20 employees during one week was as follows.

1,087	850	1,084	792
924	1,226	1,012	1,205
1,265	1,028	1,230	1,182
1,086	1,130	989	1,155
1,134	1,166	1,129	1,160

An **ungrouped frequency distribution** would not be a helpful way of presenting the data, because each employee has produced a different number of units in the week.

The range of output from the lowest to the highest producer is 792 to 1,265, a range of 473 units. This range could be divided into classes of say, 100 units (the **class width** or **class interval**), and the number of employees producing output within each class could then be grouped into a single frequency, as follows.

Output Units	Number of employees (frequency)
700 – 799	1
800 – 899	1
900 – 999	2
1,000 – 1,099	5
1,100 – 1,199	7
1,200 – 1,299	4
	20

3.3 Cumulative frequency distributions

A **cumulative frequency distribution** can be used to show the total number of times that a value above or below a certain amount occurs.

Example: Grouped cumulative frequency distribution

The volume of output produced in one day by each of 20 employees is as follows, in units.

18	29	22	17
30	12	27	24
26	32	24	29
28	46	31	27
19	18	32	25

We could present a grouped frequency distribution as follows.

Output (Units)	Number of employees (frequency)
Under 15	1
15 or more, under 20	4
20 or more, under 25	3
25 or more, under 30	7
30 or more, under 35	4
35 or more	1
	20

The two possible **cumulative frequency distributions** for the same data are as follows.

	Distribution 1			Distribution 2
	Cumulative frequency			Cumulative frequency
≥ 0	20		< 15	1
≥ 15	19		< 20	5
≥ 20	15		< 25	8
≥ 25	12		< 30	15
≥ 30	5		< 35	19
≥ 35	1		< 47	20

3.3.1 Using symbols to state classes

The following symbols provide a convenient way to state classes.

- The symbol > means 'greater than'
- The symbol ≥ means 'greater than, or equal to'
- The symbol < means 'less than'
- The symbol ≤ means 'less than or equal to'.

The first **cumulative frequency distribution** shows that of the total of 20 employees:

- 19 produced 15 units or more
- 15 produced 20 units or more
- 12 produced 25 units or more and so on

The second **cumulative frequency distribution** shows that of the total of 20 employees:

- 1 produced less than 15 units
- 5 produced less than 20 units
- 8 produced less than 25 units and so on

Activity 16.3

The commission earnings for January 20X0 of the salespeople in Mill Stream Ltd were as follows (in pounds).

60	35	53	47	25	44	55	58	47	71
63	67	57	44	61	48	50	56	61	42
43	38	41	39	61	51	27	56	57	50
55	68	55	50	25	48	44	43	49	73
53	35	36	41	45	71	56	40	69	52
36	47	66	52	32	46	44	32	52	58
49	41	45	45	48	36	46	42	52	33
31	36	40	66	53	58	60	52	66	51
51	44	59	53	51	57	35	45	46	54
46	54	51	39	64	43	54	47	60	45

Task

Prepare a grouped frequency distribution classifying the commission earnings into categories of £5 commencing with '£25 and less than £30'.

4 Charts

Instead of presenting data in a table, it might be preferable to provide a visual display in the form of a **chart**.

The purpose of a chart is to convey the data in a way that will demonstrate its meaning or significance more clearly than a table of data would. Charts are not always more appropriate than tables, and the most suitable way of presenting data will depend on the following.

- What the data are intending to show
- Who is going to use the data

Types of chart that might be used to present data include the following.

- Pie charts
- Bar charts
- Histograms

5 Pie charts

A **pie chart** is a chart which is used to show pictorially the relative size of component elements of a total.

It is called a pie chart because it is **circular**, and so has the **shape of a pie** in a round pie dish and because the 'pie' is then cut into slices. Each slice represents a part of the total.

5.1 Drawing pie charts

Pie charts have sectors of varying sizes, and you need to be able to draw sectors fairly accurately. To do this, you need a **protractor**. Working out sector sizes involves converting parts of the total into **equivalent degrees of a circle**. A complete 'pie' = 360°: the number of degrees in a circle = 100% of whatever you are showing. An element which is 50% of your total will therefore occupy a segment of 180°, and so on.

Alternatively, you could use a computer with either **graphics software** or a **spreadsheet** with **graphing capability** (such as **ChartWizard** in Microsoft Excel).

Two pie charts are shown as follows.

Breakdown of air and noise pollution complaints, 1

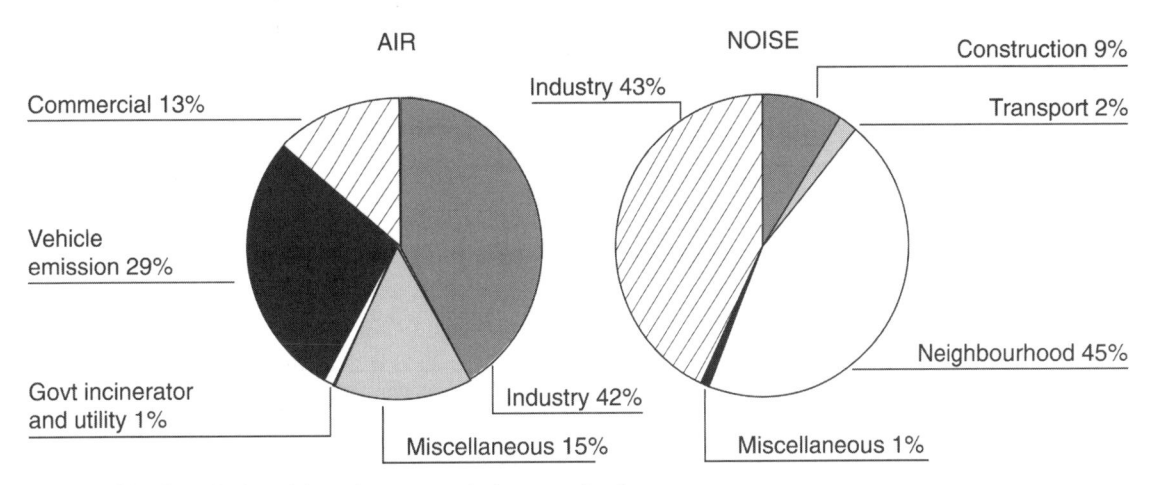

- **Shading** distinguishes the segments from each other.
- **Colour** can be used to distinguish segments also.

Example: Pie charts

The costs of materials at the Cardiff Factory and the Swansea Factory of Mill Stream Ltd during January 20X0 were as follows.

	Cardiff factory		Swansea factory	
	£'000	%	£'000	%
Material W	70	35	50	20
Material A	30	15	125	50
Material L	90	45	50	20
Material E	10	5	25	10
	200	100	250	100

Show the costs for the factories in pie charts.

Solution

To convert the components into degrees of a circle, we can use either the **percentage figures** or the **actual cost figures**.

Using the percentage figures

The total percentage is 100%, and the total number of degrees in a circle is 360°. To convert from one to the other, we multiply each percentage value by 360°/100% = 3.6.

	Cardiff factory		Swansea factory	
	%	Degrees	%	Degrees
Material W	35	126	20	72
Material A	15	54	50	180
Material L	45	162	20	72
Material E	5	18	10	36
	100	360	100	360

Using the actual cost figures

Using this method, we would multiply each cost by the number of degrees and divide by the total cost.

Cardiff factory: $\dfrac{360}{200} = 1.8$

Swansea factory: $\dfrac{360}{250} = 1.44$

	Cardiff factory		Swansea factory	
	£'000	Degrees	£'000	Degrees
Material W	70	126	50	72
Material A	30	54	125	180
Material L	90	162	50	72
Material E	10	18	25	36
	200	360	250	360

A pie chart could be drawn for each factory.

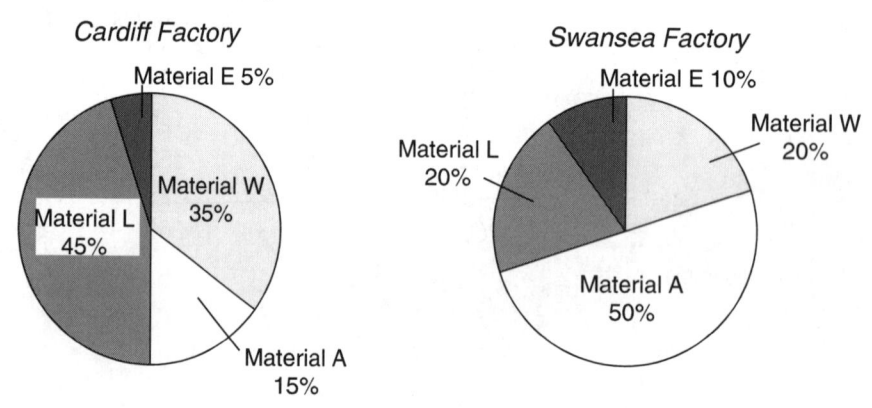

Cardiff Factory
- Material E 5%
- Material W 35%
- Material L 45%
- Material A 15%

Swansea Factory
- Material E 10%
- Material W 20%
- Material L 20%
- Material A 50%

Note:

If the pie chart is drawn manually, a protractor must be used to measure the degrees accurately to obtain the correct sector sizes.

5.2 Using computers

Using a computer makes the process much simpler, especially using a spreadsheet. We explain this process in Chapter 17.

Activity 16.4

The European division of Mill Stream Ltd, has just published its accounts of the year ended 30 June 20X0. The sales director made the following comments.

'Our total sales for the year were £1,751,000, of which £787,000 were made in the United Kingdom, £219,000 in Italy, £285,000 in France and £92,000 in Germany. Sales in Spain and Holland amounted to £189,000 and £34,000 respectively, while the rest of Europe collectively had sales of £145,000 in the twelve months to 30 June 20X0.'

Task

Present the above information in the form of a pie chart. Show all of your workings.

6 Bar charts

The bar chart is one of the most common methods of presenting data in a visual form.

A **bar chart** is a chart in which quantities are shown in the form of bars.

6.1 Types of bar chart

There are a number of types of bar chart.

- Simple bar charts
- Component bar charts, including percentage component bar charts
- Multiple (or compound) bar charts
- Histograms, which are a special type of bar chart

6.2 Simple bar charts

A **simple bar chart** is a chart consisting of one or more bars, in which the length of each bar indicates the magnitude of the corresponding data item.

Example: Simple bar chart

A company's total sales for the years from 20X1 to 20X6 are as follows.

Year	£'000
20X1	800
20X2	1,200
20X3	1,100
20X4	1,400
20X5	1,600
20X6	1,700

The data could be shown on a simple bar chart as follows.

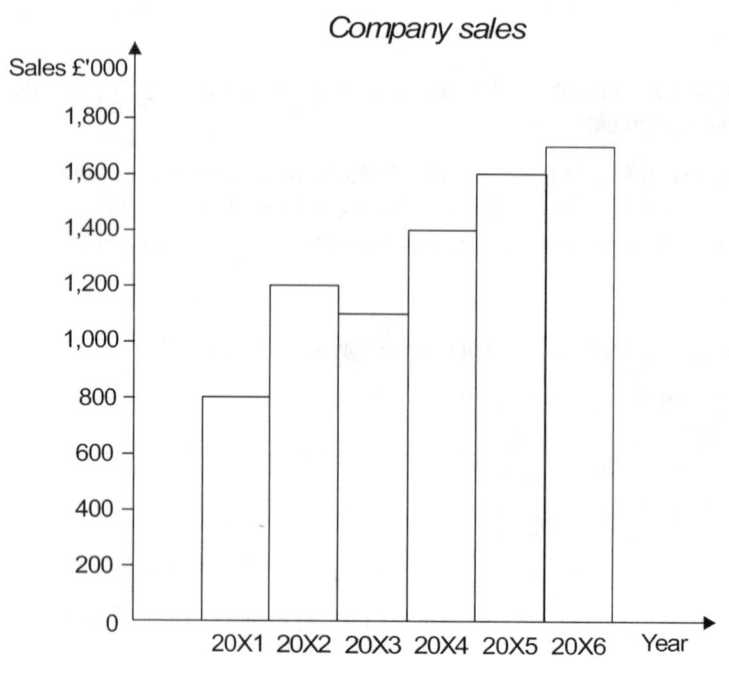

Company sales bar chart: Sales £'000 on y-axis (0 to 1,800), Year on x-axis (20X1 to 20X6). Values approximately: 20X1: 800, 20X2: 1,200, 20X3: 1,100, 20X4: 1,400, 20X5: 1,600, 20X6: 1,700.

- Each axis of the chart must be clearly labelled
- There must be a scale to indicate the magnitude of the data
- Note that the y axis shows the value of the sales

Simple bar charts serve two purposes.

- They show the **actual magnitude** of each item
- By comparing the lengths of bars it is easy to compare magnitudes

Activity 16.5

Luke Skywalker Ltd is preparing its published accounts and the finance director has requested that the turnover of the company be compared in the form of a bar chart for the last five years. The data are contained in the following table.

	1998	1999	2000	2001	2002
	£'000	£'000	£'000	£'000	£'000
Turnover	981	1,020	1,121	1,244	1,306

Tasks

(a) Construct a simple bar chart which represents the given data relating to turnover.
(b) Comment on the turnover for Luke Skywalker Ltd over the five year period.

6.3 Component bar charts

A **component (or multiple or compound) bar chart** is a bar chart that gives a breakdown of each total into its components.

Example: Component bar chart

A component bar chart would show the following.

- How total sales have changed from year to year
- The components of each year's total

Charbart plc's sales for the years from 20X7 to 20X9 are as follows.

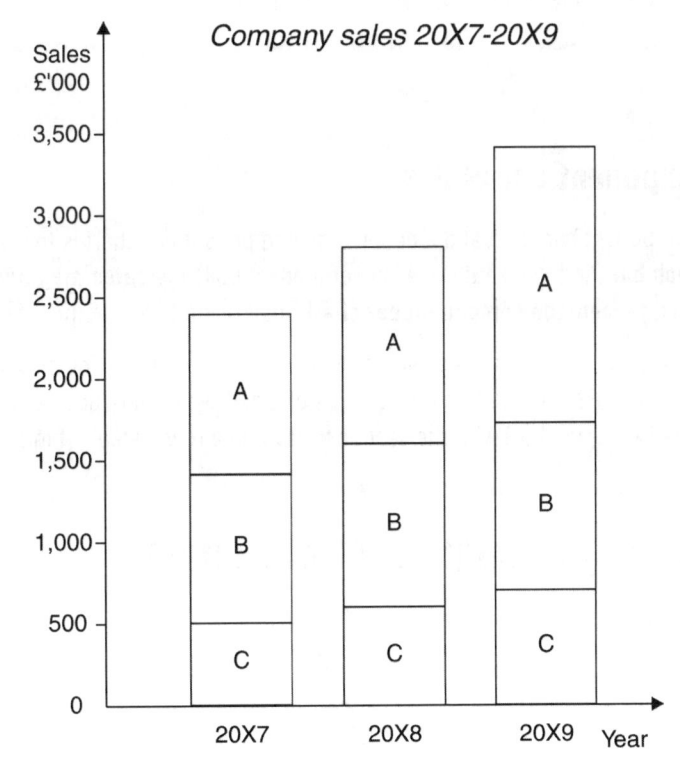

	20X7	20X8	20X9
	£'000	£'000	£'000
Product A	1,000	1,200	1,700
Product B	900	1,000	1,000
Product C	500	600	700
Total	2,400	2,800	3,400

The bars in a component bar chart can be drawn in the following ways.

- Side by side
- With no gap between them
- With gaps between them, as in the diagram here

In this diagram the **growth in sales** is illustrated and the significance of growth in product A sales as the reason for the total sales growth is also fairly clear.

Activity 16.6

Your company is preparing its published accounts and the chairman has requested that the assets of the company be compared in a component bar chart for the last five years. The data are contained in the following table.

Asset	20X3 £'000	20X4 £'000	20X5 £'000	20X6 £'000	20X7 £'000
Property	59	59	65	70	74
Plant and machinery	176	179	195	210	200
Stock and work in progress	409	409	448	516	479
Debtors	330	313	384	374	479
Cash	7	60	29	74	74

Tasks

(a) Construct the necessary component bar chart.
(b) Comment on the movements in the assets over the five year period.

6.4 Percentage component bar charts

The difference between a component bar chart and a percentage component bar chart is that with a component bar chart, **the total length of each bar** (and the length of each component in it) **indicates magnitude**. A bigger amount is shown by a longer bar. With a **percentage component bar chart**, total magnitudes are not shown.

If two or more bars are drawn on the chart, the total length of each bar is the same. The only varying lengths in a percentage component bar chart are the lengths of the sections of a bar, which vary according to the **relative sizes** of the components. So it is a bit like a **pie chart** with the sections drawn in a row instead of in a circle.

Example: Percentage component bar chart

Charbart plc's sales for the years from 20X7 to 20X9 are as follows.

	20X7 £'000	20X8 £'000	20X9 £'000
Product A	1,000	1,200	1,700
Product B	900	1,000	1,000
Product C	500	600	700
Total	2,400	2,800	3,400

In a percentage component bar chart, **all the bars are of the same height**.

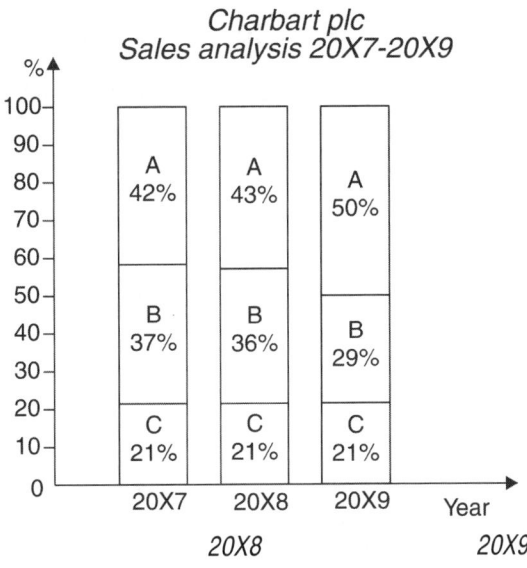

Charbart plc
Sales analysis 20X7-20X9

Workings	20X7		20X8		20X9	
	£'000	%	£'000	%	£'000	%
Product A	1,000	42	1,200	43	1,700	50
Product B	900	37	1,000	36	1,000	29
Product C	500	21	600	21	700	21
Total	2,400	100	2,800	100	3,400	100

Chart percentages:
- 20X7: A 42%, B 37%, C 21%
- 20X8: A 43%, B 36%, C 21%
- 20X9: A 50%, B 29%, C 21%

This chart shows that sales of C have remained a steady proportion of total sales, but the proportion of A in total sales has gone up quite considerably, while the proportion of B has fallen correspondingly.

Activity 16.7

The sales of September Ltd's four products A, B, C and D over the period 20X0-20X2 were as follows.

	Units sold			
	A	B	C	D
20X0	560	330	810	400
20X1	620	300	760	520
20X2	650	270	710	670

Tasks

(a) Represent the data given above in the form of a percentage component bar chart.
(b) Comment on the trends in sales of the products.

6.5 Multiple bar charts (compound bar charts)

A **multiple bar chart (or compound bar chart)** is a bar chart in which two or more separate bars are used to present sub-divisions of data.

Example: Multiple bar chart

(a) The output of Rodd Ltd in the years from 20X6 to 20X8 is as follows.

	20X6 '000 units	20X7 '000 units	20X8 '000 units
Product X	180	130	50
Product Y	90	110	170
Product Z	180	180	125
Total	450	420	345

(b) The data could be shown in a multiple bar chart as follows.

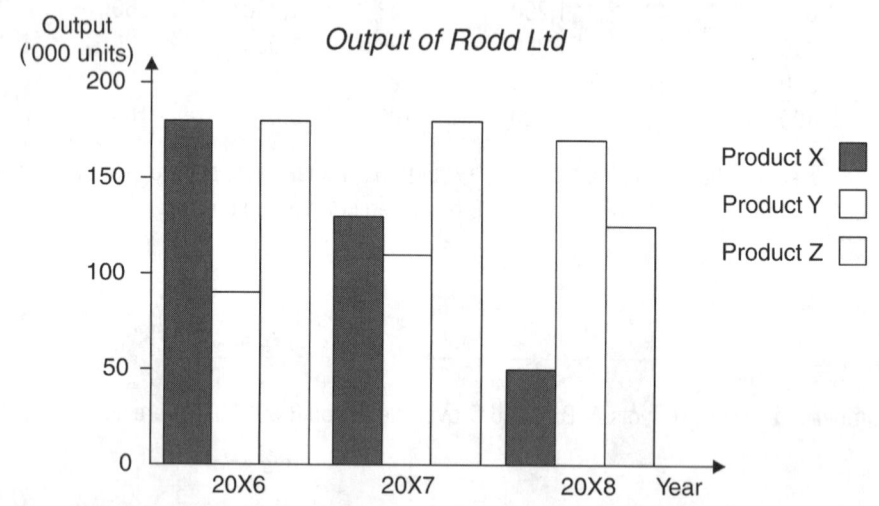

Output of Rodd Ltd — bar chart with Output ('000 units) on y-axis (0 to 200) and Year (20X6, 20X7, 20X8) on x-axis. Legend: Product X (shaded), Product Y (white), Product Z (white).

A multiple bar chart uses **several bars for each total**. In the above example, the sales in each year are shown as **three separate bars**, one for each product, X, Y and Z. Multiple bar charts are sometimes drawn with the bars **horizontal** (extending from the y axis) instead of vertical.

Multiple bar charts do not show grand totals (in the above example, the total output each year) whereas component bar charts do.

Multiple bar charts illustrate the comparative magnitudes of the components more clearly than component bar charts.

Note. Spreadsheet software such as Microsoft Excel simplifies the process of producing a wide range of charts. We explain how to use Excel to produce graphs and charts in Chapter 17.

7 Histograms

A **histogram** is a form of bar chart but with important differences. It is used when **grouped data of a continuous variable** are presented. It can also be used for discrete data, by treating the data as continuous so there are no gaps between class intervals: for example with an athlete's times in the 100 metres, using $\geq 9.75 < 10.0$, $\geq 10.00 < 10.25$, ≥ 10.25, < 10.5 etc.

The number of observations in a class is represented by **the area covered by the bar**, rather than by its height.

Example: Histograms

The following grouped frequency distribution represents the values on a printing machine's console which is read at the end of every day.

Reading	Number of occasions
$> 800 \leq 1,000$	4
$> 1,000 \leq 1,200$	10
$> 1,200 \leq 1,400$	12
$> 1,400 \leq 1,600$	10
$> 1,600 \leq 1,800$	4
	40

Task

Prepare a histogram.

Solution

There is a **standard bar width** of 200. Don't worry – you are unlikely to come across a situation where the bar widths are not all the same. The values of the readings are plotted on the x axis and the number of days are plotted on the y axis as shown below.

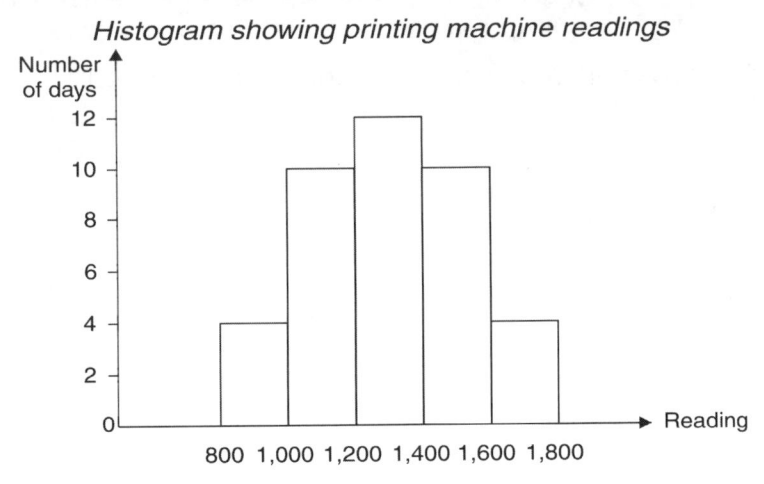

Histogram showing printing machine readings

8 Frequency polygons

A histogram can be converted into a **frequency polygon**.

A frequency polygon is drawn from a histogram as follows.

- Marking the mid-point of the top of each bar in the histogram
- Joining up all these points with straight lines

The ends of the diagram (the mid-points of the two end bars) should be joined to the base line at the mid-points of the next class intervals outside the range of observed data.

Example: Frequency polygon

Convert the histogram in the example above into a frequency polygon.

Solution

Frequency polygon showing printing machine readings

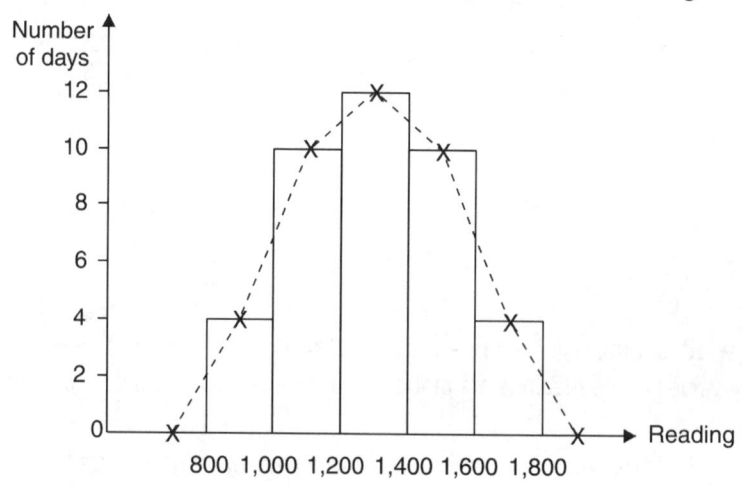

The mid-points of the class intervals outside the range of observed data are 700 and 1,900.

Key learning points

- **Tabulation** means putting data into tables. A **table** is a matrix of data in rows and columns.
- **Charts** often convey the meaning or significance of data more clearly than would a table.
- A **piechart** is used to show in picture form the relative sizes of component elements of a total.
- In order to draw pie charts accurately in an assessment remember that you will need to use a **protractor**. You will also need to be able to calculate the number of degrees which will occupy each different sector of the pie by multiplying the percentage value by 360°/100%.
- A **barchart** is a way of presenting data where quantities are shown in the form of bars on a chart. The different types of bar chart are as follows.
    - Simple
    - Component
    - Multiple
    - Histogram
- **Frequency distributions** are used if values of particular variables occur more than once.
- In an assessment, you will probably be told the type of chart that you are required to draw. If not, then you need to think carefully about the information that you are trying to communicate in your chart. For example, if you wish information about grand totals to be communicated, you will probably want to draw a **component bar chart** since this type of chart conveys such information. If however, it is more important to communicate the comparative magnitudes, then you will probably want to draw a **multiple bar chart**.

Quick quiz

1. What are the main guidelines for tabulation?

2. What is 843.668 correct to:

(i)	one decimal place	
(ii)	two decimal places?	

3. A grouped frequency distribution can be drawn as a(n) histogram/ogive, whereas a cumulative frequency distribution can be graphed as a(n) ogive/histogram.

4. $217 \leq 217$

   True [ ]

   False [ ]

5. List four different types of bar chart

   (a) ....

   (b) ....

   (c) ....

   (d) ....

Answers to quick quiz

1. (a) The table should have a clear title.
   (b) All columns should be clearly labelled.
   (c) Clear sub-totals should be included.
   (d) Columns should be totalled showing a total figure.
   (e) Tables should be spaced out, so that the information presented may be read easily.

2.
(i)	843.7
(ii)	843.67

3. A grouped frequency distribution can be drawn as a **histogram**, whereas a cumulative frequency distribution can be graphed as an **ogive**.

4. True ✓

5. (a) Simple bar chart
   (b) Component bar chart
   (c) Multiple bar chart
   (d) Histogram

16: PRESENTING INFORMATION: TABLES AND CHARTS

Activity checklist

This checklist shows which performance criteria, range statement or knowledge and understanding point is covered by each activity in this chapter. Tick off each activity as you complete it.

Activity

16.1	☐	This activity deals with Knowledge and Understanding point 14 regarding the diagrammatic and tabular presentation of information
16.2	☐	This activity deals with Knowledge and Understanding point 14 regarding the diagrammatic and tabular presentation of information
16.3	☐	This activity deals with Knowledge and Understanding point 14 regarding the diagrammatic and tabular presentation of information
16.4	☐	This activity deals with Knowledge and Understanding point 14 regarding the diagrammatic and tabular presentation of information
16.5	☐	This activity deals with Knowledge and Understanding point 14 regarding the diagrammatic and tabular presentation of information
16.6	☐	This activity deals with Knowledge and Understanding point 14 regarding the diagrammatic and tabular presentation of information
16.7	☐	This activity deals with Knowledge and Understanding point 14 regarding the diagrammatic and tabular presentation of information

chapter 17

Presenting information: graphs

Contents

1. Introduction
2. Drawing and using graphs
3. Straight line graphs
4. Scattergraphs
5. Ogives
6. Using Excel to produce charts and graphs
7. Spreadsheet skills and Unit 7

Knowledge and understanding

13. Tabulation of accounting and other quantitative information using spreadsheets
14. Methods of presenting information: written reports; diagrammatic; tabular

1 Introduction

In Chapter 16 we looked at some of the ways in which information can be presented using **tables** and **charts**.

In this chapter we are going to be looking at some of the ways in which data can be presented diagrammatically in the form of **graphs**.

This chapter looks at how to draw graphs (straight line graphs) and it also introduces two special types of graph – the **scattergraph** and the **ogive**.

2 Drawing and using graphs

A **graph** is a form of **visual display**. A graph shows, by means of either a straight line or a curve, the relationship between two variables.

2.1 Variables

Graphs show how the value of one variable changes given changes in the value of the other variable.

For example, a graph might be used to show the following.

- Sales turnover changes over time
- A country's population changes over time
- How total costs of production vary with the number of units produced

The variable whose value is influenced by the value of the other variable is referred to as the **dependent variable**.

The variable whose value affects the value of the dependent variable is known as the **independent variable**.

The **relationship between variables** can often be presented more clearly in graph form than in a table of figures, and this is why graphs are used so often.

Activity 17.1

If you were to draw a graph showing how the total costs of producing a product varies with the number of units produced, which variable would be the dependent variable and which one would be independent?

Dependent variable = [ ]

Independent variable = [ ]

2.2 Using graphs well

A graph has a **horizontal axis**, the x axis, and a **vertical axis**, the y axis.

- The x axis is used to represent the **independent variable**.
- The y axis is used to represent the **dependent variable**.
- The intersection of the x axis and the y axis is known as the **origin** and is labelled 0.

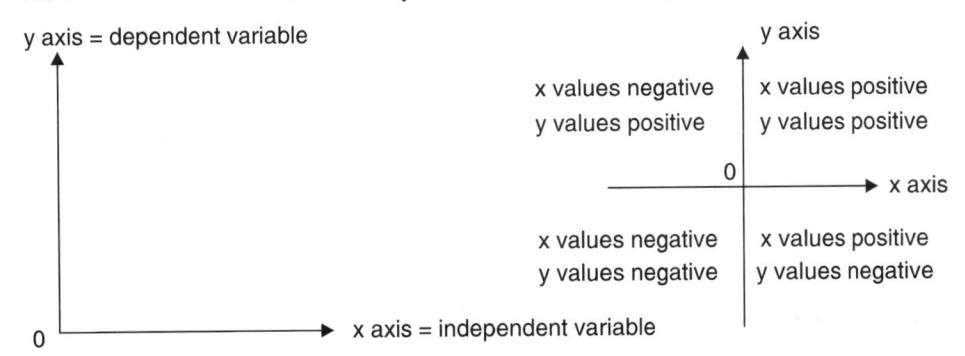

If time is one variable, it is always treated as the independent variable. When time is represented by the x axis on a graph, we have a **time series**. The analysis of time series is covered in Chapter 18 of this Interactive Text.

2.3 Rules for drawing graphs

The following rules should be applied when drawing graphs.

- **All axes should be labelled**, with the variable which they represent and the scale in which they are measured.

- Show any workings in a **neat table**. Use as much of the available space as possible. **Do not cramp a graph into one corner of the page.**

- **Break the axis** concerned, as follows, if it is best not to start a scale at zero.

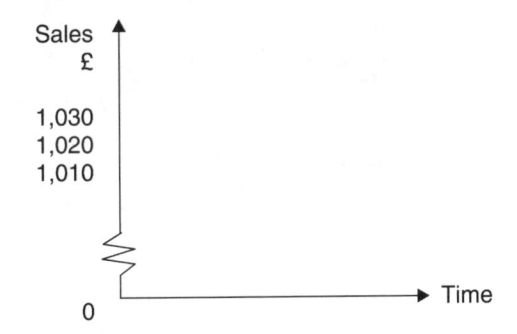

- The scales on the x axis and the y axis should be marked.

- A graph should not be overcrowded with too many lines.

- **A graph must always be given a title**, and where appropriate, a reference should be made to the source of data.

- Use graph paper when total accuracy is required.

3 Straight line graphs

A **straight line graph** is one which can be expressed by a formula y = a + bx where a and b are fixed, constant values and x and y are the variables.

Here are some examples of the equations of straight line graphs.

- y = 100 + 3x
- y = 1,000 + 0.2x
- y = −60 + 12x

There are no x^2, x^3, x^4, $\sqrt{x}$ or 1/x terms. If there were, the corresponding graphs would not be straight lines.

To draw a straight line graph, we need only plot two points and join them up with a straight line.

Example: Straight line graph

To draw y = 50 + 2x we can take any two points, for example these two.

- When x = 0, y = 50
- When x = 10, y = 50 + 20 = 70

These can be plotted on graph paper, or input into a modern spreadsheet package, and the points joined up and the line extended as follows.

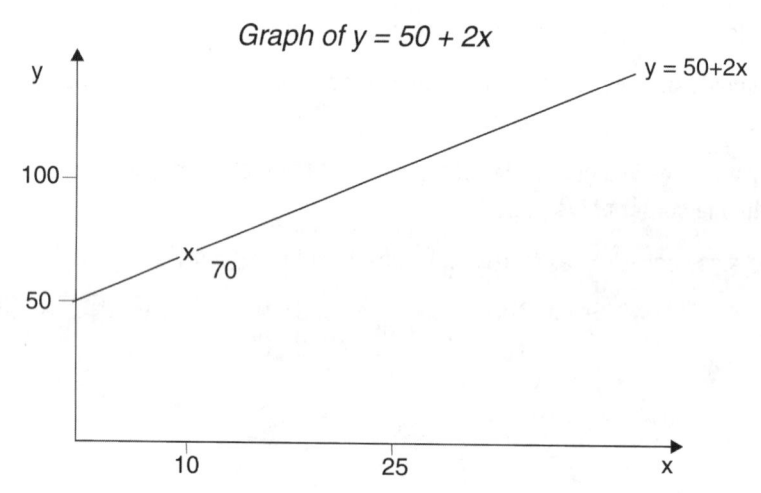

Graph of y = 50 + 2x

Activity 17.2

Plot the graph of y = 4x + 5

Consider the range of values from x = 0 to x = 10

4 Scattergraphs

Scattergraphs are graphs which are used to exhibit data, rather than equations which produce simple lines or curves, in order to compare the way in which two variables vary with each other.

The **x axis** of a scattergraph is used to represent the **independent variable** and the **y axis** represents the **dependent variable**.

To construct a **scattergraph** or **scatter diagram**, we must have several pairs of data, with each pair showing the value of one variable and the corresponding value of the other variable.

Each pair of data is plotted on a graph. The resulting graph will show a number of pairs, scattered over the graph. The scattered points might or might not appear to follow a **trend**.

Example: Scattergraph

The output at a factory each week for the last ten weeks, and the cost of that output, were as follows.

Week	1	2	3	4	5	6	7	8	9	10
Output (units)	10	12	10	8	9	11	7	12	9	14
Cost (£)	42	44	38	34	38	43	30	47	37	50

The data could be shown on a **scattergraph** as follows.

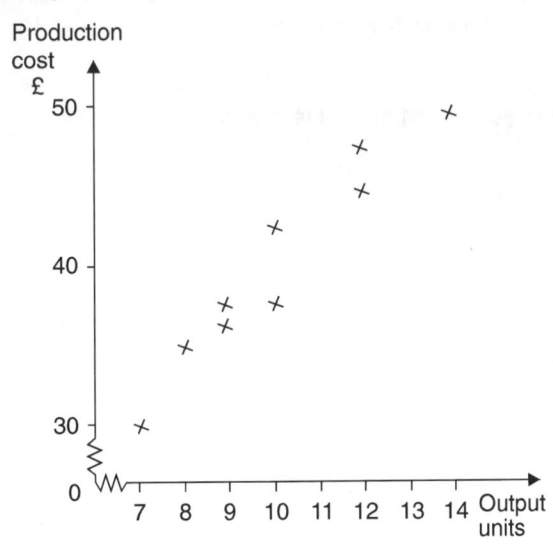

- The cost depends on the volume of output
- Volume is the independent variable and is shown on the x axis
- The plotted data lie approximately on a rising trend line
- Higher total costs compared with higher output volumes
- The lower part of the y axis has been omitted – this is indicated by the jagged line

4.1 Curve fitting

Scattergraphs are used to try to identify **trend lines**.

If a trend can be seen in a scattergraph, the next step is to try to draw a trend line. Fitting a line to scattergraph data is called **curve fitting**.

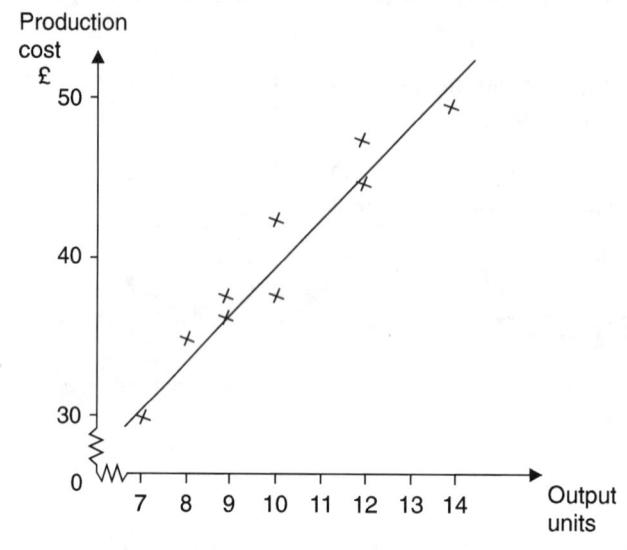

The reason for wanting to do this is to make **predictions**. In the previous example, we have drawn a **trend line** from the scattergraph of output units and production cost. This trend line might turn out to be, say, y = 10 + 3x. We could then use this trend line to **forecast** what we think costs ought to be, if output were, say, 10 units or 15 units in any week.

The trend line could be a straight line, or a curved line. The simplest technique for drawing a trend line is to make a **visual judgement** about what the **closest-fitting trend line** seems to be.

Activity 17.3

The quantities of units produced by April Ltd during the year ended 31 August 20X3 and the related costs were as follows.

Month	Production '000	Factory cost £'000
20X2		
September	7	45
October	10	59
November	13	75
December	14	80
20X3		
January	11	65
February	7	46
March	5	35
April	4	30
May	3	25
June	2	20
July	1	15
August	5	35

Tasks

(a) Draw a scatter diagram related to the data provided above, and plot on it the line of best fit.

(b) Using the graph you have drawn, estimate the factory cost if 12,000 units had been produced in a particular month.

(c) Estimate April Ltd's monthly fixed cost.

5 Ogives

5.1 Cumulative frequency curves

An **ogive** (pronounced 'oh-jive'), also known as a cumulative frequency curve, shows the cumulative number of items with a value less than or equal to, or alternatively greater than or equal to, a certain amount.

Example: Ogives

Consider the following discrete frequency distribution.

Number of faulty units rejected on inspection	Frequency f	Cumulative frequency
1	5	5
2	5	10 (5 + 5)
3	3	13 (10 + 3)
4	1	14 (13 + 1)
	14	

An ogive would be drawn as follows.

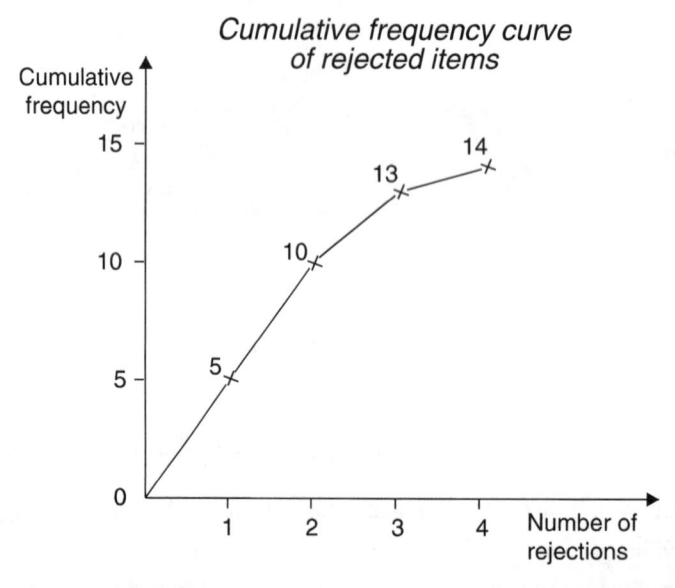

Cumulative frequency curve of rejected items

The ogive is drawn by plotting the **cumulative frequencies** on the graph, and joining them with straight lines. Although many ogives are more accurately curved lines, you can use straight lines in drawing an ogive in work for an assessment.

For **grouped frequency distributions**, where we work up through values of the variable, the cumulative frequencies are plotted against the **upper** limits of the classes.

For the class 'over 200, up to and including 250', the cumulative frequency should be plotted against 250.

For the class 'from 100 up to but not including 150' the cumulative frequency for a continuous variable should be plotted against 150. For a discrete variable, it would be plotted against the highest value less than 150, probably 149.

5.2 What information does an ogive provide?

An ogive represents a **cumulative frequency distribution** and it can be used to show what range of values contains given proportions of the total population. For example, it can be used to find the following:

- Median
- Upper quartile
- Lower quartile

The **median** is the value of the middle member of a distribution which corresponds to a cumulative frequency of 50%. It is also known as the **second quartile**.

The **upper quartile** is the value of the item which is 75% of the way through the cumulative frequencies. It is also known as the **third quartile**.

The **lower quartile** is the value of the item which is 25% of the way through the cumulative frequencies. It is also known as the **first quartile**.

Example: Information from ogives

The following data relate to the production output recorded at a factory for the last 40 weeks.

Class	Frequency f	Cumulative frequency
341 – 370	17	17
371 – 400	9	26
401 – 430	2	28
431 – 460	10	38
461 – 490	2	40
	40	

Plot an ogive using the information in the above table. Use your graph to establish the following.

(a) Median of the distribution
(b) Upper quartile of the distribution
(c) Lower quartile of the distribution

Solution

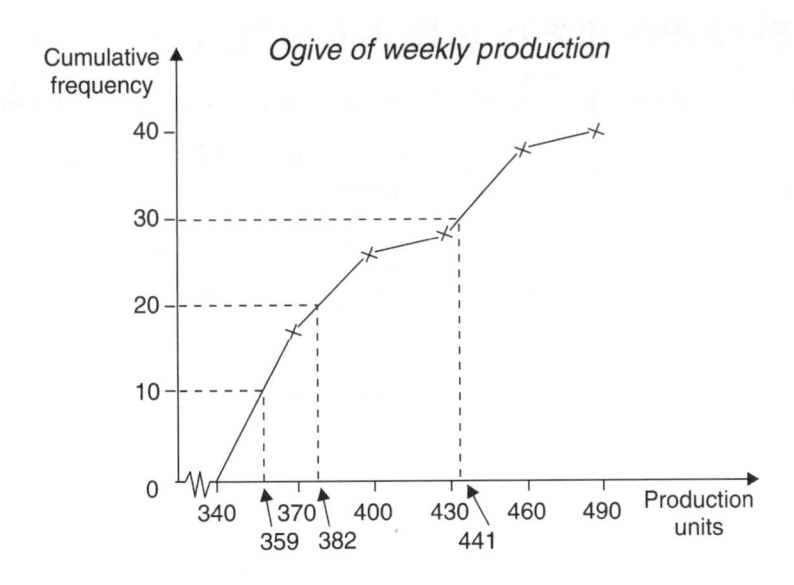

Ogive of weekly production

(Graph shows cumulative frequency plotted against production units, with dashed lines indicating:
- Lower quartile ≈ 359
- Median ≈ 382
- Upper quartile ≈ 441)

(a) The **median** is the ½ × 40 = 20th value. Reading off from the ogive, this value is 382 units per week.
(b) The **upper quartile** is the ¾ × 40 = 30th value. Reading off from the ogive, this value is 441 units.
(c) The **lower quartile** is the ¼ × 40 = 10th value. Reading off from the ogive, this value is 359 units.

Activity 17.4

Annual profit data from 50 similar companies in 20X8 are as follows.

Annual profit £million	Number of companies
–10 to under –5	2
–5 to under 0	0
0 to under 5	2
5 to under 10	3
10 to under 15	6
15 to under 20	11
20 to under 25	13
25 to under 30	9
30 to under 35	4

Tasks

(a) Construct a cumulative frequency distribution and draw the ogive (cumulative frequency curve) on graph paper.

(b) Use your ogive to estimate the three quartiles (to the nearest £ million) and explain their meaning.

6 Using Excel to produce charts and graphs

Today, the vast majority of **charts** and **graphs** produced in a business setting are prepared using **spreadsheet software**.

This section assumes you are reasonably competent in the basics of Microsoft Excel. The level of prior knowledge assumed is the level required to prove competency at AAT Foundation Level.

6.1 Using Microsoft Excel to produce charts and graphs

Using Microsoft Excel, It is possible to display data held in a range of spreadsheet cells in a variety of charts or graphs. We will use the Discount Traders Ltd spreadsheet shown below to generate a chart.

	A	B	C	D	E
1	Discount Traders Ltd				
2	*Sales analysis - April 200X*				
3	Customer	Sales	5% discount	Sales (net)	
4		£	£	£	
5	Arthur	956.00	0.00	956.00	
6	Dent	1423.00	71.15	1351.85	
7	Ford	2894.00	144.70	2749.30	
8	Prefect	842.00	0.00	842.00	
9					
10					

The data in the spreadsheet could be used to generate a chart, such as those shown below. We explain how later in this section.

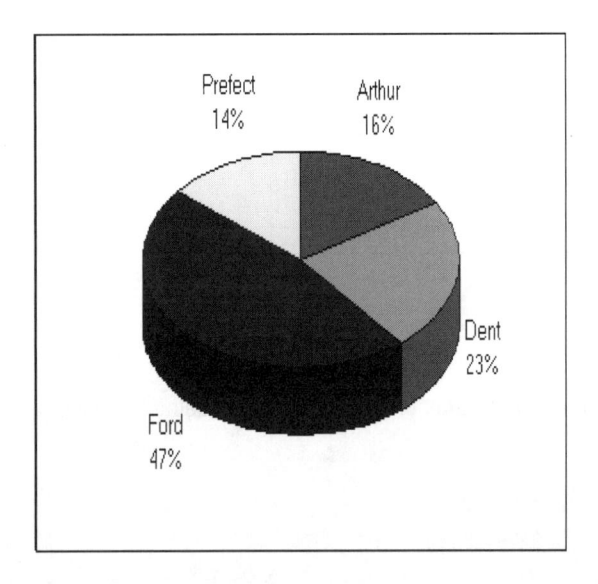

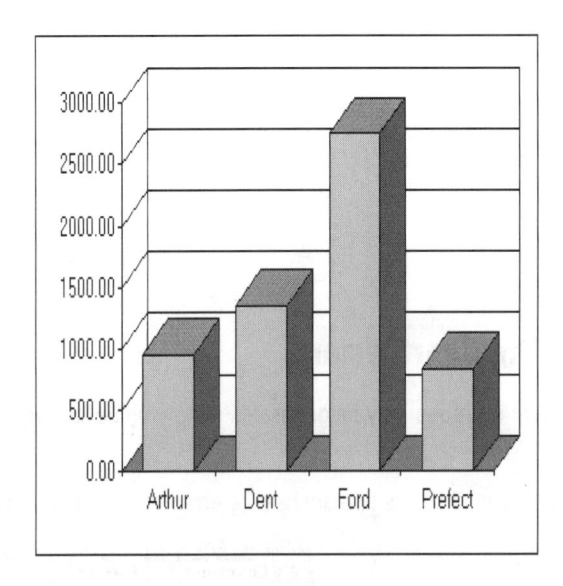

The Chart Wizard, which we explain in a moment, may also be used to generate a line graph. A line graph would normally be used to track a tend over time. For example, the chart below graphs the Total Revenue figures shown in Row 7 of the following spreadsheet.

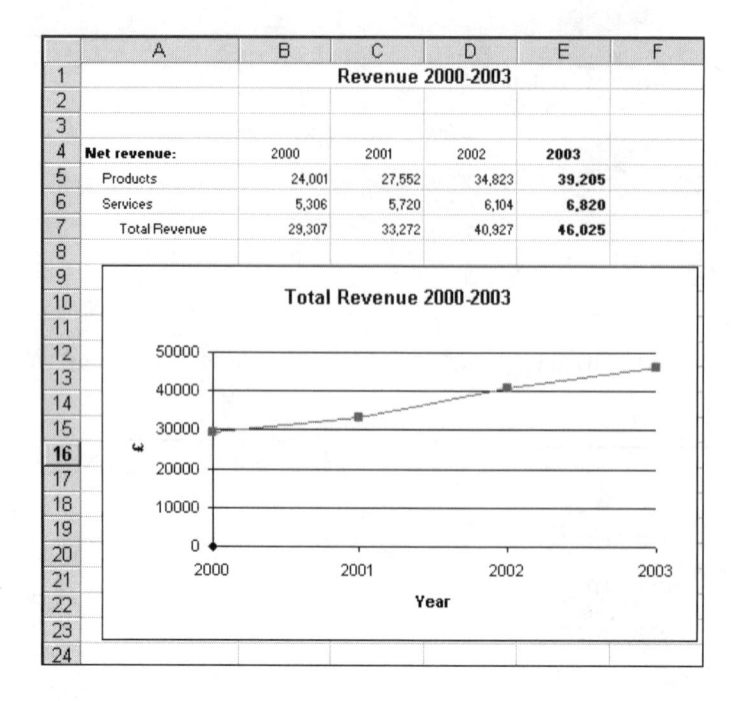

	A	B	C	D	E	F
1			Revenue 2000-2003			
2						
3						
4	Net revenue:	2000	2001	2002	**2003**	
5	Products	24,001	27,552	34,823	**39,205**	
6	Services	5,306	5,720	6,104	**6,820**	
7	Total Revenue	29,307	33,272	40,927	**46,025**	

(Rows 8–24 contain a chart titled "Total Revenue 2000-2003" showing total revenue increasing from approximately 30,000 in 2000 to about 46,000 in 2003, with Year on the x-axis and £ on the y-axis.)

6.2 The Chart Wizard

Charts and graphs may be generated simply by **selecting the range** of figures to be included, then using Excel's Chart Wizard.

The Discount Traders spreadsheet referred to earlier is shown again below.

	A	B	C	D	E
1	Discount Traders Ltd				
2	*Sales analysis - April 200X*				
3	Customer	Sales	5% discount	Sales (net)	
4		£	£	£	
5	Arthur	956.00	0.00	956.00	
6	Dent	1423.00	71.15	1351.85	
7	Ford	2894.00	144.70	2749.30	
8	Prefect	842.00	0.00	842.00	
9					
10					

To chart the **net sales** of the different **customers**, follow the following steps.

Step 1. Highlight cells A5:A8, then move your pointer to cell D5, hold down **Ctrl** and drag to also select cells D5:D8.

Step 2. Look at the **toolbar** at the top of your spreadsheet. You should see an **icon** that looks like a small bar chart. Click on this icon to start the 'Chart Wizard'.

The following steps are taken from the Excel 2000 Chart Wizard. Other versions may differ slightly.

Step 3. Pick the type of chart you want. We will choose chart type **Column** and then select the sub-type we think will be most effective. (To produce a graph, select a type such as **Line**).

17: PRESENTING INFORMATION: GRAPHS

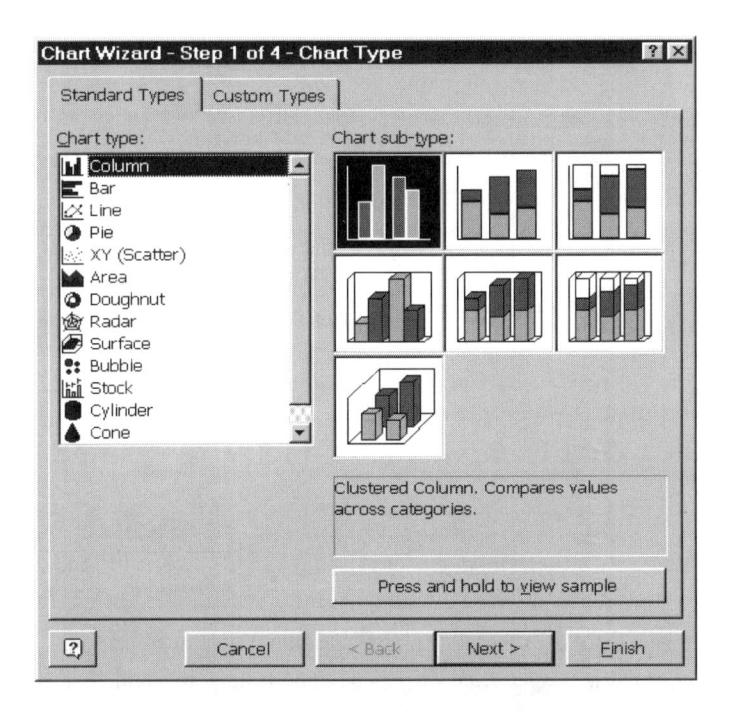

Step 4. This step gives us the opportunity to confirm that the data we selected earlier was correct and to decide whether the chart should be based on **columns** (eg Customer, Sales, Discount etc) or **rows** (Arthur, Dent etc). We can accept the default values and click Next.

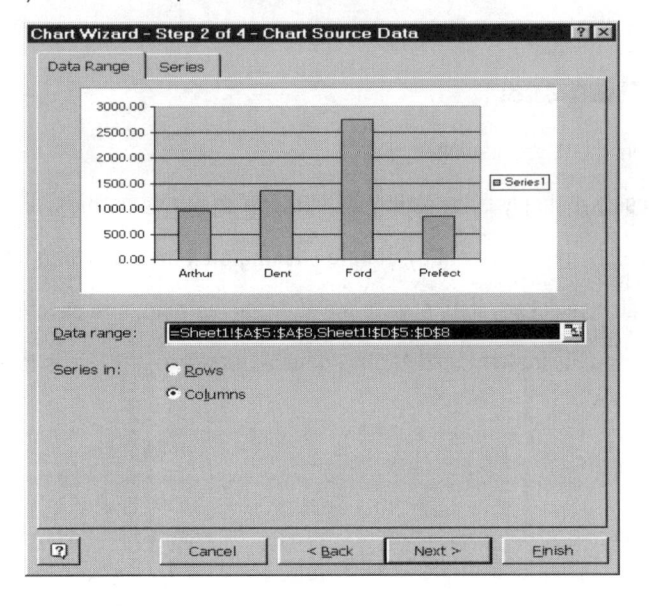

Step 5. Next, specify your chart **title** and axis **labels**. Incidentally, one way of remembering which is the **X axis** and which is the **Y axis** is to look at the letter Y: it is the only letter that has a vertical part pointing straight up, so it must be the vertical axis! Click Next to move on.

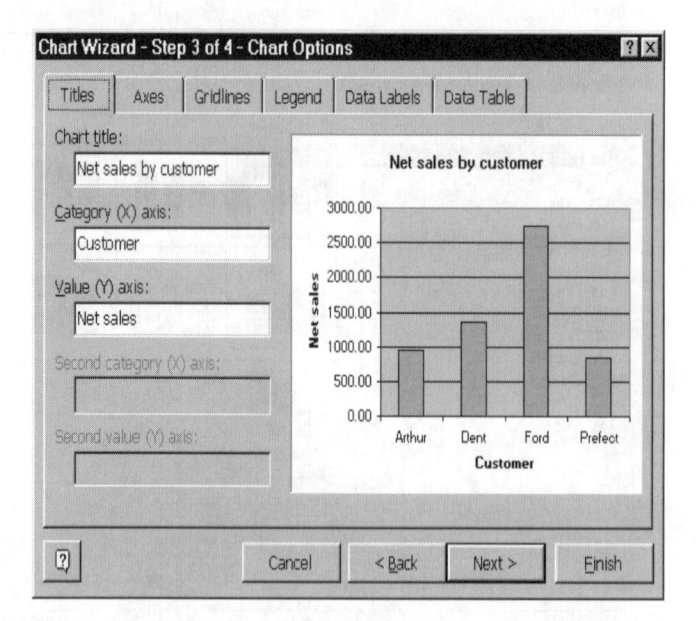

As you can see, there are other index tabs available. You can see the effect of selecting or deselecting each one in **preview** - experiment with these options as you like then click Next.

Step 6. The final step is to choose whether you want the chart to appear on the same worksheet as the data or on a separate sheet of its own. This is a matter of personal preference – for this example choose to place the chart as an object within the existing spreadsheet.

6.3 Changing existing charts

Even after your chart is 'finished', you can change it.

(a) You can **resize it** simply by selecting it and dragging out its borders.

(b) You can change **each element** by **double clicking** on it then selecting from the options available.

(c) You could also select any item of **text** and alter the wording, size or font, or change the **colours** used.

(d) In the following illustration, the user has double-clicked on the Y axis to enable them to **change the scale**.

17: PRESENTING INFORMATION: GRAPHS

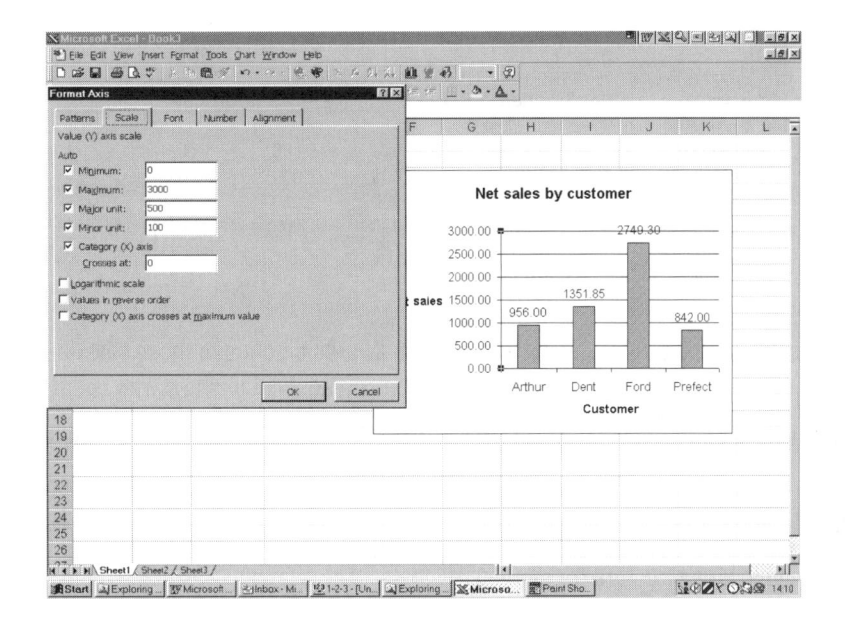

7 Spreadsheet skills and Unit 7

In addition to the ability to produce charts and graphs, other spreadsheet skills may be relevant to Unit 7. For example the Performance Criteria 7.1 F requires students to be able to 'Prepare reports in the appropriate form and present them to management within the required timescales'. You should therefore be competent in the use of **basic spreadsheet functions**, as covered at AAT **Foundation** Level.

The AAT has issued additional guidance for Unit 7. This specifies that students should be able to use spreadsheet **rounding** and **sorting** facilities, and should be able to use **conditional formulae**. We will now explain these three areas.

7.1 Formulae with conditions

You should be familiar with simple spreadsheet formulae such as addition, subtraction, multiplication and division. Spreadsheets offer a range of more complex functions and formulae. You should experiment with these yourself – searching the word 'function' in Excel's Help facility is a good starting point.

We will now look at an example of conditional formulae using an **IF statement**.

Example: IF statement

The following spreadsheet has been set up showing the difference between actual sales and target sales for four salesmen, and expressing the difference as a percentage of target sales.

	A	B	C	D	E	F
1	Sales team comparison of actual against budget sales					
2	Name	Sales (Budget)	Sales (Actual)	Difference	% of budget	
3		£	£	£	£	
4	Northington	275,000	284,000	9,000	3.27	
5	Souther	200,000	193,000	(7,000)	(3.50)	
6	Weston	10,000	12,000	2,000	20.00	
7	Easterman	153,000	152,000	(1,000)	(0.65)	
8						
9	Total	638,000	641,000	3,000	0.47	
10						

Suppose the company employing the salesmen in this example awards a bonus to those salesmen who exceed their target by more than £1,000. A formula could be entered into the spreadsheet to show who is entitled to the bonus.

To do this we would enter the appropriate formula in cells F4 to F7. For salesperson Easterman, we would enter the following in cell F7:

=IF(D4>1000,"BONUS"," ")

IF statements follow the following structure (or syntax).

=IF(logical_test,value_if_true,value_if_false)

The logical_test is any value or expression that can be evaluated to Yes or No. For example, D4>1000 is a logical expression; if the value in cell D4 is over 1000, the expression evaluates to Yes. Otherwise, the expression evaluates to No.

Value_if_true is the value that is returned if the answer to the logical_test is Yes. For example, if the answer to D4>1000 is Yes, and the value_if_true is the text string "BONUS", then the cell containing the IF function will display the text "BONUS".

Value_if_false is the value that is returned if the answer to the logical_test is No. For example, if the value_if_false is two sets of quote marks "" this means display a blank cell if the answer to the logical test is No. So in our example, if D4 is not over 1000, then the cell containing the IF function will display a blank cell.

Note the following symbols which can be used in formulae with conditions:

<	less than (like L (for 'less') on its side)
<=	less than or equal to
=	equal to
>=	greater than or equal to
>	greater than
<>	not equal to

Care is required to ensure **brackets** and **commas** are entered in the right places. If, when you try out this kind of formula, you get an error message, it may well be a simple mistake, such as leaving a comma out.

7.1.1 Examples; formulae with conditions

A company offers a discount of 5% to customers who order more than £1,000 worth of goods. A spreadsheet showing what customers will pay might look like this.

	A	B	C	D	E	F
1	Discount Traders Ltd					
2	*Sales analysis - April 200X*					
3	Customer	Sales	5% discount	Sales (net)		
4		£	£	£		
5	Arthur	956.00	0.00	956.00		
6	Dent	1423.00	71.15	1351.85		
7	Ford	2894.00	144.70	2749.30		
8	Prefect	842.00	0.00	842.00		
9						
10						

The formula in cell C5 is: =IF(B5>1,000,(0.05*B5),0). This means, if the value in B5 is greater than £1,000 multiply it by 0.05, otherwise the discount will be zero. Cell D5 will calculate the amount net of discount, using the formula: =B5-C5. The same conditional formula with the cell references changed will be found in cells C6, C7 and C8. **Strictly**, the variables £1,000 and 5% should be entered in a **different part** of the spreadsheet.

Here is another example. Suppose the pass mark for an examination is 50%. You have a spreadsheet containing candidate's scores in column B. If a score is held in cell B10, an appropriate formula for cell C10 would be:

=IF(B10<50,"FAILED","PASSED").

7.2 Rounding numbers

Most spreadsheet programs contain facilities for presenting numbers in a particular way. In Excel you simply click on **Format** and then **Cells ...**to reach these options.

(a) **Fixed format** displays the number in the cell rounded off to the number of decimal places you select.

(b) **Currency format** displays the number with a '£' in front, with commas and not more than two decimal places, eg £10,540.23.

(c) **Comma format** is the same as currency format except that the numbers are displayed without the '£'.

(d) **General format** *is* the format assumed unless another format is specified. In general format the number is displayed with no commas and with as many decimal places as entered or calculated that fit in the cell.

(e) **Percent format** multiplies the number in the display by 100 and follows it with a percentage sign. For example the number 0.548 in a cell would be displayed as 54.8%.

(f) **Hidden format** is a facility by which values can be entered into cells and used in calculations but are not actually displayed on the spreadsheet. The format is useful for hiding sensitive information.

The ability to display numbers in a variety of formats (eg to no decimal places) can result in a situation whereby totals that are correct may actually look incorrect.

Example: Rounding errors

The following example shows how apparent rounding errors can arise.

	A	B	C	D
1	*Petty cash*			
2	*Week ended 16 August 200X*			
3		£		
4	Opening balance	231		
5	Receipts	33		
6	Payments	-105		
7	Closing balance	160		
8				

	A	B	C	D
1	*Petty cash*			
2	*Week ended 16 August 200X*			
3		£		
4	Opening balance	231.34		
5	Receipts	32.99		
6	Payments	(104.67)		
7	Closing balance	159.66		
8				

Cell B7 contains the formula =SUM(B4:B6). The spreadsheet on the left shows that 231 + 33 - 105 is equal to 160, which is not true (check it). The **reason for the discrepancy** is that both spreadsheets actually contain the values shown in the spreadsheet on the right.

However, the spreadsheet on the left has been formatted to display numbers with **no decimal places**. So, individual numbers display as the nearest whole number, although the actual value held by the spreadsheet and used in calculations includes the decimals.

Solution

One solution, that will prevent the appearance of apparent errors, is to use the **ROUND function.** The ROUND function has the following structure: ROUND (value, places). 'Value' is the value to be rounded. 'Places' is the number of places to which the value is to be rounded.

The difference between using the ROUND function and formatting a value to a number of decimal places is that using the ROUND function actually **changes** the **value**, while formatting only changes the **appearance** of the value.

In the example above, the ROUND function could be used as follows. The following formulae could be inserted in cells C4 to C7.

C4 = ROUND(B4,0)   C5 = ROUND(B5,0)   C6 = ROUND(B6,0)   C7 = SUM(C4:C6)

Column B could then be hidden by highlighting the whole column (by clicking on the B at the top of the column), then selecting Format, Column, Hide from the main menu. Try this for yourself, hands-on.

Note that using the ROUND function to eliminate decimals results in slightly inaccurate calculation totals (in our example 160 is actually 'more correct' than the 159 obtained using ROUND. For this reason, some people prefer not to use the function, and to make users of the spreadsheet aware that small apparent differences are due to rounding.

7.3 Sorting

Data in a range of cells may be sorted using Excel's Sort facility. The Sort function allows users to sort column and row data in ascending or descending order. This allows the user to customise how data is displayed. To sort data held within an Excel spreadsheet follow the steps below.

Step 1. Open the spreadsheet and highlight the range of cells containing the data you wish to Sort.

Step 2. To sort the data selected, chose **Data, Sort** from the main menu. The Sort dialogue box appears.

Step 3. In the Sort dialogue box, specify the column the data should be sorted on and the order (ascending or descending). Click OK. The data will be sorted according to your specification.

Note. To quickly sort data in ascending order, click on the ⇣ button. To **Undo** a Sort go to **Edit, Undo** immediately following the sort.

Key learning points

- **Graphs** are a form of visual display. They show the relationship between two variables.
- A **dependent variable** is one whose value is influenced by the value of another variable. An **independent variable** is one whose value affects the value of the dependent variable.
- A graph has a **horizontal axis** (x axis) and a **vertical axis** (y axis). These axes intersect at the **origin**.
- In the modern office, graphs and charts are produced using spreadsheet software such as Microsoft Excel.
- If time is one variable, and is represented by the x axis, we have a **time series**.
- An axis break can be used to indicate a non-zero starting point.
- A straight line graph may be drawn by plotting only two points and joining them with a straight line.
- **Scattergraphs** exhibit data rather than equations. They are drawn to compare the way in which two variables may vary with each other. They are generally used to identify trend lines.
- An **ogive** is a curve which shows the cumulative number of items with a value less than or equal to, or greater than or equal to a certain amount.
- Make sure that you have a sharp pencil, an eraser and a ruler when drawing graphs in your assessments.

Quick quiz

1 A linear equation has the general form y = a + bx where

    y   independent variable
    x   constant (fixed amount)
    b   ?   constant (coefficient of x)
    a   dependent variable

2 The horizontal axis on a graph is known as the y axis.

    True ☐

    False ☐

3 The intercept is ....

4 On a scattergraph, which axis represents the independent variable?

5 List four pieces of statistical information provided by an ogive.

    (a) ....

    (b) ....

    (c) ....

    (d) ....

Answers to quick quiz

1   y = dependent variable
      x = independent variable
      b = constant (coefficient of x)
      a = constant (fixed amount)

2   ✓ False

3   The point at which a straight line crosses the y axis

4   The x axis

5   (a)   Range of data
        (b)   Median
        (c)   Lower quartile
        (d)   Upper quartile

Activity checklist

This checklist shows which performance criteria, range statement or knowledge and understanding point is covered by each activity in this chapter. Tick off each activity as you complete it.

Activity

17.1	☐	This activity deals with Knowledge and Understanding point 14 regarding the diagrammatic presentation of information
17.2	☐	This activity deals with Knowledge and Understanding point 14 regarding the diagrammatic presentation of information
17.3	☐	This activity deals with Knowledge and Understanding point 14 regarding the diagrammatic presentation of information
17.4	☐	This activity deals with Knowledge and Understanding point 14 regarding the diagrammatic presentation of information

chapter 18

Averages and time series

Contents

1 Introduction
2 Averages
3 Time series analysis
4 The trend
5 Seasonal variations
6 Cyclical and random variations

Knowledge and understanding

9 Time series analysis

1 Introduction

The standards of competence for Unit 7 require you to have a knowledge and understanding of **time series analysis**, which involves statistics recorded over a period of time. Before being able to study time series analysis in detail, we need to be clear about the concept of an **average**.

In this chapter, we shall be looking at the three main types of average and how they are calculated. Once you have got to grips with averages, we will use this knowledge to look at the analysis of time series.

A time series is a series of figures or values recorded over time and **moving averages** are used in time series analysis to identify the **trend** of a series.

2 Averages

2.1 Types of average

An **average** is a representative figure that is used to give some impression of the size of all the items in a population.

The three main types of average are as follows.

- The arithmetic mean
- The mode
- The median

An average, whether it is a mean, a mode or a median, is a **measure of central tendency**. By this we mean that while a population may range in values, these values will be distributed around a **central point**. This central point, or average, is therefore in some way **representative** of the population as a whole.

2.2 The arithmetic mean

This is the best known type of average. For **ungrouped data**, it is calculated by the formula shown below.

$$\text{Arithmetic mean} = \frac{\text{Sum of values of items}}{\text{Number of items}}$$

Example: Arithmetic mean

The demand for a product on each of 20 days was as follows (in units).

3	12	7	17	3	14	9	6	11	10
1	4	19	7	15	6	9	12	12	8

The **arithmetic mean** of daily demand is calculated as follows.

$$\frac{\text{Sum of daily demand}}{\text{Number of days}} = \frac{185}{20} = 9.25 \text{ units}$$

The **arithmetic mean** of a variable x is shown as $\bar{x}$ (**'x bar'**).

Thus in the above example $\bar{x}$ = 9.25 units.

In the above example, demand on any one day is never actually 9.25 units. The arithmetic mean is merely an **average representation** of demand on each of the 20 days.

2.2.1 The arithmetic mean of data in a frequency distribution

The concept of the frequency distribution was explained earlier. In our previous example, the frequency distribution would be shown as follows.

Daily demand	Frequency	Demand × frequency
x	f	fx
1	1	1
3	2	6
4	1	4
6	2	12
7	2	14
8	1	8
9	2	18
10	1	10
11	1	11
12	3	36
14	1	14
15	1	15
17	1	17
19	1	19
	20	185

$$\bar{x} = \frac{185}{20} = 9.25$$

2.2.2 Sigma, Σ

The statistical notation for the arithmetic mean of a set of data uses the symbol Σ (sigma).

Σ **(sigma)** means 'the sum of' and is used as shorthand to mean the sum of a set of values.

Thus, in the previous example:

(a) Σ f would mean the sum of all the frequencies, which is 20.

(b) Σ fx would mean the sum of all the values of 'frequency multiplied by daily demand', that is, all 14 values of fx, so Σ fx = 185.

2.2.3 The symbolic formula for the arithmetic mean

Using the Σ sign, the formula for the arithmetic mean of a frequency distribution is given as follows.

Arithmetic mean of a frequency distribution, $\bar{x} = \dfrac{\Sigma fx}{n}$ or $\dfrac{\Sigma fx}{\Sigma f}$

where n is the number of values recorded, or the number of items measured.

Activity 18.1

For the week ended 13 June, the annual salaries earned by the 20 sales staff employed by Bridge Ltd were as follows.

Annual salary £	Number of sales staff
12,000	3
12,500	1
13,000	1
13,500	1
14,000	2
14,500	4
15,000	1
16,000	5
18,000	2
	20

Task

Calculate the arithmetic mean annual salary of the sales staff of Bridge Ltd for the week ended 13 June.

2.3 The mode

The **mode** is an average which means 'the most frequently occurring value'.

Example: The mode

The daily demand for stock in a ten day period is as follows.

Demand Units	Number of days
6	3
7	6
8	1
	10

The **mode** is 7 units, because it is the value which occurs **most frequently**.

2.4 The median

The third type of average is the **median**. We met the **median** earlier in this Interactive Text in Chapter 17 when we were studying **ogives**.

The **median** is the value of the middle member of a distribution.

The median of a set of ungrouped data is found by arranging the items in ascending or descending order of value, and **selecting the item in the middle of the range**. A list of items in order of value is called an **array**.

Example: The median

The **median** of the following nine values:

    8   6   9   12   15   6   3   20   11

is found by taking the **middle item** (the fifth one) in the array:

    3   6   6   8   9   11   12   15   20

The **median** is 9.

The **median** of the following ten values

    8   6   7   2   1   11   3   2   5   2

would be the fifth item in the array, that is 3.

    1   2   2   2   3   5   6   7   8   11

With an even number of items, we could take the **arithmetic mean** of the two middle ones (in this example, (3 + 5)/2 = 4).

2.5 Weighted averages

Weighted averages are used whenever a simple average fails to give an accurate reflection of the **relative importance of the items being averaged**.

One use of the weighted average includes **calculating the average cost of a product** which is made up from different amounts of components which have different prices. This sort of problem is also dealt with by the use of **index numbers**, which we will look at in the next chapter.

Example: Average cost

Suppose you went shopping and spent £36.40 as follows.

Item	Cost
	£
CD	13.00
Cassette	9.00
Book	6.00
Battery	3.40
Lunch	5.00
	36.40

What would you say was the average cost of the items you bought that afternoon?

The total cost was £36.40, and five items were purchased.

Average unit cost = $\dfrac{£36.40}{5}$ = £7.28

Example: Weighted average cost

Suppose you went shopping and spent a total of £135 as follows.

Item	Number purchased	Cost per item	Total cost
		£	£
CDs	3	13.00	39
Cassettes	5	9.00	45
Books	2	6.00	12
Batteries	10	3.40	34
Lunch	1	5.00	5
	21		135

The total cost was £135, and 21 items were purchased

Average unit cost = $\dfrac{£135}{21}$ = £6.43

Note that in the second example, different numbers of each item were purchased, so they were given **different weights** when the average cost was calculated. For instance, twice as many batteries were bought as cassettes, so the 'weight' for battery cost was twice that for cassette cost. Now you can see why the average unit cost came down from £7.28 to £6.43 in the second example – more 'weight' was being given to the items which cost less.

2.6 Moving averages

Moving averages are a special type of average used in connection with time series analysis.

A **moving average** is an average of the results of a fixed number of periods.

Since a moving average is an **average** of several time periods, it is related to the mid-point of the overall period.

Moving averages could, for example, cover the sales of a shop over periods of seven days (Monday to the next Sunday, Tuesday to the next Monday, Wednesday to the next Tuesday, and so on), or a business's costs over periods of four quarters.

Example: Moving averages

Year	Sales (units)
20X0	390
20X1	380
20X2	460
20X3	450
20X4	470
20X5	440
20X6	500

Task

Calculate a moving average of the annual sales over a period of three years.

Solution

(a) Average sales in the three year period 20X0 – 20X2 were

$$\frac{390+380+460}{3} = \frac{1,230}{3} = 410$$

This average relates to the middle year of the period 20X1.

(b) Similarly, average sales in the three year period 20X1 – 20X3 were

$$\frac{380+460+450}{3} = \frac{1,290}{3} = 430$$

This average relates to the middle year of the period 20X2.

(c) The average sales can also be found for the periods 20X2 – 20X4, 20X3 – 20X5 and 20X4 – 20X6, to give the following.

Year	Sales Units	Moving total of 3 years sales Units	Moving average of 3 years sales (÷ 3) Units
20X0	390		
20X1	380	1,230	410
20X2	460	1,290	430
20X3	450	1,380	460
20X4	470	1,360	453.3
20X5	440	1,410	470
20X6	500		

UNIT 7 PREPARING REPORTS AND RETURNS

Note

The **moving average series** has five figures relating to the years from 20X1 to 20X5. The original series had seven figures for the years from 20X0 to 20X6.

There is an **upward trend** in sales, which is more noticeable from the series of moving averages than from the original series of **actual** sales each year.

The above example averaged over a three year period. Over what period should a moving average be taken? The answer to this question is that **the moving average which is most appropriate will depend on the circumstances and the nature of the time series**.

Activity 18.2

Sales in pounds of a particular product for the last five years have been: 100, 110, 108, 112, 106.

Task

Calculate a 3-year moving average to the nearest pound.

3 Time series analysis

3.1 Time series

A **time series** is a series of figures or values recorded over time.

Examples of **time series** are as follows.

- Output at a factory each day for the last month
- Monthly sales over the last two years
- Total annual costs for the last ten years
- The Retail Prices Index each month for the last ten years
- The number of people employed by a company each year for the last 20 years

3.2 Historigrams

A **historigram** is a graph of a time series. (Note the 'r' and the second 'i'; this is not the same as a histogram.)

Example: Historigram

Consider the following time series.

Year	Sales £'000
20X0	20
20X1	21
20X2	24
20X3	23
20X4	27
20X5	30
20X6	28

The historigram for this data is as follows.

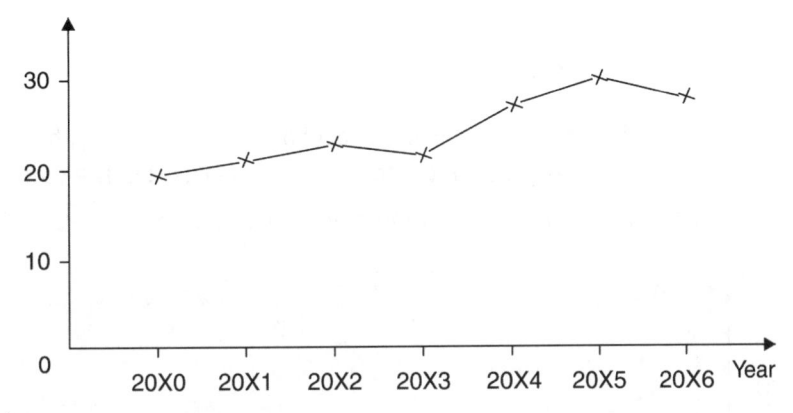

Note the following points.

- The horizontal axis is always chosen to represent time
- The vertical axis represents the values of the data recorded

3.3 Features of a time series

There are several features of a time series which it may be necessary to identify.

- A trend
- Seasonal variations or fluctuations
- Cycles, or cyclical variations
- Non-recurring, random variations

4 The trend

The **trend** or 'underlying trend' is the underlying long-term movement over time in the values of the data recorded.

4.1 Types of trend

The following examples of time series relate to Freedom Ltd and show three types of trend.

	Time series (A) Output per labour hour (units)	Time series (B) Cost per unit £	Time series (C) Number of employees
20X4	30	1.00	100
20X5	24	1.08	103
20X6	26	1.20	96
20X7	22	1.15	102
20X8	21	1.18	103
20X9	17	1.25	98

Example: Downward trend

In time series (A) there is a **downward** trend in the output per labour hour. Output per labour hour did not fall every year, because it went up between 20X5 and 20X6, but **the long-term movement is clearly a downward one**.

Graph showing trend of output per labour hour in years 20X4-X9

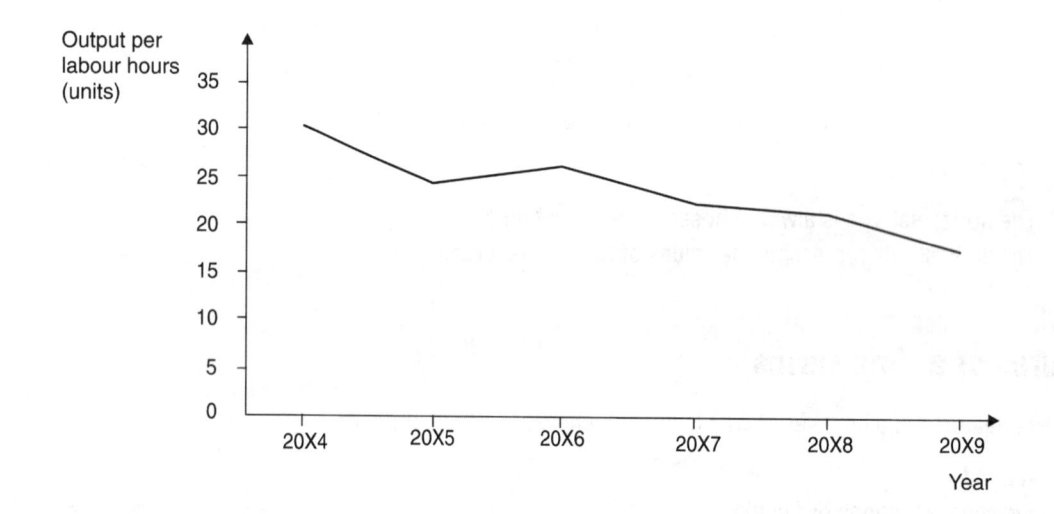

Example: Upward trend

In time series (B) there is an **upward** trend in the cost per unit. Although unit costs went down in 20X7 from a higher level in 20X6, **the basic movement over time is one of rising costs**.

Graph showing trend of costs per unit in years 20X4-X9

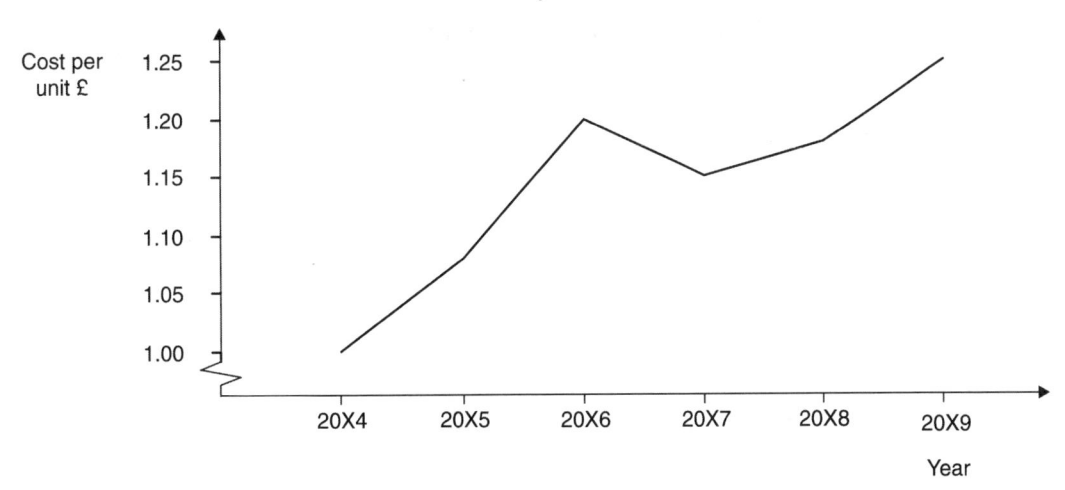

Example: Static trend

In time series (C) there is **no clear movement up or down**, and the number of employees remained fairly constant around 100. The trend is therefore a **static**, or level one.

Graph showing trend of number of employees in years 20X4-X9

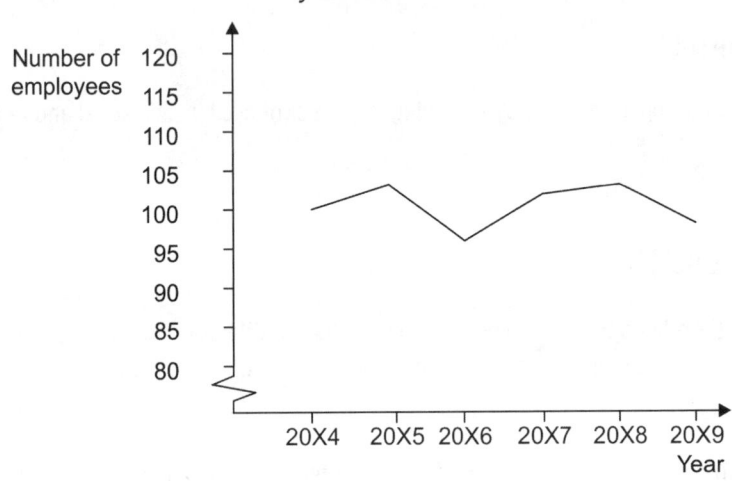

A trend may be of great significance to a manager who will want to know whether his or her company's results are on an upward or a downward trend. **The difficulty is to isolate a trend from the other factors that cause variations in results.**

4.2 Finding the trend

There are three principal methods of finding a trend from time series data.

- Inspection
- Regression analysis by the least squares method
- Moving averages

4.2.1 Inspection

The trend line can be drawn by eye on a graph in such a way that it appears to lie evenly between the recorded points.

4.2.2 Regression analysis by the least squares method

This is a statistical technique used to calculate the **'line of best fit'**. This method, which we do not need to discuss in detail here, makes the assumption that the trend line, whether up or down, is a **straight line**.

4.2.3 Moving averages

This method attempts to **remove seasonal (or cyclical) variations** by a process of averaging. We studied moving averages earlier in this chapter.

4.3 The underlying trend

The underlying trend is the trend which is revealed by removing the effect of cyclical, seasonal and random variations from the time series data.

5 Seasonal variations

Seasonal variations are short-term fluctuations in recorded values, due to different circumstances which affect results at different times of the year, on different days of the week, at different times of day, or whatever.

Examples of seasonal variations

- Sales of ice cream will be higher in summer than in winter, and sales of overcoats will be higher in autumn than in spring.
- Shops might expect higher sales shortly before Christmas, or in their winter and summer sales.
- Sales volumes might be higher on Friday and Saturday than on Monday.

'Seasonal' is a term which may appear to refer to the seasons of the year. However, its meaning in time series analysis is somewhat broader, as the examples given above show.

Example: Seasonal variations

The number of customers served by a company of travel agents over the past four years is shown in the following historigram.

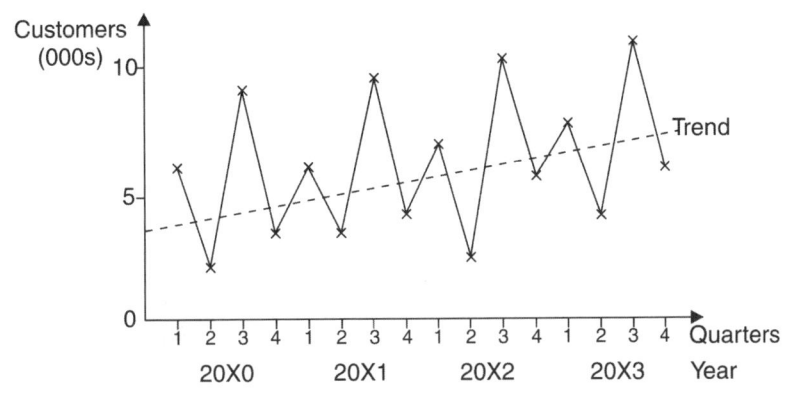

In this example, there would appear to be **large seasonal variations** in demand, but there is also a **basic upward trend**.

6 Cyclical and random variations

6.1 Cyclical variations

Cyclical variations are changes in results caused by circumstances which repeat in cycles.

In business, cyclical variations are commonly associated with **economic cycles**, which are successive booms and recessions in the economy.

In a **boom**, the rate of increase in economic activity (economic growth) is **higher than normal**, while in a **recession**, the level of economic activity (the output of goods and services) is **falling**.

Economic cycles may last a few years. Cyclical variations are therefore **longer term than seasonal variations**.

Activity 18.3

The following figures relate to the sales of a product during the period January 20X1 to April 20X2.

Month		Sales £'000
20X1	January	55
	February	52
	March	45
	April	48
	May	65
	June	70
	July	62
	August	55
	September	58
	October	75
	November	80
	December	77
20X2	January	55
	February	73
	March	85
	April	90

Task

Draw a graph showing the sales month by month for the period. Include on your graph the five-month moving average line.

6.2 Random variations

Random variations may be caused by **unforeseen circumstances** such as the following.

- A change in the government of a country
- A war
- The collapse of a company
- Technological change

Key learning points

- An **average** is a **measure of central tendency**. The three main types of average are:
  - The arithmetic mean
  - The mode
  - The median

- The **arithmetic mean** is the best known type of average. The value of every item is included in the computation of the arithmetic mean.

- The **mode** is an average which means 'the most frequently occurring value'.

- The **median** is the value of the middle member of a distribution.

- **Weighted averages** take account of the relative importance of the items being averaged.

- **Moving averages** are a special type of average used in connection with time series analysis. A moving average is an average of the results of a fixed number of time periods.

- A **time series** is a series of figures or values recorded over time.

- A **graph** of a time series is called a **historigram**.

- The **trend** in a time series is the underlying long term movement over time in the values of the data recorded. Trends must always be interpreted with care.

- The three main types of trend are as follows.
  - Downward trend
  - Upward trend
  - Static trend

- **Seasonal variations** are short-term fluctuations in recorded values, resulting from different circumstances which affect results in different periods.

- **Cyclical variations** are medium-term changes resulting from circumstances which repeat in cycles.

- The trend, seasonal variations and cyclical variations need to be distinguished from **random** or **one-off variations** in a set of results over a period of time.

- When completing an assessment, do make sure that you have a reliable calculator with you in order to calculate averages and analyse time series quickly and accurately. Make sure also that you have a spare set of batteries or a spare calculator – and beware of the dangers of using a solar powered calculator!

UNIT 7 PREPARING REPORTS AND RETURNS

Quick quiz

1. The arithmetic mean of the following numbers is ☐ (to 2 decimal places)

   23 21 20 32 71 50 23 19 19

2. What is the median of the following numbers?

   23 21 20 32 71 50 23 19 19

3. What is the weighted average price of the following books?

   12 × Great Britain Road Atlas (£10 each)
   3 × Pride and Prejudice (£7 each)
   9 × The Little Book of Calm (£2 each)

4. The name of the graph of a time series is an ☐

5. The main identifiable features of a time series are as follows.

   (a) ....
   (b) ....
   (c) ....
   (d) ....

6. What is a moving average?

7. What are seasonal variations?

8. What are cyclical variations?

Answers to quick quiz

1. ☐ 30.89 ☐ (to 2 decimal places)

   Arithmetic mean $= \dfrac{\Sigma x}{n}$

   $= \dfrac{23 + 21 + 20 + 32 + 71 + 50 + 23 + 19 + 19}{9}$

   $= \dfrac{278}{9} = 30.89$ (to 2 decimal places)

2. 23.

   Arranged in ascending order

   19, 19, 20, 21, 23, 23, 32, 50, 71

   Middle item = 23

3   Weighted average = $\dfrac{[(12 \times £10) + (3 \times £7) + (9 \times £2)]}{12 + 3 + 9}$ = $\dfrac{£120 + £21 + £18}{24}$

$\qquad\qquad\qquad\qquad\qquad\qquad\qquad\qquad$ = $\dfrac{£159}{24}$ = £6.625

4   Historigram

5   (a)   A trend
    (b)   Seasonal variations or fluctuations
    (c)   Cycles or cyclical variations
    (d)   Non-recurring, random variations

6   An average of the results of a fixed number of time periods.

7   Short-term fluctuations in recorded values, due to different circumstances which affect results at different times of the year, on different days of week and so on.

8   Changes in results caused by circumstances which repeat in cycles.

Activity checklist

This checklist shows which performance criteria, range statement or knowledge and understanding point is covered by each activity in this chapter. Tick off each activity as you complete it.

Activity

18.1	☐	This activity deals with Knowledge and Understanding point 9 regarding time series analysis
18.2	☐	This activity deals with Knowledge and Understanding point 9 regarding time series analysis
18.3	☐	This activity deals with Knowledge and Understanding point 9 regarding time series analysis

chapter 19

Using index numbers

Contents

1 Introduction
2 What is an index number?
3 Calculating index numbers
4 Chain based index numbers
5 Using index numbers to compare results

Performance criteria

7.1.C Compare results over time using an appropriate method that allows for changing price levels

Knowledge and understanding

10 Use of index numbers

1 Introduction

If we are making **comparisons** of costs and revenues over time to see how well a business is performing, we need to take account of the fact that there will be a **general shift** in costs (ie prices).

If a business achieves an increase in sales of 10% in **monetary** (cash) terms over a year, this result becomes less impressive if we are told that there was **general price inflation** of 15% over the year.

Index numbers therefore provide a **standardised way of comparing values** of the following over time.

- Prices
- Wages
- Volume of output

They are extensively used in business and government.

2 What is an index number?

An **index** is a measure, over a period of time, of the average changes in the values (prices or quantities) of a group of items.

2.1 Retail prices index

The **Retail Prices Index** (RPI) is probably the most well-known index in Britain. It measures changes in the cost of items of expenditure of the average household. The RPI includes the following.

- Bread
- Butter
- Meat
- Rent
- Insurance

The RPI used to be called the **'cost of living' index.**

2.2 The Footsie 100 share index

Another example which you may have heard reported in the news is the **FT-SE** (or 'footsie') 100 share index, which measures how the top 100 share prices in general have performed from one day to the next.

2.3 Index points

The term **'points'** is used to measure the difference between the index value in one year and the value in another year. For example, if the RPI was 120 in 1999 and 132 in 2001, we can say that the Retail Prices Index has risen 12 points during this period.

2.4 The base period

The **base period** is also known as the **base year** or the **base date**.

Index numbers are normally expressed as **percentages**, taking the value for a **base date** as 100. The choice of a base date or base year is not significant, except that it should normally be **'representative'**.

3 Calculating index numbers

Once a base year has been established, it is given an index of 100, and all other years are compared with the base year in order to calculate index numbers for these years. The calculation of index numbers is best explained by means of an example.

Example: Calculating index numbers for prices

The price of a cup of coffee in the Café Frederick was 40p in 2000, 50p in 2001 and 76p in 2002.

Task

Calculate index numbers for the price of a cup of coffee for the years 2001 and 2002 using 2000 as the base year.

Solution

Index number $= \dfrac{\text{Current year's figure}}{\text{Base year figure}} \times 100$

2001 index $= \dfrac{\text{Price in 2001}}{\text{Price in 2000}} \times 100$

$= \dfrac{50}{40} \times 100$

$= 125$

2002 index $= \dfrac{\text{Price in 2002}}{\text{Price in 2000}} \times 100$

$= \dfrac{76}{40} \times 100$

$= 190$

Note that index numbers are not just calculated for prices. They can also be calculated for quantities in order to show how sales volumes (for example) have changed over a period of time.

Example: Calculating index numbers for volumes

The Café Frederick sold 500,000 cups of coffee in 2000, 700,000 cups in 2001, and 600,000 in 2002.

Task

Calculate index numbers for the number of cups of coffee sold in the years 2001 and 2002 using 2000 as the base year.

Solution

$$\text{2001 Index} = \frac{\text{Quantity in 2001}}{\text{Quantity in 2000}} \times 100$$

$$= \frac{700,000}{500,000} \times 100$$

$$= 140$$

$$\text{2002 index} = \frac{\text{Quantity in 2002}}{\text{Quantity in 2000}} \times 100$$

$$= \frac{600,000}{500,000} \times 100$$

$$= 120$$

Activity 19.1

An index measuring the price of a litre of milk over the period 2000-2003 is as follows.

Year	Index
2000	96
2001	98
2002	100
2003	113

Tasks

(a) What year has been chosen for the base year of this index, as far as you can tell from the table above?
(b) By how many points has the index risen between 2000 and 2002?
(c) By what percentage has the index risen between 2000 and 2002?
(d) If a litre of milk cost £0.54 in 2001, how much did it cost in 2003?

Activity 19.2

Sales revenues for a company over a five-year period were as follows.

Year	Sales
	£'000
1998	35
1999	42
2000	40
2001	45
2002	50

Task

Calculate a sales index using 1999 as the base year.

4 Chain based index numbers

In all the previous examples in this chapter, we have used a **fixed base** method of indexing, whereby a base year is selected (index 100) and all subsequent changes are measured against this base.

The **chain base** method of indexing is an alternative approach, whereby the changes in prices (or volumes) are taken as a percentage of the period **immediately before**.

Chain based index numbers are best explained by means of an example.

Example: The chain base method

The price of a particular model of car varied as follows over the years 2000 to 2003.

Year	2000	2001	2002	2003
Price	£10,000	£11,120	£12,200	£13,880

Task

Construct a chain based index for the years 2001 to 2003.

Round your answer to the nearest index point.

Solution

A chain based index is calculated using the **percentage increase** (or decrease) on the previous year, rather than on a base year.

Year		Index
2000	£10,000	100
2001	$\frac{£11,120}{£10,000} \times 100 =$	111
2002	$\frac{£12,200}{£11,120} \times 100 =$	110
2003	$\frac{£13,880}{£12,200} \times 100 =$	114

The chain based index shows the rate of change from year to year, whereas the fixed base index shows the change more directly against the base year.

Activity 19.3

Sales for a company over a five-year period were as follows.

Year	Sales £'000
1998	70
1999	84
2000	80
2001	90
2002	100

Task

Calculate a chain based index number for the years 1999 to 2002 to the nearest index point.

Round your answer to the nearest whole number.

4.1 Rebasing index numbers

It is sometimes necessary to change the base of a time series (to **rebase**) perhaps because the **base time point is too far in the past**. The following time series has a base date of 1970 which would probably be considered too out of date.

	1990	1991	1992	1993	1994	1995
Index (1970 = 100)	451	463	472	490	499	505

To change the base date, divide each index by the index corresponding to the new base time point and multiply the result by 100.

Activity 19.4

The price index of a company's major raw material is as follows.

1998	1999	2000	2001	2002
100	110	112	106	120

Task

Rebase the index for the years 2001 and 2002 using 2000 as the base year. (Answers to the nearest whole number.)

---

5 Using index numbers to compare results

For the purpose of internal management reporting, results recorded over a number of periods can be adjusted using an appropriate price index to convert the figures from money terms to **'real' terms**.

As well as the Retail Prices Index (RPI) which measures the average level of prices of goods and services purchased by most households in the United Kingdom, the Office for National Statistics publishes a large number of producer price indices for different sectors of industry as well as index numbers of agricultural prices.

The various price indices for specific industry sectors will usually provide a more useful way of comparing results in different periods than more general indices such as the RPI. The RPI measures price changes over a varied 'basket' of retail goods and services, including housing costs. The price trends facing a wholesaler or producer in any particular industry may be very different.

Once the index to be used is agreed, the index is **'rebased'** to the period required and the various data are **adjusted** using the rebased index.

Example: Using index numbers to compare results

Fuchsias Unlimited is a garden centre that specialises in all varieties of fuchsia. The following information is available for the years 1999-2003.

	1999	2000	2001	2002	2003
Sales value (£)	20,000	26,000	30,780	28,710	36,000
Selling price per fuchsia (£)	1.25	1.30	1.35	1.45	1.60
UK Retail Price Index	125	127	129	133	136

Tasks

(a) Calculate the number of fuchsias sold in the years 1999-2003.

(b) Calculate the adjusted sales values to take account of price rises since 1998 when the RPI was 123.5 (to the nearest £).

Solution

(a)
	1999	2000	2001	2002	2003
Number of fuchsias sold (Sales value ÷ selling price)	16,000	20,000	22,800	19,800	22,500
(b) Actual sales value (£)	20,000	26,000	30,780	28,710	36,000
Adjusted sales value (at 1998 prices) (£)	19,744	25,204	29,331	26,659	32,476

Sales value at 1998 prices

$$1999 = £20,000 \times \frac{123.5}{125.1} = £19,744$$

$$2000 = £26,000 \times \frac{123.5}{127.4} = £25,204$$

$$2001 = £30,780 \times \frac{123.5}{129.6} = £29,331$$

$$2002 = £28,710 \times \frac{123.5}{133.0} = £26,659$$

$$2003 = £36,000 \times \frac{123.5}{136.9} = £32,476$$

Activity 19.5

The following information relates to Lily Ltd's sales figures for the four quarters in 2002.

	2002			
	Quarter 1 £	Quarter 2 £	Quarter 3 £	Quarter 4 £
Sales revenue	533,280	495,700	525,400	506,210

The sales director has requested that in addition to reporting quarterly sales revenue figures in the sales report, he would like the accounting technician to adjust these sales figures to take account of price rises. He has identified suitable index numbers as follows.

First quarter 2001 (Base period) = 179.1
First quarter 2002 = 184.2
Second quarter 2002 = 189.4
Third quarter 2002 = 185.9
Fourth quarter 2002 = 187.6

Calculate the adjusted sales revenue figures to be included in the sales report (to the nearest whole number).

19: USING INDEX NUMBERS

Key learning points

- **Index numbers** provide a standardised way of comparing values over time of prices, volumes and so on.

- An **index** is a measure, over a period of time, of the average changes in the values (prices or quantities) of a group of items.

- The most well-known indexes in Britain are the **Retail Prices Index** and the **Footsie 100 Share Index.**

- **Index points** measure the difference between one year's index and another year's index.

- The **base period** is also known as the **base year** or the **base date**. A **base period** is usually assigned a value of 100.

- **Fixed base method** of indexing involves measuring all changes against the base year.

    $$\text{Index number} = \frac{\text{Current year's figure}}{\text{Base year figure}} \times 100$$

- **Chain base method** of indexing involves measuring all changes against the previous year rather than against a base year.

    $$\text{Index number} = \frac{\text{Current year's figure}}{\text{Previous year's figure}} \times 100$$

- **Rebasing** involves changing the base date of an index. This is sometimes necessary when the base point is **too far in the past.**

- For the purpose of internal management reporting, results recorded over a number of periods can be adjusted using an appropriate price index to convert the figures from money terms (actual results) to **'real'** terms.

Quick quiz

1. What does an index measure?

2. When calculating index numbers the value normally assigned to the base year = ☐

3. Fixed base method] ? [Changes are measured against base period
   Chain base method   Changes are measured against the previous period

4. An index of machine prices has year 1 as the base year, with an index number of 100. By the end of year 9 the index had risen to 180 and by the end of year 14 it had risen by another 18 points.

   What was the percentage increase in machine prices between years 9 and 14?

   A 2%
   B 9%
   C 10%
   D 18%

5. The mean weekly take-home pay of the employees of Staples Ltd and a price index for the 11 years from 20X0 to 20Y0 are as follows.

Year	Weekly wage £	Price index (20X0 = 100)
20X0	150	100
20X1	161	103
20X2	168	106
20X3	179	108
20X4	185	109
20X5	191	112
20X6	197	114
20X7	203	116
20X8	207	118
20X9	213	121
20Y0	231	123

Complete the following table in order to construct a time series of real wages for 20X0 to 20Y0 using a price index with 20X6 as the base year.

Year	Index	Real weekly wage
		£
20X0		
20X1		
20X2		
20X3		
20X4		
20X5		
20X6		
20X7		
20X8		
20X9		
20Y0		

Answers to quick quiz

1   The change in the value of a group of items over time.

2   100

3   Fixed base method ⟶ Changes are measured against the base period

    Chain base method ⟶ Changes are measured against the previous period

4   C   To find the percentage increase since year 9, we must take the increase in the index as a percentage of the year 9 value. The increase in the index of 18 points between year 9 and year 14 is therefore a percentage increase of $(18/180 \times 100\%) = 10\%$.

    The correct answer is therefore C.

    If you selected option D you interpreted the increase of 18 points as an increase of 18% which is incorrect.

5

Year	Index	Real wage
		£
20X0	88	170
20X1	90	179
20X2	93	181
20X3	95	188
20X4	96	193
20X5	98	195
20X6	100	197
20X7	102	199
20X8	104	199
20X9	106	201
20Y0	108	214

The index number for each year with 20X6 as the base year will be the original index number divided by 1.14, and the real wages for each year will be (money wages × 100)/rebased index number for the year.

Activity checklist

This checklist shows which performance criteria, range statement or knowledge and understanding point is covered by each activity in this chapter. Tick off each activity as you complete it.

Activity

19.1	☐	This activity deals with Performance Criteria 7.1.C regarding the comparison of results over time and the use of index numbers
19.2	☐	This activity deals with Performance Criteria 7.1.C regarding the comparison of results over time and the use of index numbers
19.3	☐	This activity deals with Performance Criteria 7.1.C regarding the comparison of results over time and the use of index numbers
19.4	☐	This activity deals with Performance Criteria 7.1.C regarding the comparison of results over time and the use of index numbers
19.5	☐	This activity deals with Performance Criteria 7.1.C regarding the comparison of results over time and the use of index numbers

chapter 20

Reporting performance

Contents

1 Introduction
2 Management accounts
3 Cost centres, cost units and profit centres
4 Separate organisational units and the consolidation of information
5 Reporting non-financial information

Performance criteria

7.1.A **Consolidate information** derived from different units of the organisation into the appropriate form

7.1.B Reconcile **information** derived from different information systems within the organisation

7.1.D Account for transactions between separate units of the organisation in accordance with the organisation's procedures

Range statement

7.1 **Information:**
- Costs
- Revenue

7.1 **Methods of presenting information:**
- Written report containing diagrams
- Table

Knowledge and understanding

2 Relevant performance and quality measures
8 Use of standard units of inputs and outputs
13 Tabulation of accounting and other quantitative information using spreadsheets
14 Methods of presenting information: written reports; diagrammatic; tabular

1 Introduction

Much of the material in this chapter may be familiar to you from your studies for Unit 4 – **Supplying Information for Management Control** and Unit 6 – **Recording and Evaluating Costs and Revenue**.

Where material has been covered in earlier studies, it provides essential background information for the performance criteria covered in this chapter.

We begin this chapter by giving an overview of **management accounts** and then looking at **cost centres**, **cost units** and **profit centres**.

Sections 2 and 3 of this chapter provide the background needed before we get into the real nitty gritty of reporting performance. One of the objectives of this chapter is that you will be able to consolidate information derived from different units of the organisation into the appropriate form – we look at this specifically in Section 4.

In addition to reporting financial performance (we study this further in the next chapter) some organisations may find it useful to report non-financial results where these might give more meaningful information. We consider this in the final section of this chapter.

2 Management accounts

2.1 Financial accounts

As you already know, most financial accounts aim to provide **summarised information about the state of a business as a whole**. **Financial accounts** are generally of limited use for those who manage a business, because they look at past data and do not distinguish between different sections of the same business.

2.2 Management accounts

Most large businesses also produce **internal accounts** on a regular basis for the purposes of **management control**. Such accounts are generally referred to as **management accounts** and they allow managers to see what is happening in business operations.

Management accounts should be familiar to you as you will have studied the AAT's Unit 4 – **Supplying Information for Management Control** at the foundation level. Your Unit 6 – **Recording and Evaluating Costs and Revenues** studies (at the beginning of this Interactive Text) also provide some useful background to this chapter, and the next (Chapter 21) as we look at reporting performance and analysing results.

As you will remember, there is no obligation to produce management accounts and no set layout; they are solely for **internal use** and are produced in whatever format is convenient and useful to managers.

2.2.1 Reasons for producing management accounts

The main reasons for producing management accounts are as follows.

- To generate **up-to-date information** for management purposes
- To provide an **analysis of results** from various sections of the business

Because management accounts are primarily concerned with the **analysis of costs** they are also known as **cost accounts** and the person who produces them is sometimes referred to as a **cost accountant**.

2.2.2 Presentation and issue of management accounts

The analysis of costs and expenses shown in management accounts is at the **discretion of the management**. The way the figures are presented will depend on what kind of information the managers require to **control the business**.

The allocation of costs to the various profit and loss account categories in a **published profit and loss account**, which all companies are required to produce, will be much more restricted.

It is common for management accounting reports to be issued **monthly**. For certain types of report, **weekly** or **quarterly** reporting may be more appropriate.

It may be helpful to include **running annual totals**, adding the last month or quarter and dropping the equivalent month or quarter from the previous year each time. This can be particularly worthwhile if there are **seasonal patterns** and can help to indicate whether a **longer-term trend** is developing.

2.2.3 Rounding management accounts

In general, the first **two significant digits** of a number are those which matter. For example, for most reporting purposes, the important part of the figure £29,120 are the figures 2 and 9: the figure might as well be rounded to £29,000. A third digit may be included to avoid too much rounding: for example, the figure might be presented as 29.1 in a column headed £'000.

2.2.4 Consolidating management accounts

Where information on costs and revenues from different units of the organisation is aggregated (or **'consolidated'**) together, it will be necessary to make sure that the resulting consolidated figures are compiled in a **consistent way**. This may involve ensuring that costs are **categorised** in a reasonable way and adopting the methods which have been used in past management reports.

VAT should be excluded from sales turnover. The current VAT position is reflected in the accounts by showing in the balance sheet net amounts due to or repayable by HM Customs and Excise. We shall be studying VAT in more detail in Chapters 23 and 24 of this Interactive Text.

2.3 Manufacturing accounts

2.3.1 Preparing manufacturing accounts

A **manufacturing account** might be prepared by a manufacturing company, in order to establish the cost of the goods it has produced during a period of time. When a manufacturing account is prepared, it precedes the trading, profit and loss account, so that there are the following accounts.

- A **manufacturing** account, to establish the cost of goods produced
- A **trading** account, to establish the cost of goods sold and gross profit
- A **profit and loss** account, to establish the net profit

Manufacturing accounts are **not obligatory** for manufacturing companies, because they can prepare a trading, profit and loss account without a manufacturing account if they wish to do so. However, a manufacturing account is needed if management want to know what the cost of producing goods has been, for **internal information**.

2.3.2 Direct and indirect costs

A manufacturing account is basically a list of the costs of producing the goods in a factory, or in several factories, during a period. These costs consist of the following.

- The cost of **raw materials and components** that are used to make up the products **(direct materials)**.
- The cost of the **labour** that makes the products. As this is labour that is directly involved in producing an item of output, it is called **direct labour**.
- **Other** costs incurred in the factory, which cannot be attributed to the production of any specific output but which are incurred to keep the factory running. These **indirect production costs**, or **production overheads**, include the salaries of supervisors, factory rent and so on.

The total direct costs of production are often known as **prime cost**, and the total of direct costs plus production overheads is known as **factory cost** or total production cost (or **works cost**).

2.3.3 Fixed and variable costs

A further distinction is often made between variable costs and fixed costs.

- **Variable costs** are costs that **vary** with the number of goods produced, or the number of hours worked.
- **Fixed costs** are the costs which are the **same** total amount for a period of time, regardless of the number of units produced or the number of hours worked.

Unit 6 – Recording and Evaluating Costs and Revenues studies manufacturing costs in detail. For the purposes of **Preparing Reports and Returns** (Unit 7) you need to have some **knowledge and understanding** of costs, which we have provided for you in this chapter.

20: REPORTING PERFORMANCE

We have used manufacturing accounts in order to illustrate the different types of cost that an organisation incurs. In a skills based assessment, however, you might be faced with a situation relating to various types of organisation, not just a manufacturing business.

3 Cost centres, cost units and profit centres

3.1 Allocation of costs to cost centres

We have already established that costs consist of the following.

- Direct materials
- Direct labour
- Direct expenses
- Production overheads
- Administration overheads
- General overheads

But how does an accounting technician set about **recording** in practice the actual expenses incurred under any one of these classifications?

3.2 Recording costs

To begin with, all costs should be recorded as a direct cost of a **cost centre**. Even 'overhead costs' are directly traceable to an office or an item of expense and there should be an **overhead cost centre** to cater for these costs.

A **cost centre** is a location, person or item of equipment for which costs may be ascertained and related to cost units for control purposes.

When costs are incurred, they are generally allocated to a **cost centre**. Examples of cost centres are as follows.

- A department
- A machine
- A project
- A new product

Charging costs to a cost centre involves two steps.

Step 1   **Identifying** the cost centre for which an item of expenditure is a direct cost.
Step 2   **Allocating** the cost to the cost centre.

3.3 Cost unit

In general, departments are termed **cost centres** and the product produced by an organisation is termed the **cost unit**. Once costs have been traced to cost centres, they can be further analysed in order to establish a **cost per cost unit**.

343

Alternatively, some items of cost may be charged directly to a cost unit, for example direct materials and direct labour costs.

Example: Cost units

Organisation	Possible cost unit
Steelworks	Tonne of steel produced Tonne of coke used
Hospital	Patient/day Operation Out-patient visit
Freight organisation	Tonne/kilometre
Passenger transport organisation	Passenger/kilometre
Accounting firm	Audit performed Chargeable hour
Restaurant	Meal served

A **cost unit** is a unit of product or service in relation to which costs are ascertained.

3.4 Cost codes

The allocation of the cost to the cost centre is usually by means of a **cost code.** We studied cost codes earlier on in this Interactive Text in Chapters 4 and 8.

A **cost code** is a shorthand description of a cost using numbers, letters or a combination of both.

In order to provide accurate information for management, it is important that costs are **allocated correctly**. Each individual cost should therefore be identifiable by its **code**.

3.5 Profit centres

In some businesses, management establish **profit centres** of operations, with each centre held accountable for making a profit. The manager of the profit centre is made responsible for its good or bad results.

3.6 Transfers of goods or services

Where there are transfers of goods or services between divisions of a **divisionalised organisation**, the transfers could be made **'free'** or **'as a favour'** to the division receiving the benefit.

Example: Transfers of goods or services

If a garage and car showroom has two divisions, one for car repairs and servicing and the other for car sales, the servicing division will be required to service cars before they are sold and delivered to customers. There is no requirement for this service work to be charged for: the servicing division could do its work for the car sales division without making any record of the work done. However, unless the cost or value of such work is recorded, management cannot keep a proper check on the amount of resources (like labour time) being used up on new car servicing. It is necessary for control purposes that **some record of the inter-divisional services should be kept**, and one way of doing this is through the accounting system. Inter-divisional work can be given a cost or charge: a **transfer price**.

3.6.1 Transfer price

A **transfer price** is the price at which goods or services are transferred from one process or department to another.

It is particularly important in the case of transferred goods that a transfer price should be charged. A proper system of accounting demands that **goods should be costed as they progress through work in progress to finished goods** and so the need for a transfer cost or transfer price should be clear.

A transfer price may be based upon the following.

- Marginal cost (at marginal cost or with a gross profit margin on top)
- Full cost (at full cost, or at a full cost plus)
- Market price
- Negotiated or discounted price

4 Separate organisational units and the consolidation of information

4.1 Departmental and branch accounts

Many organisations are large enough for a certain degree of **divisionalisation** to take place. Organisations may be divided into the following.

- Departments
- Sales areas
- Divisions
- Branches

Where an organisation is increasing in size and/or is intending to diversify its activities, it may find it necessary to control operations by using a system of **departmental or branch accounting**.

As each department or branch is established as a **separate accounting centre**, the net profit per branch can be found and accumulated to arrive at the profit for the whole business. A **profit target** might be set for each unit of the organisation.

Organisations operating through branches

- Banks
- Building societies
- Estate agents
- Travel agents
- Department stores

4.2 Consolidation of information

Where a complete and independent set of records is maintained by individual branches trading and profit and loss accounts and balance sheets can be prepared for each branch and for the head office. Accounts for the business as a whole can then be produced by **combining the individual accounts**.

At the end of an accounting period trial balances are extracted from the head office and branch ledgers. Using the trial balances, accounts may be prepared for the following.

- The head office
- The branch
- The combined firm or company

Generally, the trading and profit and loss accounts and balance sheets are produced in columnar form, the head office and branch being treated almost as if they were **separate legal entities**. The organisation is only regarded as a **single concern** in the **'combined' columns** which are arrived at by totalling appropriate items in the head office and branch columns. In the **combined balance sheet** the branch current account is replaced by the underlying assets and liabilities.

In some situations it might be necessary to make **adjustments** if there have been any **transfers of goods** between different organisational units.

Example: Consolidation of information

Departmental trading and profit and loss accounts for AllSales Ltd are as follows.

ALLSALES LIMITED
DEPARTMENTAL TRADING AND PROFIT AND LOSS ACCOUNTS
FOR THE YEAR ENDED 31 DECEMBER 20X0

	Furniture dept		Electrical goods dept	
	£	£	£	£
Sales		180,000		270,000 [1]
Cost of sales:				
Opening stock	36,000		45,000	
Purchases	105,000 [2]		162,000	
	141,000		207,000	
Less closing stock	39,000		54,000	
		102,000		153,000
Gross profit		78,000		117,000
Less expenses:				
Selling & distribution	22,800		34,200	
Administration	17,450		26,450	
Lighting & heating	1,000		4,800	
Rent & rates	19,000		9,500	
		60,250		74,950
Net profit		17,750		42,050

Note:

(1) Includes sales to the furniture department at cost of £23,000.
(2) This figure includes purchases from the electrical goods department of £23,000.

Task

Calculate the consolidated trading and profit and loss account for Allsales Limited for the year ended 31 December 20X0 showing clearly any adjustments which should be made.

Solution

	Furniture dept		Electrical goods dept		Adjustment	Total	
	£	£	£	£	£	£	£
Sales		180,000		270,000	23,000		427,000
Cost of sales:							
Opening stock	36,000		45,000			81,000	
Purchases	105,000		162,000		23,000	244,000	
	141,000		207,000			325,000	
Less closing stock	39,000		54,000			93,000	
		102,000		153,000			232,000
Gross profit		78,000		117,000			195,000
Less expenses:							
Selling & distribution	22,800		34,200			57,000	
Administration	17,450		26,450			43,900	
Lighting & heating	1,000		4,800			5,800	
Rent & rates	19,000		9,500			28,500	
		60,250		74,950			135,200
Net profit		17,750		42,050			59,800

Activity 20.1

Consolidated departmental trading and profit and loss accounts for Harry Ltd are as follows.

HARRY LTD
DEPARTMENTAL TRADING AND PROFIT AND LOSS ACCOUNTS
FOR THE YEAR ENDED 28 FEBRUARY 20X1

	Dept A		Dept B		Total	
	£	£	£	£	£	£
Sales		360,000		540,000		900,000
Cost of sales:						
Opening stock	72,000		90,000		162,000	
Purchases	210,000		324,000		534,000	
	282,000		414,000		696,000	
Less closing stock	78,000		108,000		186,000	
		204,000		306,000		510,000
Gross profit		156,000		234,000		390,000
Less expenses:						
Selling & distribution	45,600		68,400		114,000	
Administration	34,900		52,900		87,800	
Light & heating	2,000		9,600		11,600	
Rent & rates	38,000		19,000		57,000	
		120,500		149,900		270,400
Net profit		35,500		84,100		119,600

Task

Your manager has asked you to check the figures in the above consolidated accounts. He also tells you that Department A transferred £48,000 of goods to Department B at cost but that £2,000 of these sales is in respect of a job not completed until 5 March 20X1. Produce a revised consolidated set of accounts for Harry Ltd showing clearly any adjustments which should be made.

5 Reporting non-financial information

5.1 Non-financial results

In addition to reporting financial information, some organisations may find it useful to report **non-financial results** where these might give more meaningful information.

Examples of organisations which might find it useful to report non-financial results are as follows.

- Hospitals
- Railways
- Hotels
- Educational establishments (colleges and schools)

5.2 Hospitals

The **financial management departments** of most hospitals will be concerned with financial results such as **monthly management accounts** and year-end published accounts. Cost accountants will also be involved with costing the services provided by the hospital, for example, the cost of a hip replacement operation and so on.

In addition to the large volume of financial information passing through this department, there will also be a large amount of **relevant non-financial data**.

- The number of inpatients
- The number of outpatient attendances
- The number of daycases
- The number of beds available
- The average stay per inpatient (days)
- The average number of beds occupied

Organisations such as those listed in 5.1 above are usually required to complete returns (to the Area Health Authority, for example) that summarise both financial and non-financial data for certain periods.

Example: Reporting non-financial information

The following data relates to two hospitals, the Trent South Hospital and the Brigden Royal Hospital.

	Trent South		Brigden Royal	
	Inpatients £	Outpatients £	Inpatients £	Outpatients £
Cost of services				
Direct patient care	23,400,000	3,600,000	15,000,000	650,000
Medical support services				
X Ray	1,400,000	1,100,000	395,000	165,000
Pathology	2,500,000	1,700,000	650,000	295,000
Pharmacy	4,700,000	1,950,000	4,040,000	72,000
Non-medical support services				
Laundry	415,000	42,500	35,400	19,700
Catering	725,000	17,500	525,000	4,950
Administration	6,540,000	1,890,000	5,980,000	1,250,000
Other data				

	Trent South	Brigden Royal
Number of inpatients	31,900	1,620
Average stay per inpatient	16 days	179 days
Number of beds available	1,250	750
Average number of beds occupied	890	690
Number of outpatient attendances	329,500	26,400

Number of inpatient days

Number of inpatients × average stay per inpatient = number of inpatient days

Trent South = 31,900 × 16 = 510,400 inpatient days
Brigden Royal = 1,620 × 179 = 289,980 inpatient days

Bed occupancy rates

$$\text{Bed occupancy rate} = \frac{\text{Average number of beds occupied}}{\text{Number of beds available}} \times 100\%$$

Trent South $= \frac{890}{1,250} \times 100\% = 71.2\%$

Brigden Royal $= \frac{690}{750} \times 100\% = 92\%$

Armed with information such as the number of **inpatient days** for each hospital, it is possible to produce more meaningful financial information. For example, the hospitals might wish to compare the costs of their X Ray departments per inpatient day.

For Trent South, the **cost per inpatient day** for the **X Ray department** = $\dfrac{£1,400,000}{510,400}$ = £2.70.

For the Brigden Royal, the **cost per inpatient day** for the **X Ray department** = $\dfrac{£395,000}{289,980}$ = £1.40.

5.2.1 Bed occupancy rates

The data in the example above shows **bed occupancy rates** of 71.2% and 92% for the hospitals under consideration. Such information is very useful, since if bed occupancy rates in any hospital were below a certain level then the Area Health Authority might wish to investigate the reasons for this.

5.3 Railways

Railway companies are also likely to be interested in reporting non-financial information. For example, they might be interested in the following.

- Number of passengers using their trains in a given period
- The number of train services running
- The average number of seats per train
- The number of passengers per train service
- The percentage of seats filled per train service

5.4 Hotels

In order to compare the performances of different hotels, information such as the number of rooms let and room occupancy rates might prove useful.

Activity 20.2

The Grand Garden Bench Company manufactures high quality garden benches. Wyn Lotkins is manager of the main factory based in Hay-on-Wye in Wales. There is a second factory in Tonbridge in Kent. The production department is made up of the following sections.

1. Moulding
2. Assembly
3. Finishing

Wyn Lotkins has collected performance data from her two factories which is given below.

	Quarter 1	Quarter 2	Quarter 3	Quarter 4
Benches completed				
Hay-on-Wye	4,800	5,400	5,600	5,200
Kent	4,000	4,200	4,600	4,400

Budgeted labour hours per bench
Moulding   13.6
Assembly   17.2
Finishing   25.6

	Quarter 1	Quarter 2	Quarter 3	Quarter 4
Actual hours worked				
Hay-on-Wye				
Moulding	16,800	17,280	19,040	19,760
Assembly	19,800	23,180	23,980	22,896
Finishing	29,728	34,980	37,260	34,248
Kent				
Moulding	14,400	14,280	16,100	15,240
Assembly	16,852	18,120	20,480	19,500
Finishing	25,828	28,084	31,060	27,648

Task

Wyn Lotkins is concerned about the performance of the factory in Hay-on-Wye, compared to that of the factory in Kent, and would like you (her accounting assistant) to calculate the following for her.

- The total actual hours worked in each factory.
- The actual hours per bench manufactured in each factory (to two decimal places).

Key learning points

- ☑ **Management accounts** are **internal accounts** produced on a regular basis for the purposes of management control.

- ☑ A **cost centre** is a location, person or item of equipment for which costs may be ascertained and related to cost units for control purposes.

- ☑ A **cost unit** is a unit of product or service in relation to which costs are ascertained.

- ☑ A **cost code** is a shorthand description of a cost using numbers, letters or a combination of both.

- ☑ **Profit centres** are similar to cost centres except that each centre is held accountable for **making a profit.**

- ☑ A **transfer price** is the price at which goods or services are transferred from one process or department to another.

- ☑ Many organisations are large enough to have separate organisational units, such as the following.
    - Departments
    - Sales areas
    - Divisions
    - Branches

- ☑ If separate organisational units of a business transfer goods between different units, it might be necessary to make adjustments when consolidating information.

- ☑ The following organisations might find it useful to report **non-financial results** in addition to reporting financial information.
    - Hospitals
    - Railways
    - Hotels
    - Colleges and schools

- ☑ In an assessment, be prepared to report *and* comment upon non-financial data as well as financial data. Always draw on any experience that you have gained in the work place when tackling skills based assessments – you are much more likely to impress the assessor if you do so!

Quick quiz

1. Give two reasons why organisations produce management accounts.
2. Give four examples of cost centres.
3. What are the two steps involved in charging costs to a cost centre?

   Step 1. ....

   Step 2. ....

4. If Department A transfers goods to Department B, which two accounts will need to be adjusted when the departments' results are consolidated?
5. List three examples of organisations operating through branches.

   (a) ....

   (b) ....

   (c) ....

6. Why do some organisations find it useful to report non-financial results?

Answer to quick quiz

1. (a) To generate up-to-date information for management purposes
   (b) To provide an analysis of results from various sections of the business

2. (a) A department
   (b) A machine
   (c) A project
   (d) A new product

3. **Step 1.** Identifying the cost centre for which an item of expenditure is a direct cost
   Step 2. Allocating the cost to the cost centre

4. The sales account and the purchases accounts will need to be reduced by the value of the goods transferred.

5. Any three of the following.

   (a) Banks
   (b) Building societies
   (c) Estate agents
   (d) Travel agents
   (e) Department stores

6. Because sometimes non-financial results give more meaningful information than financial results and they can usefully supplement the financial information given.

Activity checklist

This checklist shows which performance criteria, range statement or knowledge and understanding point is covered by each activity in this chapter. Tick off each activity as you complete it.

Activity

20.1 ☐ This activity deals with Performance Criteria 7.1.A, 7.1.B and 7.1.D regarding the consolidation and reconciliation of information derived from separate units of an organisation in accordance with the organisation's procedures

20.2 ☐ This activity deals with Performance Criteria 7.1.A, 7.1.B and 7.1.D regarding the consolidation and reconciliation of information derived from separate units of an organisation in accordance with the organisation's procedures

chapter 21

Measuring performance

Contents

1. Introduction
2. Productivity
3. Cost per unit
4. Resource utilisation
5. Profitability

Performance criteria

7.1.E Calculate **ratios** and **performance indicators** in accordance with the organisation's procedures

7.2.B Ensure calculations of **ratios** and performance indicators are accurate

Range statement

7.1 **Ratios:**
& 7.2
- Gross profit margin
- Net profit margin
- Return on capital employed

7.1 **Performance indicators:**
- Productivity
- Cost per unit
- Resource utilisation
- Profitability

UNIT 7 PREPARING REPORTS AND RETURNS

Knowledge and understanding

2   Relevant performance and quality measures
11 Main types of performance indicators: productivity; cost per unit; resource utilisation; profitability
12 Ratios: gross profit margin; net profit margin; return on capital employed

1 Introduction

The **profitability** and **productivity** of different products and departments respectively, give us some indication of how a product or department is performing. Generally, the terms profitability and productivity are known as **performance indicators**.

Performance indicators can be used to compare the performances of different cost centres and profit centres with each other, during one accounting period. Performance indicators may also be used to compare the performance of a single cost centre or profit centre over a number of accounting periods.

For Unit 7 – **Preparing Reports and Returns**, you are expected to have an awareness of relevant performance and quality measures. You are also expected to be able to calculate accurately ratios and performance indicators in accordance with the organisation's procedures.

This chapter will explain the following performance indicators, and show the ways in which they may be measured.

- Productivity
- Cost per unit
- Resource utilisation measures
- Profitability

Make sure that you have got a calculator when you work through this chapter as there are lots of numerical examples and activities for you to have a go at.

2 Productivity

2.1 Production and productivity

It is important to distinguish between the terms **production** and **productivity**.

- **Production** is the quantity or volume of output produced. It is the number of units produced, or the actual number of units produced converted into an equivalent number of 'standard hours of production'.

- **Productivity** is a measure of the efficiency with which output has been produced. It can also be thought of as a measure of how hard an organisation's employees are working.

We are going to look at three productivity measures.

- Productivity per labour hour
- Productivity per employee
- Productivity ratio

2.2 Productivity per labour hour

Productivity per labour hour $= \dfrac{\text{Output in the period}}{\text{Hours worked in the period}}$

Example: Productivity per labour hour

Transhiner Ltd has produced 550,000 units of Product S in a period. The company's 110 employees have worked a total of 132,000 hours in order to produce these units.

The expected production level in this period was 600,000 units of Product S in 150,000 hours.

Productivity per labour hour $= \dfrac{\text{Output in the period}}{\text{Hours worked in the period}}$

$= \dfrac{550{,}000 \text{ units}}{132{,}000 \text{ hours}}$

= 4.17 units per labour hour

Expected productivity = 600,000 units in 150,000 hours

$= \dfrac{600{,}000 \text{ units}}{150{,}000 \text{ hours}}$

= 4 units per labour hour

Actual productivity (4.17 units per labour hour) is therefore greater than expected productivity (4 units per labour hour) in the same period.

2.3 Productivity per employee

We can calculate the productivity per employee for Transliner Ltd as follows.

Productivity per employee $= \dfrac{\text{Output in the period}}{\text{Number of employees producing output}}$

$= \dfrac{550{,}000 \text{ units}}{110 \text{ employees}}$

= 5,000 units per employee

Activity 21.1

Transliner Ltd has a sales department which is made up of 25 staff who all process telephone orders. In a period the sales team processed 1,400 orders.

Task

Calculate the productivity per employee for Transliner Ltd's sales department.

2.4 Productivity ratio

Productivity is a **relative** measure of the output actually produced compared with the output expected for the hours worked.

It is expressed as a percentage and calculated as follows.

$$\text{Productivity ratio} = \frac{\text{Actual production}}{\text{Expected production}} \times 100\%$$

Example: Productivity ratio

Suppose that an employee is expected to produce three units in every hour worked. The **standard rate of productivity** is therefore three units per hour, and one unit is valued at $1/3$ of a standard hour of output. If, during one week, the employee makes 126 units in 40 hours of work:

Production = 126 units per week

In 40 hours, production is expected to be (× 3)   120 units
Actual production was   126 units

$$\text{Productivity ratio} = \frac{\text{Actual production}}{\text{Expected production}} \times 100\%$$

$$= \frac{126}{120} \times 100\%$$

$$= 105\%$$

A productivity ratio greater than 100% indicates that actual productivity is better than the expected or 'standard' level of productivity.

2.5 Controlling production levels

Management will wish to plan and control both production levels and labour productivity.

Production levels can be increased in the following ways.

- Working overtime
- Hiring extra staff
- Sub-contracting some work to an outside firm

- Raising productivity – ie managing the work force so as to achieve more output in a given number of hours worked.

Production levels can be reduced in the following ways.

- Cancelling overtime
- Laying off staff

Managers will also wish to avoid paying employees (in full) for doing nothing (ie idle time payments) and will also wish to avoid a drop in productivity.

Productivity, if improved, will enable a company to achieve its production targets in fewer hours of work, and therefore at a lower cost.

Activity 21.2

Fred works for Bassett Ltd. He is expected to produce 7 units in every hour that he works. During one particular week he makes 280 units in 35 hours of work.

Tasks

(a) What is the standard rate of productivity?
(b) What is the productivity ratio?

3 Cost per unit

Once costs have been traced to cost centres, they can be further analysed in order to establish a **cost per cost unit**.

The **cost per unit** of a product is another type of **performance indicator**, like productivity and profitability. The unit which is selected must be appropriate to the organisation, and **must** be a meaningful measure.

The **cost per unit** of a product or service may be calculated as follows.

$$\text{Cost per unit} = \frac{\text{Cost of input}}{\text{Units of output}}$$

Example: Cost per unit

Tandridge Ltd makes two products, the 'Oxted' and the 'Edenbridge'. Management believe that the company is performing more efficiently since the introduction of a bonus scheme for its factory workers one year ago. The following information relates to the costs and production of Tandridge Ltd for 20X7 and 20X8.

	20X7		20X8	
	Oxted	Edenbridge	Oxted	Edenbridge
	£	£	£	£
Direct material	20,000	16,000	18,000	14,000
Direct labour	15,000	20,000	14,000	18,000
Direct expenses	12,000	12,000	10,000	10,000
Total direct costs	47,000	48,000	42,000	42,000
Output (units)	10,000	16,000	12,000	18,000

Using cost per unit as a performance indicator, comment on the performance of the company in the years 20X7 and 20X8.

Solution

Firstly, we need to calculate the cost per unit for each product for each of the years 20X7 and 20X8.

			Cost per unit	
			20X7	20X8
			£	£
Oxted				
20X7	=	$\dfrac{£47,000}{10,000}$	4.70	
20X8	=	$\dfrac{£42,000}{12,000}$		3.50
Edenbridge				
20X7	=	$\dfrac{£48,000}{16,000}$	3.00	
20X8	=	$\dfrac{£42,000}{18,000}$		2.33

The results show that the cost per unit for both the Oxted and the Edenbridge has fallen quite significantly between 20X7 and 20X8. This is an example of a situation in which the **cost per unit** may be used as a **performance indicator**.

Activity 21.3

The following information relates to two hospitals for the year ended 31 December 20X8.

	The General	The County
Number of in-patients	15,400	710
Average stay per in-patient	10 days	156 days
Total number of out-patient attendances	130,000	3,500
Number of available beds	510	320
Average number of beds occupied	402	307

Cost analysis	The General		The County	
	In-patients £	Out-patients £	In-patients £	Out-patients £
Patient care services				
Direct treatment services and supplies (eg nursing staff)	6,213,900	1,076,400	1,793,204	70,490
Medical supporting services				
Diagnostic (eg pathology)	480,480	312,000	22,152	20,650
Other services (eg occupational therapy)	237,160	288,600	77,532	27,790
General services				
Patient related (eg catering)	634,480	15,600	399,843	7,700
General (eg administration)	2,196,760	947,700	1,412,900	56,700

Note. In-patients are those who receive treatment while remaining in hospital. Out-patients visit hospital during the day to receive treatment.

Tasks

(a) Prepare separate statements for each hospital for each cost heading.

    (i) Cost per in-patient day, £ to two decimal places.
    (ii) Cost per out-patient attendance, £ to two decimal places.

(b) Calculate for each hospital the bed-occupation percentage.

(c) Comment briefly on your findings.

4 Resource utilisation

4.1 Inputs and outputs

Resource utilisation is usually measured in terms of **productivity**, which is the ratio of outputs to inputs. As usual, the ease with which this may be measured varies according to the service being delivered.

The main resource of a firm of accountants, for example, is the **time** of various grades of staff. The main output of an accountancy firm is **chargeable hours**.

In a restaurant it is not nearly so straightforward. **Inputs** are the ingredients for the meal, the chef's time and expertise, the waiter's time and expertise, the surroundings, the music, the other customers, and the customers' own likes and dislikes. A customer attitude survey might show whether or not a customer enjoyed the food, but it could not ascribe the enjoyment or lack of it to the quality of the ingredients, say, rather than to the skill of the chef or the speed of the waiter.

Here are some examples of resource utilisation ratios.

Business	Input	Output
Consultancy firm	Hours available	Chargeable hours
Hotel	Rooms available	Rooms occupied
Rail company	Passenger miles available	Passenger miles achieved
Bank	Number of staff	Number of accounts

4.2 Return on capital employed

Return on capital employed (ROCE (also called **return on investment (ROI))** is calculated as (profit/capital employed) × 100% and shows how much profit has been made in relation to the amount of resources invested.

Profits alone do not show whether the return achieved by an organisation is sufficient, because the profit measure takes no account of the **volume of assets committed**.

Example: Return on capital employed

If company A and company B have the following results, identify which company would have the better performance.

	A £	B £
Profit	5,000	5,000
Sales	100,000	100,000
Capital employed	50,000	25,000

Company A ROCE $= \dfrac{\text{Profit}}{\text{Capital employed}} \times 100\%$

$= \dfrac{£5,000}{£50,000} \times 100\%$

$= 10\%$

Company B ROCE $= \dfrac{£5,000}{£25,000} \times 100\%$

$= 20\%$

The profit of each company is the same but company B only invests £25,000 to achieve these results whereas company A needs £50,000. Therefore, Company B would have the better performance.

ROCE may be calculated in a number of ways, but accounting technicians usually prefer to exclude from profits all revenues and expenditures which are not related to the operation of the business itself (such as interest payable and income from trade investments). **Profit before interest and tax** is therefore often used.

Similarly **all assets of a non-operational nature** (for example trade investments and intangible assets such as goodwill) **should be excluded** from capital employed.

Profits should be related to average capital employed but, in practice, the **ratio is usually computed using the year-end capital employed**.

What does the ROCE tell us? What should we be looking for? There are **two principal comparisons** that can be made.

- The change in ROCE from one year to the next
- The ROCE being earned by other entities operating in the same line of business

4.3 Asset turnover

Asset turnover is a measure of how well the assets of a business are being used to a generate sales. It is calculated as (sales ÷ capital employed).

Example: Asset turnover

Two companies each have capital employed of £100,000. Company A makes sales of £400,000 per annum whereas Company B makes sales of only £200,000 per annum.

Task

Calculate the asset turnover ratio for both companies.

Solution

$$\text{Asset turnover} = \frac{\text{Sales}}{\text{Capital employed}}$$

Company A asset turnover $= \dfrac{£400,000}{£100,000} = 4$ times

Company B asset turnover $= \dfrac{£200,000}{£100,000} = 2$ times

Company A is therefore generating an asset turnover which is twice that of Company B.

Asset turnover is **expressed as 'x times' so that assets generate x times their value in annual turnover.** Here, Company A's asset turnover is 4 times and B's 2 times.

5 Profitability

In addition to productivity ratios, cost per unit and resource utilisation measures, you need to be able to calculate and explain **profitability** for Unit 7 skills based assessments.

Profitability is a measure of how profitable something is. Profit has two components, cost and income. All parts of an organisation and all activities within it incur costs, and so their success needs to be judged in relation to costs. Only some parts of an organisation earn income, for example **profit centres,** and their success should be judged in terms of both cost and income, ie **profit.**

The main indicator of profitability in profit centres and in individual organisations is the **profit margin.**

5.1 Profit margin

The **profit margin (profit to sales ratio)** is calculated as (profit ÷ sales) × 100%.

The profit margin is a particularly useful way of analysing information.

- It provides a measure of performance for management.
- Investigation of unsatisfactory profit margins enables control action to be taken, either by reducing excessive costs or, possibly, by raising selling prices.

Profit margin is usually **calculated using operating profit**.

Example: Profit to sales ratio

Trading Places plc compares its 20X1 results with 20X0 results as follows.

	20X1 £	20X0 £
Sales	160,000	120,000
Cost of sales		
Direct materials	40,000	20,000
Direct labour	40,000	30,000
Production overhead	22,000	20,000
Marketing overhead	42,000	35,000
	144,000	105,000
Operating profit	16,000	15,000
Profit to sales ratio	10%	12½%

Ratio analysis on the above information shows that there is a decline in profitability in spite of the £1,000 increase in profit, because the profit margin is less in 20X1 than 20X0.

5.2 Gross profit margin

The **pure trading activities of a business can be analysed** using the gross profit margin, which is calculated as follows.

Gross profit margin = $\dfrac{\text{Gross profit}}{\text{Turnover}} \times 100\%$.

Remember that gross profit excludes non-production overheads.

For Trading Places plc the gross profit margins would be calculated as follows.

20X1 $\dfrac{16,000 + 42,000}{160,000} \times 100\% = 36.25\%$

20X0 $\dfrac{15,000 + 35,000}{120,000} \times 100\% = 41.67\%$

5.3 Net profit margin

Another ratio which you need to be aware of is the net profit margin, which is calculated as follows.

Net profit margin = $\dfrac{\text{Net profit}}{\text{Turnover}} \times 100\%$

Remember that non-production overheads are included in the net profit calculation.

For Trading Places plc, the net profit margins would be as follows.

20X1 $\dfrac{16,000}{160,000} \times 100\% = 10\%$

20X0 $\dfrac{15,000}{120,000} \times 100\% = 12.5\%$

Activity 21.4

The following results are for Macbeth Ltd, a company which has just two profit centres A and B.

	20X4		20X5		20X6	
	A	B	A	B	A	B
	£'000	£'000	£'000	£'000	£'000	£'000
Sales	25	44	60	47	62	49
Net profit	10	11	24	14	27	16

Task

Calculate the net profit margin for each profit centre in each of the years 20X4, 20X5 and 20X6, and comment on your results.

5.4 Performance reports

As we have already mentioned, the management accounting system should be capable of preparing performance reports for each cost centre, profit centre, product or department. Once the management accounting information has been consolidated, it may be used by management to measure the performance of different aspects of the organisation.

Remember that there is no single correct formula to use when calculating ratios. You *must* understand the concepts underlying the ratios. For example, when considering the return on capital employed, both the return and the capital employed might be measured in different ways. Different ratios for ROCE may therefore be used for different purposes at different times.

Key learning points

- **Productivity, cost per unit, resource utilisation measures** and **profitability** are all different types of **performance indicator**.

- **Productivity** is a measure of the efficiency with which output has been produced.

- The three main measures of productivity are as follows.
  - Productivity per labour hour
  - Productivity per employee
  - Productivity ratio

- The **cost per unit** of a product or service = $\dfrac{\text{Costs of input}}{\text{Units of output}}$

- **Resource utilisation** is usually measured in terms of productivity ($\dfrac{\text{Outputs}}{\text{Inputs}}$).

- **Return on capital employed (ROCE)** shows how much profit has been earned in relation to the amount of resources invested. It is calculated as $\dfrac{\text{Profit}}{\text{Capital employed}} \times 100\%$.

- **Asset turnover** is a measure of how well the assets of a business are being used to generate sales. It is calculated as (sales ÷ capital employed).

- **Profitability** measures how profitable something is. Profit is the difference between income and costs. It is an important performance indicator used to evaluate the performance of profit centres.

- The **profit margin** determines the profitability of an operation, and is calculated as $\dfrac{\text{Profit}}{\text{Sales}} \times 100\%$. The gross profit margin and the net profit margin use the gross profit and net profit respectively in this calculation.

- Remember that there is no single formula that is the correct one to use when calculating ratios. You *must* understand the concepts underlying the ratios.

Quick quiz

1. List four types of performance indicator.

   (a) ……………………………………………………..

   (b) ……………………………………………………..

   (c) ……………………………………………………..

   (d) ……………………………………………………..

2. What is productivity?

3. Cost per unit of a product or service = $\dfrac{A}{B}$ where A = ……………………………………………………

   B = ……………………………………………………

4. How is resource utilisation measured?

5. What is the formula for return on capital employed?

6. What is the most suitable indicator of the profitability of a profit centre?

7. What is the formula for gross profit margin?

Answers to quick quiz

1. (a) Productivity
   (b) Cost per unit
   (c) Resource utilisation measures
   (d) Profitability

2. A measure of how efficiently output has been produced.

3. A = Cost of input
   B = Units of output

4. In terms of productivity, and is calculated as $\dfrac{\text{Outputs}}{\text{Inputs}}$

5. $\dfrac{\text{Profit}}{\text{Capital employed}} \times 100\%$

6. Profit margin

7. $\dfrac{\text{Gross profit}}{\text{Sales}} \times 100\%$

Activity checklist

This checklist shows which performance criteria, range statement or knowledge and understanding point is covered by each activity in this chapter. Tick off each activity as you complete it.

Activity

21.1	☐	This activity deals with Performance Criteria 7.1.E and 7.2.B regarding the calculation of ratios and performance indicators
21.2	☐	This activity deals with Performance Criteria 7.1.E and 7.2.B regarding the calculation of ratios and performance indicators
21.3	☐	This activity deals with Performance Criteria 7.1.E and 7.2.B regarding the calculation of ratios and performance indicators
21.4	☐	This activity deals with Performance Criteria 7.1.E and 7.2.B regarding the calculation of ratios and performance indicators

chapter 22

Preparing reports and returns

Contents

1. Introduction
2. What is a report?
3. Format of a report
4. Writing a report
5. Information for your report
6. Standard forms

Performance criteria

- 7.1.F Prepare reports in the appropriate form and present them to management within the required timescales
- 7.2.A Identify, collate and present relevant information in accordance with the conventions and definitions used by outside agencies
- 7.2.C Obtain authorisation for the despatch of completed **reports and returns** from the appropriate person
- 7.2.D Present reports and returns in accordance with outside agencies' requirements and deadlines

Range statement

- 7.2 **Reports and returns:**
  - Written report
  - Return on standard form

Knowledge and understanding

14 Methods of presenting information: written reports; diagrammatic; tabular

1 Introduction

The standards of competence for Unit 7: **Preparing Reports and Returns** require you to be able to prepare **written reports** in a clear and intelligible form.

The term 'reports' here embraces the **periodic performance reports** of an organisation which you may be required to prepare in your workplace.

External agencies of various kinds, such as grant-awarding agencies, may also require written reports, as well as forms and other returns, to be submitted to them.

The standards of competence expect you to be able to deal with written reports on specific issues as well as reports of a more routine nature.

2 What is a report?

Report is a general term and one that may suggest a wide range of formats. If you give someone a verbal account, or write him a message in a letter or memorandum informing him of facts, events, actions you have taken, suggestions you wish to make as a result of an investigation and so on, you are 'reporting'. In this sense the word means simply 'telling' or 'relating'.

The **format and style of a report**

- Formal or informal
- Routine
- Occasional
- Special
- Professional or non-professional

Formal or informal reports. You may think of reports as huge documents with lots of sections, subsections, paragraphs and so on. There are extensive, complex reports like this, but a single page memorandum may often be sufficient.

Routine reports are produced at regular intervals. Examples of routine reports are as follows.

- Budgetary control reports
- Sales reports
- Progress reports

Occasional reports include an **accident report** or a **disciplinary report**.

Special reports may be commissioned for **'one-off'** planning and decision making situations such as a **market research report**, or a report on a **proposed project**.

Reports may be **professional**, or for a **wider audience** of laymen or people from other backgrounds, who will not necessarily understand or require the same information or language.

For the purposes of Unit 7, you will be required to prepare **short, formal reports.**

3 Format of a report

In this section we shall consider the general format of a short formal report. It is worth noting that different organisations may have different report formats.

3.1 Planning a report

Whether you are completing an assignment for your course of studies, compiling a report at work or researching a hobby of your own, you will need to know how to put information together **effectively**. You will therefore have to **plan** your report.

You will need to consider the following when planning a report.

- Who is the user?
- What type of report will be most useful to him/her?
- What exactly does he/she need to know, and for what purpose?
- How much information is required, how quickly and at what cost?
- Do you need to give recommendations and so on (or just information)?

The detailed structure of a report will include the following.

- To/from/date/subject/details ⎫
- Confidentiality   ⎬ BEGINNING
- Introduction   ⎪
- Summary   ⎭
- Findings   } MIDDLE
- Conclusion   ⎫
- Recommendations   ⎬ END
- Appendices   ⎭

3.2 To/from/date/subject details

It is important to identify clearly the names and job titles of the people that the report is being sent to. Similarly, the name or job title of the person preparing the report should be clearly stated at the top of the report, along with the date on which the report was prepared.

The subject of the report must also be highlighted at the beginning of the report so that the report users know what the report is dealing with.

3.3 Confidentiality

At the beginning of the report, just after the To/from/date/details, you should insert a **clear warning as to the status of the report** if its contents are **confidential.**

3.4 Introduction

The introduction (or **'terms of reference'**) explains the reasons why the report has been written and includes the following.

- The name of the person who requested the report
- The date by which the report must be circulated to report users
- The areas that the report must cover
- The purpose of the report

3.4.1 Purpose of a report

Reports will usually communicate information that will be used by the report users to make a decision. In addition to providing information in a report, you might also be required to analyse the information that you have provided and make recommendations for the future.

3.5 Summary

It is usual, at the beginning of a report, to include a summary which gives a brief outline of the report and any conclusions and recommendations made. This enables the report users to get an overview of the report's contents before reading it in detail.

3.6 Findings

The information requested (or findings) is set out in the main body of the report. If the report covers more than one topic, it is a good idea to divide this section into a number of sub-sections, each with an appropriate heading.

Any detailed calculations or data are included at the end of the report in an **appendix.**

3.7 Conclusion

This section provides a summary of the report's **main findings** and any conclusions which may be drawn from the information provided.

3.8 Recommendations

If the terms of reference require recommendations to be made, they are included in this section of the report.

3.9 Appendices

Not all of the information obtained will be included in the main body of a report – some of it will be included in an appendix at the end of a report. For example, if your report findings are based on detailed calculations, diagrams and graphs, the main points are included in the '**findings**' section and the detailed calculations, graphs and diagrams are included in the **appendix**.

Information contained within an appendix should be referenced to the main body of the report.

Example: Format of a report

```
To:        Joe Bloggs, Manager
From:      Joanne Bloggs, Accounting Technician
Subject    What the report is about
Date:      XX.XX.XX
```

CONFIDENTIAL

INTRODUCTION

- Reasons for report
- Areas covered by report
- Purpose of report

SUMMARY

- Brief outline of report
- Conclusions in outline
- Recommendations in outline

FINDINGS

- Significant information
- Section headings if applicable

CONCLUSION

- Summary of main findings and conclusions

RECOMMENDATIONS

- Included if required

APPENDICES

- Detailed calculations
- Graphs
- Diagrams
- Supplementary information

Activity 22.1

(a) Where in a report might its conclusions be set out?
(b) What is meant by 'the terms of reference' of a written report?
(c) For what reasons might parts of a report be contained in appendices?

4 Writing a report

In order to write a successful report you need to be able to communicate your findings clearly and concisely. You should bear the following points in mind when writing a report.

4.1 Length of report

Your reports should be as brief as possible. Keep sentences a short as possible but do make sure that no items of important information are omitted.

4.2 Easily understood

- Avoid **unnecessary technical language** and **jargon**.
- Information should be organised in a **logical sequence**.
- Main areas of the report should be **highlighted by headings**.
- Use adequate spacing to separate different sections of the report.
- Use CAPITALS, **bold**, *italics* or underlining to highlight important points.
- Keep vocabulary, sentences and paragraphs as simple as possible.

4.3 Timeliness

As with all information, a report may be of no use at all if it is not produced **on time**. There is no point in presenting a report to influence a decision if the decision has already been made by the time the report is issued.

4.4 Objectivity

In more formal reports, **impersonal constructions** should be used rather than 'I', 'we' etc., which carry personal and possibly subjective associations. In other words, first person subjects should be replaced with third person.

I/we found that...	It became clear that...
	(Your name) found that...
	Investigation revealed that...

4.5 Completeness

Make sure that all pages of your report are present by checking each copy for completeness before circulating it to the report users.

4.6 Presentation

Your report should be as free from errors as possible – that includes checking for spelling mistakes! Use the spellchecker facility on your computer once you have completed your report to ensure that you haven't made any spelling mistakes.

Finally, make sure that the pages of your report are clean and fresh. If your report is covered in coffee mug stains you will not be creating a good impression!

Activity 22.2

Tender Ltd is a member of a trade association which operates an inter-company comparison scheme. The scheme is designed to help its member companies to monitor their own performance against that of other companies in the same industry.

At the end of each year, the member companies submit detailed annual accounts to the scheme organisers. The results are processed and a number of performance ratios are published and circulated to members. The ratios indicate the average results for all member companies.

Your manager has given you the following extract, which shows the average profitability and asset turnover ratios for the latest year. For comparison purposes, Tender Ltd's accounts analyst has added the ratios for your company.

	Results for year 4	
	Trade association average	*Tender Ltd*
Return on capital employed	20.5%	18.4%
Net profit margin	5.4%	6.8%
Asset turnover	3.8 times	2.7 times
Gross profit margin	14.2%	12.9%

Tasks

As one of the accounting technicians for Tender Ltd, your manager has asked you to prepare a report for the Senior Management Committee. The report should cover the following points.

(a) An explanation of what each ratio is designed to show.

(b) A conclusion which identifies how Tender Ltd's profitability and asset turnover compare with the trade association average.

4.7 Distribution

Reports should not be late – managers could be waiting for them and wanting to use them. It is usual for regular reports such as monthly reports to be printed to a specified timetable and deadline. For the reports to be up-to-date, this means having to make sure that all the relevant data has been input and processed.

Reports, once printed, should be distributed promptly. When data is confidential, the reports should be sent in sealed envelopes, with the recipient's name and the words 'STRICTLY CONFIDENTIAL' clearly shown.

Reports may be distributed on paper, or sent via fax or e-mail.

Completed reports should only be despatched once **authorisation** has been given by the appropriate person. For example, internal reports such as a payroll summary which might be submitted to cost centre managers once a month should only be despatched when the payroll manager authorises this to be done. The payroll clerk preparing this report should therefore send a covering note or memorandum to the payroll manager which highlights the fact that the report is ready for despatch **subject to his authorisation.**

5 Information for your report

5.1 Information

Because your report is providing information, it should pay attention to the qualities of good information which we saw in Chapter 14.

- Relevance
- Accuracy
- Reliability
- Timeliness
- Appropriateness of communication
- Cost effectiveness

The information contained in your report can come from one of the two sources which we saw in Chapter 3.

- External sources
- Internal sources

Revisit Chapter 15 if you cannot remember the principal sources of primary and secondary data and the main internal sources of information.

5.2 Including graphs and charts in your reports

Some software packages give the user an option to produce and print **graphs** or **charts** from **numerical data**. This is a facility with all graphics packages (software written specifically for the production of graphs and diagrams). It is also available with some other types of software, including spreadsheet packages such as Microsoft Excel. Remember to include graphs and charts at the end of your report in an **appendix.**

Example: Including graphs and charts in your reports

Carter Doyle Ltd achieved the following sales turnover last year.

Quarter	Sales
	£'000
1	75
2	100
3	175
4	150
Total	500

If this data were input into a program with a graph production facility, any of the following graphs or charts shown below could be prepared.

Pie chart: Annual sales

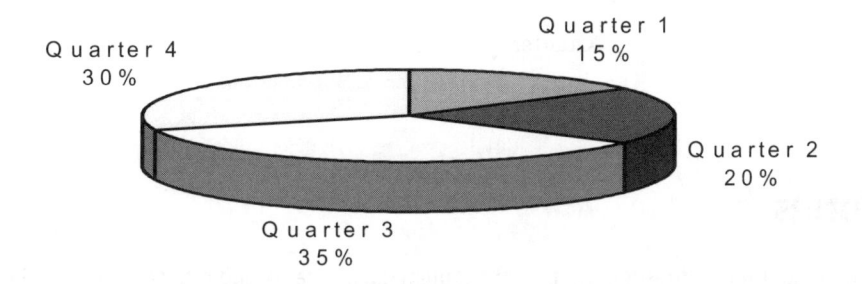

- Quarter 1: 15%
- Quarter 2: 20%
- Quarter 3: 35%
- Quarter 4: 30%

Graph: Time series

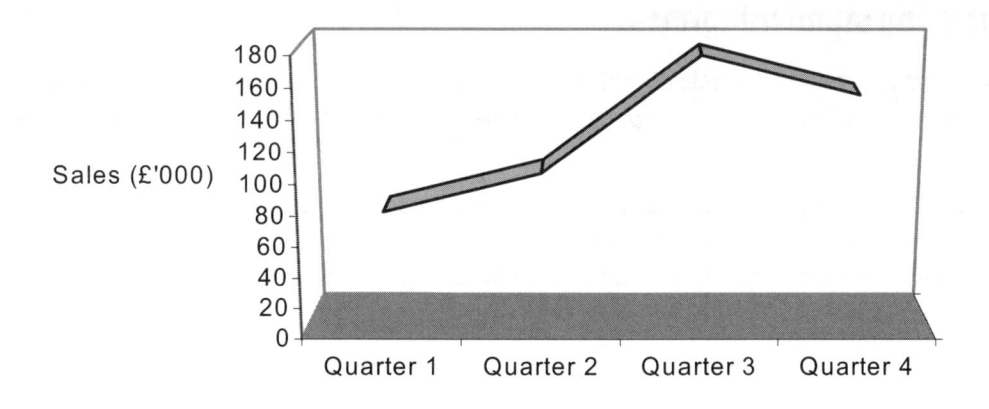

Sales (£'000) plotted against Quarter 1, Quarter 2, Quarter 3, Quarter 4.

Histogram: Sales per quarter

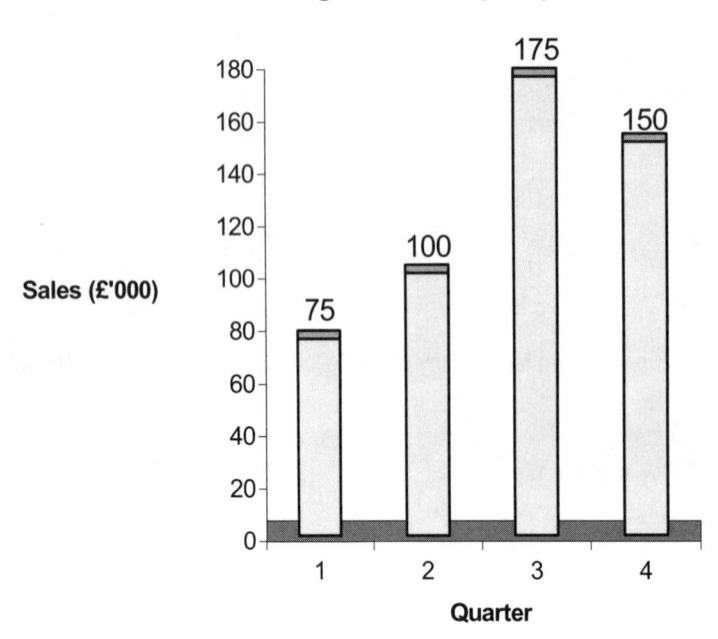

Sales (£'000) by Quarter:
- Quarter 1: 75
- Quarter 2: 100
- Quarter 3: 175
- Quarter 4: 150

6 Standard forms

In **recording data** and in **presenting routine reports** to management, accountants and others in organisations make frequent use of **standard forms**.

A **form** can be defined as a schedule which is to be filled in with details and has a prescribed layout, arrangement and wording. Forms are standard documents which are used regularly to 'capture' data and communicate information.

6.1 Advantages of using standard forms

Forms ensure that **all the information required is actually obtained**, or at least that any gaps in the information can be easily recognised. In other words, they help to ensure **completeness** of the data or information when the form is initially filled in.

Because they are in a standard format, they are more easily **understood**. Users of forms know where to look on the form for items of information. If there is anything users do not understand, they can check the meaning in an office procedures manual, which should describe the functions of forms used by the organisation.

6.2 Form filling

A well-designed form should be **easy to fill in**. It may not **look** very easy, if it requires a large amount of complex information, but you should find the required items indicated for you, and sufficient instruction to enable you to insert the desired data in the right place and manner. Many forms do the work for you, leaving you only with small insertions, crosses or ticks in 'choice' boxes, either/or deletions and so on.

Hints for form-filling

- **Scan the form first**, for main headings and topic areas.
- **Obey any instructions about what to include**.
- **Obey instructions about how to provide data**, eg 'Write in block capitals'.
- **Plan any prose descriptions or narratives requested**.
- **Keep to a relevant content and clear written style**.

6.3 Forms in computer systems

In computer systems source documents may have to be transcribed into a **machine readable medium** (eg magnetic disk or tape), but they may have other functions in addition to data capture for computer processing.

Computer-produced forms or even other printed forms might be turn-round documents – which start by providing output to a user, are then used (filled in) and re-input to a computer, and so re-processed. Examples of turn-round documents are **bank giro payment slips** (as at the bottom of telephone bills and electricity bills).

6.4 Timeliness

Like reports, returns made on standard forms must be **presented on time**. In the case of a form for an external agency, there will usually be a **deadline** by which the form must be submitted. As with reports, lateness may make a standard return worthless or may lead to **penalties** for late submission. For example, a late VAT return may attract **penalties**, and a late grant application might **not be accepted** at all.

Key learning points

- **Report** means 'telling' or 'relating'. Reports may be **formal**, **informal**, **routine**, **occasional** or **special**.

- The general format of a short formal report includes the following.
    - To/from/date/subject details
    - Confidentiality
    - Introduction
    - Summary
    - Findings
    - Conclusion
    - Recommendations
    - Appendices

- You should bear the following points in mind when writing a report.
    - Keep your report as **brief** as possible
    - Make sure your report is **easy to understand**
    - Your report should be produced **on time**
    - Check your report for **completeness**
    - Your report should be as **error-free** as possible
    - Your report should be **clear**

- Information for your reports might be contained within **graphs** and **charts** – remember to include such information at the end of your report in an **appendix**.

- A **form** is a schedule which is filled in with details and has a prescribed layout, arrangement and wording. Forms are standard documents which are used regularly to 'capture' data and communicate information.

- Hints for form-filling
    - Scan the form first
    - Obey instructions
    - Plan how you will fill out the form
    - Keep content relevant
    - Write in a clear style

- Reports and returns should be presented **on time** by a certain **deadline**. **Penalties** may exist for late submission.

- Completed reports and returns should only be distributed once **authorisation** has been given by the appropriate person.

Quick quiz

1. What four sections are included in the beginning of a report?

    (a) ……………………………………………………..

    (b) ……………………………………………………..

    (c) ……………………………………………………..

    (d) ……………………………………………………..

2. Every report will have recommendations.

    ☐ True

    ☐ False

3. What sort of items would you include in an appendix?

4. How can important information contained within a report be highlighted?

5. Completed reports can be distributed as soon as they are completed.

    ☐ True

    ☐ False

6. List two advantages of standard forms.

    (a) ……………………………………………………..

    (b) ……………………………………………………..

Answers to quick quiz

1. (a) To/from/date/subject details
   (b) Confidentiality
   (c) Introduction
   (d) Summary

2. ✓ False.

    A report will only have recommendations if they are required by the person who requested the report.

3. (a) Graphs
   (b) Charts
   (c) Detailed calculations
   (d) Supplementary information

4. By using CAPITALS, **bold**, *italics* or underlining.

UNIT 7 PREPARING REPORTS AND RETURNS

5   [✓] False.

Completed reports should only be distributed when authorisation to do so has been given by the appropriate person.

6   (a)   They ensure all required information is obtained
    (b)   They are more easily understood because they are in a standard format.

Activity checklist

This checklist shows which performance criteria, range statement or knowledge and understanding point is covered by each activity in this chapter. Tick off each activity as you complete it.

Activity

22.1   [ ]   This activity deals with Range Statement 7.2: Reports and returns

22.2   [ ]   This activity deals with Range Statement 7.2: Reports and returns

chapter 23

The VAT charge and VAT returns

Contents

1. Introduction
2. Basic principles of VAT
3. The scope of VAT
4. Invoices and records
5. Registration for VAT

Performance criteria

7.3.A Complete and submit VAT returns correctly, using data from the appropriate **recording systems**, within the statutory time limits

7.3.B Correctly identify and calculate relevant **inputs and outputs**

Range statement

Recording systems:
- Computerised ledgers
- Manual control account
- Cash book

Knowledge and understanding

4   Basic law and practice relating to all issues covered in the range statement and referred to in the performance criteria
    Specific issues include: the classification of types of supply; registration requirements; the form of VAT invoices; tax points

5   Sources of information on VAT; Customs & Excise Guide

15 How the accounting systems of an organisation are affected by its organisational structure, its administrative systems and procedures and the nature of its business transactions

17 Background understanding that a variety of outside agencies may require reports and returns from organisations and that these requirements must be built into administrative and accounting systems and procedures

1 Introduction

VAT applies to many business transactions, and you will often see it mentioned on invoices and in price lists and advertisements. In your work you will not be able to deal with sales, purchases, receipts and payments correctly unless you understand how VAT works.

You will find that the style of this part of the Interactive Text is very different from the style of Part A. This is because VAT was created by law, and the law has to be precise and detailed to prevent people from avoiding the tax. If any loopholes are left in the law, someone will use them in order to pay less tax than they should.

Because there are a lot of hard and fast rules to learn (instead of recommended approaches), you may find it helpful to try new approaches to study. Here are some suggestions.

- Start by quickly reading through the whole of this section of the Interactive Text twice.
- Do not spend time puzzling out the meaning of a paragraph which is not clear to you, but move on so that you get an overall view.
- Then read through the section much more carefully.
- Work through each activity as you reach it during the chapter.
- Finally, try the activities and the end of chapter quizzes again.

2 Basic principles of VAT

2.1 Computing VAT due

VAT is a tax on sales, not on income or profit. Whenever goods or services are sold, VAT (usually at a rate of 17.5%) may be due. The VAT is added to the price, so the money is collected by the seller. The seller then pays over the VAT collected by him to HM Customs & Excise, who administer VAT.

The system is arranged so that VAT is collected at each stage in the sales chain. VAT on the full value of the item sold is borne by the final consumer. Everybody except the final consumer goes through the following procedure.

- Work out the VAT on sales (the **output VAT**).
- Work out the VAT on purchases (the **input VAT**).
- **Pay to HM Customs & Excise the output VAT minus the input VAT, or claim from HM Customs & Excise the input VAT minus the output VAT.**

Example: the VAT charge

Anne makes a table from some wood she has grown herself. She sells it to Bob for £100, who sells it to Christine for £150. Christine sells it to David for £280. All these prices exclude VAT and David is the final consumer.

Tasks

(a) Show the profits made by Anne, Bob and Christine, ignoring VAT.
(b) Show the effect of imposing VAT at 17.5%.

Solution

(a)

	Selling price £	Purchase price £	Profit £
Anne	100	0	100
Bob	150	100	50
Christine	280	150	130

(b) In the following table, the selling and purchase prices have all been increased by 17.5%, to take account of the VAT. The VAT payable is the output VAT minus the input VAT. The profit is the selling price minus the purchase price minus the VAT payable.

	Selling price £	Purchase price £	Output VAT £	Input VAT £	VAT payable £	Profit £
Anne	117.50	0	17.50	0	17.50	100
Bob	176.25	117.50	26.25	17.50	8.75	50
Christine	329.00	176.25	49.00	26.25	22.75	130
					49.00	

The imposition of VAT has made no difference to any of Anne, Bob and Christine. Each of them makes the same profit as before. The two parties who are affected are:

(i) David, who pays £329 for the table instead of £280, so he is £49 worse off;
(ii) HM Customs & Excise, who collect £49 in VAT. They collect £17.50 from Anne, £8.75 from Bob and £22.75 from Christine.

2.2 Accounting for VAT

A trader does not in practice pay over to Customs the VAT due every time he sells something. **Instead he works out the total VAT due for a VAT period** (usually three months). **He fills in a VAT return (form VAT 100) for the period.** The return shows **the total output VAT, the total input VAT and the total VAT due or repayable**. He then sends this return to HM Customs & Excise, together with any VAT due. HM Customs & Excise then send him a return for the next period. Every VAT return shows a trader's name, address and VAT registration number.

Output VAT is the VAT charged on sales of goods or provision of services.

Input VAT is the VAT suffered when goods or services are purchased by a business.

Example: VAT for a VAT period

In a VAT period, Susan sold goods for £10,000 (excluding VAT). She bought goods for £7,050 (including VAT). Show the VAT figures for her VAT return for the period.

Solution

The output VAT is £10,000 × 17.5% = £1,750.

The input VAT is 17.5% of the purchases excluding VAT, so it is 17.5/117.5 = 7/47 of the purchases including VAT. This fraction of 7/47, the VAT in an amount including VAT, is called the **VAT fraction**.

The input VAT is £7,050 × 7/47 = £1,050.

The VAT payable is £(1,750 − 1,050) = £700.

2.3 VAT periods

Most VAT periods last for one quarter (three months). They may end on the last day of

- June, September, December and March;
- July, October, January and April; or
- August, November, February and May.

A trader is allocated to one of these groups (called Stagger Groups) depending on the type of trade carried on. He may ask to be put into the stagger group which will fit in with his own accounting year.

Some traders regularly get refunds of VAT (see the next chapter). **Such traders can elect to have monthly VAT periods, so that they get their refunds more quickly**.

Some traders can have annual VAT periods. This **annual accounting scheme** is dealt with in the next chapter.

2.4 Paying VAT

The VAT return is due within one month after the end of the VAT period. Any VAT due must be paid within the same time limit.

If a repayment to the trader is due, the trader may receive it through the post or, if he prefers, by credit transfer directly to his bank account.

2.5 Substantial traders

If a trader's total VAT liability over 12 months to the end of a VAT period exceeds £2,000,000, he is a substantial trader. He must thereafter make payments on account of each quarter's VAT liability during the quarter. Payments are due a month before the end of the quarter and at the end of the quarter. A final payment is due at the usual time, a month after the end of the quarter. Payments must be made electronically, not by a cheque through the post.

Each payment on account is 1/24 of the total annual VAT liability. Thus if a trader had, last year, a VAT liability of £3,000,000, each payment would be £3,000,000/24 = £125,000. If, in the quarter to 30 June, the VAT liability was £400,000, the trader would pay

- £125,000 on 31 May
- £125,000 on 30 June
- £150,000 on 31 July as a balancing payment

The payments on account are recomputed annually, using the latest annual VAT liability. They are also recomputed in-between annual reviews if the total liability for the past 12 months changes by more than 20% (up or down).

Traders can choose to switch from making quarterly returns to monthly returns instead of making the payments on account calculated by Customs.

Traders can also choose to pay their actual monthly liability without having to make monthly returns. Customs can refuse to allow a trader to continue to do this if they find he has abused the facility by not paying enough. The trader will then either have to make payments on account or switch to making monthly returns.

A trader has the right to appeal to a VAT tribunal if Customs refuse to allow him to make monthly returns of his VAT liability.

Activity 23.1

In January 20X3, Sam weaves wicker panels using materials which he acquired at negligible cost. In March 20X3, he sells ten screens to Jan for £400 excluding VAT.

Jan immediately buys materials for £70.50 including VAT which she uses to join the panels to make a large screen. She sells the screen to Josh in May 20X3 for £700 excluding VAT. Josh keeps the screen for his own use.

Sam, Jan and Josh are all registered for VAT and account for VAT quarterly. Sam and Josh have tax periods ending at the end of June, September, December and March and Jan's tax periods end at the end of August, November, February and May.

Task

Show all payments to HM Customs & Excise arising from these transactions, and the due dates.

2.6 The boxes on a VAT return

The boxes on a VAT return which a trader must fill in are as follows.

- **Box 1**: the VAT due in the period on sales and other outputs
- **Box 2**: the VAT due on acquisitions from other EC member states
- **Box 3**: the total of boxes 1 and 2
- **Box 4**: the VAT reclaimed in the period on purchases and other inputs
- **Box 5**: the net VAT to be paid or reclaimed: the difference between boxes 3 and 4
- **Box 6**: the total value (before cash discounts) of sales and all other outputs in the period, excluding VAT but including the total in box 8
- **Box 7**: the total value (before cash discounts) of purchases and all other inputs in the period, excluding VAT but including the total in box 9
- **Box 8**: the total value of all sales and related services to other EC member states, excluding VAT
- **Box 9**: the total value of all purchases and related services from other EC member states, excluding VAT

Amounts in boxes 1 to 5 are given in pounds and pence. All other amounts are given to the nearest pound below.

Value Added Tax Return

For the period
01 06 X4 to 31 08 X4

For Official Use

Registration number: 483 8611 98
Period: 08 X4

You could be liable to a financial penalty if your completed return and all the VAT payable are not received by the due date.

MS S SMITH
32 CASE STREET
ZEDTOWN
ZY4 3JN

Due date: 30 09 X4

For Official Use

Before you fill in this form please read the notes on the back and the VAT Leaflet *"Filling in your VAT return"*.
Fill in all boxes clearly in ink, and write 'none' where necessary. Don't put a dash or leave any box blank. If there are no pence write "00" in the pence column. Do not enter more than one amount in any box.

For official use			£	p
	VAT due in this period on sales and other outputs	1		
	VAT due in this period on acquisitions from other EC Member States	2		
	Total VAT due (the sum of boxes 1 and 2)	3		
	VAT reclaimed in this period on purchases and other inputs (including acquisitions from the EC)	4		
	Net VAT to be paid to Customs or reclaimed by you (Difference between boxes 3 and 4)	5		
	Total value of sales and all other outputs excluding any VAT. Include your box 8 figure	6		00
	Total value of purchases and all other inputs excluding any VAT. Include your box 9 figure	7		00
	Total value of all supplies of goods and related services, excluding any VAT, to other EC Member States	8		00
	Total value of all acquisitions of goods and related services, excluding any VAT, from other EC Member States	9		00

If you are enclosing a payment please tick this box.

DECLARATION: You, or someone on your behalf, must sign below.

I, _____ declare that the
(Full name of signatory in BLOCK LETTERS)
information given above is true and complete.

Signature_____ Date .... 20 ....
A false declaration can result in prosecution.

VAT100(half)

You might be asked to complete a VAT return in a devolved assessment. **It is essential that you are familiar with the VAT return** and understand which numbers are entered into each box. Get hold of a real VAT return and read the notes on the back. The notes on the back of a return are reminders of what goes in which box, of how to correct errors and of how to pay VAT.

2.7 Errors in previous periods

Where errors were made in previous periods and the net error is £2,000 or less, the error may be corrected on the **next VAT return**. A 'net error' is the error in VAT payable less the error in VAT allowable. The VAT return is amended for the net error by changing the figures in boxes 1, 2 and 4 as appropriate. If an amount was overstated, the figure must be reduced. If a figure becomes negative because of this, it should be shown in brackets.

Larger errors must be separately notified to the local VAT office, either on form VAT 652 or by letter.

2.8 The time of a supply

Because sales and purchases (supplies by and to a business) are grouped together in VAT periods, rules are needed to fix the time of a supply. It can then be decided which VAT period a supply falls into. This time of supply is the **tax point**.

2.8.1 Basic tax point

The basic tax point is the date on which goods are removed or made available to the customer, or the date on which services are completed.

2.8.2 Earlier tax point

If a VAT invoice is issued or payment is received before the basic tax point, the earlier of these dates automatically becomes the tax point.

2.8.3 Later tax point

If the VAT invoice is issued within 14 days after the basic tax point the invoice date becomes the tax point. This rule does not apply if the earlier tax point in 2.8.2 applies. The trader can elect to use the basic tax point for all his supplies if he wishes.

The 14 day period may be extended to accommodate, for example, monthly invoicing. The tax point is then the VAT invoice date or the end of the month, whichever is applied consistently.

2.8.4 Sale or return goods

Goods supplied on sale or return are treated as supplied on the earlier of:

- adoption by the customer, or
- 12 months after despatch.

2.8.5 Continuous services

Continuous supplies of services paid for periodically normally have tax points on the earlier of:

- receipt of each payment and
- issue of each VAT invoice.

However, if one invoice covering several payments is issued in advance for up to a year, the tax point becomes the earlier of each due date or date of actual payment.

Special rules apply for certain continuous supplies made between connected persons (eg group companies).

Activity 23.2

D Ltd has made sales and purchases as indicated by the following documents.

```
D LTD

Job Ltd                                            1 Long Lane
45 Broad Street                                        Anytown
Newtown                                               AN4 5QP
NE7 2LH                             VAT reg no GB 212 7924 36

Invoice no. 324
Date: 4 July 20X5
Tax point: 4 July 20X5              VAT rate
                                        %                  £
Sale of 300 pens                      17.5             600.00
Sale of 400 calculators               17.5           2,500.00
Total excluding VAT                                  3,100.00
Total VAT at 17.5%                                     542.50
Total payable within 30 days                         3,642.50
```

D LTD

Brahms GmbH
Peterstr 39
Hamburg
Germany

1 Long Lane
Anytown
AN4 5QP
VAT reg no GB 212 7924 36

VAT reg no DE 99369326 5
Invoice no. 325
Date: 5 July 20X5
Tax point: 5 July 20X5

	VAT rate %	£
Sale of 500 rulers	0.0	50.00
Sale of 2,000 calculators	0.0	12,500.00
Total excluding VAT		12,550.00
Total VAT at 0.0%		0.00
Total payable within 30 days		12,550.00

D LTD

Mickle plc
12 Narrow Road
Oldtown
OL4 7TC

1 Long Lane
Anytown
AN4 5QP
VAT reg no GB 212 7924 36

Invoice no. 326
Date: 24 August 20X5
Tax point: 24 August 20X5

	VAT rate %	£
Sale of 700 staplers	17.5	756.00
Sale of 3,000 rulers	17.5	300.00
Total excluding VAT		1,056.00
Total VAT at 17.5%		184.80
Total payable within 30 days		1,240.80

D LTD	
Job Ltd	1 Long Lane
45 Broad Street	Anytown
Newtown	AN4 5QP
NE7 2LH	VAT reg no GB 212 7924 36

Credit note no. 28
Date: 18 September 20X5

	VAT rate %	£
Return of defective goods: 30 calculators (invoice no. 324, date 4 June 20X5)	17.5	187.50
Total credited excluding VAT		187.50
Total VAT credited at 17.5%		32.81
Total credited including VAT		220.31

ANGEL PLC
78 Madras Road, London NW14 2JL
VAT registration number 187 2392 49

Invoice to: D Ltd
1 Long Lane
Anytown
AN4 5QP

Date: 3 August 20X5
Tax point: 3 August 20X5
Invoice no. 873

	£
Sale of 10,000 pens	4,200.00
VAT at 17.5%	735.00
Amount payable	4,935.00

Terms: strictly net 30 days

UNIT 7 PREPARING REPORTS AND RETURNS

INVOICE
QUANTUM LTD

To: D Ltd

472 Staple Street   1 Long Lane
London   Anytown
SE4 2QB   AN4 5QP

VAT reg no 162 4327 56
Date: 7 September 20X5
Tax point: 7 September 20X5
Invoice no. 634

	VAT rate %	Net £	VAT £	Gross £
Sale of 600 calculators	17.5	2,700.00	472.50	3,172.50
Sale of 1,000 rulers	17.5	80.00	14.00	94.00
		2,780.00	486.50	3,266.50

£3,266.50 is payable by 7 October 20X5. Interest will be charged thereafter at 1.5% per month.

Input VAT for the VAT period ended 30 June 20X5 was overstated by £800.

Task

Complete the following VAT return to 30 September 20X5 for D Ltd.

23: THE VAT CHARGE AND VAT RETURNS

Value Added Tax Return
For the period
01 07 X5 to 30 09 X5

For Official Use

Registration number: 212 7924 36
Period: 09 X5

You could be liable to a financial penalty if your completed return and all the VAT payable are not received by the due date.

D LTD
1 LONG LANE
ANYTOWN
AN4 5QP

Due date: 31 10 X5

For Official Use

Before you fill in this form please read the notes on the back and the VAT Leaflet *"Filling in your VAT return"*.
Fill in all boxes clearly in ink, and write 'none' where necessary. Don't put a dash or leave any box blank. If there are no pence write "00" in the pence column. Do not enter more than one amount in any box.

For official use			£	p
	VAT due in this period on sales and other outputs	1		
	VAT due in this period on acquisitions from other EC Member States	2		
	Total VAT due (the sum of boxes 1 and 2)	3		
	VAT reclaimed in this period on purchases and other inputs (including acquisitions from the EC)	4		
	Net VAT to be paid to Customs or reclaimed by you (Difference between boxes 3 and 4)	5		
	Total value of sales and all other outputs excluding any VAT. Include your box 8 figure	6		00
	Total value of purchases and all other inputs excluding any VAT. Include your box 9 figure	7		00
	Total value of all supplies of goods and related services, excluding any VAT, to other EC Member States	8		00
	Total value of all acquisitions of goods and related services, excluding any VAT, from other EC Member States	9		00

If you are enclosing a payment please tick this box. ☐

DECLARATION: You, or someone on your behalf, must sign below.

I, ... declare that the
(Full name of signatory in BLOCK LETTERS)
information given above is true and complete.

Signature.. Date .... 20 ....
A false declaration can result in prosecution.

VAT100 (half)

3 The scope of VAT

VAT is charged on supplies of goods and services, provided that the following conditions are met.

- Taxable supplies
- Made in the UK
- Made by a taxable person
- Made in the course or furtherance of any business carried on by that taxable person

VAT is charged on imports of goods into the UK, whether or not made by a taxable person or for business purposes.

VAT may also be charged on certain types of services received from abroad. This is called the **reverse charge**.

Special rules, covered in the next chapter, apply to trade with other European Community (EC) countries and overseas countries in general.

3.1 Types of supply

Supplies may be **taxable** or **exempt**.

- **Exempt supplies** are not subject to VAT.
- **Taxable supplies** may be **standard rated** or **zero rated**.
- **Standard rated supplies** are subject to VAT at 17.5%.
- **Zero rated supplies** are subject to VAT at 0%.

Some supplies have a lower standard rate applying, for example, domestic fuel at a rate of 5%.

Examples of standard rated, zero rated and exempt supplies are given in the next chapter.

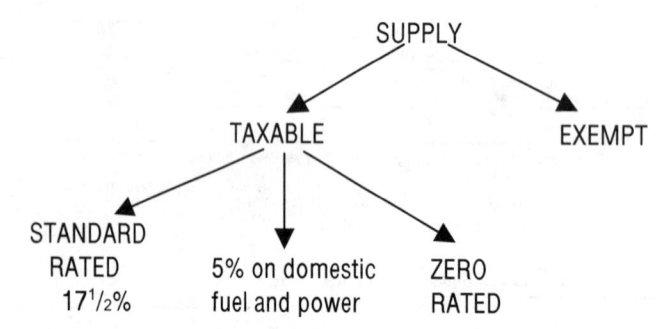

```
                    SUPPLY
                   /      \
               TAXABLE    EXEMPT
              /   |   \
       STANDARD  5% on    ZERO
        RATED   domestic  RATED
        17½%   fuel and power
```

There is a difference between exempt and zero rated supplies. A trader making exempt supplies cannot recover the VAT paid to purchase goods and services for use in his business. A trader making zero rated supplies can.

3.2 Taxable person

A **taxable person** is someone who is or ought to be registered for VAT. Such a person may be an individual, a partnership, a company, a club, an association or a charity.

4 Invoices and records

4.1 VAT invoices

A taxable person making a taxable supply to a VAT registered person must supply a VAT invoice within 30 days of the time of supply. A copy of the invoice must be kept. The recipient of a supply can only claim the VAT he paid on the purchase as input VAT if he holds a valid VAT invoice. VAT invoices need not be issued for zero rated supplies except for supplies to other EC member states.

4.1.1 What VAT invoices must show

There is no set form for a VAT invoice, but it must show the following.

- The supplier's name, address and registration number.
- The date of issue, the tax point and an invoice number.
- The name and address of the customer.
- The type of supply (sale, hire purchase, loan, exchange, hire, goods made from the customer's materials, sale on commission, sale or return etc).
- A description of the goods or services supplied, giving for each description the quantity, the rate of VAT and the VAT exclusive amount.
- The rate of any cash discount.
- The total invoice price excluding VAT (with separate totals for zero rated and exempt supplies).
- Each VAT rate applicable, the amount of VAT at each rate and the total amount of VAT.

4.1.2 Credit notes

Credit notes must give the reason for the credit (such as 'returned goods') **and the number and date of the original VAT invoice.** If a credit note makes no VAT adjustment, it should state this.

For supplies to other EC member states, the type of supply may be omitted. However the supplier's VAT registration number must be prefixed by 'GB'. The customer's registration number (including the state code, such as DE for Germany) must also be shown. Less detailed invoices (4.1.3) are not allowed.

4.1.3 Invoice total of £100 or less

A less detailed VAT invoice may be issued by a retailer where the invoice is for a total including VAT of up to £100. Such an invoice must show the following.

- The supplier's name, address and registration number.
- The date of the supply.
- A description of the goods or services supplied.

- The rate of VAT chargeable.
- The total amount chargeable including VAT.

Zero rated and exempt supplies must not be included in less detailed invoices.

4.1.4 Payments of up to £25

VAT invoices are not required for payments of up to £25 including VAT which are

- **for telephone calls**
- **for car park fees**
- **made through cash operated machines**

In such cases, input VAT can be claimed without a VAT invoice.

Activity 23.3

D Ltd holds the following invoices from suppliers.

(a)

```
                        ALPHA plc
                   VAT reg no 337 4849 26
D Ltd
1 Long lane
Anytown
AN4 5QP

Invoice no. 3629
Date: 6 May 20X7
Tax point: 6 May 20X7
                                              £
Sale of 2,000 handbags                   50,000
VAT at 17.5%                              8,750
Total                                    58,750

Terms: strictly net 14 days
```

(b)

```
                        HYM LTD
1 Market Square
Bluetown
BL1 8VA
                                                        D Ltd
                                                   1 Long Lane
                                                       Anytown
                                                      AN4 5QP
Invoice no.
Date: 12 June 20X7
Tax point: 12 June 20X7
                                    Net         VAT         Total
                                    £           £           £
400 necklaces                       2,000.00    350.00      2,350.00
800 hair slides                     2,500.00    437.50      2,937.50
400 pairs of earrings               5,880.00      0.00      5,880.00
                                   10,380.00    787.50     11,167.50
```

(c)

```
                      MUSTER & CO
          36 Lubeck Street, Gatestown. GN2 SY4
                  VAT reg no 499 3493 27
Date: 15 June 20X7

3 felt hats sold for £35.25 including VAT at 17.5%.
```

23: THE VAT CHARGE AND VAT RETURNS

(d)

```
VAT reg no 446 9989 57                                    KLUNK PLC
Date: 16 June 20X7                                  254 Metric Street
Tax point: 16 June 20X7                                     Ruletown
Invoice no. 328                                             RL3 7CM

D Ltd
1 Long Lane
Anytown
AN4 5QP

Sales of goods
```

Type	Quantity	VAT rate %	Net £
Earrings	700	17.5	700.00
Silver chains	800	17.5	240.00
Hair slides	4,000	0.0	200.00
Hair bands	1,200	0.0	120.00
			1,260.00
VAT at 17.5%			156.28
Payable within 60 days			1,416.28
Less 5% discount if paid within 14 days			63.00
			1,353.28

Task

For each of the above invoices, state whether it is a valid VAT invoice. Give your reasons.

4.2 Records

Every VAT registered trader must keep records for six years. HM Customs & Excise may sometimes grant permission for their earlier destruction. Records may be kept on:

- paper
- microfilm
- microfiche
- computer

However, there must be adequate facilities for HM Customs & Excise to inspect records.

All records must be kept up to date and in a way which allows the following:

- The calculation of VAT due.
- Officers of HM Customs & Excise to check the figures on VAT returns.

4.2.1 What records are needed?

The following records are needed:

- Copies of VAT invoices, credit notes and debit notes issued
- VAT invoices, credit notes and debit notes received
- Records of goods received from and sent to other EC member states
- Documents relating to imports from and exports to countries outside the EC
- A VAT account (see Paragraph 4.2.5 below)
- Order and delivery notes
- Correspondence
- Appointment books and job books
- Purchases and sales books
- Cash books
- Account books
- Records of takings (such as till rolls)
- Bank paying-in slips
- Bank statements
- Annual accounts
- Records of zero rated and exempt supplies
- Details of gifts or loans of goods
- Records of taxable self-supplies (see the following Chapter)
- Details of any goods taken for non-business use

4.2.2 Record of supplies made

A summary of supplies made must be kept, in the same order as the copies of VAT invoices retained. It must enable the trader to work out the following totals for each VAT period.

- The VAT chargeable on supplies
- The values of standard rated and zero rated supplies excluding VAT (note)
- The value of exempt supplies (note)
- The value of all supplies, excluding VAT (note)
- The VAT due on goods imported by post
- The VAT due on services received from abroad to which the reverse charge applies

Note: Credits allowed should be deducted but cash discounts should not be deducted

4.2.3 Record of supplies received

A summary of supplies received must be kept, in the same order as the VAT invoices received. It must enable the trader to work out the following totals for each VAT period.

- The VAT charged on goods and services received
- The VAT due on goods imported by post and on services received from abroad to which the reverse charge applies

- The value excluding VAT of all supplies received, deducting credits received from suppliers but not deducting cash discounts

The summaries described in Paragraphs 4.2.2 and 4.2.3 above could be obtained by adding appropriate columns to sales and purchases day books. The cash book can alternatively be used for the summary of supplies received.

4.2.4 VAT credits

When credits are given or received, the **VAT should be adjusted**. As an example Sam sells goods for £10,000 plus £1,750 VAT. Goods worth £1,000 plus £175 VAT are returned. The VAT to be accounted for by Sam should be shown as £(1,750 – 175) = £1,575. However, no adjustment need be made if both parties agree and the buyer makes no exempt supplies.

4.2.5 The VAT account

A VAT account must be kept, made up for each VAT period.

The **VAT payable portion (the credit side)** shows the following.

- The output VAT due for the period on UK sales
- The output VAT due on acquisitions from other EC member states for the period
- Any corrections to VAT payable for previous periods, provided that the net error is not more than £2,000
- Any adjustments to the VAT on supplies made in previous periods which are evidenced by credit or debit notes
- Any other adjustment to the VAT payable for the period

The **VAT allowable portion (the debit side)** shows the following.

- The input VAT allowable for the period on UK purchases
- The input VAT allowable on acquisitions from other EC member states for the period
- Any corrections to VAT allowable for previous periods, provided that the net error is not more than £2,000
- Any adjustments to the VAT on supplies received in previous periods which are evidenced by credit or debit notes
- Any other adjustment to the VAT allowable for the period

Example: A VAT account

D Ltd has the following transactions in the VAT period from January to March 2003.

	Net £	VAT £	Gross £
Sales	15,000	2,625	17,625
Purchases	8,000	1,400	9,400
Credits allowed (current period's sales)	400	70	470
Credits allowed (previous periods' sales)	200	35	235
Credits received (current period's purchases)	800	140	940
Credits received (previous periods' purchases)	600	105	705

The finance director of D Ltd discovered in March 2003 that she had under-declared the VAT payable for the VAT period from October to December 2000 by £74.

Show D Ltd's VAT account for the period from January to March 2003.

Solution

VAT ACCOUNT FOR THE PERIOD FROM JANUARY TO MARCH 2003

VAT allowable	£	VAT payable	£
Input VAT allowable £(1,400 – 140)	1,260	Output VAT due £(2,625 – 70)	2,555
Adjustment for credits received	(105)	Correction of error	74
		Adjustment for credits allowed	(35)
	1,155		2,594
Cash (payment to HM Customs & Excise)	1,439		
	2,594		2,594

Activity 23.4

Suzie runs a candle shop supplying both trades people and the general public, and is registered for VAT. She does not use the cash accounting scheme or any retail scheme. All her purchases and sales are standard rated.

Suzie's transactions within a single VAT period included the following.

(a) A retail cash sale for £56.40 including VAT, made using a till. The customer was registered for VAT.

(b) A retail sale on credit for £39.95 including VAT. The debtor paid by cheque two weeks later. The customer was not registered for VAT.

(c) A purchase for £270 plus VAT, paid for by cheque immediately.

Task

State what records should be kept reflecting the impact of these transactions, and what they should show.

Activity 23.5

D Ltd had the following transactions in the quarter ended 31 July 20X7.

Date	Type	Net amount £	VAT rate %
2 May	Purchase	4,200	17.5
7 May	Purchase	6,700	17.5
12 May	Sale	10,000	0.0
12 May	Sale	3,900	17.5
22 May	Sale	12,800	17.5
29 May	Sale	1,400	0.0
7 June	Purchase	20,000	0.0
8 June	Purchases returned	500	17.5
20 June	Sale	2,300	0.0
23 June	Sale	5,500	17.5
4 July	Sales returned	800	0.0
8 July	Purchase	730	17.5
14 July	Purchases returned	120	0.0
22 July	Sale	1,700	0.0
31 July	Sales returned	340	17.5

All returns of goods are evidenced by credit notes for both the net price and (where applicable) the VAT. All returns related to current period transactions, except for the return on 8 June.

On the previous period's VAT return, output VAT was overstated by £1,450 and input VAT was understated by £520. These errors are to be corrected through the VAT account for this quarter.

Task

Prepare D Ltd's VAT account for the quarter.

5 Registration for VAT

Once a trader is registered for VAT, he must charge VAT on sales and may reclaim VAT on purchases. A registered trader has a VAT registration number, which must be shown on all VAT invoices issued. It must also be quoted in all correspondence with HM Customs & Excise.

A trader has one registration covering all his business activities. The turnovers of all such activities are added together (no matter how different the business activities are) to determine whether the trader must register.

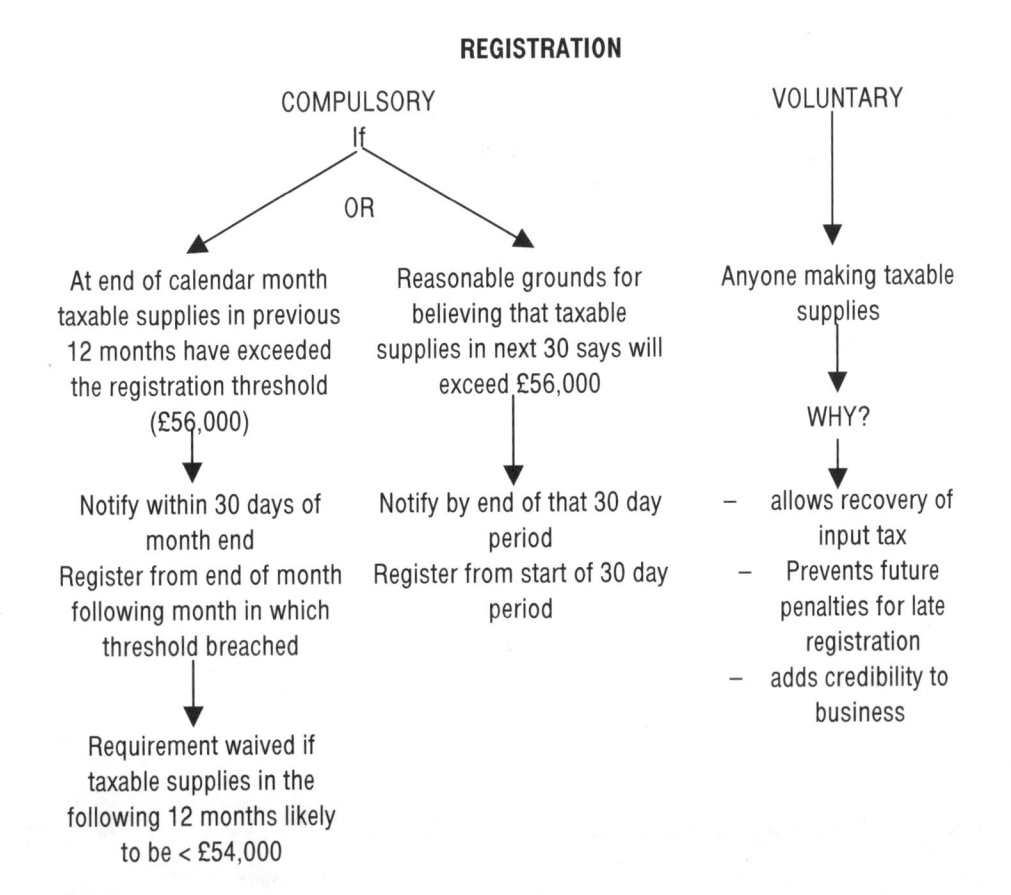

REGISTRATION

```
                    COMPULSORY                                    VOLUNTARY
                        If
                        OR

    At end of calendar month      Reasonable grounds for        Anyone making taxable
    taxable supplies in previous  believing that taxable              supplies
    12 months have exceeded       supplies in next 30 says will
    the registration threshold         exceed £56,000
            (£56,000)                                                  WHY?

    Notify within 30 days of      Notify by end of that 30 day     - allows recovery of
           month end                       period                      input tax
    Register from end of month    Register from start of 30 day    - Prevents future
    following month in which              period                      penalties for late
       threshold breached                                              registration
                                                                   - adds credibility to
      Requirement waived if                                            business
      taxable supplies in the
      following 12 months likely
         to be < £54,000
```

5.1 Compulsory registration

5.1.1 Supplies made to date

A trader making taxable supplies becomes liable to register for VAT if the value of his taxable supplies (excluding VAT) exceeds the registration limit. The registration limit is £56,000 from 10 April 2003. Supplies in the last 12 consecutive calendar months are cumulated. For a new business the turnover total may be exceeded in a shorter than 12 month period.

The trader must notify HM Customs & Excise within 30 days of the end of the month when the registration limit was exceeded. HM Customs & Excise will then register the trader with effect from the end of the month following that period. Registration may be from an earlier date if Customs and the trader agree. **When looking at turnover only taxable (standard and zero rated) supplies are considered.**

Registration is not required if HM Customs & Excise are satisfied that the value of the trader's taxable supplies (excluding VAT) in the year starting at the end of the period will not exceed £54,000 from 10 April 2003.

The **registration limit** from 10 April 2003 is £56,000. If the value of taxable turnover in a specified period exceeds this value the trader must become VAT registered.

5.1.2 Supplies in next 30 days

A trader is also liable to register at any time under a second, different rule. **Registration is due if there are reasonable grounds for believing that his taxable supplies (excluding VAT) in the following 30 days will exceed the registration limit.** HM Customs & Excise must be notified by the end of the 30 day period. Registration will be with effect from the beginning of that period.

Example: Compulsory registration

A trader had the following monthly turnovers of taxable supplies (excluding VAT) from the start of trade on 1 April 2002.

Period	Monthly turnover
	£
1 April – 31 December 2002	3,350
1 January – 30 September 2003	7,375
1 October 2003 onwards	7,750

By what date must the trader notify his liability to register for VAT?

Solution

9 × £3,350 = £30,150, so the registration limit is clearly not exceeded in 2002.

12 months to end of	Working	Turnover
		£
January 2003	(9 × £3,350) + 7,375	37,525
February 2003	(9 × £3,350) + (2 × 7,375)	44,900
March 2003	(9 × £3,350) + (3 × 7,375)	52,275
April 2003	(8 × £3,350) + (4 × 7,375)	56,300

The registration limit is exceeded in the 12 months to 30 April 2003, so the trader must notify his liability to register by 30 May 2003. Customs will register the trader from 1 June 2003.

5.2 More on compulsory registration

A trader's taxable supplies for the purposes of the £56,000 tests is after ignoring supplies of goods and services that are capital assets. However we do not ignore non-zero-rated supplies of interests in land.

When a trader should have registered in the past, it is his responsibility to pay any VAT due. If he is unable to collect it from those to whom he made taxable supplies, the VAT burden will fall on him. A trader must start keeping VAT records and charging VAT to customers as soon as he is required to register.

However, VAT should not be shown separately on any invoices until the registration number is known. The invoice should show the VAT inclusive price. Customers should be informed that a VAT invoice will be forwarded once the registration number is known. Formal VAT invoices should then be sent to such customers within 30 days of receipt of the registration number.

5.2.1 How to notify

Notification of liability to register must be made on form VAT 1. Simply writing to, or telephoning, a local VAT office is not enough.

5.3 Voluntary registration

A trader may decide to become VAT registered even though his taxable turnover falls below the registration threshold. Unless a trader is registered he cannot recover the input VAT he pays on supplies to him.

5.3.1 Why voluntary registration?

Voluntary registration is advantageous where a person wishes to recover input VAT on supplies to him. For example, consider a trader who has one input during the year which cost £1,000 plus £175 VAT. He works on the input which becomes his sole output for the year. He decides to make a profit of £1,000.

- If he is not registered for VAT he will charge £2,175 and his customer will obtain no relief for any VAT (since none was charged).
- If he is registered for VAT he will charge £2,000 plus VAT of £350. His customer will have input VAT of £350 which he will be able to recover if he, too, is registered for VAT.

If the customer is not registered he will prefer the first option as the cost to him is £2,175 instead of £2,350. If he is registered he will prefer option 2 as the net cost is £2,000 instead of £2,175. Thus, a decision whether or not to register may also depend upon the status of customers.

5.3.2 Intending trader registration

A trader may choose to register for VAT as an intending trader if:

- He satisfies HM Customs & Excise that he is carrying on a business; and
- He intends to make taxable supplies

But, once registered, he is obliged to notify HM Customs & Excise within 30 days if he no longer intends to make taxable supplies.

5.4 Exemption from registration

If a trader makes zero rated supplies but no standard rated supplies, he may request exemption from registration. The trader must notify any material change in the nature of his supplies.

HM Customs & Excise may also allow exemption from registration if only a small proportion of supplies are standard rated, provided that the trader would normally receive repayments of VAT if registered.

5.5 Group registration

U.K. Companies under common control may apply for **group registration.** This allows two or more group companies who would normally register separately for VAT to register jointly for VAT.

5.5.1 Effect of group registration

Broadly, the effects of group registration are as follows.

- Each VAT group must appoint a representative member which must account for the group's output VAT and input VAT.
- All members of the group are liable for any VAT due from the representative member.
- Any supply of goods or services by a member of the group to another member of the group is disregarded for VAT purposes.
- Any other supply of goods or services by or to a group member is treated as a supply by or to the representative member.
- Any VAT payable on the import of goods by a group member is payable by the representative member.

A group registration is not compulsory – it is voluntary. Customs just require written notification to establish or amend a VAT group registration. Such a registration can be cancelled at any time.

5.6 Divisional registration

A company which is divided into several units which each prepare accounts can apply for divisional registration. Divisional registration is for administrative convenience. The separate divisions do not become separate taxable persons and the company is itself still liable for the VAT.

5.6.1 Conditions

Broadly, the conditions for divisional registration are as follows.

- Each division must be registered even where that division's turnover is beneath the registration limit
- The divisions must be independent, self-accounting units, carrying on different activities or operating in separate locations
- Input VAT attributable to exempt supplies must be so low that it can all be recovered (see next chapter)
- Each division must make VAT returns for the same VAT periods
- VAT invoices must not be issued for supplies between the divisions of the same company

5.7 Deregistration

A trader is eligible for voluntary deregistration if the value of his taxable supplies in the following 12 month period will not exceed £54,000. The £54,000 deregistration limit applies from 10 April 2003.

However, deregistration will not be allowed if the reason for the expected fall in value of taxable supplies is the cessation of trading. Neither is it available for the suspension of taxable supplies for a period of 30 days or more in that following year. Thus a trader cannot deregister just because he will soon retire.

HM Customs & Excise will cancel a trader's registration from the date the request is made or from an agreed later date.

5.7.1 Compulsory deregistration

Traders may suffer **compulsory deregistration**. Failure to notify a requirement to deregister may lead to a penalty.

A person may be **compulsorily deregistered** if he is no longer making nor intending to make taxable supplies.

Changes in legal status also require **cancellation of registration**. Examples include the following.

- A sole trader becoming a partnership
- A partnership reverting to a sole trader
- A business being incorporated
- A company being replaced by an unincorporated business

5.7.2 What happens on deregistration

On deregistration, a special final VAT return (form VAT 193) is completed. The form has the same boxes 1 to 9 as an ordinary return. **VAT is chargeable on all stocks and capital assets in a business on which input VAT was claimed. This is because the registered trader is in effect making a taxable supply to himself as a newly unregistered trader. If the VAT chargeable does not exceed £1,000 it need not be paid.**

The VAT charge on deregistration does not apply if the business is sold as a **going concern to another taxable person**. Such transfers are generally outside the scope of VAT. If the original owner ceases to be taxable, the new owner of the business may also take over the existing VAT number. If he does so, he takes over the rights and liabilities of the transferor as at the date of transfer. The transfer of a going concern may also apply to parts of a business.

If HM Customs & Excise are misled into granting registration then the registration is treated as void from the start.

5.8 Pre-registration input VAT

VAT incurred before registration is known as **pre-registration input VAT**. It can be treated as input VAT and recovered from HM Customs & Excise (on the trader's first VAT return) subject to certain conditions.

5.8.1 Conditions – goods

If the claim is for **input VAT paid on goods** bought prior to registration then the following conditions must be satisfied.

- The goods were acquired for the purposes of a business
- The goods have not been supplied onwards or consumed before the date of registration
- **The VAT must have been incurred in the three years prior to registration.**

5.8.2 Conditions – services

If the claim is for **input VAT paid on a supply of services** prior to registration then the following conditions must be satisfied.

- The services were supplied for the purposes of a business
- **The services were supplied within the six months prior to the date of registration.**

Activity 23.6

D Ltd has incurred the following expenses. Only the documentation noted is held. All amounts are shown including VAT.

Ref	Item	Documentation	Amount £
(a)	Purchase of goods	Full VAT invoice (D Ltd's registration number not shown)	82.25
(b)	Purchase of goods	Less detailed VAT invoice	105.75
(c)	Car park charge	None	10.00
(d)	Purchase of goods	Full VAT invoice (D Ltd's address not shown)	869.50
(e)	Purchase of goods	Less detailed VAT invoice	98.70
(f)	Computer repair services	Full VAT invoice (total price excluding VAT not shown)	383.05

Task

Compute the amount of VAT which D Ltd may recover as input VAT.

Key learning points

- ☑ VAT is collected in stages along the production chain, but is effectively a burden on the final consumer.
- ☑ VAT is accounted for one VAT period at a time. The trader completes a VAT return.
- ☑ A VAT return period is usually three months long but can, at the trader's request, be monthly.
- ☑ The tax point for a supply is in practice usually the invoice date.
- ☑ Supplies may be standard rated (usually 17.5% VAT), zero rated or exempt.
- ☑ VAT invoices must show specified information.
- ☑ Traders must keep full records, including a VAT account.
- ☑ Registration for VAT is compulsory if annual taxable turnover exceeds the registration threshold, unless exemption is granted.
- ☑ The registration threshold is £56,000 from 10 April 2003.
- ☑ Voluntary registration, group registration and divisional registration are also possible.
- ☑ Pre-registration input VAT can be reclaimed if certain conditions are satisfied.

Quick quiz

1. Peter is a VAT registered trader. In the quarter to 31 March 2003 Peter sold goods for £40,000 (excluding VAT) and bought stock to sell for £17,900 (including VAT). Show the VAT figures for his VAT return for this quarter.

2. When will the VAT return to 30 June 2003 be due for submission to Customs

    A   30 June 2003
    B   1 July 2003
    C   31 July 2003
    D   1 August 2003

3. What is the basic tax point of a supply of services?

4. John delivers 6 boxes of chocolates to Mrs Smith on Monday 4 May 2003. On Friday 8 May John issues an invoice to Mrs Smith for the goods. Mrs Smith pays John on 18 May 2003. What is the tax point of the sale for John?

5. How do you notify Customs you need to be registered for VAT?

6. Zoë started in business last June but registered for VAT in May 2003. Zoë can claim some of the VAT she incurred on purchases of goods made before her business was VAT registered

    ☐ True

    ☐ False

7. A retailer may issue a less detailed VAT invoice where sales are made directly to the public and the supply is for £100 or less. Such an invoice must set out the time of supply and the name, address and VAT registration number of the retailer.

    What further information must be shown on the invoice?

8. In his first year of trading to 31 December 2002 Monty's turnover from his restaurant was £3,100 a month.

    For the first seven months of 2003 his turnover was as follows.

	£
January 2003	4,500
February 2003	5,100
March 2003	5,500
April 2003	6,000
May 2003	8,000
June 2003	8,700
July 2003	9,000

    By which date is Monty required to register for VAT?

    A   30 June 2003
    B   30 July 2003
    C   31 July 2003
    D   1 August 2003

Answers to quick quiz

1.
	£
Output VAT (£40,000 × 17.5%)	7,000
Input VAT (£17,900 × 7/47)	(2,666)
Net VAT payable	4,334

2. C A VAT return is usually due within one month after the end of the VAT period. The return to 30 June 2003 will be due to be received by Customs by 31 July 2003 at the latest.

3. The date the service is completed.

4. Basic tax point is Monday 4 May but John raises an invoice within the next 14 days so the invoice date 8 May 2003 is the real tax point for this supply.

5. By completing and submitting form VAT 1.

6. True.   Zoë can claim VAT on any goods still on hand in May 2003.

7. The total amount payable inclusive of VAT.

   A description sufficient to identify the goods or services supplied

   The rate of VAT in force at the time of supply

8. B When the value of taxable supplies in previous twelve months exceeds £56,000 he is required to register within 30 days ie 30 July 2003 – 30 days after the twelve months to 30 June 2003 (12 month turnover then £56,400) and registration takes effect from 1 August 2003.

Activity checklist

This checklist shows which performance criteria, range statement or knowledge and understanding point is covered by each activity in this chapter. Tick off each activity as you complete it.

Activity

23.1	☐	This activity deals with Performance Criteria 7.3.B regarding the correct identification and calculation of relevant inputs and outputs
23.2	☐	This activity deals with Performance Criteria 7.3.A regarding the correct submission of VAT returns using data from the appropriate recording systems within statutory time limits
23.3	☐	This activity deals with Knowledge and Understanding point 4
23.4	☐	This activity deals with Range Statement 7.3 regarding: recording systems; computerised ledgers; manual control account; cash book
23.5	☐	This activity deals with Range Statement 7.3 regarding recording systems; computerised ledgers; manual control account; cash book
23.6	☐	This activity deals with Performance Criteria 7.3.B regarding the correct identification and calculation of relevant inputs and outputs

chapter 24

The computation and administration of VAT

Contents

1. Introduction
2. Finding the VAT on a supply
3. Standard rated, zero rated and exempt supplies
4. The deduction of input VAT
5. Partial exemption
6. Relief for bad debts
7. Imports and exports and EC Trade
8. Special schemes
9. Administration
10. Penalties

Performance criteria

7.3.A   Complete and submit VAT returns correctly, using data from the appropriate **recording systems** within the statutory time limits
7.3.B   Correctly identify and calculate relevant **inputs and outputs**
7.3.C   Ensure submissions are made in accordance with current legislation
7.3.D   Ensure guidance is sought from the VAT Office when required, in a professional manner

Range statement

Recording systems:
- Computerised ledgers
- Manual control account
- Cash book

Inputs and outputs:
- Standard supplies
- Exempt supplies
- Zero rated supplies
- Imports
- Exports

UNIT 7 PREPARING REPORTS AND RETURNS

Knowledge and understanding

4 Basic law and practice relating to all issues covered in the range statement and referred to in the performance criteria
Specific issues include the classification of types of supply; registration requirements; the form of VAT invoices; tax points
5 Sources of information on VAT: Customs & Excise Guide
6 Administration of VAT: enforcement
7 Special schemes: annual accounting; cash accounting; bad debt relief
8 Use of standard units of inputs and outputs
15 How the accounting systems of an organisation are affected by its organisational structure, its administrative systems and procedures and the nature of its business transactions
17 Background understanding that a variety of outside agencies may require reports and returns from organisations and that these requirements must be built into administrative and accounting systems and procedures
18 Background understanding that recording and accounting practices may vary between organisations and different parts of organisations
19 The basis of the relationship between the organisation and the VAT Office

1 Introduction

This chapter is all about how VAT is charged on a supply and at what rate. Different supplies carry different rates of VAT. When items are purchased by a business VAT may be paid to the seller. If certain conditions are met this VAT can be reclaimed by a business.

We shall also look at various schemes for accounting for VAT. In order to ensure VAT is accounted for accurately and paid on time there are various penalties that Customs & Excise can levy on wrongdoers. We shall also look at this penalty system.

2 Finding the VAT on a supply

2.1 Introduction

The VAT on a standard rated supply is 17.5% of the price excluding VAT, or 17.5/117.5 = 7/47 of the price including VAT.

2.1.1 Discounts

If a discount is offered for prompt payment, VAT is computed on the amount after deducting the discount (at the highest rate offered), **even if the discount is not taken**. (However, for imports from outside the EC, VAT is computed on the full price unless the discount is actually taken up.) If goods are sold to staff at a discount, VAT is charged on the reduced price.

A trader may charge different prices to customers paying with credit cards and those paying by other means. In such a case the VAT due on each standard rated sale is the full amount paid by the customer $\times$ 7/47.

2.1.2 Rounding rules

The rules on the rounding of amounts of VAT are as follows.

(a) If amounts of VAT are calculated for individual lines on an invoice, they must be:

- rounded down to the nearest 0.1p, so 86.76p would be shown as 86.7p; or
- rounded to the nearest 0.5p, so 86.7p would be shown as 87p and 86.3p would be shown as 86.5p.

(b) If amounts of VAT are calculated from an amount of VAT per unit or article, the amount of VAT should be:

- calculated to the nearest 0.01p and then rounded to the nearest 0.1p, so 0.24p would be rounded to 0.2p; or
- rounded to the nearest 0.5p, but with a minimum of 0.5p for any standard rated item, so 0.2p would be rounded to 0.5p rather than to 0p.

(c) The total VAT shown on an invoice should be rounded down to the nearest 1p, so £32.439 would be shown as £32.43.

Example: The VAT on supplies

Find the VAT on each of the following supplies.

(a) Goods with a normal retail price of £10,000 excluding VAT are sold net of

- a trade discount of 20%
- a cash discount of 5% for payment within ten days
- a cash discount of 3% for payment within 21 days

The customer takes 30 days to pay.

(b) Goods would normally be sold for £109 including VAT to a customer paying by cash or cheque. However the goods are sold to a customer paying by credit card subject to a 4% surcharge.

Solution

(a)

	£
Normal retail price	10,000
Less trade discount £10,000 × 20%	2,000
	8,000
Less cash discount £8,000 × 5%	400
Amount on which VAT is calculated	7,600

VAT = £7,600 × 17.5% = £1,330

(b) Price including VAT = £109 × 1.04 = £113.36

VAT = £113.36 × 7/47 = £16.88

2.2 Finding the VAT due in unusual circumstances

When goods are permanently taken from a business for non-business purposes, VAT must be accounted for on their market value. If services bought for business purposes are used for non-business purposes (without charge), then VAT must be accounted for on their cost. The VAT to be accounted for is not allowed to exceed the input VAT deductible on the purchase of the services.

2.2.1 Mixed supplies

Different goods and services are sometimes invoiced together at an inclusive price (a mixed supply). Some items may be chargeable at the standard rate and some at the zero rate. In such cases the supplier must account for VAT separately on the standard rated and zero rated elements. This is done by splitting the total amount payable in a fair proportion between the different elements and charging VAT on each at the appropriate rate. There is no single way of doing this. One method is to split the amount according to the cost to the supplier of each element. Another is to use the open market value of each element. Note that 'multiple supply' is another term used for 'mixed supply'.

An example of a mixed supply is a pack of audio-visual materials containing slides (standard rated) and books (zero rated). The item may be sold at an inclusive price.

2.2.2 Composite supplies

Where a supply cannot be split into components, there is a composite supply and one VAT rate applies to the whole supply. The rate depends on the nature of the supply as a whole. A supply of air transport including an in-flight meal has been held to be a single, composite supply of transport (zero rated). This was rather than a supply of transport (zero rated) and a supply of a meal (standard rated). Note that 'compound supply' is another term used for 'composite supply'.

2.2.3 Gifts

Gifts of goods must normally be treated as sales at cost (so VAT is due). However, business gifts are not supplies (so VAT need not be accounted for) if:

- in any period of 12 months, the cost of gifts given to a recipient does not exceed £50. If it does, then VAT output tax will be due in full on all of the gifts.
- the gift is a sample. However, if two or more identical samples are given to the same person, all but one of them are treated as supplies.

2.3 Errors on invoices

If an invoice shows too much VAT, the full amount shown must be accounted for. This will not apply if the error is corrected by issuing a credit note to the customer.

If an invoice shows too little VAT, a supplementary invoice will normally be issued to the customer to collect the extra VAT. The full correct amount of VAT must then be accounted for.

If an invoice shows too little VAT but the extra VAT is not collected from the customer, the VAT must still be accounted for. The VAT due is calculated as the gross amount shown × 7/47.

3 Standard rated, zero rated and exempt supplies

3.1 Introduction

A supply is a standard rated supply unless it is a zero rated supply or an exempt supply. This is not a helpful definition but unfortunately it is an accurate description of a standard rated supply. So the approach to take is as follows.

3.1.1 Categorising supplies

Step 1. Is the supply on the list of zero rated supplies (see 3.2 below). If yes, the supply is zero rated. If no move to step 2.

Step 2. Is the supply on the list of exempt supplies (see 3.3 below). If yes the supply is an exempt supply. If not the supply is standard rated.

There is no 'list' of standard rated supplies. If the supply is not zero-rated or exempt then it is standard rated.

3.1.2 Reduced rate supplies

There are some standard rated supplies which are taxable at 5% rather than the usual 17.5%.

Such reduced VAT rate supplies are listed in the VAT legislation and include the following.

- Domestic fuel and power (for use in homes and for charity use).
- The installation of energy saving materials (including solar panels) in homes.
- The installation, maintenance and repair of central heating systems and home security goods in the homes of less well-off and the installation of heating measures in the homes of the less well-off where funded by Government grants.
- Women's sanitary products.
- Children's car seats.

3.1.3 Zero rated supplies

Zero rated supplies are taxable at 0%. A registered trader whose outputs are zero rated but whose inputs are standard rated will obtain VAT repayments. Here is an example.

	Net £	VAT £	Gross £
Sales	160	0.00	160.00
Less purchases	100	17.50	117.50
	60	17.50	42.50

The trader gets a repayment of the £17.50 of VAT he paid on his purchases. Thus his own profit after this repayment is £160 (takings) – £117.50 (paid to supplier) + £17.50 (VAT repayment) = £60.

3.1.4 Exempt supplies

Exempt supplies are not so advantageous. In exactly the same way as for a non-registered trader, a trader making exempt supplies is unable to recover VAT on inputs. The exempt trader thus has to shoulder the burden of VAT.

Of course, he may increase his prices to pass on the charge. However he cannot issue a VAT invoice which would enable a registered customer to obtain a credit for VAT. This is because no VAT is chargeable on exempt supplies thus no VAT invoice is due.

Example: standard rated, zero rated and exempt supplies

Here are figures for three traders, the first with standard rated outputs, the second with zero rated outputs and the third with exempt outputs. All their inputs are standard rated. All have purchases of £20,000 excluding VAT and sales of £30,000 excluding VAT.

	Standard rated £	Zero rated £	Exempt £
Inputs	20,000	20,000	20,000
VAT	3,500	3,500	3,500
	23,500	23,500	23,500
Outputs	30,000	30,000	30,000
VAT	5,250	0	0
	35,250	30,000	30,000
Pay/(reclaim)	1,750	(3,500)	0
Net profit	10,000	10,000	6,500

3.2 Zero rated supplies

The following goods and services are zero rated.

- Human and animal **food**, although pet food and certain luxury items, such as confectionery are standard rated. **Food supplied in the course of catering (which includes all hot takeaways) is standard rated**. Most beverages are standard rated, but milk, tea (excluding iced tea), coffee and cocoa are zero rated unless supplied in the course of catering.

- **Sewerage services and water.**
- Periodicals, **books** and leaflets.
- **New construction work or the sale of new buildings** by builders, where the buildings are to be used for residential or non-business charitable purposes.
- **Passenger transport in** vehicles with 10 or more seats.
- Large residential **caravans and houseboats**.
- **Drugs and medicines on prescription** or provided in private hospitals.
- **Exports of goods to outside the EC.**
- Supplies to VAT registered traders in other EC states where the purchaser's VAT registration number is shown on the invoice.
- **Clothing and footwear for young children** and certain protective clothing.

3.3 Exempt supplies

The following supplies are exempt.

- **Sales of freeholds** (over three years old) **and leaseholds of land and buildings** by someone other than the builder.
- **Financial services**. But note that investment advice is standard rated.
- **Insurance**.
- **Postal services provided by the Post Office**.
- **Betting and gaming**, except admission charges and subscriptions.
- **Educational and vocational training** supplied by a school, a university or an independent private tutor, and tuition in English as a foreign language.
- **Health services**, including medical, nursing, dental and ophthalmic treatment and hospital accommodation.
- **Burial and cremation** services.

Activity 24.1

D Ltd supplied the following goods and services to Ferguson Ltd on 12 May 20X2. All amounts exclude any VAT. All amounts are totals, not unit costs.

	Quantity	£
Personal computer	1	980
Microscopes	3	360
Books	20	200
Periodicals	500	450
Insurance		1,200
Medical treatment services		400

Task

Complete the following invoice for all these supplies, giving only the figures which must be shown on VAT invoices and the overall totals with and without the cash discount.

D LIMITED
32 Hurst Road,
London NE20 4LJ
VAT reg no 730 4148 37

To: Ferguson Ltd　　　　　　　　　　Date: 12 May 20X2
75 Link Road　　　　　　　　　　　Tax point: 12 May 20X2
London NE25 3PQ　　　　　　　　　Invoice no. 2794

Item	Quantity	VAT rate %	Net £	VAT £
Sales of goods				
Personal computer	1	17.5	980.00	164.64
Microscopes	3	17.5	360.00	60.48
Books	20	0	200.00	–
Periodicals	500	0	450.00	–
Insurance		Exempt	1,200.00	–
Medical treatment services		Exempt	400.00	–
			3,590.00	225.12

Total without discount: £3,590.00 + £225.12 = £3,815.12
Total with 4% cash discount: £3,446.40 + £225.12 = £3,671.52

Terms: 30 days, 4% discount if paid within 10 days.

Activity 24.2

What type of VAT supply is each of the following?

(a) sale of child's jumper (age 4-5)
(b) supply of life assurance policy
(c) supply of 10 first class stamps by Jesmond Post Office
(d) sale of hot meat pie by Joe's takeaway
(e) sale of coat for man size 40 inch chest

4 The deduction of input VAT

For input VAT to be deductible, the payer must be registered for VAT, with the supply being to him in the course of his business. In addition a VAT invoice must be held. For payments of up to £25 including VAT which are for telephone calls, car park fees or made through cash operated machines a VAT invoice is not necessary.

There are a few special cases where the input VAT is not deductible. These are listed below.

4.1 Entertaining

VAT on **business entertaining**, except entertaining staff is not deductible.

4.2 Domestic accommodation

VAT on expenses incurred on **domestic accommodation for directors** is not deductible.

4.3 Non-business items

VAT on **non-business items passed through the business accounts is not deductible.** However, when goods are bought partly for business use, the buyer may:

- deduct all the input VAT, and account for output VAT in respect of the private use; or
- deduct only the business proportion of the input VAT.

Where services are bought partly for business use, only the first method may be used.

If services are initially bought for business use but the use then changes, a fair proportion of the input tax (relating to the private use) is reclaimed. This is actioned by HM Customs & Excise by making the trader account for output VAT.

VAT which does not relate to the making of supplies by the buyer in the course of a business is not deductible.

Where non-deductible input VAT arises the VAT inclusive amount will be included in the trader's accounts.

4.4 Motoring expenses

VAT on motor cars not used wholly for business purposes is never reclaimable. This does not apply if a car is acquired new

- for resale or
- is acquired for use in or leasing to a taxi business, a self drive car hire business or a driving school.

Private use by a proprietor **or an employee** is non-business use unless the user pays a full commercial hire charge (not a reimbursement of costs). **If a car is used wholly for business purposes** (including leasing) **the input VAT is recoverable. However the buyer must account for VAT when he sells the car.**

4.4.1 Accessories

If accessories are fitted and invoiced at a later date to the original purchase then the VAT on the accessories can be recovered. The accessories must be for business use.

4.4.2 Leased cars

If a car is leased and the lessor recovered the input VAT then that VAT may not be fully recoverable. If the lessee makes some private use of the car the lessee can only recover 50% of the input VAT on the lease charges.

The VAT charged when a car is hired for business purposes may be reclaimable. If there is some non-business use and the hire company reclaimed VAT on the original purchase of the car, only 50% of the VAT on hire charges can be reclaimed by the hirer. A hiring for five days or less is assumed to be wholly for business use.

4.4.3 Other points

If a car is used for business purposes then any VAT charged on repair and maintenance costs can be treated as input VAT. No apportionment has to be made for private use.

If an employee accepts a reduced salary in exchange for being allowed to use his employer's car privately there is no supply. Thus VAT is not due on the salary reduction. However, VAT is due on charges for running costs. VAT is also due on charges for employee use in the rare cases where the charge is a full commercial rate. This will occur where the employer has recovered input VAT on the cost or on leasing charges in full.

4.4.4 Fuel

The VAT incurred on fuel used for business purposes is fully deductible as input VAT. If the fuel is bought by employees who are reimbursed for the actual cost or by a mileage allowance, the employer may deduct the VAT.

Fuel may be supplied for private use at less than the cost of that fuel to the business. In such a case, all input VAT on the fuel is allowed but the business must account for output VAT. This is done using set scale charges per quarter or per month, based on the cylinder capacity of the car's engine.

The scale charges (from 1 May 2003) are as follows:

Cylinder capacity	Scale figure (deemed supply including VAT)		VAT due (scale figure × 7/47)	
	Quarter	Month	Quarter	Month
cc	£	£	£	£
Diesel engines				
Up to 2,000	225	75	33.51	11.17
Over 2,000	283	94	42.14	14.00
Non-diesel engines				
Up to 1,400	237	79	35.29	11.76
1,401 – 2,000	300	100	44.68	14.89
Over 2,000	442	147	65.82	21.89

Example: Recovering input tax

Mr Gumby is registered for VAT and makes wholly taxable supplies.

During the quarter to 31 March 2003 he incurred the following amounts of VAT on his business expenses

	£
Purchase of goods for resale	12,163
Business telephone	105
Fixtures and fittings	350
Electricity	70
new delivery van	1,750
New car for Mr Bgumbt	2,164
Staff Christmas party	210
Gifts of wines and spirits for customers	174
	16,987

Tasks

How much input VAT may be reclaimed for the quarter?

Explain the reasons for any input VAT that is irrecoverable

Solution

All of the input VAT with the exception of that on the motor car and business entertainment may be reclaimed, the input VAT on these expenses being specifically 'blocked'. Thus £14,648 (£16,987 – £2,164 – £175) of input VAT may be reclaimed.

Note. It is arguable that the gifts of wines and spirits are not 'entertainment' if there is no element of hospitality. The £50 gifts rule could then apply. It is assumed that either only employees (not spouses etc) attended the Christmas party or a charge was made for non-employees. Otherwise Customs view the non-employee element as irrecoverable.

Activity 24.3

Pete runs a plumbing business in Brighton. He owns a Vauxhall Astra 2.8L petrol car which he uses for business and private purposes. He reclaims the input VAT on all petrol purchases.

Task

For the VAT quarter to 31 December 2003 how much output VAT must Pete pay to Customs in respect of the car?

5 Partial exemption

A taxable person may only recover the VAT he has paid on supplies to him so far as it is attributable to taxable supplies made by him. Where a trader makes a mixture of taxable and exempt supplies, his business falls within the concept of **partial exemption**. Where a trader is partially exempt, not all his input VAT is recoverable because some of it is attributable to exempt supplies made by him. A person able to recover all input VAT (except as in section 4.1-4.4 above) is a **fully taxable person**.

A partially exempt business has the problem of trying to analyse the input tax suffered into two categories.

- **Attributable to making taxable supplies** (fully recoverable)
- **Attributable to making exempt supplies** (not recoverable unless very small)

Customs may agree various methods with a trader to allow this apportionment to be calculated. The most popular method used is called the **standard method**.

5.1 The standard method

The **standard method** of attributing input VAT involves the following steps.

Step 1. Calculate the amount of input VAT suffered on supplies made to the taxable person in the period.

Step 2. Calculate how much of the input VAT suffered relates to supplies which are wholly used or to be used by him in making taxable supplies. This input VAT is deductible in full.

Step 3. Calculate how much of the input VAT suffered relates to supplies which are wholly used or to be used by him in making exempt supplies. This input VAT is not deductible.

Step 4. Calculate how much of any remaining input VAT is deductible. This is calculated using a percentage. The percentage is (taxable turnover excluding VAT/total turnover excluding VAT) × 100%, rounded to the nearest whole percentage above.

```
                           INPUT TAX
           ┌──────────────────┼──────────────────┐
           ▼                  ▼                  ▼
       TAXABLE          UNATTRIBUTABLE         EXEMPT
       SUPPLIES         (eg Overheads)        SUPPLIES
           │                  │                  │
           ▼                  ▼                  ▼
         Fully            Partially         Not recoverable
      recoverable       recoverable ie     unless 'Irrecoverable'
                                              Input Tax =
                                                  │
                                                  ▼
                  Unattributable   (value of taxable supplies)   (a) < £625 per month
                   input tax    ×  ─────────────────────────         on average
                                   (value of total supplies)     (b) is 50% of total
                                        RECOVERABLE                   input tax

                                                                 If so, RECOVER
```

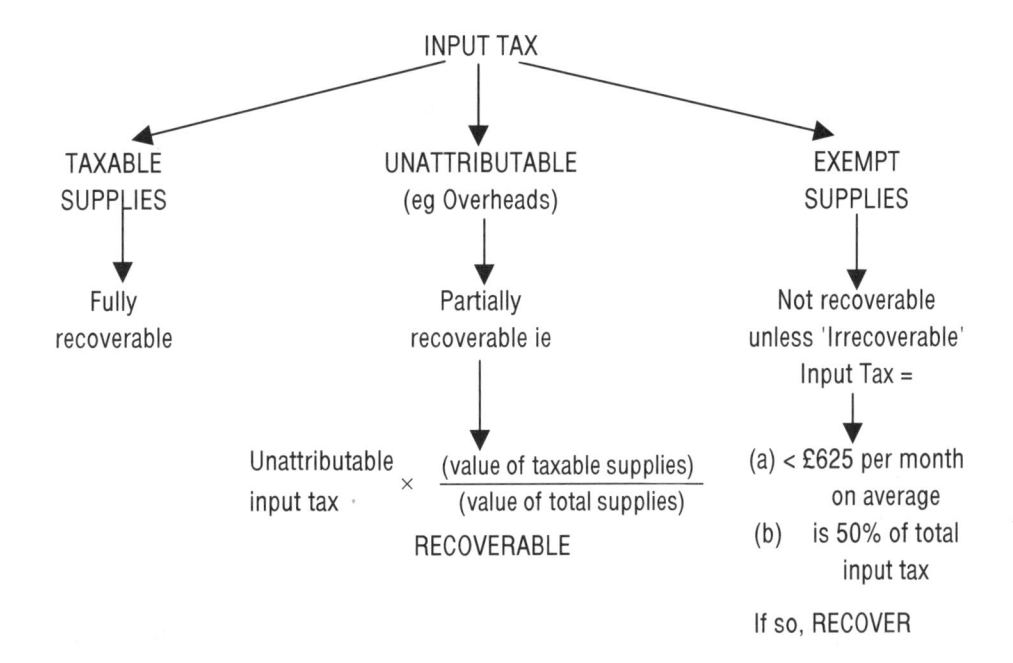

Example: The standard method of attributing input VAT

In a three month VAT period, Mr A makes both exempt and taxable supplies. £100,000 of supplies are exempt and £320,000 taxable. Most of the goods purchased are used for both types of supply. This means that much of the input VAT cannot be directly attributed to either type of supply. After directly attributing as much input VAT as possible the following position arises.

	£
Attributed to taxable supplies	1,200
Attributed to exempt supplies	600
Unattributed VAT	8,200
	10,000

How much input VAT can Mr A recover?

Solution

The amount of unattributed VAT which is attributable to the making of taxable supplies is $£\dfrac{320,000}{420,000} = £76.19047\%$ ie rounded up is 77%

77% × £8,200 = £6,314

Mr A can therefore recover £1,200 + £6,314 = £7,514 of input VAT.

Alternative bases of attributing input VAT may be agreed with HM Customs & Excise. These are called *special methods* as opposed to the standard method.

5.2 De minimis limit

If the exempt input tax is small it can be recovered. To be 'small' two conditions must be met.

- the input VAT wholly attributable to exempt supplies plus the VAT apportioned to exempt supplies is no more than £625 a month on average
- the exempt input tax is also no more than 50% of all input VAT

This limit is known as the **de minimis limit**.

5.3 More on partial exemption

An annual adjustment is made, covering the year to 31 March, 30 April or 31 May (depending on when the return periods end). A computation of recoverable input VAT is made for the whole year, using the same method as for individual returns. The '£625 a month on average and 50%' test is also applied to the year as a whole. If the de minimis test is passed then all input VAT for the year is recoverable.

The result for the whole year is compared with the total of results for the individual return periods.

The result for the whole year may show that less input VAT is recoverable than has been recovered period by period. **The difference is accounted for** as output VAT **on the next VAT return after the end of the year.**

The result for the whole year may show that more input VAT is recoverable than has been recovered period by period. The difference is claimed as input VAT on the next VAT return after the end of the year.

5.3.1 Definition of 'year'

It may be that there was no exempt input VAT for the preceding year. In this case, the 'year' for the purposes of the annual adjustment starts at the beginning of the first return period in which there was exempt input VAT.

In the year of registration, the 'year' starts on the day when exempt input VAT was first incurred.

If a trader ceases to be taxable, the 'year' ends when he ceases to be taxable.

Activity 24.4

D Ltd had the following sales and purchases in the three months ended 30 September 20X2. All amounts exclude any VAT, and all transactions were with United Kingdom traders.

	£
Sales	
Standard rated	450,000
Zero rated	237,000
Exempt	168,000
Purchases	
Standard rated:	
Attributable to taxable supplies	300,000
Attributable to exempt supplies	75,000
Unattributable	240,000
Zero rated	4,200
Exempt	7,900

Task

Compute the figures which would be entered in boxes 1 to 5 of D Ltd's VAT return for the period.

5.4 New rule

A new rule was introduced from midnight on 17 April 2002. This new rule requires businesses using the standard method to override the standard method in cases where the result achieved does not reflect the use made of purchases. The rule will apply especially in cases of abuse. The rule does not apply to businesses using a 'special method' to apportion their input tax.

Businesses will be required to adjust the input tax deductible under the standard method at the end of their VAT year if that amount is 'substantially' different from an attribution based on purchases.

5.4.1 'Substantially' different

'Substantially' is defined as:

- £50,000 or greater; or
- 50% or more of the value of the residual input tax but not less than £25,000.

Where the amount of residual input tax is less than £50,000 per year the override calculation is not required and the business can rely purely on the standard method. There is, however, one exception to this; businesses that are defined as 'groups' under the Companies Act 1985 will have to follow the new rule where residual input tax is greater than £25,000 per year.

5.5 Self supply

5.5.1 What is self-supply?

As we have seen, a trader making exempt supplies cannot reclaim input VAT charged on goods and services bought to make those supplies. This could lead to distortion of competition.

Traders with exempt outputs could obtain a VAT advantage by producing their own goods or making use of their own services rather than buying them. The Treasury has power to deal with such distortions by making regulations taxing self supplies.

The most common regulations made in practice cover cars. Prior to 1 June 2002 there was also a regulation covering the self-supply of stationery.

5.5.2 Effect of a self supply

The effect of a **self supply** is that the trader is treated as supplying the goods or services to himself. Output VAT is thus due to HM Customs & Excise. If the cars have some non-business use the VAT cannot be fully recovered as input VAT. Thus the business suffers a VAT cost.

The amount of the self supply is excluded from both the numerator and the denominator of the fraction used in the partial exemption calculation.

6 Relief for bad debts

6.1 Bad debts

If a trader supplies goods or services on credit, he may well account for the VAT on the sale before receiving payment.

For example, a trader prepares a VAT return for January to March. He will include VAT on sales invoiced in March and will pay that VAT at the end of April. This will be the case even though the customer may not pay him until May.

VAT may therefore have to be paid to HM Customs & Excise before the trader knows that he is going to be paid at all. **The customer might never pay. Without a special relief, the trader might lose both the amount of the bad debt excluding VAT and the VAT on the sale.**

Under **VAT bad debt relief**, the trader can reclaim VAT already accounted for on debts which have gone bad. The VAT is reclaimed on the creditor's VAT return, by adding it to the figure for VAT reclaimed on purchases. The amount must be debited to a 'refunds for bad debts' account. The debit is then transferred to the VAT allowable portion of the VAT account.

6.2 Conditions

All of the following **conditions must be met for VAT bad debt relief to be available.**

- **The debt is over six months old** (measured from the date payment was due).
- The **debt has been written off** in the creditor's accounts.
- The consideration was not in excess of the market value of the goods or services.
- **The creditor has a copy of the VAT invoice**.

The trader must keep records to show that VAT on the supply has been accounted for and that the debt has been written off.

6.3 Part payments

If the debtor has paid some, but not all, of what he owes, the most recent debts are treated as the ones still owed.

If some payment from the debtor is later received, a corresponding part of the VAT must be paid back to HM Customs & Excise.

6.4 How to claim BDR

A claim for bad debt relief is made by including it in the input tax box (ie box 4) of a VAT return. The conditions for relief must have been met by the end of the period for which the return is made. Relief must be claimed within three years from the later of

- the date when the consideration became payable and
- the tax point for the supply concerned.

Prior to the Finance Act 2002 the **supplier** was required to **notify the customer that the debt** was **being written off**.

This is no longer required.

6.5 The debtor

Any business that has claimed input tax on a supply but has not paid for the goods or the services within six months of the supply (or if later the date due for payment) must repay such input tax. He does this by making a negative input tax entry on the return for the period in which the end of the six months falls. This rule was brought in by the Finance Act 2002.

If the non-paying business subsequently makes payment, the input tax can be claimed again on the return covering the date of payment.

6.6 Practical aspects

The debtors listing should periodically be reviewed. Debts over six months old can be 'written off' to a VAT Bad Debts account to allow bad debt relief to be claimed. Such relief is claimed on the next VAT return. It is not also necessary to write off the debt as bad through the accounts for VAT bad debt relief to be available.

7 Imports and exports and EC trade

Imports and exports are purchases from and sales to countries other than EC members.

7.1 Imports

Imports are chargeable to VAT when the same goods supplied in the home market by a registered trader would be chargeable to VAT. Imports are thus charged at the same rate.

An importer of goods from outside the EC must calculate VAT on the value of the goods imported. He must account for VAT at the point of entry into the UK. He can then deduct the VAT payable as input VAT on his next VAT return.

If security can be provided, the deferred payment system can be used. Under this system VAT is automatically debited to the importer's bank account each month rather than payment being made for each import when imported.

HM Customs & Excise issue monthly certificates to importers showing the VAT paid on imports.

VAT is chargeable on the sale of the goods in the UK in the normal way.

7.1.1 Incidental expenses

All incidental expenses incurred up to the arrival of the goods in the UK should be included in the value of imported goods. Additionally, the goods may travel to a further destination in the UK or another member State. If this is known at the time the goods are imported, any costs incurred in transporting the goods to that place must also be included.

Example: Imports

Tiptree Ltd, a company making taxable supplies and registered for VAT, imported three computers from Canada costing £3,000 (exclusive of VAT) each.

Explain how the VAT will have been accounted for on the VAT return for the quarter in which the purchase took place.

Solution

A purchase from Canada is an import.

VAT of £1,575 (3,000 × 3 × 17.5%) will have been accounted for at the time of importation

On the VAT return in which the purchase took place, Tiptree Ltd can claim input VAT of £1,575.

7.2 Exports

Exports of goods are zero rated (even if a sale of the same goods in the UK would be standard rated or exempt). However the exporter should retain evidence of export (such as commercial documents).

7.3 Services

There is also a system of paying VAT on imports of services (from inside or outside the EC), **known as the reverse charge.** A registered trader belonging in the UK who obtains certain services from abroad for business purposes is treated as supplying the services. Thus VAT must be paid on those services to Customs.

7.4 Trade in goods within the EC

The general approach for trade in goods within the EC is outlined below.

For goods sold between registered traders, the seller zero rates the supply. The buyer must pay VAT at his country's rate on the supply to him. He can treat it as input VAT. Thus the buyer's country's VAT rate is substituted for the seller's country's VAT rate.

On a sale to an unregistered buyer, the seller simply applies VAT at his own country's rate. Thus he treats the sale in the same way as he would for a sale within his own country.

If the seller makes substantial sales to unregistered buyers in one country, he may have to register in that country and apply its VAT rate. 'Substantial sales' are those over set limits. Each EU country sets it own limit. In the UK it is £70,000.

7.4.1 Taxable acquisitions

VAT is charged on **taxable acquisitions** (the term 'imports' is not used) of goods from other EC member states.

An acquisition is taxable if it meets all of the following conditions.

- The acquirer is a taxable person
- The goods were acquired in the course or furtherance of a business, or of an activity of any corporate or unincorporated body
- The acquirer carries on the business or activity
- The supplier is taxable on the supply in another member state of the EC
- The supply to the acquirer is not an exempt supply

No VAT is charged on an acquisition of zero rated goods.

7.4.2 Time of supply

The time of supply of an acquisition is not determined by the usual tax point rules. It is the earlier of:

- the date of issue of a VAT invoice;

- the 15th of the month following removal of the goods.

7.4.3 Other points

When goods are acquired, the VAT due is accounted for as output VAT on the return form. If the goods are for business purposes, it may also be treated as input VAT if a VAT invoice issued by the supplier is held. The invoice must show both the supplier's VAT registration number (prefixed by the state code) and the acquirer's VAT registration number (prefixed by GB).

7.5 Statistical returns required

7.5.1 EC sales list

The EC Sales List (ESL) must be produced for each calendar quarter. It must be submitted to Customs within 42 days of the quarter end.

The ESL is submitted on form VAT 101. It consists of a list of all customers elsewhere in the EC to whom supplies of goods have been made in the period. It shows their VAT registration numbers (including country prefixes) and the value of supplies of goods to them during the period.

Traders whose total taxable supplies are low may apply to submit ESLs annually instead of quarterly.

7.5.2 SSD

The Supplementary Statistical Declaration (SSD or INTRASTAT) is a monthly return detailing all movements of goods between the UK and other EC states. It covers transfers between branches of the same business as well as purchases and sales of goods. It provides the information needed for the trade statistics.

The obligation to submit SSDs arises separately for acquisitions and despatches and depends on the value of the movements. The threshold is £233,000 pa.

The SSD must give details of each shipment, including such matters as

- the detailed trade classification of the goods,
- quantities,
- shipping costs,
- countries of departure and arrival etc.

The SSD must be submitted BY THE END OF THE FOLLOWING MONTH.

8 Special schemes

8.1 The cash accounting scheme

The **cash accounting scheme** enables businesses to account for VAT on the basis of cash paid and received. That is, the date of payment or receipt determines the return in which the transaction is dealt with.

The scheme can only be used by a trader whose annual taxable turnover (excluding VAT) does not exceed £600,000. A trader can join the scheme only if all returns and VAT payments are up to date. It is possible to still join if arrangements have been made to pay outstanding VAT by instalments.

If the value of taxable supplies exceeds £750,000 in the 12 months to the end of a VAT period, the trader must leave the scheme.

A trader using the scheme should use his records of cash paid and received (for example his cash book) to prepare returns.

Traders cannot use the cash accounting scheme

- For sales of goods and services invoiced in advance of the supply being made
- For sales where payment is not due for more than six months after the invoice date

8.1.1 How the scheme works

If the cash accounting scheme is in operation you need only look at the entries in the cash book to determine the input VAT and output VAT to include in the VAT return. However, do ensure that there are proper VAT invoices relating to the supplies to support your claim. Thus the regular rule of 'tax point' is ignored.

8.1.2 Automatic BDR

A plus point of the scheme is that it gives automatic bad debt relief. The output tax is only paid over to Customs when it is collected by the supplier from the customer.

Activity 24.5

D Limited has opted to use the cash accounting scheme. Some of the company's sales are standard rated, some are zero rated and some are exempt. Transactions for which the sale, the purchase or the receipt or payment of cash fell in the three months ended 31 August 20X4 are as follows. All amounts include any VAT. No input VAT is attributable to any particular type of supply. There are no transactions with anyone outside the United Kingdom.

Date of Transaction	Date cash received or paid	VAT rate %	Amount £
Sales			
14.5.X4	2.6.X4	17.5	270.35
29.5.X4	15.6.X4	17.5	420.00
2.6.X4	2.6.X4	17.5	620.74
4.6.X4	7.6.X4	0.0	540.40
10.6.X4	22.6.X4	0.0	680.18
14.6.X4	14.6.X4	17.5	200.37
27.6.X4	4.7.X4	Exempt	180.62
4.7.X4	12.7.X4	0.0	235.68
10.7.X4	12.7.X4	17.5	429.32
21.7.X4	21.7.X4	Exempt	460.37
31.7.X4	20.8.X4	Exempt	390.12
3.8.X4	3.8.X4	0.0	220.86
12.8.X4	2.9.X4	Exempt	800.28
20.8.X4	23.8.X4	17.5	350.38
25.8.X4	5.9.X4	17.5	380.07
Purchases			
20.5.X4	4.6.X4	17.5	521.44
3.6.X4	3.6.X4	17.5	516.13
22.6.X4	1.7.X4	0.0	737.48
1.7.X4	4.7.X4	17.5	414.68
12.7.X4	12.7.X4	Exempt	280.85
4.8.X4	1.9.X4	17.5	779.13
23.8.X4	7.9.X4	17.5	211.73

Suzanne Smith, the Managing Director of D Limited took fuel from the business (without payment) for use in her 1,700 cc petrol engined car, which she does not drive for business purposes. The scale charge is £283.

Task

Complete the following VAT return for D Limited.

24: THE COMPUTATION AND ADMINISTRATION OF VAT

Value Added Tax Return
For the period
01 06 X4 to 31 08 X4

For Official Use

Registration number: 212 7924 36
Period: 08 X4

You could be liable to a financial penalty if your completed return and all the VAT payable are not received by the due date.

D LIMITED
1 LONG LANE
ANYTOWN
AN4 5QP

Due date: 30 09 X4

For Official Use

Before you fill in this form please read the notes on the back and the VAT Leaflet *"Filling in your VAT return"*.
Fill in all boxes clearly in ink, and write 'none' where necessary. Don't put a dash or leave any box blank. If there are no pence write "00" in the pence column. Do not enter more than one amount in any box.

For official use			£	p
	VAT due in this period on sales and other outputs	1		
	VAT due in this period on acquisitions from other EC Member States	2		
	Total VAT due (the sum of boxes 1 and 2)	3		
	VAT reclaimed in this period on purchases and other inputs (including acquisitions from the EC)	4		
	Net VAT to be paid to Customs or reclaimed by you (Difference between boxes 3 and 4)	5		
	Total value of sales and all other outputs excluding any VAT. Include your box 8 figure	6		00
	Total value of purchases and all other inputs excluding any VAT. Include your box 9 figure	7		00
	Total value of all supplies of goods and related services, excluding any VAT, to other EC Member States	8		00
	Total value of all acquisitions of goods and related services, excluding any VAT, from other EC Member States	9		00

If you are enclosing a payment please tick this box.

DECLARATION: You, or someone on your behalf, must sign below.

I, _____ declare that the
(Full name of signatory in BLOCK LETTERS)
information given above is true and complete.

Signature_____ Date _____ 20 _____
A false declaration can result in prosecution.

VAT 100 (HALF)

8.2 The annual accounting scheme

The annual accounting scheme is only available to traders who regularly pay VAT to HM Customs & Excise, not to traders who normally get repayments. It is available for traders **whose annual taxable turnover (excluding VAT) does not exceed £600,000.**

8.2.1 How the scheme works

Traders opting for the **annual accounting scheme** make VAT returns only once a year. However, throughout the year they make payments on account of the ultimate liability.

HM Customs & Excise estimate the annual liability based on the past performance of the business. The trader must pay 90% of this estimate during the year by means of nine monthly direct debit payments. The first payment is due in the fourth month of the year.

Smaller payments are made for smaller businesses. A business with turnover below £150,000 using the scheme pays three quarterly payments on account. Each payment is each equal to 20 per cent of the previous year's liability. However, if the previous year's liability was below £2,000, no interim payments are required. Interim payments may be made by credit transfer or direct debit, as the trader chooses.

At the end of the year the trader completes an annual VAT return. This is submitted to HM Customs & Excise along with any payment due by two months after the end of the year.

8.2.2 Conditions

It is not possible to join the annual accounting scheme if input VAT exceeded output VAT in the year prior to application. In addition, all returns must have been made up to date.

If the value of a trader's taxable supplies exceeds £750,000 notice must be given to HM Customs & Excise within 30 days. The trader will then have to leave the scheme.

A trader can be expelled from the scheme if he

- fails to make the regular payments required by the scheme
- fails to make the final payment for a year
- has not paid all VAT shown on returns made before joining the scheme

For businesses with a turnover between £600,000 and £150,001 there is a requirement to have been VAT registered for at least 12 months before being allowed to join the annual accounting scheme.

From 10 April 2003 there is no need for a person with a taxable turnover of up to £150,000 to have been VAT registered for at least 12 months prior to joining the scheme.

The Finance Act 2002 also introduced an option for businesses to pay three larger interim instalments instead of the usual nine interim payments.

8.3 Retail schemes

Retail schemes exist to facilitate VAT accounting by shops, particularly those making a mixture of standard rated, zero rated and exempt supplies. Some schemes rely on separate totals being kept for different sorts of supply. Others make estimates of VAT due by reference to purchases. Customs may agree a bespoke scheme with an individual retailer or allow a retailer to operate one of a number of standard schemes.

8.4 The secondhand goods scheme

Under the secondhand goods scheme VAT is calculated on the trader's margin, rather than on the entire amount charged on reselling the goods. The trader has to account for VAT at 7/47 of the difference between his buying price and his selling price.

The scheme applies to all secondhand goods, apart from precious metals and gemstones. It also applies to works of art, collectors' items and antiques.

A trader does not have to apply the scheme: he can account for VAT in the normal way if he chooses.

No VAT invoice is issued, so a customer cannot reclaim the input VAT suffered.

8.4.1 Global accounting

A dealer in large volumes of low value goods (purchase price £500 or less per item) **can use 'global accounting'. This is where he accounts for VAT of 7/47 of his total margin for a period, instead of working out each profit margin individually.**

Global accounting cannot be used for motor vehicles, motorcycles, caravans, motor caravans, aircraft, boats, outboard motors, horses or ponies.

The margin for a period may be negative where purchases have exceeded sales. In such a case the negative amount is carried forward and set against the margin for a future period.

8.4.2 Conditions

The secondhand goods scheme can only be applied where the goods have been purchased from a person

- who did not charge VAT on the supply or
- who was operating the secondhand goods scheme

The scheme cannot be used for goods which have been obtained VAT free as part of the transfer of a business as a going concern.

In order to apply the second-hand goods scheme, the trader must keep certain records specified by Customs. The principal records required are a stock book and purchase and sale invoices.

8.5 Optional Flat Rate Scheme

The optional flat rate scheme is a simplification measure which enables businesses to calculate the net VAT due simply by applying a flat rate percentage to their tax-inclusive turnover.

8.5.1 How the scheme works

Under the scheme, businesses will be able to calculate their net VAT due by applying a flat rate percentage to their tax inclusive turnover, ie the total turnover generated, including all reduced, zero-rated and exempt income. The flat rate percentage will depend upon the trade sector into which a business falls for the purposes of the scheme. The percentage ranges from 5% for retailing food, confectionery, tobacco, newspapers or children's clothing to 14.5% for computer and IT consultancy. The flat rate percentage for accountancy and bookkeeping is 13.5% and for financial services is 12%.

Businesses using the scheme will still need to issue VAT invoices to their VAT registered customers but will not have to record all the details of the invoices issued or purchase invoices received to calculate the VAT due. Invoices issued will show VAT at the normal rate rather than the flat rate.

8.5.2 Conditions

The optional flat rate scheme came into effect in 2002. Businesses can only join the new flat rate scheme if they meet certain entry requirements. These requirements are (from 1 May 2003);

- a tax exclusive annual taxable turnover of up to £150,000; and
- a tax exclusive annual total turnover, including the value of exempt and/or other non-taxable income, of up to £187,500.

Example

An accountant undertakes work for individuals and for business clients. In a VAT year, the business client work amounts to £35,000 and the accountant will issue invoices totalling £41,125 (£35,000 plus VAT at 17.5%). Turnover from work for individuals totals £18,000, including VAT. Total gross sales are therefore £59,125. The flat rate percentage for an accountancy business is 13.5%.

VAT due to Customs will be 13.5% × £59,125 = £7,981.88.

Under the normal VAT rules the output tax due would be:

	£
£35,000 × 17.5%	6,125.00
£18,000 × 7/47	2,680.85
	8,805.85

Whether the accountant is better off under the scheme depends on the amount of input tax incurred as this would be offset, under normal rules, from output tax due.

9 Administration

9.1 Sources of information

The sources of law on VAT are as follows.

- The Value Added Tax Act 1994 (VATA 1994)
- Subsequent legislation contained in finance acts
- Statutory instruments
- Some sections of HM Customs & Excise Notice 700, The VAT guide

Information on VAT is also available in notices and leaflets obtainable from local VAT offices. *VAT notes* is a newsletter sent with the VAT return.

9.1.1 Local VAT offices

Customs has several head office divisions that deal with central administrative issues and policy matters. There are 14 regional collections that are responsible for VAT matters within specified geographical areas. Each regional collection contains a number of local VAT offices.

Local VAT offices are responsible for the local administration of VAT. They also provide advice to registered persons whose principal place of business is in their area.

The local VAT office (LVO) deals with

- registration
- deregistration
- debt collection
- visits to VAT-registered businesses

The head of the local VAT office is an Assistant Collector. The office comprises a number of sections, called districts. One surveyor is in charge of each district supervising Senior Officers, Officers and clerical staff within that district.

Completed VAT returns should be sent to the VAT Central Unit at Southend, not to a local VAT office.

9.1.2 Control visits

Customs carry out VAT inspections periodically. As a rule, a Senior Officer or an Officer inspects a trader's VAT accounting records during such an inspection. The frequency and duration of the inspections depends on the

- size
- complexity and
- VAT compliance record of the business.

Usually, the visiting officer makes an appointment for the inspection. Before the inspection a business should ensure that all the records are available (usually six years, or from the date of the last inspection). Key staff should be available on the day of the inspection.

It is also useful to review the periods covered by the inspection. Any unusual activities that might have caused VAT errors should be identified, for possible disclosure at the start of the inspection.

9.1.3 Custom's powers

Customs have many powers to assist them in the administration and control of VAT. These include the power to issue assessments for tax due if VAT returns have not been rendered or they consider that tax has been understated. There is a time limit on Customs' powers to assess of three years from the end of the prescribed accounting period concerned. This is extended to 20 years in the case of fraud.

9.1.4 Practical aspects

Immediately following a VAT inspection it is advisable to make a record of what took place, eg records inspected, points discussed, verbal agreements.

A point to remember is that a VAT inspection is not an audit. The fact that an officer did not challenge a particular point on one VAT inspection does not preclude another officer raising the point on a subsequent inspection.

A record of each inspection will assist in any future dealings with Customs. It is also important to obtain any advice given by Customs during the visit or any Customs' rulings in writing. The full facts that might affect these rulings should be provided to the officer in writing.

9.2 Seeking guidance

If there is any doubt in respect of any aspect of VAT it is advisable to seek guidance from the local VAT office. A letter should be sent outlining all the information necessary for the local office to be able to make an informed decision. That decision should be requested in writing. If any telephone conversations are held records should be kept and again requests made for Customs to conclude their decisions in writing.

It is essential that when the letter seeking guidance is sent to Customs all relevant information is disclosed. If this condition is complied with and it later turns out that Custom's ruling was incorrect the trader is protected from a retrospective claim. This protection is under a concession known as the 'Sheldon Statement'.

However this concession only applies if full details were supplied to Customs. Thus it only applies if the local VAT office was not misled or manipulated into giving a particular decision.

9.2.1 Disputes

In the event of a dispute with Customs it is necessary for a trader to decide what action to take. Generally this will involve deciding whether to **request the local VAT office to review the disputed decision or to formally appeal to a tribunal**.

While a local VAT office can review any decision they make, not every decision can go to tribunal.

In some situations a local review will lead, relatively quickly, to a satisfactory solution. It also avoids the need for a more formal tribunal appeal.

The request for a local review should be made to the local VAT office within 30 days.

9.3 Appeals to VAT and duties tribunals

VAT and duties tribunals, which are independent of HM Customs & Excise, provide an alternative method of dealing with disputes. Provided that VAT returns and payments shown thereon have been made, appeals can be heard by a tribunal.

A tribunal can waive the requirement to pay all tax shown on returns before an appeal is heard in cases of hardship. It cannot allow an appeal against a purely administrative matter such as Customs refusal to apply an extra statutory concession.

9.3.1 How to go to a tribunal

An appeal must be lodged with the tribunal (not the local VAT office) **within 30 days of the decision date by HM Customs & Excise.** In addition to this the trader may also ask the local VAT office to reconsider their decision. He should apply within 30 days of the decision to the relevant VAT office. If such a local review is also required, the local VAT office may either:

- confirm the original decision
- send a revised decision

If the original decision is confirmed the taxpayer has 21 days from the date of that confirmation in which to lodge an appeal.

In the case of a revised decision the taxpayer has 30 days from the date of the decision in which to lodge an appeal.

9.3.2 Types of appeal heard by a tribunal

A decision of Customs is appealable only if it concerns one of the matters listed below.

- Registration or cancellation of registration
- The tax chargeable on the supply of any goods
- The amount of any input tax allowable
- A claim for a refund because of a bad debt
- Any liability of Customs to pay interest
- A direction by Customs that the value of supplies shall be their open market value, eg supplies between connected persons
- Any requirements by Customs in respect of computer invoices
- An assessment to tax or the amount of an assessment
- Any liability to a penalty or surcharge under the Civil Penalty provisions
- The amount of any penalty, interest or surcharge under the Civil Penalty provisions
- A refusal to permit the use of the cash accounting provisions appeal to a tribunal

9.3.3 After the hearing

If one of the parties is dissatisfied with the decision of the tribunal on a point of law he may appeal to the courts. Tribunals may award costs.

Activity 24.6

You are employed by D Limited which owns a chain of shops selling Herbal goods and wholefoods to the public. D Limited is about to start selling a new product called Catha Edulis which is a herbal remedy. You are having difficulty in deciding whether the new product constitutes 'food' and will be a zero rated sale or rather is a non-food item and standard rated.

The product is imported by the business from Abyssinia where it is known locally as Srih and drunk as a tea.

Task

Draft a letter to your local VAT office requesting guidance on the correct treatment of the sale of this product.

10 Penalties

There are many different penalties for failure to comply with VAT law.

10.1 Late notification

A trader who makes taxable supplies must tell HM Customs & Excise if supplies exceed the registration limit. A penalty can be levied for failure to notify a liability to register by the proper date. In addition, the VAT which would have been accounted for had the trader registered on time, must be paid.

10.1.1 Late notification penalty

The penalty for late notification is based on the net tax due from the date when the trader should have been registered to

- the date when notification is made or,
- the date on which HM Customs & Excise become aware of the trader's liability to be registered if earlier.

The penalty varies as follows.

Number of months registration late by	Percentage of tax
Up to 9	5%
Over 9, up to 18	10%
Over 18	15%

A minimum penalty of £50 applies. However Customs can waive the penalty if the trader has a 'reasonable excuse' for the late registration.

10.1.2 Amnesty

In order to encourage traders not presently within VAT to register Customs commenced an amnesty from late registration penalty on 10 April. The amnesty is from any penalty applying to late registration for VAT. However any VAT due on supplies made during the period the trade was liable to be registered must be paid in full. No penalty notice will be issued provided the trader makes all VAT returns and payments due on time for the 12 months following registration. The amnesty period runs until 30 September 2003.

10.2 The unauthorised issue of invoices

This penalty applies where a person who is not registered for VAT nevertheless issues VAT invoices. The penalty is 15% of the VAT involved with a minimum penalty of £50.

10.3 The default surcharge

This penalty has the aim of encouraging tax payers to submit their VAT returns (and the VAT due) on time.

10.3.1 What is a default?

A **default** occurs when a trader either submits his VAT return late, or submits the return on time but pays the VAT late. If a taxpayer defaults, HM Customs & Excise will serve a **surcharge liability notice** on the taxpayer. The notice specifies a **surcharge period.** This runs from the date of the notice to the anniversary of the end of the period for which the taxpayer is in default.

If a further default occurs during the surcharge period the original surcharge period will be amended. It is extended to the anniversary of the end of the period to which the new default relates. In addition, if the default involves a late payment of VAT (as opposed to simply a late return) **a surcharge is levied.**

10.3.2 How much surcharge?

The surcharge depends on the number of defaults involving late payment of VAT which have occurred in the surcharge period, as follows.

Default involving late payment of VAT in the surcharge period	Surcharge as a percentage of the VAT outstanding at the due date
First	2%
Second	5%
Third	10%
Fourth and over	15%

Any surcharge of less than £30 is increased to £30. Surcharges at the 2% and 5% rates are not normally demanded unless the amount would be at least £400.

Customs have the power to waive the penalty if the trader has a 'reasonable excuse' for submitting the return late or paying the VAT late.

10.3.3 Practical points

If a trader submits one year's returns and pays the VAT shown on them on time he will break out of the surcharge regime.

Example: Default surcharge

Mr Sloppy is frequently late with his VAT returns and payments and he was issued with a surcharge liability notice running from 1 July 2003.

His subsequent returns have been submitted as follows.

Return period	VAT payment due	Date submitted
Quarter to 30 September 2003	£16,384	27 October 2003
Quarter to 31 December 2003	£21,500	21 February 2004
Quarter to 31 March 2004	£15,400	23 May 2004

On each occasion he paid the VAT outstanding at the time of submission of the return.

Task

Compute the default surcharges payable if any, in respect of the three return periods and state the effect of any subsequent default.

Solution

A default occurs when a trader either submits his VAT return late, or submits the return on time but submits the payment late.

Quarter to 31 December 2003 – first default £21,500 × 2% = £430
Quarter to 31 March 2004 – second default £15,400 × 5% = £770

A further default in respect of a return ending during the surcharge period causes the original surcharge period to be extended to the anniversary of the end of the period to which the new default relates. The surcharge period is thus extended to 31 March 2005.

Activity 24.7

D Ltd often submits its VAT returns and payments late, as shown in the following schedule.

Quarter ended	VAT due £	Return and payment
30.6.X2	4,000	On time
30.9.X2	2,500	Late
31.12.X2	5,000	On time
31.3.X3	4,000	On time
30.6.X3	5,000	Late
30.9.X3	9,000	Late
31.12.X3	7,000	On time
31.3.X4	3,500	Late
30.6.X4	4,500	Late
30.9.X4	500	Late
31.12.X4	3,600	On time

Task

Compute the default surcharges arising from the above.

10.3.4 Small businesses and default surcharge

From 1 May 2002 the application of the default surcharge regime to small businesses has been modified. The definition of small business here is one with a turnover below £150,000. The changes have the aim of amending Customs approach so that small businesses are first offered advice and support when they are late with payments, rather than an automatic penalty.

Under the new system when a business is late submitting a VAT return or paying VAT it will receive a letter from Customs offering help. No penalty will be charged. Four such letters will be issued without penalty. However on the issue of a fifth letter a 10% penalty will apply which increases to 15% on the issue of a sixth or subsequent letter.

10.4 The misdeclaration penalty: very large errors

The making of a return which understates a person's true liability or overstates the repayment due to him may result in a penalty. The penalty is 15% of the VAT which would have been lost if the return had been accepted as correct. The same penalty applies when the trader fails to notify Customs that an assessment issued understates the VAT due within 30 days of the issue.

10.4.1 When does the penalty apply?

These penalties apply only where the VAT which would have been lost is 'large'. For an incorrect return 'large' equals or exceeds the lower of £1m or 30% of the sum of the true input VAT and the true output VAT. This sum is known as the gross amount of tax (GAT).

In the case of an incorrect assessment 30% of the true amount of tax, the VAT actually due from or to the trader, is used instead of GAT.

The penalty may be mitigated.

10.4.2 Practical points

Errors on a VAT return of up to £2,000 may be corrected on the next return without giving rise to a misdeclaration penalty or interest. Larger errors must be notified to Customs as a voluntary disclosure. On such notified errors no penalty will arise although interest may be charged.

10.5 The misdeclaration penalty: repeated errors

Another penalty applies if **a trader submits an inaccurate return containing a 'smaller' error. If the error equals or exceeds the lower of £500,000 or 10% of the GAT, the inaccuracy is material.**

Before the end of the fourth tax period following the period of a material inaccuracy, HM Customs & Excise may issue a penalty liability notice. This specifies a **penalty period** of eight VAT periods starting with the one in which the notice is issued.

If there are material inaccuracies for two or more VAT periods falling within the penalty period a penalty may be imposed. For each such inaccuracy apart from the first one a penalty of 15% of the VAT which would have been lost is levied.

Example: Misdeclaration penalty

Aquila and Priscilla are unconnected traders who happen to have the same VAT quarterly periods.

In the quarter ended 31 December 2003 each trader submitted an erroneous VAT return, as follows.

	Aquila £	Priscilla £
Output tax returns	275,000	600,000
Input tax returned	450,000	425,000
Output tax understated	375,000	200,000

State in each case whether an immediate penalty arises in respect of these errors, quantifying the penalty where appropriate.

Solution

Aquila: the error is over 30% of the gross amount of tax (£1,100,000), so an immediate penalty arises of 15% of £375,000 = £56,250.

Priscilla: the error is < 30% of the GAT (£1,225,000) but > 10% of it.

Has she already been issued with a penalty liability notice within the last two years?

If so, and this is her second error exceeding 10% in the VAT return period outlined in the notice, she has an immediate penalty of 15% of £200,000 = £30,000.

If not, no immediate penalty arises.

10.6 Interest

Interest (not deductible in computing taxable profits) may be **charged on VAT which is recovered by an assessment. Assessments are raised where returns were not made or were incorrect**.

Interest runs from the reckonable date until the date of payment.

10.6.1 What is the reckonable date?

The reckonable date is when the VAT should have been paid (one month from the end of the return period). In the case of VAT repayments to traders which should not have been made, the reckonable date is seven days from the issue of the repayment order.

Where VAT is charged by an assessment interest does not run from more than three years before the date of assessment.

Where the VAT was paid before an assessment was raised, interest is still due. However interest does not run for more than three years before the date of payment.

Activity 24.8

D Ltd submitted the return for 31 March 2003 on time but it contained an error in it which the company notified Customs of 6 months later when a new accountant discovered it. The extra £18,000 of VAT due was also paid at this time which was 2 October 2003.

Task

What penalties or interest will D Ltd suffer in respect of this error?

10.7 Repayment supplement

Repayment supplement may be due where a trader is entitled to a repayment of VAT and the original return was rendered on time. HM Customs & Excise should issue a written instruction for the repayment to be made within 30 days of receiving the return. If not then the trader will receive a supplement of the greater of £50 and 5% of the amount due.

If, however, the return states a refund due which differs from the correct refund by more than the greater of

- 5% of the correct refund and
- £250

no supplement is added.

Days spent in raising and answering reasonable enquiries in relation to the return do not count towards the 30 day period.

10.8 Interest on overpayments due to official errors

Interest may be due if VAT is overpaid or a credit for input VAT is not claimed because of an error by HM Customs & Excise. The trader may claim interest on the amount eventually refunded, running from the date on which

- he paid the excessive VAT
- HM Customs & Excise might reasonably be expected to have authorised a VAT repayment owing to him

to the date on which HM Customs & Excise authorise a repayment.

Interest must be claimed within three years of the date on which the trader discovered the error. Interest is not available where a repayment supplement is available. Interest does not run for periods relating to reasonable enquiries by HM Customs & Excise into the matter in question.

10.9 New civil penalty procedure

Businesses importing and exporting goods from and to outside the EU will be subject to a new civil penalty regime to commence in the autumn of 2003. There will be penalties for non compliance (including errors) and for evasion.

10.9.1 The new penalties

The non compliance penalties are intended to apply in cases of:

- Occasional serious error involving at least £10,000 of import VAT
- Persistent failure to comply with regulatory obligations, including low level errors in declarations, and
- Failure to put right deficiencies in systems, operations or physical security when directed to do so by Customs and Excise.

10.9.2 How the new penalties will be applied

Warning notices will be issued, and traders who still remain non compliant will incur a penalty of up to £2,500. Less serious cases of evasion of VAT will be liable to civil penalties of up to 100% of the VAT evaded.

Activity 24.9

In one VAT period, D Ltd has the following transactions in goods which would be standard rated if supplied in the UK. All amounts exclude any VAT. All goods sold are sent to the buyers' countries by D Ltd.

(a) Buys goods from a UK supplier for £12,000

(b) Sells goods to an Italian customer for £7,300. The customer's VAT registration number is shown on the invoice

(c) Sells goods to a Danish customer for £470. The customer is not registered for VAT. The relevant Danish VAT rate is 25%

(d) Sells goods to an Australian customer for £2,500

(e) Buys goods from a VAT registered German supplier for £3,000. The invoice shows D Ltd's VAT registration number and the goods are transferred to the UK

Task

Compute the VAT payable to or recoverable from HM Customs & Excise for the period.

Key learning points

- ☑ VAT is computed on the price after discounts.
- ☑ Mixed supplies are split, but composite supplies are not.
- ☑ Some supplies are taxable at either the standard or zero rate, while others are exempt.
- ☑ Input VAT on some supplies, including many cars, is not recoverable.
- ☑ If a trader makes some exempt supplies, the proportion of his input VAT that relates to making these supplies is not recoverable unless it is small.
- ☑ VAT bad debt relief is available after six months.
- ☑ VAT is generally due on imports, but exports are zero rated.
- ☑ Special schemes for the smaller business include the cash accounting scheme, the annual accounting scheme and the optional flat rate scheme.
- ☑ Returns are sent to the VAT Central Unit, but a trader may have dealings with his local VAT office or with a VAT tribunal.
- ☑ The most important penalties are the default surcharge and the misdeclaration penalty.

Quick quiz

1. David runs a grocery business. Every week his wife does the weekly shop for the family at the business premises and does not pay David for the groceries taken. How should this situation be treated for VAT?

2. Draw a line to match the turnover limits to the appropriate cash accounting, annual accounting and optional flat rate schemes.

Cash accounting	£150,000
Annual accounting	£187,500
Optional flat rate	£600,000

   - taxable turnover
   - total turnover

3. Where are completed VAT returns sent to?

4. What is the time limit for lodging an appeal against a disputed Custom's decision?

   A   10 days
   B   30 days
   C   45 days
   D   60 days

5. Peter was 2 months late registering his business for VAT in 2004. The first VAT return completed was for this 2 month period and showed VAT due of £4,200. What penalty, if any, is also due?

6. Tatkolat Ltd, a company registered for VAT, buys an aeroplane to be used for business purposes. The aeroplane is priced at £300,000 (exclusive of VAT).

   Tatkolat bought the aeroplane on hire purchase. The company will make 20 quarterly payments of £20,000. VAT will be paid with the first instalment.

   The company's sales are all standard rated for VAT purposes.

   How will the input VAT on the aeroplane be accounted for?

7. Frances commenced to trade on 1 January 2003. Her taxable supplies are normally £5,000 per month

   On 2nd June 2003 she was offered a contract to supply goods for the month of June only. The value of this contract is £60,000.

   Assuming that the contract related to taxable supplies, underline the date by which Frances should inform Customs and Excise of her liability to register for VAT, and the date from which she will be registered, if she decides to accept the contract?

Notify Customs by	Registered from
2 June 2003	2 July 2003
30 June 2003	30 June 2003
2 July 2003	2 July 2003
31 July 2003	31 July 2003

UNIT 7 PREPARING REPORTS AND RETURNS

8   Catherine's return of Value Added Tax for the quarter ended 31 March 2003, as submitted, was as follows.

	£
Output tax	252,650
Input tax	200,350
Tax due and paid	52,300

Catherine now finds that her output tax for the period has been understated by £140,000. She had made no previous errors on her returns and has discovered this error herself.

State, giving your reasons:

(1) Whether a penalty is due, and, if so, its amount

(2) If there were a penalty (regardless of your answer to (1)), what steps she could take to avoid having to pay it.

9   Jacky started to trade on 1 January 2003. She makes taxable supplies of £8,100 per month and incurs input VAT of £500 per month.

Jacky registers for VAT from 1 February 2004.

What is the amount of any penalty due to Customs and Excise, when Jacky registers for VAT?

A   £176
B   £225
C   £297
D   £346

10   S Normal has produced the following invoice for the sale of goods to one of his major customers.

	£
200 widgets @ £25 each	5,000
Less: quantity discount 20%	(1,000)
	4,000

The invoice also states that a further 5% discount is available if payment is received within 14 days of the invoice date.

How much VAT should be shown on the invoice?

A   £596
B   £665
C   £700
D   £875

Answers to quick quiz

1. This situation is 'goods taken from a business for non-business use' and VAT should be accounted for on their market value

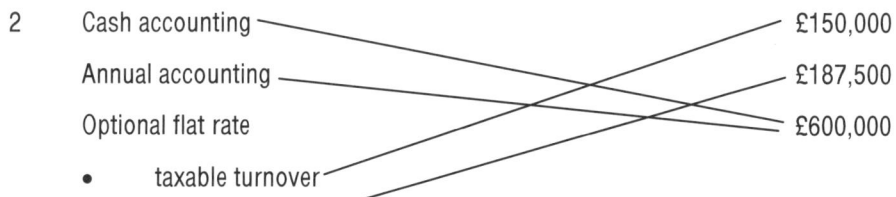

2. Cash accounting — £187,500
   Annual accounting — £600,000
   Optional flat rate
   - taxable turnover — £150,000
   - total turnover — £600,000

   (Cash accounting → £600,000; Annual accounting → £600,000; Optional flat rate taxable turnover → £150,000; total turnover → £187,500)

3. VAT Central Unit at Southend

4. B   Within 30 days of the date of Custom's decision

5. A 5% penalty totalling £210 (£4,200 × 5%) is payable by Peter

6. Input VAT of £52,500 will be reclaimed on the VAT return for the quarter in which the contract commenced.

7. Registered for VAT from the date grounds first existed, ie when the contract was made on 2nd June 2003.

   Inform Customs and Excise 30 days after this date ie 2 July 2003.

8. (1) No, a misdeclaration penalty is not due: the error £140,000 < 'gross amount of tax' (£252,650 + £200,350 + £140,000) at 30% = £177,900

   (2) She should notify Customs and Excise by way of voluntary disclosure and pay over the tax due.

9. A   Taxable supplies exceed £56,000 on 31.7.03 being £56,700 at that point. Jacky should have been registered from 1.9.03. Registration is therefore 5 months late.

	£
VAT due to Customs and Excise	
Output tax 8,100 × 5 × 7/47	6,032
Input tax 500 × 5	(2,500)
	3,532
Penalty 5% × 3,532	£176

   If the trader dealt with VAT registered businesses, she would try to recover the VAT on the supplies. This would then mean that the penalty is based on 17.5% × 5 × £8,100. It would also be possible to reduce this amount if there was pre-registration VAT recoverable.

10. B   Where a discount is offered for prompt payment, VAT is chargeable on the net amount regardless of whether the discount is taken up.

    Where a quantity discount is offered VAT is charged on the reduced price.

    £4,000 × 95% = £3,800 × 17.5% = £665 of VAT chargeable.

UNIT 7   PREPARING REPORTS AND RETURNS

Activity checklist

This checklist shows which performance criteria, range statement or knowledge and understanding point is covered by each activity in this chapter. Tick off each activity as you complete it.

Activity

24.1	☐	This activity deals with Knowledge and Understanding point 4
24.2	☐	This activity deals with Knowledge and Understanding point 4
24.3	☐	This activity deals with Performance Criteria 7.3.B regarding the correct identification and calculation of relevant inputs and outputs
24.4	☐	This activity deals with Performance Criteria 7.3.B regarding the correct identification and calculation of relevant inputs and outputs
24.5	☐	This activity deals with Knowledge and Understanding point 4
24.6	☐	This activity deals with Performance Criteria 7.3.D regarding seeking guidance from the VAT office when required, in a professional manner
24.7	☐	This activity deals with Performance Criteria 7.3.C regarding making submissions in accordance with current legislation *and* Knowledge and Understanding point 6
24.8	☐	This activity deals with Performance Criteria 7.3.C regarding making submissions in accordance with current legislation *and* Knowledge and Understanding point 6
24.9	☐	This activity deals with Range Statement: Inputs and outputs

Answers to activities

Answers to activities

Chapter 2

Answer 2.1

(a) Metal, rubber, plastic, glass, fabric, oil, paint, glue

(b) Cereals, plastic, cardboard, glue. You might have included sugar and preservatives and so on, depending upon what you eat for breakfast

(c) Sand, gravel, cement, bricks, plaster, wood, metal, plastic, glass, slate

(d) You will have to mark your own answer. If you work for a service organisation like a firm of accountants, you could view the paper (and binding) of sets of accounts sent out to clients as raw materials, although in practice such materials are likely to be regarded as indirect costs

Answer 2.2

Direct materials can be traced directly to specific units of product or service whereas **indirect materials** cannot.

Answer 2.3

(a) Direct
(b) Direct
(c) Indirect
(d) Direct
(e) Direct

Answer 2.4

Raw materials are goods purchased for incorporation into products for sale, but not yet issued to production. **Work in progress** is the name given to the materials while they are in the course of being converted to the final product. **Finished goods** are the end products when they are ready to be sold.

Answer 2.5

(a) The name and address of the ordering organisation
(b) The date of the order
(c) The order number
(d) The address and date for delivery or collection
(e) Details of the goods or services ordered

Answer 2.6

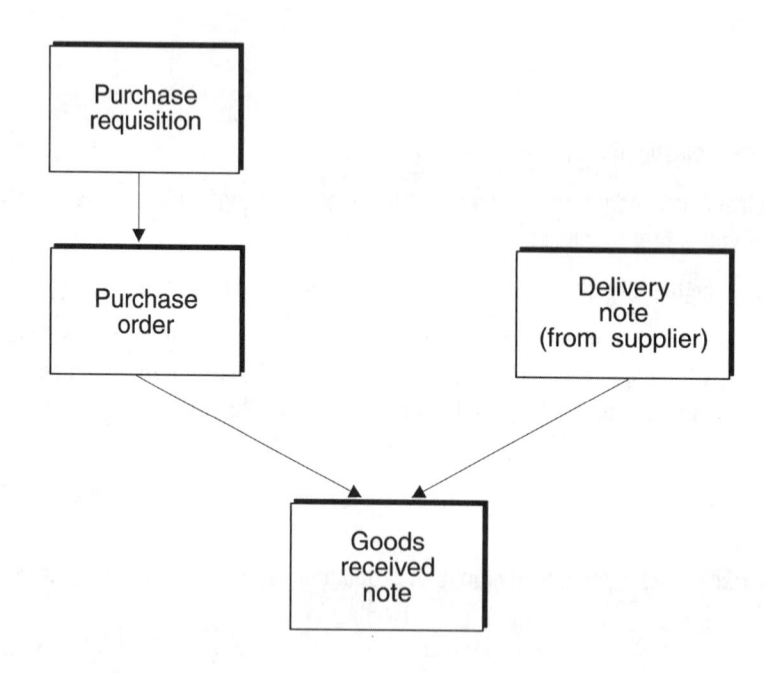

```
       Purchase
       requisition
           |
           v
       Purchase              Delivery
        order                  note
           \               (from supplier)
            \                  /
             v                v
              Goods received
                  note
```

Answer 2.7

(a) **FIFO**

Date of issue	Quantity Units	Value	£	Cost of issues £
4 May	200	100 at £2.00	200	
		100 at £2.10	210	
				410
11 May	400	300 at £2.10	630	
		100 at £2.12	212	
				842
20 May	100	100 at £2.12		212
Total cost of issues				1,464
Closing stock value	200	100 at £2.12	212	
		100 at £2.40	240	
				452
				1,916

ANSWERS TO ACTIVITIES

The cost of materials issued plus the value of closing stock equals the cost of purchases plus the value of opening stock (£1,916).

(b) **LIFO**

Date of issue	Quantity Units	Value	£	Cost of issues £
4 May	200	200 at £2.10		420
11 May	400	300 at £2.12	636	
		100 at £2.10	210	
				846
20 May	100	100 at £2.40		240
Total cost of issues				1,506
Closing stock value	200	100 at £2.10	210	
		100 at £2.00	200	
				410
				1,916

The cost of materials issued plus the value of closing stock equals the cost of purchases plus the value of opening stock (£1,916).

(c) **Weighted average cost**

Date	Received Units	Issued Units	Balance Units	Total stock value £	Unit cost £	Price of issue £
Opening stock			100	200	2.00	
3 May	400			840	2.10	
			500*	1,040	2.08	
4 May		200		(416)	2.08	416
			300	624	2.08	
9 May	300			636	2.12	
			600*	1,260	2.10	
11 May		400		(840)	2.10	840
			200	420	2.10	
18 May	100			240	2.40	
			300*	660	2.20	
20 May		100		(220)	2.20	220
Cost of issues						1,476
Closing stock			200	440	2.20	440
						1,916

* A new average unit cost is calculated whenever a new receipt of materials occurs.

The cost of materials issued plus the value of closing stock equals the cost of purchases plus the value of opening stock (£1,916).

Answer 2.8

(a) **FIFO** has the disadvantage that if stocks are quite old they may be issued to production at a price which is well below the current market price. This gives the wrong message to production managers.

(b) **LIFO** has the advantage that stock will be issued to production at a cost close to market value, thereby helping production managers gain a realistic idea of recent costs.

(c) The **weighted average cost method** involves less cumbersome calculations than the other methods, but the issue price rarely represents an actual price that could be found in the market.

Answer 2.9

	Cost centre code no.	Expenditure code no.
Issue of packing materials to production	300	100
Issue of raw materials to machining centre	100	100
Issue of lubricating oils to maintenance	400	200
Issue of cleaning materials to finishing centre	200	200

Answer 2.10

(a) Stock quantities delivered may not have matched the quantity shown on the Goods Received Note, which is used to update the stock records.

(b) The quantity of stock issued to production may not have matched the quantity on the materials requisition note.

(c) Stock may have been returned to stores without documentation.

(d) There may be other errors in the stock records (for example casting errors).

(e) Stock may have been destroyed or broken without a record being made.

(f) Stock may have been stolen.

Answer 2.11

(a) **Reorder quantity** $= \sqrt{\dfrac{2cd}{h}}$

$= \sqrt{\dfrac{2 \times \text{ordering costs} \times \text{annual demand}}{\text{Stockholding costs}}}$

$= \sqrt{\dfrac{2 \times 200 \times 4{,}000}{10}}$

$= 400 \text{ kg}$

(b) **Reorder level** = maximum usage × maximum lead time
= 600 × 3
= 1,800 kg

(c) **Maximum stock level** = reorder level + reorder quantity − (minimum usage × minimum lead time)
= 400 + 1,800 − (100 × 1)
= 2,100 kg

Answer 2.12

Helping hand. Study the completed values of the issues to determine what stock pricing method is in use. Check the balances and order quantities against the control levels given on the stores record card.

ANSWERS TO ACTIVITIES

STORES RECORD CARD

Material: A4 paper, white
Code: PWA4
Maximum Quantity: 140 boxes
Minimum Quantity: 40 boxes
Re-order Level: 60 boxes
Re-order Quantity: 80 boxes

Date	Receipts				Issues				Stock balance		
	Document number	Qty	Price £ per box	Total £	Document number	Qty	Price £ per box	Total £	Qty	Price £ per box	Total £
1/11									60	2.30	138.00
									20	2.32	46.40
									80		184.40
3/11					389	30	2.30	69.00	30	2.30	69.00
									20	2.32	46.40
									50		115.40
5/11	123	100	2.33	233.00					30	2.30	69.00
									20	2.32	46.40
									100	2.33	233.00
									150		348.40
8/11					397	40					
						30	2.30	69.00	10	2.32	23.20
						10	2.32	23.20	100	2.33	233.00
						40		92.20	110		256.20
9/11					401	30					
						10	2.32	23.20			
						20	2.33	46.60			
						30		69.80	80	2.33	186.40
12/11	137	80	2.35	188.00					80	2.33	186.40
									80	2.35	188.00
									160		374.40

Stock has risen above the maximum level on two occasions. On 5 November the excess was caused by ordering 100 boxes instead of the pre-set level of 80 boxes. On 12 November, the correct quantity was ordered (80 boxes) but the order was placed before the stock level had reached the pre-determined reorder level of 60 boxes.

Chapter 3

Answer 3.1

(a) From the information given, the only way of analysing Walter's time is as so many hours of 'general foreman duties'. In other words his work is so diverse that it is not possible to trace it as a direct cost to individual jobs.

It would be more appropriate to ensure that details of the individual jobs were recorded in such a way that Walter's time could be equitably split between them. For example a job requiring 20 men is likely to require twice as much of Walter's attention as a job requiring 10 men.

(b) Peter's time may at first seem to be as difficult to analyse as Walter's, but in fact it is probable that he could fill in a daily or weekly time sheet, splitting out his time between the various types of work that he does. For example he may spend 3 hours at the counter in the morning, and 1 hour filing and 2 hours dealing with correspondence in the afternoon.

Answer 3.2

Job 249

Employee	Hours	Rate £	Total £
George	14	8.20	114.80
Paul	49	7.40	362.60
			477.40

Job 250

Employee	Hours	Rate £	Total £
George	2	8.20	16.40
John	107	5.30	567.10
Ringo	74	6.50	481.00
			1,064.50

Answer 3.3

The direct labour cost is the gross basic wage, £1,327.42.

Answer 3.4

None of Dave's overtime premiums should be charged to overheads and therefore both Jenny and Mel are wrong in this instance. Since the customer specifically requested that overtime be worked on his job in order that it is completed as soon as possible, the overtime premium is a **direct cost** of the job.

ANSWERS TO ACTIVITIES

Answer 3.5

OPERATION CARD					
Operators Name Shah, L				Total Batch Quantity -	
Clock No 7142				Start Time -	
Pay week No 17 Date W/E XX/XX/XX				Stop Time -	
Part No 713/V				Works Order No 14 AB	
Opertion Drilling				Special Instructions -	
Quantity Produced	No Rejected		Good Production	Rate	£
Monday 173	14		159	50p	79.50
Tuesday 131	2		129	40p	51.60
Wednesday 92	-		92	20p	18.40
Thursday 120	7		113	30p	33.90
Friday 145	5		140	40p	56.00
Insector ND			Operative LS	
Foreman AN			Date XX/XX/XX	
PRODUCTION CANNOT BE CLAIMED WITHOUT A PROPERLY SIGNED CARD					

```
                              £
Gross wage      =         79.50
                          51.60
                          18.40
                          33.90
                          56.00
                         239.40
```

Answer 3.6

	£
Time rate = 35 hours × £8	280
Time allowed for 90 units (× 0.5 hour) = 45 hours	
Therefore time saved = 10 hours	
Bonus = 40% × 10 hours × £8	32
Total gross wages	312

Answer 3.7

Helping hand. To decide on the correct code numbers, read the instructions carefully, and then make two decisions for each cost.

- Which cost centre should be charged with the labour cost?
- Is the labour cost a direct cost or an indirect cost?

WEEKLY TIME SHEET

Name: J. Wain
Staff number: 17254
Week ending: 091201

	M	T	W	T	F	TOTAL Hours	£	CODE
Direct time								
Finishing	5	4		1	3	13	143	1 0 1 0 0
Packing				6	3	9	99	2 0 1 0 0
Direct total	5	4		7	6	22	242	
Administration								
Budget meeting	2			1		3	33	
Total admin	2			1		3	33	3 0 2 0 0
Training and courses								
First Aid course		3				3	33	
Total training		3				3	33	4 0 2 0 0
Holidays, sickness								
Holiday			7			7	77	
Total leave			7			7	77	3 0 2 0 0
TOTAL	7	7	7	7	7	35	385	

Signed: RS   Authorised: LQW

Chapter 4

Answer 4.1

(a) Capital expenditure

(b) Depreciation of a fixed asset is revenue expenditure.

(c) The legal fees associated with the purchase of a property may be added to the purchase price and classified as capital expenditure. The cost of the premises in the balance sheet of the business will then include the legal fees.

(d) Capital expenditure (enhancing an existing fixed asset)

(e) Revenue expenditure

(f) Capital expenditure

(g) If customs duties are borne by the purchaser of the fixed asset, they may be added to the cost of the machinery and classified as capital expenditure.

(h) Similarly, if carriage costs are paid for by the purchaser of the fixed asset, they may be included in the cost of the fixed asset and classified as capital expenditure.

(i) Installation costs of a fixed asset are also added to the fixed asset's cost and classified as capital expenditure.

(j) Revenue expenditure

Answer 4.2

You will need to ask the operational department concerned whether the machine is used **exclusively for one product** or for several different products.

If the machine is used exclusively for one product then the whole of the depreciation charge is traceable directly to that product and the depreciation is therefore a **direct expense**. If the machine is used for several different products and it is difficult to allocate the depreciation charges to each individual product then the depreciation charge should be an **indirect expense**.

Answer 4.3

Straight line method

$$\text{Depreciation per annum} = \frac{\text{Cost} - \text{residual value}}{\text{Expected life}}$$

$$= \frac{£(75,000 - 5,000)}{5 \text{ years}}$$

$$= £14,000$$

Reducing balance method

	£
Capital cost	75,000
Year 1 charge (£75,000 × 42%)	31,500
	43,500
Year 2 charge (£43,500 × 42%)	18,270
	25,230
Year 3 charge (£25,230 × 42%)	10,597
	14,633
Year 4 charge (£14,633 × 42%)	6,146
	8,487
Year 5 charge (£8,487 × 42%)	3,565
	4,922

Answer 4.4

	£	Code
Strange (Properties) Ltd	4,000.00	0120
Yorkshire Electricity plc	1,598.27	0060
Dudley Stationery Ltd	275.24	0100
Dora David (Cleaner)	125.00	0040
BPP Publishing Ltd	358.00	0030
AAT	1,580.00	0160
British Telecom	1,431.89	0170
Kall Kwik (Stationers)	312.50	0100
Interest to 31.3.X3	2,649.33	0020
L & W Office Equipment	24.66	0090
Avis	153.72	0190
Federal Express	32.00	0100
Starriers Garage Ltd	79.80	0070

Answer 4.5

The following expenses may be chargeable directly to clients.

	£	
Kall Kwik (Stationers)	312.50	Photocopying costs: say 200 sets of accounts to be sent to shareholders?
Avis	153.72	The cost of renting a car to travel on a client's business?

The following expenses *may* be chargeable directly to departments.

	£	
Dudley Stationery Ltd	275.24	If this type of stationery is used exclusively by one department.
L & W Office Equipment	24.66	If the item is used exclusively by one department.
Starriers Garage Ltd	79.80	The car is probably used by a specific employee.

ANSWERS TO ACTIVITIES

Federal Express expenses could also fall into this category. The remaining items need to be split between departments. Training costs and AAT subscriptions could be split according to the specific staff involved, rent according to the floor area occupied and so on. (The next chapter goes into this in more detail.)

Chapter 5

Answer 5.1

(a) **Absorption costing** is a method of determining a product cost that includes a proportion of all production overheads incurred in the making of the product and possibly a proportion of other overheads such as administration and selling overheads.

(b)
- **Allocation** of costs to cost centres
- **Apportionment** of costs between cost centres
- **Absorption** of costs into cost units

Answer 5.2

	Total £	A £	B £	Assembly £	Canteen £	Maintenance £	Basis of apportionment
Indirect wages	78,560	8,586	9,190	15,674	29,650	15,460	Actual
Consumable materials	16,900	6,400	8,700	1,200	600	-	Actual
Rent and rates	16,700	3,711	4,453	5,567	2,227	742	Area
Insurance	2,400	533	640	800	320	107	Area
Power	8,600	4,730	3,440	258	-	172	Usage
Heat and light	3,400	756	907	1,133	453	151	Area
Depreciation	40,200	20,100	17,900	2,200	-	-	Value
	166,760	44,816	45,230	26,832	33,250	16,632	

Workings

(1) **Rent and rates, insurance, heat and light**

Floor area is a sensible measure to use as the basis for apportionment.

	Area Sq metres	Proportion total area	Share of rent & rates £	Share of insurance £	Share of heat & light £
Machine shop A	10,000	10/45	3,711	533	756
Machine shop B	12,000	12/45	4,453	640	907
Assembly	15,000	15/45	5,567	800	1,133
Canteen	6,000	6/45	2,227	320	453
Maintenance	2,000	2/45	742	107	151
	45,000		16,700	2,400	3,400

(2) **Power**

	Percentage %	Share of cost £
Machine shop A	55	4,730
Machine shop B	40	3,440
Assembly	3	258
Maintenance	2	172
		8,600

(3) **Depreciation**

In the absence of specific information about the fixed assets in use in each department and the depreciation rates that are applied, this cost is shared out on the basis of the **relative value of each department's machinery** to the total. In practice more specific information would (or should) be available.

Answer 5.3

	Total £	A £	B £	Assembly £	Canteen £	Maintenance £	Basis of apportionment
Total overheads	166,760	44,816	45,230	26,832	33,250	16,632	
Reapportion (W1)	-	7,600	5,890	19,760	(33,250)	-	Dir labour
Reapportion (W2)	-	4,752	11,880	-	-	(16,632)	Mac usage
Totals	166,760	57,168	63,000	46,592	-	-	

Workings

(1) **Canteen overheads**

Total direct labour hours = 35,000

Machine shop A $= \dfrac{8,000}{35,000} \times £33,250 = £7,600$

Machine shop B $= \dfrac{6,200}{35,000} \times £33,250 = £5,890$

Assembly $= \dfrac{20,800}{35,000} \times £33,250 = £19,760$

ANSWERS TO ACTIVITIES

(2) **Maintenance overheads**

Total machine hours = 25,200

Machine shop A $= \dfrac{7,200}{25,200} \times £16,632 = £4,752$

Machine shop B $= \dfrac{18,000}{25,200} \times £16,632 = £11,880$

The total overhead has now been shared, on a fair basis, between the three production departments.

Answer 5.4

Direct apportionment method

	Production 1 £	Production 2 £	Service 1 £	Service 2 £
	97,428	84,947	9,384	15,823
Apportion Service 1 costs (20:15)	5,362	4,022	(9,384)	–
	102,790	88,969	–	15,823
Apportion Service 2 costs (3:8)	4,315	11,508	–	(15,823)
	107,105	100,477	–	–

Answer 5.5

Step-down method

	Production 1 £	Production 2 £	Service 1 £	Service 2 £
	97,428	84,947	9,384	15,823
Apportion Service 1 costs (20:15:5)	4,692	3,519	(9,384)	1,173
	102,120	88,466	–	16,996
Apportion Service 2 costs (3:8)	4,635	12,361	–	(16,996)
	106,755	100,827	–	–

Answer 5.6

(a) **Overhead absorption rate** $= \dfrac{\text{Expected overheads}}{\text{Planned direct labour hours}}$

$\dfrac{£108,000}{90,000} = £1.20$ per direct labour hour

(b) **Overhead absorption rate** $= \dfrac{\text{Expected overheads}}{\text{Planned direct machine hours}}$

$\dfrac{£720,000}{50,000} = £14.40$ per direct machine hour

Answer 5.7

	Domestic	Industrial
Direct labour cost per unit	£180	£80
Rate per hour	£10	£10
Direct labour hours per unit	18	8
Production volume (units)	20,000	20,000
Total labour hours	360,000	160,000

Overhead absorption rate = $\dfrac{\text{Total overhead}}{\text{Total labour hours}} = \dfrac{£1,040,000}{(360,000 + 160,000)} = £2.00$ per hour

	Domestic £	Industrial £
Direct materials	28	40
Direct labour	180	80
Direct expenses	40	200
Direct cost	248	320
Production overhead (18 × £2.00)/(8 × £2.00)	36	16
	284	336

Answer 5.8

		£	£
Actual expenditure			176,533
Overhead absorbed			
Machine shop A	7,300 hrs × £7.94	57,962	
Machine shop B	18,700 hrs × £3.50	65,450	
Assembly	21,900 hrs × £2.24	49,056	
			172,468
Under-absorbed overhead			4,065

Chapter 6

Answer 6.1

(a)
	£
Contribution from Clouds (unit contribution = £20 − £(8 + 4 + 2 + 2) = £4 × 10,000)	40,000
Contribution from Skys (unit contribution = £30 − £(14 + 2 + 1 + 3) = £10 × 5,000)	50,000
Total contribution	90,000
Fixed costs for the period (£40,000 + £15,000 + £25,000)	80,000
Profit	10,000

(b) At a higher volume of sales, profit would be as follows.

	£
Contribution from sales of 15,000 Clouds (× £4)	60,000
Contribution from sales of 6,000 Skys (× £10)	60,000
Total contribution	120,000
Less fixed costs	80,000
Profit	40,000

Answer 6.2

A   Difference in profit = **change** in stock levels × fixed overhead absorption rate per unit = (150 – 100) × £10 × 5 = £2,500 **lower** profit, because stock levels **decreased**. The correct answer is therefore option A.

The key is the change in the volume of stock. Stock levels have **decreased** therefore absorption costing will report a **lower** profit. This eliminates options B and D.

Option C is incorrect because it is based on the closing stock only (100 units × £10 × 5 hours).

Answer 6.3

B   Difference in profit = (8,500 – 6,750) × £3 = £5,250

Absorption costing profit = £62,100 – £5,250 = £56,850

The correct answer is B.

Since stock levels reduced, the absorption costing profit will be lower than the marginal costing profit. You can therefore eliminate options C and D.

Chapter 7

Answer 7.1

(a) Mixed (semi-variable)
(b) Fixed
(c) Fixed
(d) Variable
(e) Variable

Answer 7.2

(a)

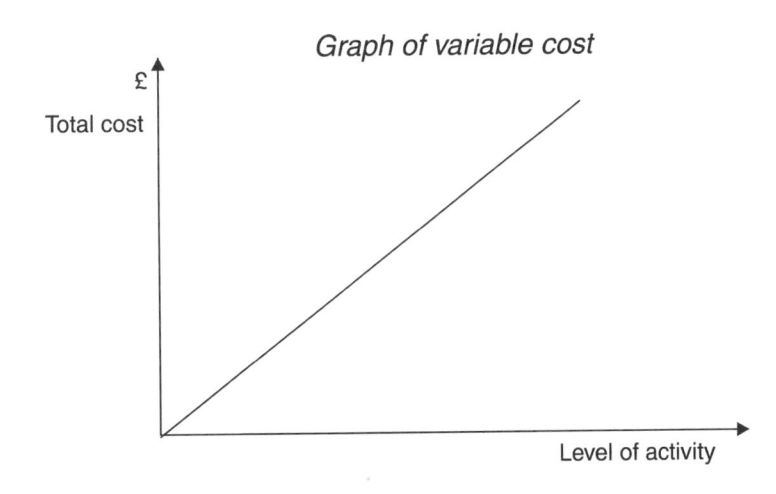

Graph of variable cost

(b)

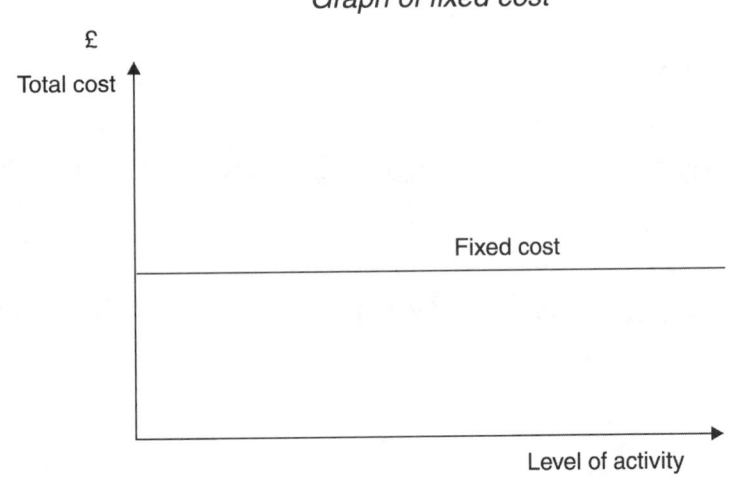

Graph of fixed cost

(c)

Graph of step cost

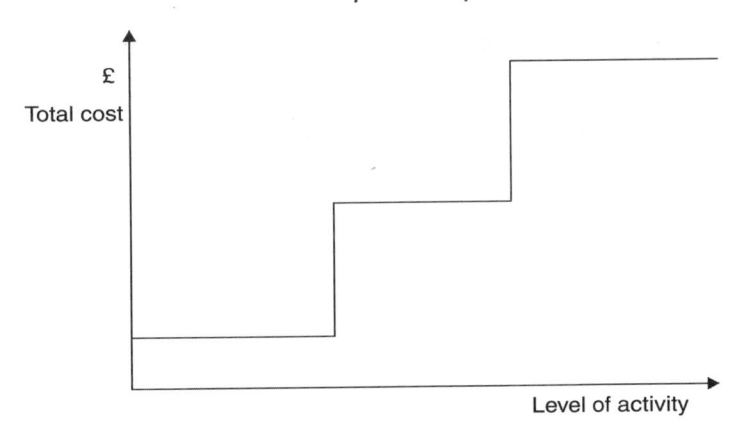

ANSWERS TO ACTIVITIES

Answer 7.3

Step 1

Period with highest activity = month 2
Period with lowest activity = month 4

Step 2

Total cost at high activity level = £115,000
Total cost at low activity level = £97,000
Total units at high activity level = 8,000
Total units at low activity level = 6,000

Step 3

Variable cost per unit $= \dfrac{\text{Total cost at high activity level} - \text{total cost at low activity level}}{\text{Total units at high activity level} - \text{total units at low level activity}}$

$= \dfrac{£(115,000 - 97,000)}{8,000 - 6,000} = \dfrac{£18,000}{2,000} = £9 \text{ per unit}$

Step 4

Fixed costs = (Total cost at high activity level) − (total units at high activity level × variable cost per unit)

= £115,000 − (8,000 × £9) = £115,000 − £72,000 = £43,000

Therefore, the costs in month 5 for an output of 7,500 units are as follows

	£
Variable costs (7,500 × £9)	67,500
Fixed costs	43,000
Total costs	110,500

Chapter 8

Answer 8.1

Helping hand. The depreciation provision is a production overhead cost incurred which is debited to the production overhead control account.

PRODUCTION OVERHEAD CONTROL ACCOUNT

	£		£
Bank account	125,478	Work in progress (27,000 × £5)	135,000
Depreciation	4,100		
Profit and loss account	5,422		
	135,000		135,000

The production overhead is over absorbed by £5,422. This amount is transferred, at the end of the period, as a credit in the profit and loss account.

Answer 8.2

(a) **Helping hand**. Since we are given no information on the issue of direct materials we need to construct a stores ledger control account.

MATERIALS CONTROL ACCOUNT

	£		£
Balance b/f	18,500	Creditors/cash (returns)	2,300
Creditors/cash	142,000	Overhead accounts (indirect materials)	25,200
		WIP (balancing figure)	116,900
		Balance c/f	16,100
	160,500		160,500

The value of the issue of direct materials during April 20X0 was £116,900.

(b) The issue of direct materials would therefore be recorded as follows.

| DR | WIP control account | £116,900 |
| CR | Materials control account | £116,900 |

Answer 8.3

				£	£
(a)	DEBIT	Materials stock		10,000	
	CREDIT	Creditors			10,000
(b)	DEBIT	Finished goods stock		50,000	
	CREDIT	Work in progress stock			50,000
(c)	DEBIT	Administration overhead/indirect materials		5,000	
	CREDIT	Materials stock			5,000
(d)	DEBIT	Production overhead control		20,000	
	CREDIT	Wages control			20,000

ANSWERS TO ACTIVITIES

Answer 8.4

Invoice no	Net sales value £	Country	Code
8730	10,360.00	Canada	R120
8731	12,750.73	Australia	R160
8732	5,640.39	Spain	R140
8733	15,530.10	Northern Ireland	R110
8734	3,765.75	South Africa	R150
8735	8,970.22	Kenya	R150
8736	11,820.45	Italy	R140
8737	7,640.00	France	R140
8738	9,560.60	Australia	R160
8739	16,750.85	Germany	R140

Chapter 9

Answer 9.1

Helping hand. Note that the profit margin is given as a percentage on selling price. If profit is 25% on selling price, this is the same as $33^{1}/_{3}$% (25/75) on cost.

			Job TN8 £		Job KT2 £
Direct material			154.00		108.00
Direct labour:	dept X	(20 × 3.80)	76.00	(16 × 3.80)	60.80
	dept Y	(12 × 3.50)	42.00	(10 × 3.50)	35.00
	dept Z	(10 × 3.40)	34.00	(14 × 3.40)	47.60
Total direct cost			306.00		251.40
Overhead:	dept X	(20 × 12.86)	257.20	(16 × 12.86)	205.76
	dept Y	(12 × 12.40)	148.80	(10 × 12.40)	124.00
	dept Z	(10 × 14.03)	140.30	(14 × 14.03)	196.42
Total cost			852.30		777.58
Profit			284.10		259.19
Quoted selling price			1,136.40		1,036.77

Answer 9.2

(a) Big units

	£	£
Direct materials		5,240
Direct labour		
Skilled 1,580 hours at £9	14,220	
Semi-skilled 3,160 hours at £7	22,120	
		36,340
Direct expenses		1,180
Administrative expenses		
4,740 hours at £0.50 (see below)*		2,370
		45,130
Selling price		48,980
Calculated profit		3,850
Divided: Staff bonus 20%		770
Profit for company 80%		3,080

*Administrative expenses absorption rate $= \dfrac{£4,400}{8,800}$ per labour hour

$= £0.50$ per labour hour

(b)

	Little units			All-purpose		
		£	£		£	£
Direct materials			6,710			3,820
Direct labour						
Skilled	1,700 hrs at £9	15,300		160 hrs at £9	1,440	
Semi-skilled	1,900 hrs at £7	13,300		300 hrs at £7	2,100	
Direct expenses		1,700			250	
Administration expenses:	3,600 hrs at £0.50	1,800		460 hrs at £0.50	230	
		32,100			4,020	
Costs to completion	20/80 × 32,100	8,025		75/25 × 4,020	12,060	
			40,125			16,080
Total costs			46,835			19,900
Selling price			43,125			25,660
Calculated profit/(loss)			(3,710)			5,760
Divided: Staff bonus 20%			-			1,152
(Loss)/profit for company			(3,710)			4,608

Note that whilst direct labour costs, direct expenses and administration expenses increase in proportion to the total labour hours required to complete the little units and the all-purpose units, there will be no further material costs to complete the batches.

Answer 9.3

Helping hand. Think about the type of production process involved and how costs would be collected.

- **A baker** would probably use batch costing. The cost units (loaves, cakes) are identical but would be produced in separately identifiable batches.

- **A transport company** would use unit costing, probably using a cost unit such as the tonne-kilometre (the cost of carrying one tonne for one kilometre).

- **A plumber** would use job costing, since every plumbing job is a separately identifiable cost unit.

- **An accountancy firm** would use job costing, since each client would require a different amount of time from employees of different skills.

- **A paint manufacturer** would use unit costing since the total costs incurred would be averaged over all the tins of paint produced in a period.

Answer 9.4

(a) **Answer: B**

The vehicle cost per passenger-kilometre (i) is appropriate for cost control purposes because it **combines the distance travelled and the number of passengers carried, both of which affect cost.**

The fuel cost for each vehicle per kilometre (ii) can be useful for control purposes because it **focuses on a particular aspect** of the cost of operating each vehicle.

The fixed cost per kilometre (iii) is not particularly useful for control purposes because it **varies with the number of kilometres travelled.**

(b) **Answer: B**

Number of occupied room-nights = 40 rooms × 30 nights × 65%
= 780

Room servicing cost per occupied room-night = $\dfrac{£3,900}{780}$ = £5

Option A is the cost per available room-night. This makes no allowance for the 65% occupancy achieved. If you selected **option C** you simply divided £3,900 by 40 rooms. This does not account for the number of nights in the period, nor the percentage occupancy achieved. If you selected **option D** you calculated the cost per **occupied room**, rather than the cost **per occupied room-night**.

Chapter 10

Answer 10.1

Cost per unit = $\dfrac{\text{Costs incurred}}{\text{Expected output}}$

Costs incurred = £100,000 + £200,000 + £100,000
= £400,000

Expected output = Actual output = 50,000

Cost per unit = $\dfrac{£400,000}{50,000 \text{ units}}$

= £8 per unit

Answer 10.2

(a) **If loss is expected**, and is an unavoidable feature of processing, it is argued by cost accountants that there is no point in charging a cost to the loss. It is more sensible to accept that the loss will occur, and spread the costs of production over the expected units of output.

$\dfrac{\text{Costs}}{\text{Expected output (90\% of 1,000)}} = \dfrac{£4,500}{900 \text{ units}}$

Cost per unit of output = $\dfrac{£4,500}{900} = £5$

Normal loss is not given any cost, so that the process account would appear as follows.

PROCESS ACCOUNT

	Units	£		Units	£
Costs incurred	1,000	4,500	Normal loss	100	0
			Output units	900	4,500
	1,000	4,500		1,000	4,500

It helps to enter normal loss into the process 'T' account, just to make sure that your memorandum columns for units are the same on the debit and the credit sides of the account.

(b) **If loss is unexpected** and occurred perhaps as a result of poor workmanship, poor quality materials, poor supervision, damage by accident, and so on, it is argued that it would be reasonable to charge a cost to the units of loss. The cost would then be transferred to an **'abnormal loss' account**, and eventually written off to the profit and loss account as an item of loss in the period. Units of 'good output' would not be burdened with the cost of the loss, so that the cost per unit remains unaltered.

$\dfrac{\text{Costs incurred}}{\text{Expected output}} = \dfrac{£4,500}{1,000 \text{ units}}$

Costs per unit   £4.50

ANSWERS TO ACTIVITIES

The process account and abnormal loss account would look like this.

PROCESS ACCOUNT

	Units	£		Units	£
Costs incurred	1,000	4,500	Abnormal loss	100	450
			Output units	900	4,050
	1,000	4,500		1,000	4,500

ABNORMAL LOSS ACCOUNT

	Units	£		Units	£
Process account	100	450	Profit and loss account	100	450

Answer 10.3

Step 1. Determine output and losses

Period 3

	Units
Actual output	850
Normal loss (10% × 1,000)	100
Abnormal loss	50
Input	1,000

Period 4

	Units
Actual output	950
Normal loss (10% × 1,000)	100
Abnormal gain	(50)
Input	1,000

Step 2. Calculate cost per unit of output and losses

For each period the cost per unit is based on expected output.

$$\frac{\text{Cost of input}}{\text{Expected units of output}} = \frac{£29,070}{900} = £32.30 \text{ per unit}$$

Step 3. Calculate total cost of output and losses

Period 3

	£
Cost of output (850 × £32.30)	27,455
Normal loss	0
Abnormal loss (50 × £32.30)	1,615
	29,070

Period 4

Cost of output (950 × £32.30)	30,685
Normal loss	0
Abnormal gain (50 × £32.30)	(1,615)
	29,070

Step 4. Complete accounts

PROCESS ACCOUNT

	Units	£		Units	£
Period 3					
Cost of input	1,000	29,070	Normal loss	100	0
			Finished goods a/c (× £32.30)	850	27,455
			Abnormal loss a/c (× £32.30)	50	1,615
	1,000	29,070		1,000	29,070
Period 4					
Cost of input	1,000	29,070	Normal loss	100	0
Abnormal gain a/c (× £32.30)	50	1,615	Finished goods a/c (× £32.30)	950	30,685
	1,050	30,685		1,050	30,685

ABNORMAL LOSS OR GAIN ACCOUNT

	£		£
Period 3		*Period 4*	
Abnormal loss in process a/c	1,615	Abnormal gain in process a/c	1,615

A nil balance on this account will be carried forward into period 5.

(*Note*. It is considered more appropriate to value all units of output at a value based on expected loss (£32.30 per unit) rather than to have random fluctuations in the cost per unit each period due to variations in the loss. Period 3 output should therefore be costed at £29,070/850 = £34.20 per unit and period 4 output at £29,070/950 = £30.60 per unit.)

Answer 10.4

Step 1. Determine output and losses

	Process 1 kgs		Process 2 kgs
Output	2,300		4,000
Normal loss (20% of 3,000 kgs)	600	(10% of 4,300)	430
Abnormal loss	100		–
Abnormal gain	–		(130)
	3,000		4,300*

* From process 1 (2,300 kgs) + 2,000 kgs added

Step 2. Determine cost per unit of output and losses

	Process 1 £		Process 2 £
Material (3,000 × £0.25)	750	(2,000 × £0.40)	800
From process 1	–	(2,300 × £0.50)	1,150
Labour	120		84
Overhead (375% × £120)	450	(496% × £84)	417
less: scrap value of **normal** loss			
(600 × £0.20)	(120)	(430 × £0.3)	(129)
	1,200		2,322
Expected output			
3,000 × 80%	2,400	4,300 × 90%	3,870
Cost per kg ($\frac{£1,320 - £120}{3,000 - 600}$)	£0.50	($\frac{£2,451 - £129}{4,300 - 430}$)	£0.60

Step 3. Determine total cost of output and losses

	Process 1 £		Process 2 £
Output (2,300 × £0.50)	1,150	(4,000 × £0.60)	2,400
Normal loss (scrap)			
(600 × £0.20)	120	(430 × £0.30)	129
Abnormal loss (100 × £0.50)	50		–
	1,320		2,529
Abnormal gain	–	(130 × £0.60)	(78)
	1,320		2,451

Step 4. Complete accounts

(a)

PROCESS 1 ACCOUNT

	kg	£		kg	£
Material	3,000	750	Normal loss to scrap a/c		
Labour		120	(20%)	600	120
General overhead		450	Production transferred to		
			process 2	2,300	1,150
			Abnormal loss a/c	100	50
	3,000	1,320		3,000	1,320

ANSWERS TO ACTIVITIES

(b)
PROCESS 2 ACCOUNT

	kg	£		kg	£
Transferred from process 1	2,300	1,150	Normal loss to scrap a/c (10%)	430	129
Material added	2,000	800	Production transferred to finished stock	4,000	2,400
Labour		84			
General overhead		417			
	4,300	2,451			
Abnormal gain	130	78			
	4,430	2,529		4,430	2,529

(c)
FINISHED STOCK ACCOUNT

	kg	£
Process 2	4,000	2,400

(d)
SCRAP ACCOUNT

	kg	£		kg	£
Normal loss (process 1)	600	120	Abnormal gain (process 2)	130	39
Normal loss (process 2)	430	129	Cash	1,000	230
Abnormal loss (process 1)	100	20			
	1,130	269		1,130	269

(e)
ABNORMAL LOSS AND GAIN ACCOUNT

	kg	£		kg	£
Process 1 (loss)	100	50	Scrap value of abnormal loss	100	20
Scrap value of abnormal gain	130	39	Process 2 (gain)	130	78
Profit and loss		9			
	230	98		230	98

Note. In this answer, a single account has been prepared for abnormal loss/gain. Your solution may have separated this single account into two separate accounts, one for abnormal gain and one for abnormal loss.

Answer 10.5

STATEMENT OF EQUIVALENT UNITS

Input litres	Output	Total litres	Process X material litres	%	Labour and overhead litres	%
50,000	Completed production	41,000	41,000	100	41,000	100
	Normal loss	2,500	-	-	-	-
	Abnormal loss	2,000	2,000	100	2,000	100
	Closing stock	4,500	4,500	100	2,250	50
50,000		50,000	47,500		45,250	

ANSWERS TO ACTIVITIES

STATEMENT OF COST PER EQUIVALENT UNIT

Input	Cost		Equivalent litres produced	Cost per litre
	£	£		£
Process X materials		47,500	47,500	1.00
Labour	3,000			
Overhead	1,525	4,525	45,250	0.10
		52,025		1.10

STATEMENT OF EVALUATION

Output	No of equivalent litres	Cost per litre		Value
			£	£
Completed production	41,000	1.10		45,100
Abnormal loss	2,000	1.10		2,200
Closing stock				
- Process X material	4,500	1.00	4,500	
- Labour and overhead	2,250	0.10	225	
				4,725
				52,025

PROCESS Y ACCOUNT

	litres	£		litres	£
Process X	50,000	47,500	Finished goods	41,000	45,100
Labour		3,000	Normal loss	2,500	-
Overhead		1,525	Abnormal loss	2,000	2,200
			Closing work in progress	4,500	4,725
	50,000	52,025		50,000	52,025

Answer 10.6

Step 1. Determine output and losses

STATEMENT OF EQUIVALENT UNITS

	Total Units	Equivalent units			
		Material		Labour	
		%	Units	%	Units
Completed production	8,000	100	8,000	100	8,000
Closing stock	1,000	80	800	50	500
Normal loss	500				
Abnormal loss	500	100	500	100	500
	10,000		9,300		9,000

Step 2. Calculate cost per unit of output, losses and WIP

STATEMENT OF COST PER EQUIVALENT UNIT

	Cost £	Equivalent units	Cost per equivalent unit £
Material (£(5,150 – 500))	4,650	9,300	0.50
Labour	2,700	9,000	0.30
	7,350		0.80

Step 3. Calculate total cost of output, losses and WIP

STATEMENT OF EVALUATION

	Equivalent units	Cost per equivalent unit £		Total £
Completed production	8,000	0.80		6,400
Closing stock: material	800	0.50	400	
labour	500	0.30	150	
				550
Abnormal loss	500	0.80		400
				7,350

Step 4. Complete accounts

PROCESS ACCOUNT

	Units	£		Units	£
Material	10,000	5,150	Completed production	8,000	6,400
Labour		2,700	Closing stock	1,000	550
			Normal loss	500	500
			Abnormal loss	500	400
	10,000	7,850		10,000	7,850

Chapter 11

Answer 11.1

Sales revenue required $= \dfrac{\text{Required contribution}}{\text{P/V ratio}}$

$= \dfrac{£50,000}{20\%}$

$= £250,000$

If selling price = £10 per unit, number of units = £250,000 ÷ £10
= 25,000 units

Answer 11.2

Breakeven point $= \dfrac{\text{Total fixed costs}}{\text{Contribution per unit}}$

$= \dfrac{£210,000}{£120 - £90}$

$= \dfrac{£210,000}{£30}$

= 7,000 units

Margin of safety = Budgeted sales volume − breakeven sales volume
= 9,000 − 7,000
= 2,000 units

Which may be expressed as $\dfrac{2,000}{9,000} \times 100\%$

= 22% (to one decimal place) of budgeted sales volume

Answer 11.3

Required contribution	=	fixed costs + profit
	=	£47,000 + £23,000
	=	£70,000
Required sales	=	14,000 units

	£
Required contribution per unit sold	5
Variable cost per unit	15
Required sales price per unit	20

Answer 11.4

	Current	Revised	Difference
	£ per unit	£ per unit	
Selling price	20	21	
Variable costs	10	9	
Contribution	10	12	
Fixed costs	£29,000	£30,000	
Breakeven point (units)	2,900	2,500	**400 lower**

$$\text{Breakeven point} = \frac{\text{Total fixed costs}}{\text{Contribution per unit}}$$

Current BEP = $\frac{£29,000}{£10}$ = 2,900 units

Revised BEP = $\frac{£30,000}{£12}$ = 2,500 units

The correct answer is therefore B.

Answer 11.5

Material required = 20,000 units × (£12/£3) = 80,000 kg

Material is therefore a limiting factor, since only 75,000 kg are available. This eliminates option D.

Labour required = 20,000 units × (£72/£8) = 180,000 hours.

Labour is not a limiting factor, since 190,000 labour hours are available. This eliminates options B and C.

Therefore the correct answer is A.

Chapter 12

Answer 12.1

(a) At 28 February 20X6, n = 3, £5,000 × 1.20^3 = £8,640
(b) At 28 February 20X7, n = 4, £5,000 × 1.15^4 = £8,745.03
(c) At 28 February 20X6, n = 3, £5,000 × 1.06^3 = £5,955.08

Answer 12.2

30 April 20X3 = Now

30 April 20X4 = time period 5

∴ n = 5
   r = 5%

Present value = £16,000 × discount rate (where n = 5 and r = 5%)
               = £16,000 × 0.784
               = £12,544

ANSWERS TO ACTIVITIES

Answer 12.3

	Cash flow	Discount factor	Present value
	£	10%	£
0	(18,000)	*1.000	(18,000)
1	6,000	0.909	5,454
2	8,000	0.826	6,608
3	5,000	0.751	3,755
4	1,000	0.683	683
		Net present value	(1,500)

*The initial cost occurs at time 0, now, and therefore the discount factor is 1.00 as £18,000 is the present value of the expenditure now.

The NPV is negative and the project is therefore not viable (since the present value of the costs is greater than the present value of the benefits).

Answer 12.4

Year	Cash flow	Discount factor	Present value
	£	11%	£
0	(28,000)	1.000	(28,000)
1	8,000	0.901	7,208
2	8,000	0.812	6,496
3	8,000	0.731	5,848
4	8,000	0.659	5,272
5	8,000	0.593	4,744
		NPV	1,568

Alternatively, you could treat the cash inflows of £8,000 for five years as an annuity.

Year	Cash flow	Discount factor	Present value
	£	11%	£
0	(28,000)	1.000	(28,000)
1-5	8,000	3.696	29,568
			1,568

Answer 12.5

Year	Cash flow	Discount factor	Present value
	£	15%	£
0	(50,000)	1.0	(50,000)
1 - ∞	9,000	1/0.15	60,000
		NPV	10,000

The net present value of the project is £10,000.

Answer 12.6

Payback period – Project X

Date	Cash inflows	Cumulative cash inflows
	£	£
31 March 20X4	50,000	50,000
31 March 20X5	150,000	200,000
31 March 20X6	150,000	350,000
31 March 20X7	70,000	420,000
31 March 20X8	130,000	550,000

The payback period is between years 2 and 3.

Payback period = 2 years + (£50,000/£150,000 × 12 months)
= 2 years + 4 months

The investment in Project X is a possibility because the payback period is less than three years.

Payback period – Project Y

Date	Cash inflows	Cumulative cash inflows
	£	£
31 March 20X4	50,000	50,000
31 March 20X5	180,000	230,000
31 March 20X6	280,000	510,000
31 March 20X7	25,000	535,000
31 March 20X8	30,000	565,000

The payback period for Project Y is also between 2 and 3 years,

Payback period = 2 years + (£70,000/£280,000 × 12 months)
= 2 years + 3 months

The investment in Project Y is also a possibility because the payback period is less than three years.

The business should invest in Project Y because it has the shortest payback period (2 years and 3 months).

Chapter 15

Answer 15.1

(a) The statement does not make clear whether the increase in sales is an increase in sales volume or sales value (or both). Were more pairs of footwear sold, or was the total sales revenue higher? Of course, the statement would also convey more information if a figure were put on the increase.

The words 'not as much as clothing' are ambiguous. Does this mean that sales of footwear are increasing at a slower percentage rate than sales of clothing? Or perhaps it means that the cash increase in footwear sales is lower than the cash increase in clothing sales.

(b) Turnover may have shown a spectacular rise because two years ago sales were particularly low. It should also be indicated whether the percentage rise is in cash terms, after adjustment for general inflation, or after adjustment for changes in prices in the company's industry.

Answer 15.2

(a) The number of diagrams in a textbook is a **discrete variable**, because it can only be counted in whole number steps. You cannot, for example, have 26½ diagrams or 47.32 diagrams in a book.

(b) Whether or not a can possesses a sticker is an **attribute**. It is not something which can be measured. A can either possesses the attribute or it does not.

(c) How long an athlete takes to run a mile is a **continuous variable**, because the time recorded can in theory take any value, for example 4 minutes 2.0643 seconds.

(d) The percentage obtained in an examination is a **discrete variable**, taking whole number values between 0% and 100%. The discrete values might include half per cent steps, if the examination is the sort where you could be awarded ½%. But it would not be possible to score, say, 62.32%, so the variable is not continuous.

(e) The height of a telegraph pole is a **continuous variable**.

Answer 15.3

C   I, II and IV are secondary data sources

Economic Trends and the *Monthly Digest of Statistics* are both sources of secondary data provided by the government. Historic sales data were not collected specifically for the preparation of forecasts, therefore they are also secondary data. Data collected through personal interview for a particular project are primary data.

Answer 15.4

(a) Employment Gazette

(b) The Monthly Digest of Statistics

(c) The Balance of Payments ('the pink book')

(d) Population Trends

Chapter 16

Answer 16.1

(i)	£1	£482,365
(ii)	£100	£482,400
(iii)	£1,000	£482,000
(iv)	£10,000	£480,000

Answer 16.2

The two dimensions of the table should be:

(a) years;
(b) each group of employees, including a category for 'others'.

It would also be possible to include percentage growth over the years.

The entries in the 'cells' of the table could be actual numbers of employees, percentages of the total work force or both.

Analysis of employee groups at Mill Stream Ltd

	1994		1997			2000			2003		
	Number empl'd	% of total	Number empl'd	% of total	% growth in total	Number empl'd	% of total	% growth in total	Number empl'd	% of total	% growth in total
Sales staff	1,176	28	2,372	31	102	4,840	38	104	7,477	36	54
Buyers	1,260	30	2,448	32	94	3,185	25	30	4,362	21	37
Administrative staff	840	20	1,607	21	91	2,550	20	59	3,739	18	47
Other groups	924	22	1,223	16	32	2,165	17	77	5,192	25	140
Total	4,200	100	7,650	100	82	12,740	100	67	20,770	100	63

Answer 16.3

We are told what classes to use, so the first step is to identify the lowest and highest values in the data. The lowest value is £25 (in the first row) and the highest value is £73 (in the fourth row). This means that the class intervals must go up to '£70 and under £75'.

ANSWERS TO ACTIVITIES

We can now set out the classes in a column, and then count the number of items in each class using tally marks.

	Tally marks	Total
£25 and less than £30	///	3
£30 and less than £35	////	4
£35 and less than £40	//// ////	10
£40 and less than £45	//// //// ////	15
£45 and less than £50	//// //// //// ///	18
£50 and less than £55	//// //// //// ////	20
£55 and less than £60	//// //// ///	13
£60 and less than £65	//// ///	8
£65 and less than £70	//// /	6
£70 and less than £75	///	3
Total		100

Answer 16.4

Workings	Sales £'000		Degrees
United Kingdom	787	(787/1,751 × 360)	162
Italy	219		45
France	285		58
Germany	92		19
Spain	189		39
Rest of Europe	145		30
Holland	34		7
	1,751		360

Mill Stream Ltd

Sales for the year ended 30 June 20X0

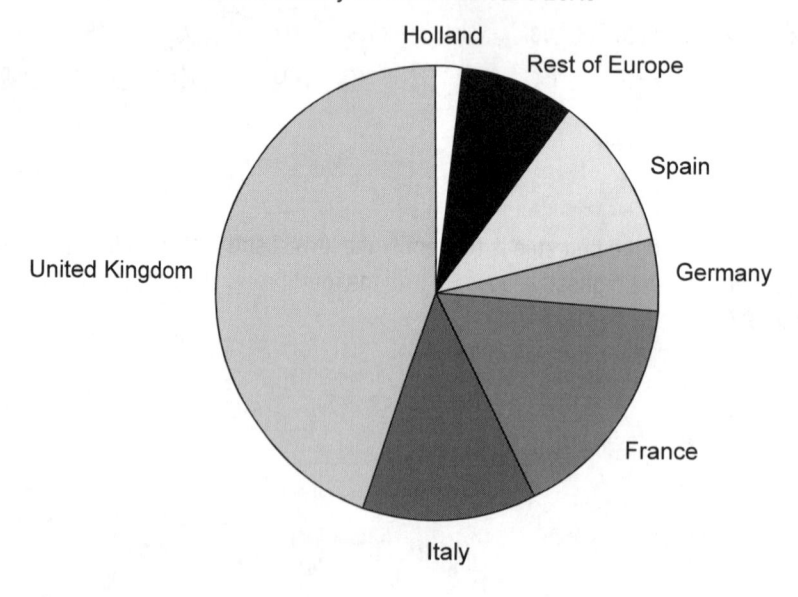

Answer 16.5

(a)

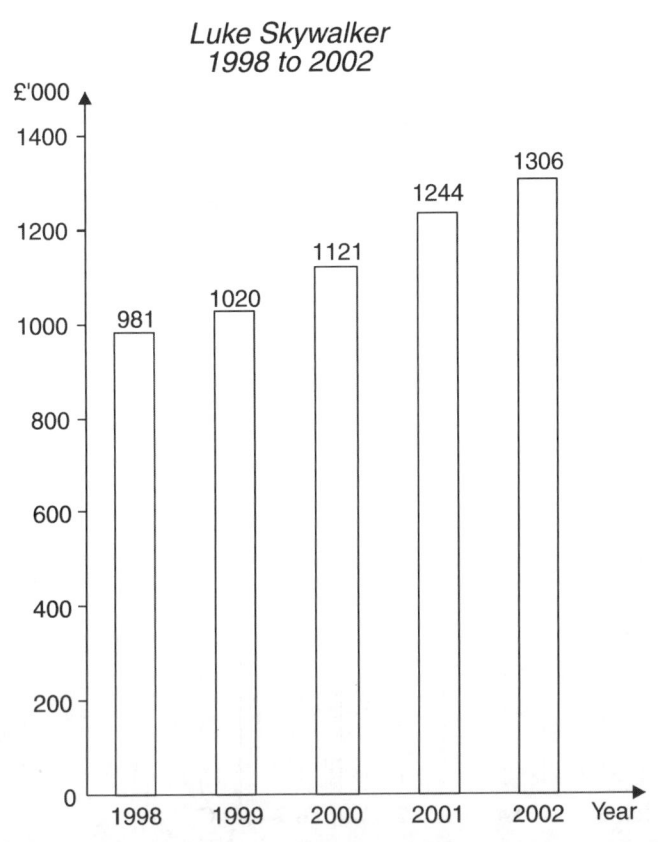

*Luke Skywalker
1998 to 2002*

[Bar chart, £'000 vs Year:
- 1998: 981
- 1999: 1020
- 2000: 1121
- 2001: 1244
- 2002: 1306]

(b) The bar chart clearly shows that turnover has increased steadily between 1998 and 2002. Turnover increased by the greatest amounts between 2000 and 2001 (£123,000 (£1,244,000 – £1,121,000)) and by the smallest amount between 1998 and 1999 (£39,000 (£1,020,000 – £981,000).

Answer 16.6

(a) Acceptable bar charts could be drawn vertically or horizontally.

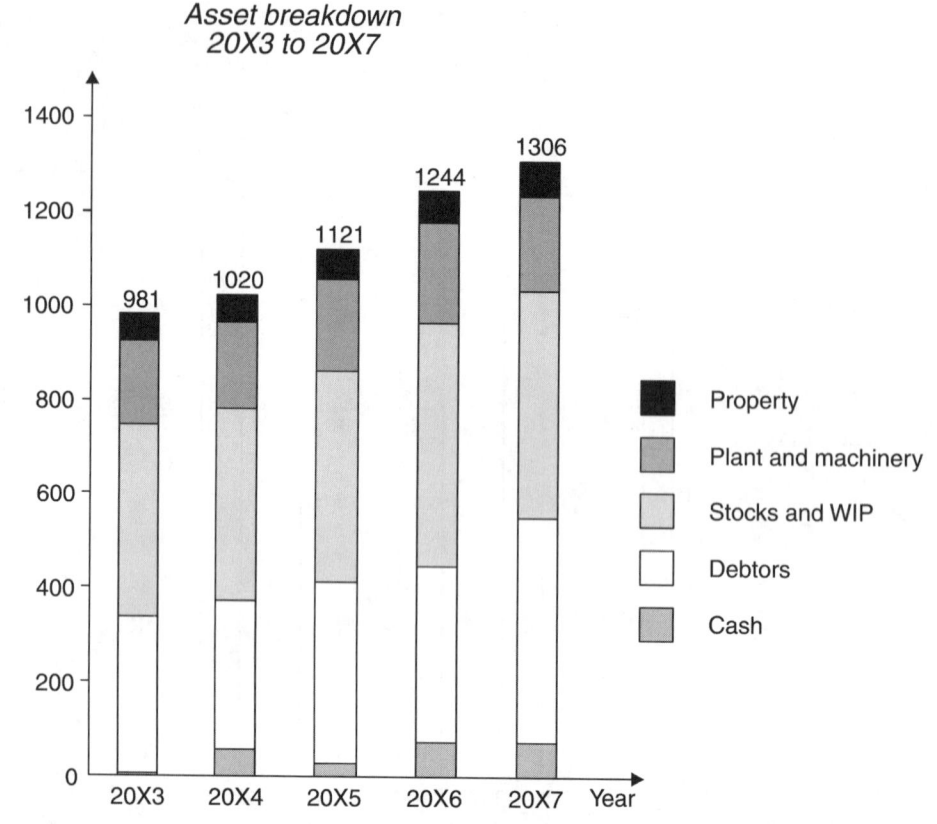

*Asset breakdown
20X3 to 20X7*

[Stacked bar chart showing totals: 20X3: 981, 20X4: 1020, 20X5: 1121, 20X6: 1244, 20X7: 1306. Components from top to bottom: Property, Plant and machinery, Stocks and WIP, Debtors, Cash.]

(b) The bar chart clearly shows that total assets have risen steadily over the five year period. Property remained static from 20X3 to 20X4, and showed only small increases from then on. Plant and machinery and stocks and work in progress both rose slowly from 20X3 to 20X4 and more steeply from 20X4 to 20X6, and then declined from 20X6 to 20X7. Debtors have behaved unevenly but with an increasing trend: total assets rose from 20X6 to 20X7 only because of the large increase in debtors over this period. Cash balances have also behaved unevenly but they exhibit an increasing trend over the five year period.

Answer 16.7

In a percentage component bar chart, all the bars are the same height. Only proportions are indicated, not absolute magnitudes.

(a) The percentages required for the bar chart are as follows.

Year	Percentage of total units sold			
	A	B	C	D
20X0	26.7	15.7	38.6	19.0
20X1	28.2	13.6	34.6	23.6
20X2	28.3	11.7	30.9	29.1

Percentage component bar chart

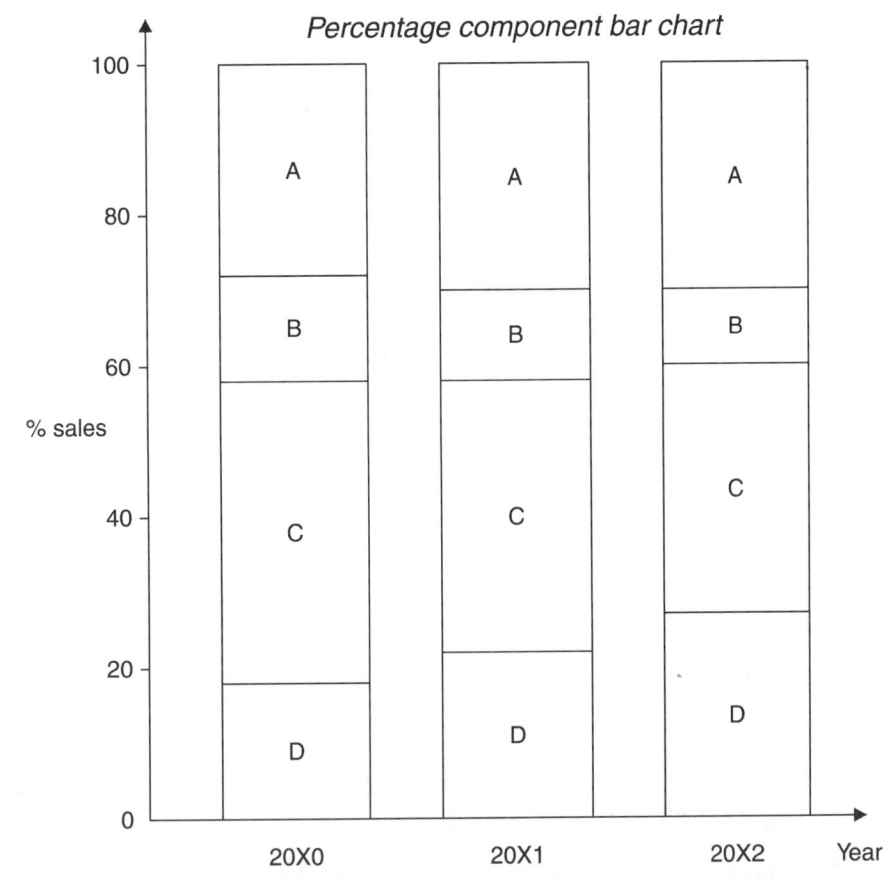

[Bar chart showing % sales for years 20X0, 20X1, 20X2 with components A, B, C, D stacked]

(b) Product D is clearly becoming increasingly important in relative terms and product C is becoming correspondingly less important. Product B's sales are also falling in percentage terms, and product A's sales are growing slightly in percentage terms. All these trends are also apparent in the figures for units sold.

Chapter 17

Answer 17.1

Dependent variable = Total costs of production

Independent variable = Number of units produced

Answer 17.2

The first step is to draw up a table for the equation. Although the problem mentions $x = 0$ to $x = 10$, it is not necessary to calculate values of y for $x = 1, 2, 3$ etc. A graph of a linear equation can actually be drawn from just two (x, y) values but it is always best to calculate a number of values in case you make an arithmetical error. We have calculated five values. You could settle for three or four.

ANSWERS TO ACTIVITIES

x	y
0	5
2	13
4	21
6	29
8	37
10	45

Graph of $y = 4x + 5$

Answer 17.3

Your answers to parts (b) and (c) may have been slightly different from those given here, but they should not have been very different, because the data points lay very nearly along a straight line.

(a) April Ltd - Scatter diagram of production and factory costs, September 20X2-August 20X3

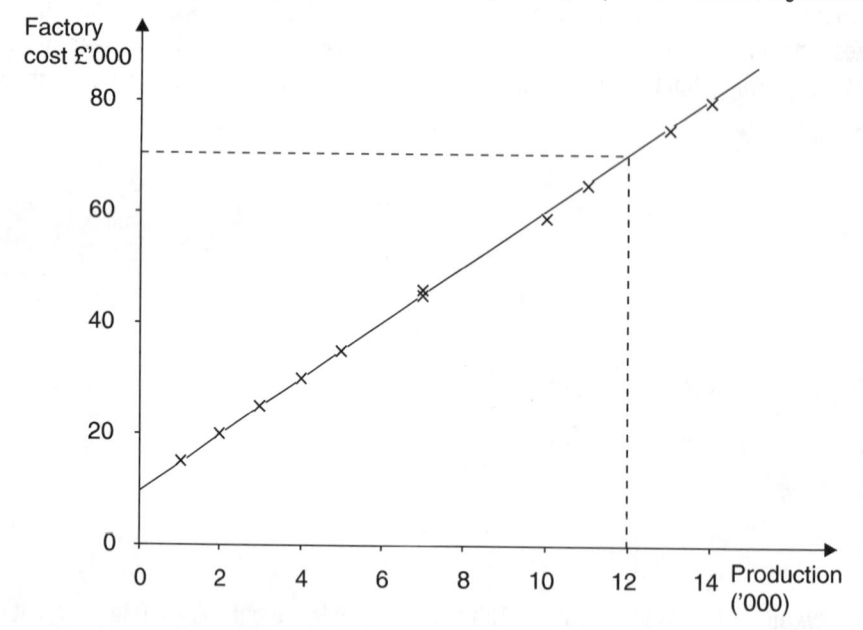

(b) Reading from the graph, the **estimated factory cost** for a production of 12,000 widgets is £70,000.

(c) The **monthly fixed costs** are indicated by the point where the line of best fit meets the y axis (costs at zero production). The fixed costs are estimated as £10,000 a month.

Answer 17.4

(a)

Profit £m Under	No. companies (frequency)	'Less than' cumulative frequency
−5	2	2
0	0	2
5	2	4
10	3	7
15	6	13
20	11	24
25	13	37
30	9	46
35	4	50
	50	

Ogive of annual profits of 50 similar companies

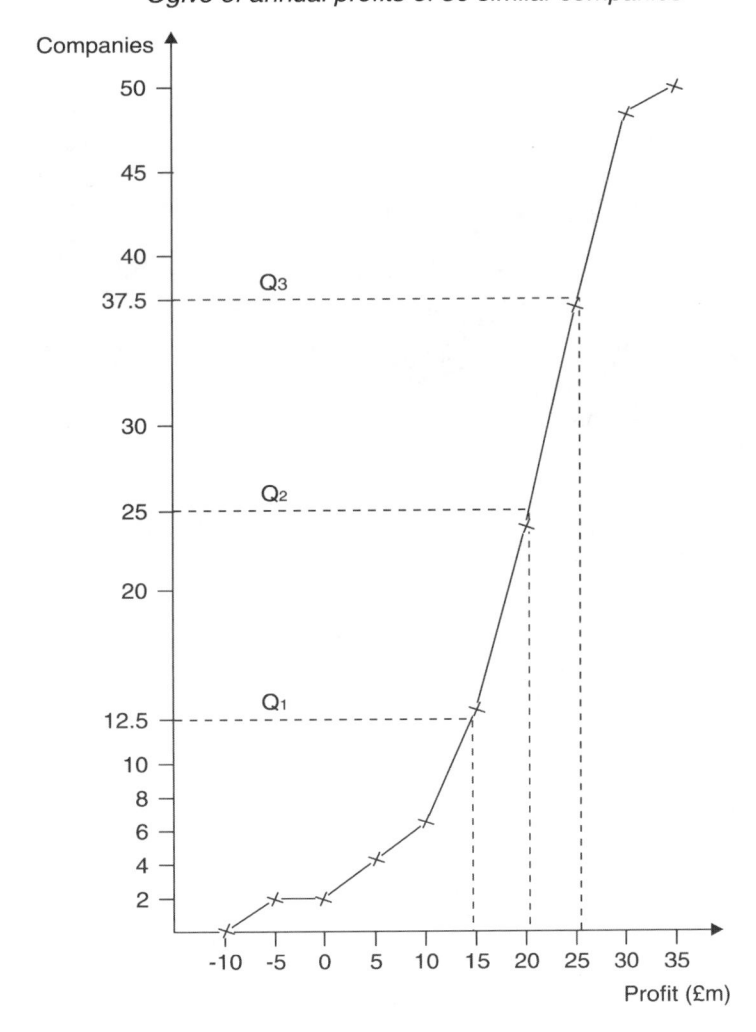

ANSWERS TO ACTIVITIES

(b) **First quartile:** 25% of companies have a profit less than this. Q_1 is £15,000,000 (to the nearest £ million).

Second quartile or median: 50% of companies have a profit less than this. Q_2 is £20,000,000 (to the nearest £ million).

Third quartile: 75% of companies have a profit less than this. Q_3 is £25,000,000 (to the nearest £ million).

Chapter 18

Answer 18.1

Annual salary x £	Frequency f	fx
12,000	3	36,000
12,500	1	12,500
13,000	1	13,000
13,500	1	13,500
14,000	2	28,000
14,500	4	58,000
15,000	1	15,000
16,000	5	80,000
18,000	2	36,000
	20	292,000

Arithmetic mean = $\dfrac{£292,000}{20}$ = £14,600

Answer 18.2

Year	Sales £	3 year total £	3 year moving average £
1	100		
2	110	318 (yrs 1, 2, 3)	106
3	108	330 (yrs 2, 3, 4)	110
4	112	326 (yrs 3, 4, 5)	109
5	106		

Answer 18.3

Helping hand. A five-month moving average is found simply by adding figures five at a time and dividing the result by five. Because five is an odd number, the averages are automatically centred on actual months.

The five-month moving average must first be calculated.

		Sales £'000	Five month total £'000	Five month average £'000
20X1	January	55		
	February	52		
	March	45	265	53
	April	48	280	56
	May	65	290	58
	June	70	300	60
	July	62	310	62
	August	55	320	64
	September	58	330	66
	October	75	345	69
	November	80	345	69
	December	77	360	72
20X2	January	55	370	74
	February	73	380	76
	March	85		
	April	90		

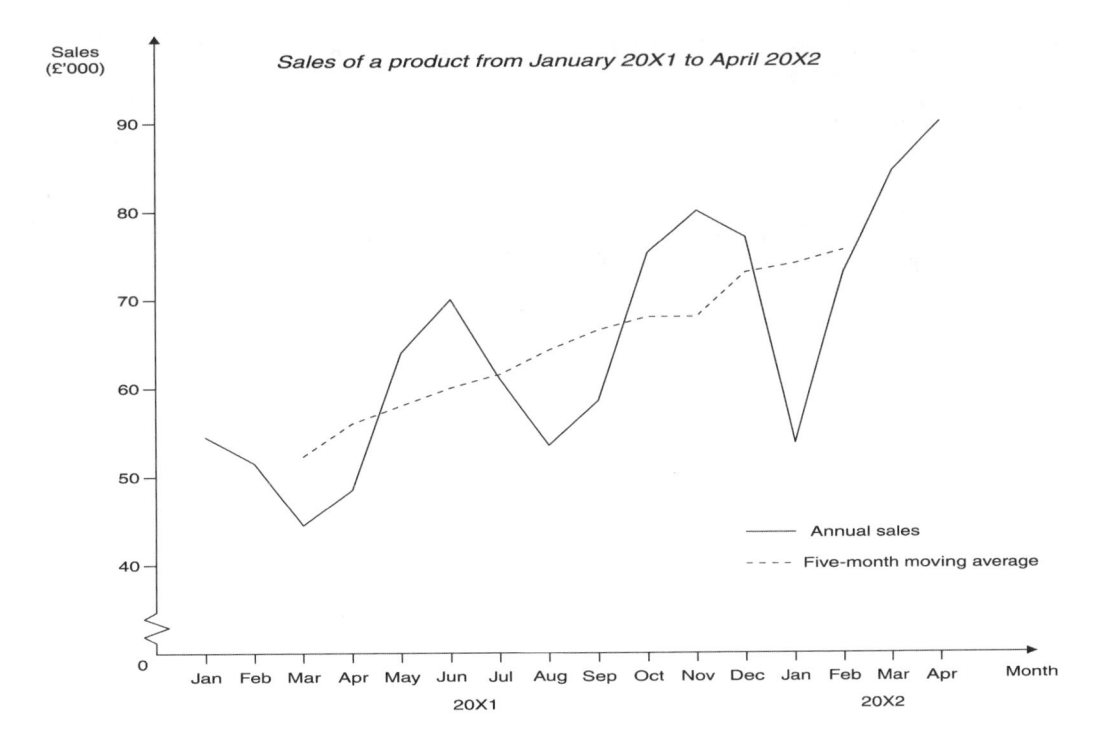

Sales of a product from January 20X1 to April 20X2

ANSWERS TO ACTIVITIES

Chapter 19

Answer 19.1

(a) The base year appears to be 2002, because the index for that year is 100. We cannot be absolutely sure about this, because the base year *could* be before 2000, and the price of a litre of milk in 2002 just happened to be the same as in the base year.

(b) The index has moved from 96 points to 100 points, a rise of 4 points.

(c) $\dfrac{4}{96} \times 100\% = 4.17\%$

(d) £0.54 × $\dfrac{113}{98}$ = £0.62

Answer 19.2

1999 index = 100

Sales for all years are compared with 1999 (£42,000)

Index = $\dfrac{\text{Current year's sales}}{\text{Sales in 1999}} \times 100$

Year	Sales (£'000)		Index
1998	35	$\dfrac{35}{42} \times 100 =$	83
1999	42	$\dfrac{42}{42} \times 100 =$	100
2000	40	$\dfrac{40}{42} \times 100 =$	95
2001	45	$\dfrac{45}{42} \times 100 =$	107
2002	50	$\dfrac{50}{42} \times 100 =$	119

Answer 19.3

Year		Index
1999	$\dfrac{84{,}000}{70{,}000} \times 100$	120
2000	$\dfrac{80{,}000}{84{,}000} \times 100$	95
2001	$\dfrac{90{,}000}{80{,}000} \times 100$	113
2002	$\dfrac{100{,}000}{90{,}000} \times 100$	111

Answer 19.4

2001 $\dfrac{106}{112} \times 100 = 94.6$, rounded to 95

2002 $\dfrac{120}{112} \times 100 = 107.1$, rounded to 107

Answer 19.5

	Quarter 1 £	Quarter 2 £	Quarter 3 £	Quarter 4 £
Adjusted sales revenue	518,515 [1]	468,743 [2]	506,181 [3]	483,274 [4]

Workings

(1) £533,280 × $\dfrac{179.1}{184.2}$ = £518,515

(2) £495,700 × $\dfrac{179.1}{189.4}$ = £468,743

(3) £525,400 × $\dfrac{179.1}{185.9}$ = £506,181

(4) £506,210 × $\dfrac{179.1}{187.6}$ = £483,274

Chapter 20

Answer 20.1

	Dept A		Dept B		Adjustments	Total	
	£	£	£	£	£	£	£
Sales		360,000		540,000	(48,000)		852,000
Cost of sales:							
Opening stock	72,000		90,000			162,000	
Purchases	210,000		324,000		(46,000)	488,000	
	282,000		414,000			650,000	
Less closing stock	78,000		108,000		2,000	188,000	
		204,000		306,000			462,000
Gross profit		156,000		234,000			390,000
Less expenses:							
Selling & distribution	45,600		68,400			114,000	
Administration	34,900		52,900			87,800	
Light & heating	2,000		9,600			11,600	
Rent & rates	38,000		19,000			57,000	
		120,500		149,900			270,400
Net profit		35,500		84,100			119,600

Answer 20.2

	Quarter 1	Quarter 2	Quarter 3	Quarter 4
Total actual hours				
Hay-on-Wye	66,328	75,440	80,280	76,904
Kent	57,080	60,484	67,640	62,388
Benches completed				
Hay-on-Wye	4,800	5,400	5,600	5,200
Kent	4,000	4,200	4,600	4,400
Hours per bench				
Hay-on-Wye	13.82	13.97	14.34	14.79
Kent	14.27	14.40	14.70	14.18

Note how the non-financial results reported here enable an easy comparison to be made between the performances of the two factories.

Chapter 21

Answer 21.1

$$\text{Productivity per employee} = \frac{\text{Output in the period}}{\text{Number of employees}}$$

$$= \frac{1{,}400 \text{ orders}}{25 \text{ employees}}$$

$$= 56 \text{ orders per employee}$$

Answer 21.2

(a) The standard rate of productivity is the number of units that Fred is expected to produce per hour. The standard rate of productivity is therefore seven units per hour.

(b) In 35 hours, production is expected to be (× 7)   245 units
Actual production was   280 units

$$\text{Productivity ratio} = \frac{280}{245} \times 100\%$$

$$= 114\%$$

Answer 21.3

This is a fairly straightforward activity if you understand the use of composite cost units. These are cost units which are made up of two parts and they are often used in service organisations. In the case of these hospitals the cost units are an in-patient day and an out-patient visit. The cost per in-patient would not be particularly meaningful because this cost could be very large or very small depending on the average length of stay. It would not be possible to compare the cost per in-patient for the two hospitals. The cost of one patient for one day (abbreviated to cost per patient-day) would however be comparable, and therefore useful for control purposes.

ANSWERS TO ACTIVITIES

(a)

	The General		The County	
	Cost per in-patient day	*Cost per out-patient attendance*	*Cost per in-patient day*	*Cost per out-patient attendance*
Number of in-patient days (*)	154,000	-	110,760	-
Number of out-patient attendances	-	130,000	-	3,500
	£	£	£	£
Patient care services				
Direct treatment	40.35	8.28	16.19	20.14
Medical support				
Diagnostic	3.12	2.40	0.20	5.90
Other services	1.54	2.22	0.70	7.94
General services				
Patient related	4.12	0.12	3.61	2.20
General	14.26	7.29	12.76	16.20
Total cost	63.39	20.31	33.46	52.38

* Number of in-patient days = number of in-patients × average stay

The General = 15,400 × 10 days = 154,000
The County = 710 × 156 days = 110,760

(b) **Bed-occupation percentages**

$$\text{The General} = \frac{402}{510} \times 100\% = 78.8\%$$

$$\text{The County} = \frac{307}{320} \times 100\% = 95.9\%$$

(c) **Cost per in-patient day**

The County has a lower cost than The General. This is partly due to the fact that The County has a higher bed-occupation percentage, which indicates that this hospital is making more efficient use of the available resources. A higher bed-occupation will mean that the fixed costs are spread over more cost units, thus reducing the unit cost.

Cost per out-patient attendance

The General has a lower cost in this case, probably owing to the large volume of patients. It is likely that more efficient systems are in operation to cope with the higher activity.

It is evident from the figures that the two hospitals care for very different types of patient. The County deals with long stays and does not attend to many out-patients. The General in-patients stay for a short time and are far fewer in number than the out-patients. Therefore despite the use of comparable cost units, caution is necessary before reaching any firm conclusions regarding the relative costs.

Answer 21.4

Net profit margin is calculated as $\frac{\text{Net profit}}{\text{Sales}} \times 100\%$

	20X4		20X5		20X6	
	A	B	A	B	A	B
Net profit margin	40%	25%	40%	30%	44%	33%

The **profit margin** is used as an **indicator of profitability**. In this example it is used to compare the profitability of profit centres A and B from 20X4 to 20X6, and also to compare the profitability of profit centre A with profit centre B.

The results show that profit centre A is as profitable in 20X4 as it is in 20X5, and that in 20X6 it appears to become more profitable.

Profit centres A and B, on the other hand, shows a **net profit margin** which is increasing steadily between 20X4 and 20X6.

In each of the years 20X4 to 20X6, profit centre A is found to be more profitable than profit centre B, as indicated by A having a higher **net profit margin** than B.

Chapter 22

Answer 22.1

(a) The conclusions of a report might be positioned either at the end (perhaps before a 'recommendations' section and any lists of sources) or alternatively after the introduction as part of the report summary.

(b) The terms of reference of a report are an explanation of the reasons for and purpose of the report and of any limitations on its scope.

(c) To keep the main body of the report short enough to hold the reader's interest, detailed explanations and tables of figures may be put into appendices to which cross reference is made in the main body of the report cross refers.

Answer 22.2

TENDER LTD

REPORT

To: Senior Management Committee
From: Accounting Technician
Subject: Profitability and asset turnover ratios
Date: 12 December year 4

Introduction

We have received the Trade Association results for year 4 and this report looks in detail at the profitability and asset turnover ratios.

Findings

What each ratio is designed to show

(i) **Return on capital employed (ROCE)/Return on investment (ROI)**

This ratio shows the percentage rate of profit which has been earned on the capital invested in the business, that is the return on the resources controlled by management. The expected return varies depending on the type of business and it is usually calculated as follows.

$$\text{Return on capital employed} = \frac{\text{Profit before interest and tax}}{\text{Capital employed}} \times 100\%$$

Other profit figures can be used, as well as various definitions of capital employed.

(ii) **Net profit margin**

This ratio shows the net profit as a percentage of turnover. The net profit is calculated before interest and tax and it is the profit over which operational mangers can exercise day to day control.

$$\text{Net profit margin} = \frac{\text{Net profit}}{\text{Turnover}} \times 100\%$$

(iii) **Asset turnover**

This ratio shows how effectively the assets of a business are being used to generate sales.

$$\text{Asset turnover} = \frac{\text{Turnover}}{\text{Capital employed}}$$

If the same figure for capital employed is used as in ROCE, then ratios (i) to (iii) can be related together as follows.

(i) ROCE = (ii) net profit margin × (iii) asset turnover

(iv) **Gross profit margin**

This ratio measures the profitability of sales.

$$\text{Gross margin} = \frac{\text{Gross profit}}{\text{Turnover}} \times 100\%$$

The gross profit is calculated as sales revenue less the cost of goods sold, and this ratio therefore focuses on the company's manufacturing and trading activities.

Conclusion

Tender Ltd's **ROCE** is lower than the trade association average, possibly indicating that the company's assets are not being used as profitably as in the industry as a whole.

Tender Ltd's **net profit margin** is higher than the trade association average, despite a lower than average gross profit margin. This suggests that non-production costs are lower in relation to sales value in Tender Ltd than in the industry as a whole.

Tender Ltd's **asset turnover ratio** is lower than the trade association average. This may mean that assets are not being used as effectively in our company as in the industry as a whole, which could be the cause of the lower than average ROCE.

Tender Ltd's **gross profit margin** is lower than the trade association average. This suggests either that Tender Ltd's production costs are higher than average, or that selling prices are lower than average.

If you would like further information please do not hesitate to contact me.

Signed: Accounting Technician

Chapter 23

Answer 23.1

Helping hand. The total collected by HM Customs & Excise is £700 × 17.5% = £122.50, the VAT on the final sale to Josh. The due date is one month after the end of the return period in question. For both Sam and Josh the relevant return is the one to 31 March 20X3. For Jan the relevant return is the one to 31 May 20X3.

Trader	Working	Amount £	Due date
Sam	£400 × 0.175	70.00	30.4.X3
Jan	£700 × 0.175 − £70 − £10.50	42.00	30.6.X3
Josh	£70.50 × 7/47	10.50	30.4.X3
		122.50	

Answer 23.2

Helping hand. All the documents calculate the correct amount of VAT, but you should have checked that this was so. If an invoice issued by D Ltd had shown too little VAT, the shortfall would have had to be accounted for.

The total VAT on sales and other outputs (Box 1) is as follows.

	£
Sale to Job Ltd	542.50
Sale to Brahms GmbH	0.00
Sale to Mickle plc	184.80
	727.30
Less credit to Job Ltd	32.81
	694.49

The Box 2 figure is 'None' so the Box 3 figure is the same as the Box 1 figure.

The total input VAT (Box 4) is as follows.

ANSWERS TO ACTIVITIES

	£
Purchase from Angel plc	735.00
Purchase from Quantum Ltd	486.50
	1,221.50
Less overstatement in previous period	800.00
	421.50

The Box 5 figure is £(694.49 − 421.50) = £272.99. Because a payment will be made, the box to the left of the declaration must be ticked.

The Box 6 figure is £(3,100.00 + 12,550.00 + 1,056.00 − 187.50) = £16,518.50, to be rounded down to £16,518.

The Box 7 figure is £(4,200 + 2,780) = £6,980.

The Box 8 figure is £12,550.

The Box 9 figure is 'None'.

ANSWERS TO ACTIVITIES

Value Added Tax Return
For the period
01 07 X5 to 30 09 X5

Registration number: 212 7924 36
Period: 09 X5

You could be liable to a financial penalty if your completed return and all the VAT payable are not received by the due date.

D LTD
1 LONG LANE
ANYTOWN
AN4 5QP

Due date: 31 10 X5

For official use

Before you fill in this form please read the notes on the back and the VAT Leaflet *"Filling in your VAT return"*.
Fill in all boxes clearly in ink, and write 'none' where necessary. Don't put a dash or leave any box blank. If there are no pence write "00" in the pence column. Do not enter more than one amount in any box.

			£	p
For official use	VAT due in this period on sales and other outputs	1	694	49
	VAT due in this period on acquisitions from other EC Member States	2	NONE	
	Total VAT due (the sum of boxes 1 and 2)	3	694	49
	VAT reclaimed in this period on purchases and other inputs (including acquisitions from the EC)	4	421	50
	Net VAT to be paid to Customs or reclaimed by you (Difference between boxes 3 and 4)	5	272	99
	Total value of sales and all other outputs excluding any VAT. Include your box 8 figure	6	16,518	00
	Total value of purchases and all other inputs excluding any VAT. Include your box 9 figure	7	6,980	00
	Total value of all supplies of goods and related services, excluding any VAT, to other EC Member States	8	12,550	00
	Total value of all acquisitions of goods and related services, excluding any VAT, from other EC Member States	9	NONE	00

If you are enclosing a payment please tick this box. ✓

DECLARATION: You, or someone on your behalf, must sign below.
I, ANNE ACCOUNTANT declare that the
(Full name of signatory in BLOCK LETTERS)
information given above is true and complete.

Signature *A Accountant* Date 25 Oct 20 X5
A false declaration can result in prosecution.

VAT 100(half)

Answer 23.3

Helping hand. Input VAT cannot be recovered unless a valid VAT invoice is held to support the claim. **You must be able to review a batch of invoices and decide if the criteria for 'valid VAT invoice' have been satisfied.** This is a typical devolved assessment task. All the invoices except (c) look superficially plausible, but in fact (c) is the only valid invoice. This shows the importance of attention to detail in applying VAT law.

(a) The invoice from Alpha plc is invalid because it does not show the supplier's address. In all other respects it meets the requirements for a valid VAT invoice.

(b) The invoice from Hym Ltd is invalid because the invoice number has been omitted, because the supplier's VAT registration number is not shown and because the type of supply (presumably a sale) is not shown.

Finally, the invoice is invalid because the applicable rates of VAT (17.5% and 0%) are not shown.

(c) The total value of the supply by Muster & Co, including VAT, does not exceed £100, so a less detailed invoice is permissible.

The invoice is valid, because it includes all the information which must be shown on a less detailed invoice.

(d) The invoice from Klunk plc is invalid because the total value of zero rated supplies is not shown.

Answer 23.4

Helping hand. Extensive records must be kept for VAT purposes. In general, these records are no more than a trader would probably keep anyway, but even if a trader could manage without some of the required records, he must still keep them.

(a) **The retail cash sale**

(i) The till roll, showing the gross sale of £56.40, must be kept.

(ii) A cash book showing the sale (or the total of the day's cash sales) must be kept.

(iii) A VAT invoice (possibly a less detailed invoice) will be issued, and a copy must be kept.

(iv) A summary of supplies must be kept, showing this sale, in such a way as to allow the trader to work out, for each VAT period:

(1) the VAT-exclusive values of standard rated supplies, zero rated supplies, exempt supplies and all supplies;

(2) the VAT chargeable on supplies.

(v) A VAT account must be kept. The VAT on the sale, £56.40 × 7/47 = £8.40, will appear on the credit (VAT payable) side of the account, probably as part of a total of VAT on several sales.

(b) **The retail credit sale**

(i) The sale must appear in the summary of supplies described in (a)(iv) above, and the VAT on the sale (£39.95 × 7/47 = £5.95) in the VAT account mentioned in (a)(v) above.

(ii) A sales day book showing the sale must be kept, and a cash book to record the eventual receipt. Records showing the debt must also be kept.

(iii) Because the customer is not registered for VAT, no VAT invoice need be issued. If one is issued (possibly a less detailed invoice), a copy must be kept.

(c) **The cash purchase**

(i) The VAT invoice received must be kept.

(ii) A cash book showing the purchase must be kept.

(iii) Any other documents relating to the purchase, such as a copy of the order or a delivery note, must be kept.

(iv) A summary of purchases must be kept, showing this purchase, in such a way as to allow the trader to work out, for each VAT period, the VAT-exclusive value of all supplies received and the VAT charged on them.

(v) The VAT on the purchase (£270 × 17.5% = £47.25) must appear (probably as part of a larger total) on the debit (VAT allowable) side of the VAT account mentioned in (a)(v) above.

Answer 23.5

Helping hand. The errors in the previous period may be corrected through the VAT account (and on the VAT return), because the net error is £(1,450 + 520) = £1,970, which does not exceed £2,000. (For more details on this see the next chapter.)

Standard rated purchases total £(4,200 + 6,700 + 730) = £11,630.

Standard rated sales total £(3,900 + 12,800 + 5,500) = £22,200.

D LTD
VAT ACCOUNT FOR THE VAT PERIOD FROM MAY TO JULY 20X7

VAT allowable	£	VAT payable	£
Input VAT allowable		Output VAT due	
£11,630 × 17.5%	2,035.25	£22,200 × 17.5%	
Adjustment for credits received		− £340 × 17.5%	3,825.50
£500 × 17.5%	(87.50)	Correction of error	(1,450.00)
Correction of error	520.00		
	2,467.75		2,375.50
		Cash (receipt from HM Customs & Excise)	92.25
	2,467.75		2,467.75

ANSWERS TO ACTIVITIES

Answer 23.6

Helping hand. VAT suffered may only be reclaimed if the correct documentation is held. This rule plays an important role in enforcing the payment of VAT: VAT registered buyers will insist that VAT registered sellers prepare proper documentation.

Ref	Comment	Recoverable VAT Gross x 7/47 £
(a)	Buyer's registration number not required	12.25
(b)	Amount including VAT exceeds £100	0.00
(c)	Amount including VAT does not exceed £25	1.49
(d)	Buyer's address required	0.00
(e)	Amount including VAT does not exceed £100	14.70
(f)	Total price excluding VAT required	0.00
		28.44

Chapter 24

Answer 24.1

Helping hand. There were two standard rated, two zero rated and two exempt supplies, and totals were needed for each category and for the invoice as a whole. Note that the total including VAT need not be shown, but in practice it always is shown. Note also that the VAT is computed on the net amount after the 4% cash discount.

```
                        D LIMITED
                32 Hurst Road, London NE20 4LJ
                    VAT reg no 730 4148 37
To:     Ferguson Ltd                                Date: 12 May 20X2
        75 Link Road                           Tax point: 12 May 20X2
        London NE25 3PQ                             Invoice no. 2794
```

Item	Quantity	VAT rate %	Net £	VAT £
Sales of goods				
Personal computer	1	17.5	980	
Microscopes	3	17.5	360	
Total of standard rated (17.5%) supplies			1,340	225.12
Books	20	0.0	200	
Periodicals	500	0.0	450	
Total of zero rated (0%) supplies			650	0.00
Supplies of services				
Insurance		Exempt	1,200	
Medical treatment services		Exempt	400	
Total of exempt supplies			1,600	
Total invoice price excluding VAT			3,590	
Total VAT				225.12

	£
Total payable within 30 days	3,815.12
Less cash discount for payment within 10 days	143.60
Total payable if paid within 10 days	3,671.52

Terms: 30 days, 4% discount if paid within 10 days.

Answer 24.2

(a) zero rated (children's clothing)
(b) exempt (insurance)
(c) exempt (postal services provided by post office)
(d) standard rated (**hot** food so not zero rated)
(e) standard rated

Answer 24.3

Due to private use of the car and full recovery of petrol input VAT Pete must account for output VAT of £65.82 in the 3 month period to 31 December 2003 using the VAT scale charges.

Answer 24.4

Helping hand. Because D Ltd makes some exempt supplies, not all the VAT on purchases can be recovered. The VAT on purchases which is not attributable to either taxable supplies or exempt supplies must be apportioned.

(a) Box 1: VAT due on outputs
The figure is £450,000 × 17.5% = £78,750.00

(b) Box 2: VAT due on acquisitions
None.

(c) Box 3: sum of Boxes 1 and 2
£78,750.00

(d) Box 4: VAT reclaimed on inputs
The figure is £86,520.00, as follows.

Apportionment percentage = (450 + 237)/(450 + 237 + 168) = 80.35%, rounded up to 81%.

	£
Tax on purchases attributable to taxable supplies £300,000 × 17.5%	52,500.00
Tax on unattributable purchases £240,000 × 17.5% × 81%	34,020.00
	86,520.00

(e) Box 5: net VAT to be paid or reclaimed
The amount reclaimable is £(86,520.00 – 78,750.00) = £7,770.00.

Answer 24.5

Helping hand. You first had to compute the relevant totals, then you had to check the position on partial exemption.

Date cash received	Standard rated turnover £	Zero rated turnover £	Exempt turnover £	VAT at 7/47 £
2.6.X4	270.35			40.26
15.6.X4	420.00			62.55
2.6.X4	620.74			92.45
7.6.X4		540.40		
22.6.X4		680.18		
14.6.X4	200.37			29.84
4.7.X4			180.62	
12.7.X4		235.68		
12.7.X4	429.32			63.94
21.7.X4			460.37	
20.8.X4			390.12	
3.8.X4		220.86		
23.8.X4	350.38			52.18
	2,291.16	1,677.12	1,031.11	341.22

ANSWERS TO ACTIVITIES

Total taxable turnover is £(2,291.16 – 341.22 + 1,677.12) = £3,627.06. Total turnover is £(3,627.06 + 1,031.11) = £4,658.17.

The output VAT in respect of fuel is £283.00 × 7/47 = £42.15, so total output VAT is £(341.22 + 42.15) = £383.37.

The scale charge net of VAT is £(283.00 – 42.15) = £240.85, so the Box 6 figure is £(4,658.17 + 240.85) = £4,899.02, rounded down to £4,899.

Date cash paid	Purchase £	VAT at 7/47 £
4.6.X4	521.44	77.66
3.6.X4	516.13	76.87
1.7.X4	737.48	
4.7.X4	414.68	61.76
12.7.X4	280.85	
	2,470.58	216.29

The purchases net of VAT (Box 7) are £(2,470.58 – 216.29) = £2,254.29, rounded down to £2,254.

Input VAT attributable to exempt supplies is 1,031.11/4,899.02 = 21.04%, rounded to 21% (*exempt* percentage *down*) × £216.29 = £45.42. As this is not more than £625 a month on average and not more than half of all input VAT, all input VAT is recoverable.

ANSWERS TO ACTIVITIES

Value Added Tax Return
For the period
01 06 X4 to 31 08 X4

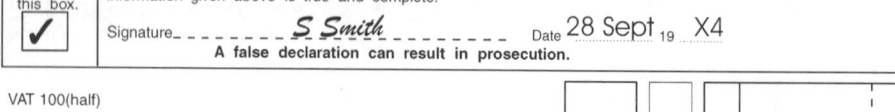

Registration number: 212 7924 36
Period: 08 X4

You could be liable to a financial penalty if your completed return and all the VAT payable are not received by the due date.

D LIMITED
1 LONG LANE
ANYTOWN
AN4 5QP

Due date: 30 09 X4

For official use

Before you fill in this form please read the notes on the back and the VAT Leaflet *"Filling in your VAT return"*.
Fill in all boxes clearly in ink, and write 'none' where necessary. Don't put a dash or leave any box blank. If there are no pence write "00" in the pence column. Do not enter more than one amount in any box.

Box	Description	£	p
1	VAT due in this period on sales and other outputs	383	37
2	VAT due in this period on acquisitions from other EC Member States	None	
3	Total VAT due (the sum of boxes 1 and 2)	383	37
4	VAT reclaimed in this period on purchases and other inputs (including acquisitions from the EC)	216	29
5	Net VAT to be paid to Customs or reclaimed by you (Difference between boxes 3 and 4)	167	08
6	Total value of sales and all other outputs excluding any VAT. Include your box 8 figure	4,899	00
7	Total value of purchases and all other inputs excluding any VAT. Include your box 9 figure	2,254	00
8	Total value of all supplies of goods and related services, excluding any VAT, to other EC Member States	None	00
9	Total value of all acquisitions of goods and related services, excluding any VAT, from other EC Member States	None	00

If you are enclosing a payment please tick this box. ✓

DECLARATION: You, or someone on your behalf, must sign below.
I, SUZANNE SMITH declare that the
(Full name of signatory in BLOCK LETTERS)
information given above is true and complete.

Signature: S Smith   Date 28 Sept 19 X4

A false declaration can result in prosecution.

VAT 100(half)

Answer 24.6

D Limited
1 Long lane
Anytown
AN4 5QP

H M Customs & Excise
Newcastle Office
1 Low Street
Newcastle

24 May 2003

Dear Sir

Classification of Catha Edulis

I am writing to request guidance with regard to a new product which will be added to our product range next month. The product is a herbal remedy imported from Abyssinia with the Latin name 'Catha Edulis'. The product is used in a similar fashion as tea.

I enclose a sample of the original product and of the product newly packaged for sale in our shops for your information. You will see from the original product enclosed that in Abyssinia the product is called Srih.

If you require any further information (or samples) please do not hesitate to contact me.

Yours faithfully

Mrs J K Buffle

Enc.

Answer 24.7

Helping hand. There must be an initial default before a surcharge liability period can start. Thus the late return to 30.9.X2 is the initial default that starts the ball rolling and sets up an initial surcharge period of 12 months to 30.9.X3. However, once the surcharge period has started it is extended by later defaults. In this case, there is a single surcharge liability period extending at least as far as 30 September 20X5. Because there is no break in the period, the percentage rate escalates right up to 15%.

Quarter ended	Working	Surcharge £	
30.6.X3	£5,000 × 2% = £100	0	(under £400)
30.9.X3	£9,000 × 5%	450	
31.3.X4	£3,500 × 10%	350	
30.6.X4	£4,500 × 15%	675	
30.9.X4	£500 × 15%	75	(surcharges under £400 are collected when at 10% or 15%)

Answer 24.8

Since the error was notified as a voluntary disclosure to Customs no misdeclaration penalty will apply. However, interest will run from the due date for the return (30 April 2003) until the date the VAT was paid (2 October 2003). Custom's set the interest rate used.

Answer 24.9

Helping hand. The current VAT system for trade with other European Community states is designed so that when goods will be resold by a VAT registered trader in the destination state, that trader will impose the local VAT rate on the final consumer; but where the sale between states is to the final consumer, VAT is charged by the seller at the rate applying in the seller's state.

		£
(a)	Input VAT £12,000 x 17.5%	(2,100.00)
(b)	Zero rated sale	0.00
(c)	Output VAT £470 x 17.5%	82.25
(d)	Zero rated export	0.00
(e)	VAT on taxable acquisition	525.00
(e)	Input VAT on taxable acquisition £3,000 x 17.5%	(525.00)
	Recoverable from HM Customs & Excise	(2,017.75)

Discount factor tables

DISCOUNT FACTOR TABLES

PRESENT VALUE TABLE

Present value of £1 ie $(1+r)^{-n}$ where r = interest rate, n = number of periods until payment or receipt.

(n)	1%	2%	3%	4%	5%	6%	7%	8%	9%	10%
1	0.990	0.980	0.971	0.962	0.952	0.943	0.935	0.926	0.917	0.909
2	0.980	0.961	0.943	0.925	0.907	0.890	0.873	0.857	0.842	0.826
3	0.971	0.942	0.915	0.889	0.864	0.840	0.816	0.794	0.772	0.751
4	0.961	0.924	0.888	0.855	0.823	0.792	0.763	0.735	0.708	0.683
5	0.951	0.906	0.863	0.822	0.784	0.747	0.713	0.681	0.650	0.621
6	0.942	0.888	0.837	0.790	0.746	0.705	0.666	0.630	0.596	0.564
7	0.933	0.871	0.813	0.760	0.711	0.665	0.623	0.583	0.547	0.513
8	0.923	0.853	0.789	0.731	0.677	0.627	0.582	0.540	0.502	0.467
9	0.914	0.837	0.766	0.703	0.645	0.592	0.544	0.500	0.460	0.424
10	0.905	0.820	0.744	0.676	0.614	0.558	0.508	0.463	0.422	0.386
11	0.896	0.804	0.722	0.650	0.585	0.527	0.475	0.429	0.388	0.350
12	0.887	0.788	0.701	0.625	0.557	0.497	0.444	0.397	0.356	0.319
13	0.879	0.773	0.681	0.601	0.530	0.469	0.415	0.368	0.326	0.290
14	0.870	0.758	0.661	0.577	0.505	0.442	0.388	0.340	0.299	0.263
15	0.861	0.743	0.642	0.555	0.481	0.417	0.362	0.315	0.275	0.239
16	0.853	0.728	0.623	0.534	0.458	0.394	0.339	0.292	0.252	0.218
17	0.844	0.714	0.605	0.513	0.436	0.371	0.317	0.270	0.231	0.198
18	0.836	0.700	0.587	0.494	0.416	0.350	0.296	0.250	0.212	0.180
19	0.828	0.686	0.570	0.475	0.396	0.331	0.277	0.232	0.194	0.164
20	0.820	0.673	0.554	0.456	0.377	0.312	0.258	0.215	0.178	0.149

Periods (n)	11%	12%	13%	14%	15%	16%	17%	18%	19%	20%
1	0.901	0.893	0.885	0.877	0.870	0.862	0.855	0.847	0.840	0.833
2	0.812	0.797	0.783	0.769	0.756	0.743	0.731	0.718	0.706	0.694
3	0.731	0.712	0.693	0.675	0.658	0.641	0.624	0.609	0.593	0.579
4	0.659	0.636	0.613	0.592	0.572	0.552	0.534	0.516	0.499	0.482
5	0.593	0.567	0.543	0.519	0.497	0.476	0.456	0.437	0.419	0.402
6	0.535	0.507	0.480	0.456	0.432	0.410	0.390	0.370	0.352	0.335
7	0.482	0.452	0.425	0.400	0.376	0.354	0.333	0.314	0.296	0.279
8	0.434	0.404	0.376	0.351	0.327	0.305	0.285	0.266	0.249	0.233
9	0.391	0.361	0.333	0.308	0.284	0.263	0.243	0.225	0.209	0.194
10	0.352	0.322	0.295	0.270	0.247	0.227	0.208	0.191	0.176	0.162
11	0.317	0.287	0.261	0.237	0.215	0.195	0.178	0.162	0.148	0.135
12	0.286	0.257	0.231	0.208	0.187	0.168	0.152	0.137	0.124	0.112
13	0.258	0.229	0.204	0.182	0.163	0.145	0.130	0.116	0.104	0.093
14	0.232	0.205	0.181	0.160	0.141	0.125	0.111	0.099	0.088	0.078
15	0.209	0.183	0.160	0.140	0.123	0.108	0.095	0.084	0.074	0.065
16	0.188	0.163	0.141	0.123	0.107	0.093	0.081	0.071	0.062	0.054
17	0.170	0.146	0.125	0.108	0.093	0.080	0.069	0.060	0.052	0.045
18	0.153	0.130	0.111	0.095	0.081	0.069	0.059	0.051	0.044	0.038
19	0.138	0.116	0.098	0.083	0.070	0.060	0.051	0.043	0.037	0.031
20	0.124	0.104	0.087	0.073	0.061	0.051	0.043	0.037	0.031	0.026

DISCOUNT FACTOR TABLES

CUMULATIVE PRESENT VALUE TABLE (ANNUITY TABLES)

This table shows the present value of £1 per annum, receivable or payable at the end of each year for *n* years

$$\frac{1-(1+r)^{-n}}{r}.$$

Periods (n)	Interest rates (r)									
	1%	2%	3%	4%	5%	6%	7%	8%	9%	10%
1	0.990	0.980	0.971	0.962	0.952	0.943	0.935	0.926	0.917	0.909
2	1.970	1.942	1.913	1.886	1.859	1.833	1.808	1.783	1.759	1.736
3	2.941	2.884	2.829	2.775	2.723	2.673	2.624	2.577	2.531	2.487
4	3.902	3.808	3.717	3.630	3.546	3.465	3.387	3.312	3.240	3.170
5	4.853	4.713	4.580	4.452	4.329	4.212	4.100	3.993	3.890	3.791
6	5.795	5.601	5.417	5.242	5.076	4.917	4.767	4.623	4.486	4.355
7	6.728	6.472	6.230	6.002	5.786	5.582	5.389	5.206	5.033	4.868
8	7.652	7.325	7.020	6.733	6.463	6.210	5.971	5.747	5.535	5.335
9	8.566	8.162	7.786	7.435	7.108	6.802	6.515	6.247	5.995	5.759
10	9.471	8.983	8.530	8.111	7.722	7.360	7.024	6.710	6.418	6.145
11	10.368	9.787	9.253	8.760	8.306	7.887	7.499	7.139	6.805	6.495
12	11.255	10.575	9.954	9.385	8.863	8.384	7.943	7.536	7.161	6.814
13	12.134	11.348	10.635	9.986	9.394	8.853	8.358	7.904	7.487	7.103
14	13.004	12.106	11.296	10.563	9.899	9.295	8.745	8.244	7.786	7.367
15	13.865	12.849	11.938	11.118	10.380	9.712	9.108	8.559	8.061	7.606
16	14.718	13.578	12.561	11.652	10.838	10.106	9.447	8.851	8.313	7.824
17	15.562	14.292	13.166	12.166	11.274	10.477	9.763	9.122	8.544	8.022
18	16.398	14.992	13.754	12.659	11.690	10.828	10.059	9.372	8.756	8.201
19	17.226	15.679	14.324	13.134	12.085	11.158	10.336	9.604	8.950	8.365
20	18.046	16.351	14.878	13.590	12.462	11.470	10.594	9.818	9.129	8.514

Periods (n)	Interest rates (r)									
	11%	12%	13%	14%	15%	16%	17%	18%	19%	20%
1	0.901	0.893	0.885	0.877	0.870	0.862	0.855	0.847	0.840	0.833
2	1.713	1.690	1.668	1.647	1.626	1.605	1.585	1.566	1.547	1.528
3	2.444	2.402	2.361	2.322	2.283	2.246	2.210	2.174	2.140	2.106
4	3.102	3.037	2.974	2.914	2.855	2.798	2.743	2.690	2.639	2.589
5	3.696	3.605	3.517	3.433	3.352	3.274	3.199	3.127	3.058	2.991
6	4.231	4.111	3.998	3.889	3.784	3.685	3.589	3.498	3.410	3.326
7	4.712	4.564	4.423	4.288	4.160	4.039	3.922	3.812	3.706	3.605
8	5.146	4.968	4.799	4.639	4.487	4.344	4.207	4.078	3.954	3.837
9	5.537	5.328	5.132	4.946	4.772	4.607	4.451	4.303	4.163	4.031
10	5.889	5.650	5.426	5.216	5.019	4.833	4.659	4.494	4.339	4.192
11	6.207	5.938	5.687	5.453	5.234	5.029	4.836	4.656	4.486	4.327
12	6.492	6.194	5.918	5.660	5.421	5.197	4.988	4.793	4.611	4.439
13	6.750	6.424	6.122	5.842	5.583	5.342	5.118	4.910	4.715	4.533
14	6.982	6.628	6.302	6.002	5.724	5.468	5.229	5.008	4.802	4.611
15	7.191	6.811	6.462	6.142	5.847	5.575	5.324	5.092	4.876	4.675
16	7.379	6.974	6.604	6.265	5.954	5.668	5.405	5.162	4.938	4.730
17	7.549	7.120	6.729	6.373	6.047	5.749	5.475	5.222	4.990	4.775
18	7.702	7.250	6.840	6.467	6.128	5.818	5.534	5.273	5.033	4.812
19	7.839	7.366	6.938	6.550	6.198	5.877	5.584	5.316	5.070	4.843
20	7.963	7.469	7.025	6.623	6.259	5.929	5.628	5.353	5.101	4.870

Index

$\sum$ (sigma), 311

Abnormal gain, 165
Abnormal loss, 165
Absence from work, 55
Absences, 50
Absorption, 80
Absorption costing, 79, 107
Absorption costing - arguments in favour of, 111
Absorption costing – calculation of profit, 106
Absorption costing and marginal costing compared, 106
Absorption costing procedures, 80
Accounting procedures and business functions, 231
Accounting procedures and geographical structure, 230
Accounting procedures and product information, 230
Accounting Standards, 245
Acquisition, 435
Administration, 443
Administration overhead, 78, 79
Adoption pay, 55
Advice note, 20
Allocation, 69, 80
Alphabetical codes, 140
Annual adjustment, 430
Annual report and accounts, 243
Annuities, 211
Annuity factors, 211
Annuity tables, 211
Appeals, 445
Apportionment, 71, 80
Arbitrary nature of absorption costing, 92
Arithmetic mean, 310
Arithmetic mean of a frequency distribution, 312
Asset turnover, 365
Attendance record, 45
Attendance time, 45
Attributes, 252
Attributing input VAT, 428
Average, 310

Bad debt relief, 432
Bar chart, 275

Base date, 329
Base period, 329
Base year, 329
Bases of absorption, 90
Bases of apportionment, 80
Basic tax point, 392
Basic wage, 44
Batch, 151
Batch costing, 151
Bin cards, 28
Blanket overhead absorption rate, 92
Bonuses, 50, 52
Branch accounts, 345
Breakeven analysis, 184
Breakeven arithmetic, 188
Breakeven chart, 191
Breakeven point, 185, 188, 191
Buffer stock, 27, 37
Business entertaining, 425
Business information, 238, 240
Buying departments, 17

C/S (contribution/sales) ratio, 186
Capital expenditure, 62
Capital items, 63
Car, 426
Cash accounting scheme, 437
Cash book, 403
Cash operated machines, 400
Central Unit, 443
Chain based index numbers, 331
Chargeable expenses, 64
Chart wizard, 298
Charts, 272, 296, 378
Classification of costs, 9
Classification of expenses, 62
Clock card, 45
Code, 139
Coding expenses, 68
Coding of job costs, 49
Coding of materials, 29
Collection of job costs, 147
Communicating information, 243
Communication, 243
Component bar chart, 277

INDEX

Composite cost unit, 155
Composite supply, 420
Compound bar chart, 277, 280
Compound interest, 207, 208
Compulsory deregistration, 411
Compulsory registration, 407
Computerised forms, 381
Computing VAT due, 386
Conditional formulae, 301
Confidentiality, 378
Consolidation of information, 346
Continuous stocktaking, 32
Continuous supplies of services, 393
Continuous variables, 252
Contribution, 102
Contribution breakeven chart, 193
Contribution information, 105
Contribution/sales ratio, 186
Control, 5
Control accounts, 130
Control visits, 443
Corporate Report, 244
Cost accounting, 7
Cost accounting systems, 7
Cost accounts, 7, 341
Cost and management accounting, 242
Cost behaviour, 116
Cost behaviour and levels of activity, 120
Cost behaviour principles, 116
Cost bookkeeping systems, 135
Cost centre, 9, 69, 343
Cost code, 344
Cost elements, 10
Cost of capital, 209
Cost of living index, 328
Cost per service unit, 155
Cost per unit, 163, 343, 361
Cost units, 8, 89, 343, 344
Costing systems, 145
Costs classification, 9
Cost-volume-profit (CVP) analysis, 184
Credit cards, 418
Credit notes, 399, 403
Cumulative frequency curve, 293
Cumulative frequency distribution, 270
Cumulative present value factors, 211

Currency format, 303
Curve fitting, 292
Customs' powers, 444
CVP analysis, 184
Cyclical variations, 321

Daily time sheets, 45
Data, 239
Day-rate system, 50
Decimal places, 266
Decision making, 6
Decision making process, 6
Deduction of input VAT, 425
Default surcharge, 447
Delivery note, 20
Departmental absorption rates, 92
Departmental accounts, 345
Dependent variable, 288
Depreciation, 65
Depreciation charge, 62
Depreciation methods, 65
Deregistration, 411
Despatch note, 20
Determining labour costs, 44
Differential piecework, 52
Direct costs, 9, 342
Direct expenses, 63, 69, 343
Direct labour, 342
Direct labour hour rate, 90
Direct materials, 342
Direct method of reapportionment, 84
Discount, 418
Discounted cash flow (DCF), 213
Discounted cash flow methods of project appraisal, 213
Discounting, 208
Discounting formula, 209
Discrete variables, 252
Distribution overhead, 78, 79
Divisional registration, 410
Domestic accommodation for directors, 425
Downward trend, 318

EC members, 434
EC Sales List, 436

EC Trade, 434
Economic cycles, 321
Economic order quantity (EOQ), 36
Employee reports, 244
Equivalent units, 173, 174
Errors in previous periods, 392
Errors on invoices, 420
Exempt supplies, 422, 423
Exemption from registration, 409
Expenses, 62
Expenses documentation, 70
Exports, 435
External agencies, 239
External reports, 232, 239
External sources of business information, 241

Factory cost, 342
Factory overhead, 79
FIFO -First In, First Out, 23
Final VAT return, 411
Finance Acts, 443
Financial accounting, 241, 242
Financial accounts, 7, 340
Financial information, 240
Financial information system, 243
First quartile, 295
Fixed assets, 62
Fixed base method of indexing, 331
Fixed costs, 10, 117, 342
Fixed format, 303
Footsie 100 share index, 328
Form, 380
Form VAT 1, 409
Form VAT 100, 388
Form VAT 193, 411
Form VAT 652, 392
Formatting numbers, 303
Formulae with conditions, 302
Framework for dealing with process costing, 164
Frequency distribution, 268
Frequency polygons, 282
Fuel used for business purposes, 426
Fully taxable person, 428
Functional organisation structure, 229

General format, 303
General ledger codes, 139
Geographical organisation structure, 228
Gifts of goods, 420
Global accounting, 441
Goods received note, 20
Government statistical publications in the UK, 255
Government statistics, 255
Graph, 288, 296, 378
Gross amount of tax (GAT), 449
Gross profit margin, 366
Group bonus schemes, 55
Group registration, 410
Grouped frequency distributions, 269
Guaranteed minimum wage, 52

Hidden format, 303
High-low technique, 121, 122
Histogram, 281
Historigram, 316
HM Customs & Excise, 386
Holding costs, 27, 34, 35
Holiday pay, 55
Horizontal axis, 289

Idle time, 48
Idle time record card, 48
IF statement, 301
Imports, 434
Imports of goods, 398
Incentives, 52
Independent variable, 288
Index, 328
Index numbers, 328
Index points, 328
Indirect costs, 10, 342
Indirect expenses, 63, 64, 69, 78
Indirect materials, 79
Indirect wages, 79
Information, 4, 239
Information for management, 4
Input VAT, 387, 425
Integrated system, 135
Interest, 206
Interest charged on VAT, 451

INDEX

Interest on overpayments due to official errors, 452
Interlocking systems, 135
Internal rate of return (IRR) method, 215
Internal reports, 232, 238
Internal sources of business information, 240
Internet, 241
Intrastat, 436
IRR (Internal Rate of Return), 215
IRR method of discounted cash flow, 215
Issuing materials, 30

Job, 146
Job account, 148
Job cards, 46
Job cost card, 148
Job cost sheet, 148
Job costing, 45, 146
Job costing and computerisation, 150
Just-in-time (JIT), 27

Labour costing system, 132
Labour costs, 9, 44
Late notification, 446
Lead time, 34
Ledger accounting, 130
Legal status, 226, 227
Less detailed VAT invoice, 399
Level of activity, 116
LIFO - Last In, First Out, 23
Limited company, 227
Limiting factor, 195
Local VAT offices, 443
Logistics information system, 243
Long term decisions, 205
Lower quartile, 294

Machine-hour method of depreciation, 67
Management accounting, 7
Management accounts, 7, 340
Management information, 4
Management information requirements, 4
Management Information System (MIS), 243
Management warnings levels, 36
Manufacturing accounts, 342

Margin of safety, 187, 191
Marginal cost, 102
Marginal cost of sales, 102
Marginal costing, 102, 105, 107
Marginal costing - arguments in favour of, 111
Marginal costing – calculation of profit, 105
Marginal costing and absorption costing compared, 106
Marginal costing principles, 103
Mark-up, 146
Material inaccuracy, 450
Materials control account, 131
Materials cost, 9
Materials costing system, 131
Materials requisition note, 30
Materials returned note, 31
Materials transfer note, 32
Maternity leave, 55
Matrix organisation structure, 229
Maximum stock level, 36
Mean, 310
Median, 294, 313
Microfiche, 402
Microfilm, 402
Minimum stock level, 36
Misdeclaration penalty: repeated errors, 450
Misdeclaration penalty: very large errors, 449
Mixed costs, 119
Mixed supply, 420
Mode, 312
Monthly VAT periods, 388
Motor cars, 426
Motoring expenses, 426
Moving average, 314, 320
Multiple bar chart, 277, 280

Net present value (NPV) method, 213
Net profit margin, 367
New civil penalty procedure, 452
Non profit making organisation, 227
Non-business items, 425
Non-business purposes, 420
Non-deductible input VAT, 425
Non-financial information, 349
Normal loss, 165

INDEX

Notice 700, 443
NPV (Net Present Value), 213
Number format, 303
Numeric codes, 140

Objective, 5
Obsolescence, 65, 68
Office for National Statistics (ONS), 241, 254
Ogive, 293
Operation card, 48
Operational information, 240
Optimal production, 197
Optimal production plan, 198
Optional Flat Rate Scheme, 442
Order form, 19
Ordering costs, 35
Organisation structure, 227
Organisations, 226
Origin, 289
Output VAT, 387
Over absorption of overhead, 93
Overhead absorption, 89, 90
Overhead absorption rate, 90
Overhead allocation, 69
Overhead apportionment, 80
Overhead recovery rates, 90
Overheads, 10, 78
Overheads costing system, 134
Overtime, 47, 50
Overtime premium, 50

P/V (profit/volume) chart, 194
P/V (profit/volume) ratio, 186
Part-finished goods, 17
Partial exemption, 428
Partnership, 227
Paternity leave, 55
Payback period, 215
Penalties, 446
Percent format, 303
Percentage component bar charts, 278
Performance indicators, 358
Performance reports, 367
Periodic performance reports, 372
Periodic stocktaking, 32

Perpetual inventory system, 29
Perpetuities, 212
Personnel information system, 243
Pie chart, 272
Piecework, 48, 52
Piecework ticket, 48
Pieceworkers, 48
Planning, 5
Population, 251, 252
Predetermined overhead absorption rate, 89, 94
Pre-registration input VAT, 411
Present value, 209
Present value of an annuity, 211, 212
Present value tables, 210
Price index, 329
Primary data, 253
Prime cost, 10, 64, 342
Principles of discounted cash flow, 208
Principles of marginal costing, 103
Process costing - closing work in progress, 173
Process costing - scrap, 169
Process costing features, 162
Process costing framework, 164
Process costing techniques, 162
Product-division structure, 228
Production costs, 9
Production levels, 360
Production overhead, 78, 79
Production overhead control account, 134
Productivity, 358, 361
Productivity per employee, 359
Productivity per labour hour, 359
Productivity ratio, 360
Profit centres, 344, 366
Profit information, 105
Profit margin, 365, 366
Profit maximisation and limiting factors, 196
Profit to sales ratio, 366
Profit/volume (P/V) ratio, 186
Profitability, 365
Profit-sharing schemes, 55
Project appraisal - discounted cash flow methods, 213
Project appraisal – payback method, 215, 217
Public sector organisations, 227
Published statistics, 254, 255
Purchase order, 20

INDEX

Purchase requisition, 18
Purchase requisition form, 18
Purchasing department, 18
Purchasing documentation, 18
Purchasing procedures, 17

Questionnaires, 254

Random variations, 322
Raw data, 264
Raw materials, 16
Real terms, 333
Reapportionment of service cost centre costs, 83
Reasonable excuse, 447, 448
Rebasing index numbers, 332
Reckonable date, 451
Recording costs and revenues, 129
Recording expenses, 68
Recording labour costs, 45
Records, 402
Reduced VAT rate supplies, 421
Reducing balance method of depreciation, 65
Refunds for bad debts account, 432
Registered trader, 402
Registration for VAT, 406
Registration limit, 407
Reorder level, 35
Reorder quantity, 36
Reordering stock, 33
Repayment supplement, 451
Report, 11, 233, 372, 378
Report confidentiality requirements, 378
Report distribution, 378
Report format, 373
Report information, 378
Report writing, 376
Reporting information, 233
Reports for external agencies, 233
Reports including graphs and charts, 378
Reports produced by an organisation's accounting information systems, 233
Representative member, 410
Resource utilisation, 363
Resource utilisation measures, 363
Responsibility accounting, 71

Responsibility centres, 71
Retail Prices Index (RPI), 328, 333
Retail schemes, 441
Return on capital employed (ROCE), 245, 364
Return on investment (ROI), 364
Revenue expenditure, 62
Revenue items, 63
Reverse charge, 398, 435
Rounding, 419
Rounding errors, 267, 303
Route cards, 47
RPI (Retail Prices Index), 328

Salaried labour, 47
Sale or return, 392
Sales revenue at breakeven point, 186
Sample, 420
Scale charges, 426
Scattergraphs, 291
Scope of VAT, 398
Scrap value, 169
Seasonal variations, 320
Second quartile, 295
Secondary data, 253, 254, 255
Secondary statistics, 265
Secondhand goods schemes, 441
Seeking guidance, 444
Self supply, 432
Selling overhead, 78, 79
Semi-fixed costs, 119
Semi-variable costs, 119
Separate departmental absorption rates, 92
Service costing, 154
Sheldon Statement, 444
Short term decision making problems, 195
Short term decisions, 183
Sickness, 55
Sigma (Σ), 311
Significant digits, 266, 341
Signing-in book, 45
Simple bar chart, 275
Simple interest, 206
Single factory-wide absorption rates, 92
Sole traders, 227
Sorting facilities, 304

Sources of information, 443
Spreadsheet calculations, 301
Spreadsheet rounding errors, 303
Standard forms, 380
Standard method, 428
Standard rated, 398
Standard time allowance, 54
Static trend, 319
Statistical data, 253
Statistical survey, 251
Statistics, 250, 255
Statutory instruments, 443
Step costs, 117
Step down method of reapportionment, 84, 86
Stepped-fixed cost, 118
Stock code, 29
Stock control, 26
Stock control checks, 29
Stock control levels, 34
Stock discrepancies, 33
Stock valuation, 22
Stock-out, 34
Stocktaking, 32
Stores record cards, 28
Straight line graph, 290
Straight line method of depreciation, 65
Strategic information, 240
Strategy, 5
Substantial traders, 389
Summary of supplies made, 403
Summary of supplies received, 403
Supplementary Statistical Declaration, 436

Tables, 264
Tabulation, 264
Tactical information, 240
Tally marks, 267
Target profit, 188, 189
Tax invoice, 393
Tax point, 393
Taxable acquisitions, 435
Taxable person, 398
Taxable supplies, 407
Third quartile, 295
Time of a supply, 392

Time recording clock, 45
Time series, 289, 316
Time sheets, 45
Time value of money, 206
Time work system, 50
Time-saved bonus, 54
Total direct cost, 64
Training, 55
Transfer price, 345
Trend, 317
Trend line, 292
Tribunals, 445
Types of expense, 64

Unauthorised issue of invoices, 447
Under absorption of overhead, 93
Under-/over-absorbed overhead account, 134
Underlying trend, 317
Unit costing, 153
United Nations, 254
Upper quartile, 294
Upward trend, 318

Value Added Tax Act 1994, 443
Variable costs, 10, 118, 342
Variables, 252
VAT, 139
VAT account, 404
VAT allowable portion, 404
VAT and duties tribunals, 445
VAT Central Unit, 443
VAT fraction, 388
VAT invoice, 392, 399
VAT notes, 443
VAT payable portion, 404
VAT period, 388
VAT registration limit, 407
VAT registration number, 406
VAT return, 388, 390
Vertical axis, 289
Volume index, 330
Voluntary deregistration, 411
Voluntary registration, 409

INDEX

Wages control account, 132
Weekly time sheets, 46
Weighted average, 313
Weighted average cost method, 23
Work in progress, 17
Written reports, 372

X axis, 289

Y axis, 289

Zero rated, 398
Zero rated supplies, 421, 422

See overleaf for information on other
BPP products and how to order

AAT Order

To BPP Professional Education, Aldine Place, London W12 8AW
Tel: 020 8740 2211. Fax: 020 8740 1184
E-mail: Publishing@bpp.com Web:www.bpp.com

TOTAL FOR PRODUCTS £ ☐

POSTAGE & PACKING

Texts/Kits	First	Each extra	
UK	£3.00	£3.00	£ ☐
Europe*	£6.00	£4.00	£ ☐
Rest of world	£20.00	£10.00	£ ☐
Passcards			
UK	£2.00	£1.00	£ ☐
Europe*	£3.00	£2.00	£ ☐
Rest of world	£8.00	£8.00	£ ☐
Tapes			
UK	£2.00	£1.00	£ ☐
Europe*	£3.00	£2.00	£ ☐
Rest of world	£8.00	£8.00	£ ☐

TOTAL FOR POSTAGE & PACKING £ ☐
(Max £12 Texts/Kits/Passcards - deliveries in UK)

Grand Total (Cheques to *BPP Professional Education*)

I enclose a cheque for (incl. Postage) £ ☐

Or charge to Access/Visa/Switch

Card Number ☐☐☐☐ ☐☐☐☐ ☐☐☐☐ ☐☐☐☐

Expiry date ☐☐☐☐   Start Date ☐☐☐☐

Issue Number (Switch Only) ☐☐

Signature _____

Mr/Mrs/Ms (Full name) _____

Daytime delivery address _____

Postcode _____

Daytime Tel _____   E-mail _____

	5/03 Texts	5/03 Kits	Special offer	8/03 Passcards	Tapes
FOUNDATION (£14.95 except as indicated)				Foundation	
Units 1 & 2 Receipts and Payments	☐	☐	Foundation Sage Bookkeeping and Excel Spreadsheets CD-ROM free if ordering all Foundation Text and Kits, including Units 21 and 22/23 ☐	£6.95 ☐	£10.00 ☐
Unit 3 Ledger Balances and Initial Trial Balance	☐	☐			
Unit 4 Supplying Information for Mgmt Control	☐	☐			
Unit 21 Working with Computers (£9.95) (6/03)	☐				
Unit 22/23 Healthy Workplace/Personal Effectiveness (£9.95)	☐				
Sage and Excel for Foundation (CD-ROM £9.95)	☐				
INTERMEDIATE (£9.95 except as indicated)					
Unit 5 Financial Records and Accounts	☐	☐		£5.95 ☐	£10.00 ☐
Unit 6/7 Costs and Reports (Combined Text £14.95)	☐	☐			
Unit 6 Costs and Revenues		☐		£5.95 ☐	£10.00 ☐
Unit 7 Reports and Returns		☐		£5.95 ☐	
TECHNICIAN (£9.95 except as indicated)					
Unit 8/9 Managing Performance and Controlling Resources	☐	☐	Spreadsheets for Technicians CD-ROM free if take Unit 8/9 Text and Kit ☐	£5.95 ☐	£10.00 ☐
Spreadsheets for Technician (CD-ROM)	☐				
Unit 10 Core Managing Systems and People (£14.95)	☐				
Unit 11 Option Financial Statements (A/c Practice)	☐	☐		£5.95 ☐	
Unit 12 Option Financial Statements (Central Govnmt)	☐	☐		£5.95 ☐	
Unit 15 Option Cash Management and Credit Control	☐	☐		£5.95 ☐	
Unit 17 Option Implementing Audit Procedures	☐	☐		£5.95 ☐	
Unit 18 Option Business Tax (FA03)(8/03 Text & Kit)	☐	☐		£5.95 ☐	
Unit 19 Option Personal Tax (FA 03)(8/03 Text & Kit)	☐	☐		£5.95 ☐	
TECHNICIAN 2002 (£9.95)					
Unit 18 Option Business Tax FA02 (8/02 Text & Kit)	☐	☐			
Unit 19 Option Personal Tax FA02 (8/02 Text & K:t)	☐	☐			
SUBTOTAL	£ ☐	£ ☐	£ ☐	£ ☐	£ ☐

We aim to deliver to all UK addresses inside 5 working days; a signature will be required. Orders to all EU addresses should be delivered within 6 working days. All other orders to overseas addresses should be delivered within 8 working days. * Europe includes the Republic of Ireland and the Channel Islands.

Review Form & Free Prize Draw – Units 6 & 7 Recording and Evaluating Costs and Revenues & Preparing Reports and Returns

All original review forms from the entire BPP range, completed with genuine comments, will be entered into one of two draws on 31 July 2003 and 31 January 2004. The names on the first four forms picked out on each occasion will be sent a cheque for £50.

Name: _____   Address: _____

How have you used this Interactive Text?
(Tick one box only)
☐ Home study (book only)
☐ On a course: college _____
☐ With 'correspondence' package
☐ Other _____

Why did you decide to purchase this Interactive Text? *(Tick one box only)*
☐ Have used BPP Texts in the past
☐ Recommendation by friend/colleague
☐ Recommendation by a lecturer at college
☐ Saw advertising
☐ Other _____

During the past six months do you recall seeing/receiving any of the following?
(Tick as many boxes as are relevant)
☐ Our advertisement in *Accounting Technician* magazine
☐ Our advertisement in *Pass*
☐ Our brochure with a letter through the post

Which (if any) aspects of our advertising do you find useful?
(Tick as many boxes as are relevant)
☐ Prices and publication dates of new editions
☐ Information on Interactive Text content
☐ Facility to order books off-the-page
☐ None of the above

Have you used the companion Assessment Kit for this subject?   ☐ Yes   ☐ No

Your ratings, comments and suggestions would be appreciated on the following areas

	Very useful	Useful	Not useful
Chapter topic lists	☐	☐	☐
Examples	☐	☐	☐
Activities and answers	☐	☐	☐

	Excellent	Good	Adequate	Poor
Overall opinion of this Text	☐	☐	☐	☐

Do you intend to continue using BPP Interactive Texts/Assessment Kits?   ☐ Yes   ☐ No

Please note any further comments and suggestions/errors on the reverse of this page.

The BPP author of this edition can be e-mailed at: lynnwatkins@bpp.com

Review Form & Free Prize Draw (continued)

Please note any further comments and suggestions/errors below

Free Prize Draw Rules

1. Closing date for 31 July 2003 draw is 30 June 2003. Closing date for 31 January 2004 draw is 31 December 2003.
2. Restricted to entries with UK and Eire addresses only. BPP employees, their families and business associates are excluded.
3. No purchase necessary. Entry forms are available upon request from BPP Publishing. No more than one entry per title, per person. Draw restricted to persons aged 16 and over.
4. Winners will be notified by post and receive their cheques not later than 6 weeks after the relevant draw date.
5. The decision of the promoter in all matters is final and binding. No correspondence will be entered into.